497 Nails

A journey of letting go.

By Dr. Garrett L. Turke

In loving memory of
Walter, My Dad

Copyright © 2015 Dr. Garrett L. Turke

All rights reserved. No part of this book may be reproduced or transmitted in any form or by any means, electronic or mechanical, including photocopying, recording, by any information storage and retrieval system, without permission in writing from the author.

ISBN 978-0-9970195-0-6

Printed by CreateSpace, An Amazon.com Company.
Available from Amazon.com, CreateSpace.com, and other retail outlets.

Cover and book interior design:
Marie Kar – www.redframecreative.com

Cover photo credit:
Profiles - Ajith Achuthan©123RF.com

Back cover painting credit:
Rosemarie Turke

When we remember those loved ones
Who traveled by our sides through life's journeys
Let us not say we are saddened
That they left us behind
But rather, let us rejoice with gratitude
That they once were with us

–traditional Russian saying

Dedication

I am dedicating this, my first book, to my family. It has been a long, difficult road back home. Without your love and support I never would have made it through.

I could not have written this book without the profound influence of all my father's guardian angels. You are too many to count. My faith in humanity, in God, and in universal balance has been restored because you all stepped forward when my dad, my family, and I needed you. I don't know if I will be able to ever thank all of you enough.

This book is dedicated to all the caregivers who quietly go about doing God's work without a thought of being recognized. I know the agony of what you all go through first hand. I want you to know that you are not alone, and that the eternal has a special place set aside for you.

Garrett

There are three things that last:
Faith, Hope, and Love.
And the greatest of these is Love.
1 Corinthians 13:13

It took me several years to build enough courage to start this book. After my father was placed in a "memory care" home, I began to ruminate about writing a book about my experience caring for him. I initially didn't really know why. Thoughts were scribbled onto napkins, recollections were dictated to my teenaged daughter while I was driving, and a few times I even woke up in the middle of the night to get my ideas down on paper so I would not forget them. Yet I was unable to ever sit down and write my story, always thinking up some excuse to put it off another day, another week, another season.

One day I decided to collect all those scraps of ideas and memories about my dad, strewn all over my desk, and put them somewhere lest I lose them. With little thought at the time, I put them inside a decorated box that my mother had made for me for my birthday over a decade before. The box was created out of an old cigar container of my father's, and had been given to me as my birthday present. Mom had lovingly painted it black and gold, lacquered and polished it until it shined, and had carefully drawn a handwritten inscription on the cover: "My Creation Box. What I put in this box vibrates and the universe will match it with the physical equivalent." Despite my internal protests that this inscription sounded rather crazy, I tolerated my Hindu influenced, artistically inclined mother and had politely accepted the gift. Embarrassed by the strange inscription, I had hidden it inside my desk drawer. I never dreamed I would actually put anything inside of it.

For the next three years, I put every last thought and memory I had about my dad into that box. When it could hold no more, I opened the box and just started writing.

This book is a non-fictional account of my struggle, agony, acceptance, and ultimately joyful spiritual awakening which occurred in ten years of care-giving for my dearly loved father stricken with Alzheimer's disease. While the sequence of events described in this book are true, the exact dates of some of these events are only estimates based on my memories and recollections. I apologize for any inaccuracies in dates and timeframes, especially in the early chapters of this book. These errors were not made intentionally, and do not detract from the book's content or message.

*What lies behind us
And what lies before us
Are tiny matters
Compared to
What lies within us.*

-Emerson

Prologue { The Last Chapter

It has been over five years since I thought I completed 497 Nails. I always felt my Dad's story was unfinished and that I had to wait until he finally passed to write the final chapter. Well, this is the final chapter, it will be shorter than I ever expected, and it is going to be put at the front of my book rather than at the end. While I suppose the story of my life with my father is unique, the lessons I learned from taking care of my father are universal. I believe these lessons are meant to be heard and experienced by all who are willing to let their hearts and minds be open.

Today my father resides at the same wonderful care-giving "facility" he has called home for over 13 years. He is surrounded by so many angels, both human and spiritual, that have taken care of him and let us know that all of us will be all right when our time comes. My father is on his final days now, his digestive system has stopped, and we know this is "the last hospice." He has beaten death several times since this book was largely written, including a bout of pneumonia where both lungs collapsed, filled with infection and countless cysts, and given just hours to live. He has "come back" each time with lessons of the "afterlife," for lack of a better word. I have over 20 handwritten pages of afterlife "events" my father has described even while in the throws of his disease. My father described these events after it appeared he had already lost all advanced cognitive faculties and almost all language. It was as if his Alzheimer's Disease lifted momentarily so he could communicate with us.

My father has been visited many times by a type of spiritual guide he described consistently as a "kind man with a grey beard." The man is described as helping him to levitate away from his body and into the air, and then they "fly" to a destination that is filled with vivid light and other beings. My father consistently described this "place" as a "land of love" where there is "no fighting, no conflict," and there are many beings about who are joyful. He has described seeing his parents and his sister, all deceased. He also described seeing his friend Connie there; a fellow facility resident who died while my father was many miles away in a hospital bed. My father often expressed a desire to stay in the afterlife but his "guide" took him back. When he "came back" to this earth we witnessed his body jolt, as if there was an electrical discharge. After this jolt, my father appeared back in his body and "present." He often traced the air in an arc over his head and said, "They are right there, waiting to take me back."

What I just described has been witnessed by most members of my family, many of his care-givers, and some of the nurses he has had. It is not something that was meant for just one person to see and experience. The experiences my father shared are independent of any one religion...one can belong to any faith or belong to none and the lessons will still apply.

Many years ago there was no way I would have believed this much less put it down in writing. I would have feared losing my career as a man of science. But there is more to this life than we can touch and feel, and count and measure. <u>Everything</u> in this world seems linked and interdependent.

My father used to tell me I was named Garrett because it meant "Mighty Spear." When the news came that my father's system was failing I was walking along a Lake Michigan beach with my daughter's Labrador Retriever, "Buddy." The winds were strong that day and the waves very high. I had forgotten Buddy's Frisbee along the beach while walking and ran back to get it. There, shimmering in the surf next to the Frisbee was a shiny object being pushed to shore. It was all by itself. Almost miraculously, I was able to reach into the frothy surf rolling in and pull it out. It was an Indian arrowhead made out of a very shiny, lightweight rock. It had many cuts or flakes in it (I counted over 40), unmistakably man-made. I later did some research on it and found out it was a 12,000 year old Paleo-Indian tool made out of obsidian rock. I also found out it was not an arrowhead at all. It was a spearhead...to me a mighty spearhead. What were the odds of finding this at just that moment? Certainly greater than any person of science could ever account for.

I will love you forever Dad. You are going to be an eternal teacher. Maybe we can all learn to treat each other a little better if we keep the "lessons" you brought us conscious in our minds and active in our hearts.

This is our story.

Garrett L. Turke, Ph.D.
October 20, 2012

1 { 497 Nails

Early June. The sun was out and spring had finally come to Michigan. The birds were in song and the air had the faint sweet smell of blossoms that only comes in springtime. I had come alone. My wife, Stacy, and daughters Shani and Miah had offered to help but I turned them away. I wanted to come by myself. I'm not sure why. I could have used the support, not to mention the help. But I was stubborn. I wanted to remain stoic. I didn't want to talk about it as I was doing it. I didn't want any distractions. I didn't want any sentiment. I didn't want to cry, although I certainly needed to. I wanted to do it fast and get it over with. Like most men would, I suppose.

Dad's home had lain dormant for almost two months. A lifetime of memories awaited me inside. It was time to take them down.

I knew I would be frightened as soon as I went through the front door. On the entranceway wall was an unobtrusive wipeboard with a five-word sentence scrawled upon it: "No help for Walter today." The words would begin to haunt me as soon as I saw them. They had been waiting there for me since April.

I had put the wipeboard up the year before, in an attempt to give some structure to Dad's increasingly chaotic world. The wipeboard contained Dad's daily schedule, essentially when my sister, my mother, my brother-in-law, and I would be out to see him. We would write what activities we would be doing that day. It was put up to reassure Dad that help would be coming each day. It was put up so he wouldn't forget that I was coming each day. The actual day and the date didn't matter. He had lost track a long time ago as to what day it was, what month it was, hell, what season or year it was for that matter.

Besides, each day was virtually the same anyway. My sister Tiffanie or brother-in-law Donald would be out in the morning to get him breakfast and give him his meds. I would be there at noon to check on him, make him lunch, and get him set up with a stack of movies to pass away the afternoon. My mother Rosemarie would often come mid afternoon to look at old photographs and reminisce about the past. I would come again at 5:30 after work, earlier if it was the weekend or I had the day off, to make dinner and get him situated for the evening. He often wanted to watch the same set of movies, having forgotten that he watched them earlier that afternoon or the day before. Gauging from his reactions, Dad thought that each time I arrived was the first time I had stopped by to see him in many weeks, if not months. He was always so excited to see me.

"No help for Walter today." Dad wrote those words on April 14, 2002, his last day of residence in his condominium home. The words stung me, but so did the way they were written. The script was childlike and unfamiliar, and could have easily passed for a seven-year-old's handwriting. In three short years my father had fallen from being a prominent psychiatrist and an involved father and grandfather to someone I no longer recognized. He seemed to have gone somewhere. Whoever remained was someone with the mind of a young child.

"No help for Walter today." The words did not appear to be a simple observation Dad was making. The words seemed angry, razor-sharp, and penetrating. They seemed tinged with feelings of abandonment and betrayal.

I knew Dad's words were directed at me. After two years of daily visits to take care of him, I could not make myself come out that one last evening. It was just too painful. I thought that evening was going to mark the end of my life with my father. I had already passed judgment on the next day. I would be taking him to his new "memory care facility," Clare Bridge of Meridian. To me, that was Dad's death sentence. His last vestiges of independence would be cradled there for a while, then lost forever.

Dad's cryptic, five-word sentence remained as an agonizing reminder that I had abandoned him that last night. Even more significantly, it was a painful, symbolic reminder that I could not save him, that I could not always be there to protect him, and that I could not shelter him from the all-permeating effects of his disease.

When Dad and I left for Clare Bridge that rainy April morning, I couldn't erase the wipeboard. I deliberately left those words up there as a haunting sort of punishment for abandoning him. A punishment I didn't really deserve.

Now, two months later, those words served as an ominous, foreboding harbinger for the painful work that I still had to do inside Dad's condo. Hundreds of memories were up on Dad's walls. It was time to take them down.

The inside of my father's home looked like some kind of bizarre museum. He had always had a flair for dramatic presentation, placing just about everything on his walls that would give him attention from others, as if he couldn't foster an identity without visible proof that he had done something worthwhile. Every house he ever lived in had this museum-like quality to it. The walls were filled with his "trophies" for the world to see and admire. There were pictures and artifacts from his trips all over the world: Tribal masks from Africa, fake shrunken heads from New Guinea, demonic looking dragons from Indonesia, a stuffed piranha from the Amazon, a spear from Fiji, a jeweled dagger from Morocco. Everything well placed and staged to draw an inquiry. And, if the point was missed, there was a large world map in the living room, dotted with over four dozen colorful pins that showed he had been to every continent at least twice.

Invariably, Dad would produce a dangerous or daredevil story in response to anyone's inquiry about his artifacts. How he danced with the cannibalistic "Mudmen of New Guinea", ate roasted bat with tribesmen in Fiji, and swam in the piranha-infested Amazon. My favorite story involved how he single-handedly talked a Moroccan sheik out of forcibly exchanging a thousand sheep for my pretty 14 year-old sister. Dad's stories were fantastic, and everyone knew they were embellished. But Dad told the stories with such conviction you thought that maybe, just maybe, some of it was true.

Filling Dad's study were images from his upbringing in New York City. All of his childhood heroes were there. The Brooklyn Dodgers. Jackie Robinson. Duke Ellington. Benny Goodman. Glenn Miller. Humphrey Bogart. Lauren Bacall. Woody Allen. A beautiful framed poster of the Brooklyn Bridge. An aerial photograph of the Manhattan skyline. A pen and ink drawing of Ebbett's Field, where my father fell in love with baseball and the Brooklyn Dodgers. And triumphantly, a big block "L", Dad's varsity letter from Franklin Lane High School, where he had been an all-city star pitcher in the late 1940's.

Then came the images from a decade of his life in Los Angeles, where my dad built a successful practice out of treating some very wealthy and neurotic "Angelinos." There were numerous photos of famous movie stars and entertainers, a few of whom he had actually known or at least met, but most he had only apparently fantasized about meeting. Marilyn Monroe. David Niven. Rod Stieger. Cliff Robertson. Neil Diamond. Judging by Dad's living room presentation, one might think he had known all these stars. In reality, however, he had only met a few famous actors and performers. Probably the biggest actor he actually did know was George "Goober" Lindsay, from the old Gomer Pyle, Mayberry RFD, and Hee Haw shows. He had met "Goober" at a North Hollywood party, and he came over to our house for dinner parties a few times.

Two and a half years after Dad was stricken with Alzheimer's disease, Dad's museum home had become more like a scene out of "A Beautiful Mind." The images that graced Dad's walls, once compulsively lined up and organized, were now all askew. There were "sticky notes" up everywhere, with cryptic messages that made sense only to Dad at the time he had written them. CD and video liner notes were taken out of their cases and pinned to the walls. Dementia-induced love letters he had written to Marilyn Monroe and Sara Brightman were scotch-taped next to their photographs. And as his Alzheimer's got progressively worse, Dad began to write personal notes to himself on the photographs, later insisting that these celebrities had actually written personalized notes just for him. There were fabricated "quotes" from Humphrey Bogart and Lauren Bacall, each expressing their love and admiration for Dad. The famous British Actor David Niven "wrote," 'To Walter, my best friend. I remember when we were at Acapulco together. Love, David." My mother later acknowledged Dad had chatted once with David Niven at LAX airport.

I had initially tried to line everything back up and to take the more bizarre notes off the walls whenever I came over to see Dad. For a while, this was a daily ritual, but he would just put more back up after I left. I eventually came to realize this was a futile exercise, not only because Dad replaced the notes I took down, but because I began to understand what I was doing: I was trying to make his place look as if someone <u>intact</u> still lived there. My wife Stacy also enlightened me: "Honey, this is his desperate way of trying to hold on to his identity. Just leave it alone." Good God, I had been undoing Dad's coping mechanism each day because of my own selfish needs to deny the reality of his disease.

Now, standing at the foot of Dad's living room, it was time. Time to take those memories down off the walls. Sixty nine years worth. I felt a surge of emotion find its way from my stomach to my throat, pressing so hard that I thought it could suffocate me. But no tears; not a one. I thought for a fleeting moment that if I let go now, the reservoir would burst and I wouldn't be able to finish the job.

One by one, the images and mementos came down, each and every one carefully placed into boxes that would later remind me who my dad was before he got sick. One by one, I pulled out the nails that had held all those memories to the walls. For some strange reason, I had to count the nails after all the keepsakes were put away. 497. 497 nails that had held 497 memories of who my dad was. I couldn't leave until I had counted every last one.

As I left, I erased the wipeboard and locked the door behind me.

The June weather was still beautiful outside; the birds were still chirping and the smell of blooming flowers fragranced the air. But I didn't notice.

I cried in the van before I drove home. The reservoir had burst.

2 { The Warning

It's hard to remember exactly when my dad got sick. There was a lot going on in all of our lives when the first warning signs emerged, and we were all too busy to really notice them. My sister was busy building a new house. I was wrapped up in the wonderful toddler years of my second daughter, Miah, coaching in my oldest daughter Shani's basketball league, and trying to adjust to a massive reorganization at work. In retrospect, Dad might have been showing symptoms of dementia for a while. The symptoms had crept up on us, at first quietly, then insidiously. Armed with hindsight and more knowledge, I now feel bad that I didn't see the warning signs sooner. But would it have mattered? I wasn't ready to accept the news anyway.

The signs were all there, as if taken out of an Alzheimer's 101 textbook: The persistent forgetfulness. The repeated calls to tell us what he had already told us the day before. The seating chart that he put together each day to remember the names of five students that he had seen daily for the past six weeks. Leaving his stove on repeatedly. Serving us packaged food out of a box without realizing the need to cook it first. Putting away badly wrinkled, soiled clothes in his dresser drawers. Hesitating at intersections as if he had momentarily forgotten what green and red meant.

Maybe any of these things could have been written off if they occurred in isolation. But the warnings were not few and far between. They were part of an aggregate of symptoms that were accumulating, and slowly worsening. I just couldn't see it yet.

Dad even told me that he was having problems with his memory, in his own way. He called me one day and said an administrative colleague from Michigan State University had come up for a site visit. The administrator asked Dad if he could ride with him for a typical afternoon, which involved consultations at several agencies across the city. Dad told me how embarrassed he was when he became disorganized while driving and "forgot" the routes he had been taking nearly every day for the past ten years. The colleague made a joke about Dad having "early Alzheimer's" and they both laughed. I laughed too when Dad told me what happened on the phone.

My wife Stacy was the first to see it, and the first to express concern. She thought his cognitive faculties were failing. I heard her, well sort of, but quickly rationalized an alternative explanation that was safer. "Yeah maybe, but I think Dad probably just had a stressful day." "Maybe he was just preoccupied and distracted, he's got a lot on his mind." Or, at worst, "Dad's started drinking again." That was terrible enough, but at least it was familiar ground.

I braced for what I thought was probably the worst of the options, Dad's intermittent bouts of drinking. I called my sister Tiffanie and told her I thought Dad was drinking again, and that we should probably have a "come to Jesus meeting" with him. A "come to Jesus meeting" was a phrase my colleagues used at work, which essentially meant getting right to the truth without any bullshit. We had had many of these meetings in the past.

Dad's personality seemed to change whenever he drank. He would start saying inappropriate things, like making sexually tinged jokes in conservative company, or telling my Jewish mother in law that some distant members of our extended family had been in the Gestapo in World War II. The shock and awe was designed to be mean and intimidating. It was painful to watch, because the father who was not drinking would never have made these comments. He would have always empathized with any victim, or any underdog. When he drank, however, Dad became the aggressor; he could be inexplicably mean, and all of his childhood conflicts emerged in a menacing eruption.

Dad's drinking had cost him. He started in the Navy in 1960, using scotch as an anesthetic to cover painful shyness and social clumsiness. He began drinking as a way to fit in with his fellow Navy officers. When he was drinking he became one of the boys, something that had eluded him during his childhood. His ultra conservative German immigrant parents had seen to that.

The cost of my father's alcoholism was catastrophic. He lost his marriage in 1981, and his relationship with his oldest daughter, Cindy, around 1990 Neither of them could put up with his bouts of drinking and verbal abuses any longer. It had been over ten long, painful years since they talked. Only Tiffanie and I remained in his life to hang on.

Tiffanie and I wanted to believe our father had finally learned his lesson from drinking the previous summer. He had vowed to stop at the last "come to Jesus" meeting. We always believed in him, even when no one else would. But now, faced with evidence mounting that Dad had some sort of worsening cognitive disorder, a return to alcoholic behavior seemed to be the preferable option.

Tiffanie and I planned a trip up to Bay City to see Dad over the Memorial Day weekend. We were going to do what we always did, tactfully and strategically confront him about his drinking. After which, Dad would do what he always did, apologize profusely, tell us he was from a "poor, dysfunctional immigrant home," and quit drinking...for a while.

The Saturday before Memorial Day was too cold to go swimming, which is what we usually did before one of our serious talks with Dad. So we went for a long walk with him instead. We did what we always did, and so did Dad. He superficially accepted responsibility, berated himself for a while, and vowed to stop drinking forever.

We ended up having a good weekend at Dad's. The sun came out, it warmed up, and everyone got some swimming in. We had a nice little barbeque, then settled in to watch a series of Dad's favorite old movies. We returned home on Monday afternoon, triumphant and happy. All was right with the world again.

Stacy wasn't as jubilant. She knew something was terribly wrong. And it wasn't the alcohol.

3 { The Champion

I always saw my father as a champion. Despite his bouts of drinking and the painful demise of his relationship with my mother and older sister, I had maintained my childhood perception of my dad as a champion throughout my adulthood. Maybe I was in denial, for he certainly had his share of character flaws and indiscretions. But I always saw the champion in him rise above his shortcomings and failures. I knew what he had overcome in his life to get where he did. I often remember what a friend of mine in college had told me when I talked about my dad. He told me, "Never judge a man by his position in life. Judge him by the number of obstacles he has had to overcome to get to where he is." I always remembered my friend Ahvay's words, and always applied them to Dad.

Although outwardly proud and sometimes boastful, inwardly my dad was a very insecure man. The son of poor, immigrant parents who had fled Hitler and Germany before World War II, he was ashamed of his ethnic identity. As a child, he was embarrassed his parents spoke German at home and was even more self conscious that they still identified with the "old country." My dad's parents had left Germany in 1928, just before the rise of the Nazi party, and they made no bones that they hated the Nazis. My father was born two years after they arrived in America, and his only sister Freda followed six years later.

Dad's perception of his heritage was of further humiliation to him. Many of Dad's peers in elementary school made fun of his parents, his German heritage, his conservative, Lederhosen-influenced clothing, and our last name, which reflected some Turkish ancestry. The kids would start laughing during roll call, when the teacher got to the S's and the name "Turke" would soon be coming up. The new teachers would invariably mispronounce his name as "turkey" and everyone would laugh. Dad eventually would develop a comeback of sorts, responding defiantly, "We are descendents of Genghis Kahn!" whenever the kids' taunted him. Although technically not a minority, my dad certainly felt like one during his youth, and his friendships with primarily African American and Jewish peers in Brooklyn bore this out.

Dad's parents tried very hard to live the American dream. His father worked long hours as a clerk in a bookstore. His mother tended dutifully to the home affairs but was very overprotective and intrusive. Dad's parents remained extremely poor throughout their lifetime and the American dream escaped them. Dad was always conflicted about his relationship with his parents, primarily due to their conservatism and extreme religiosity. In their world, if you even thought about anything bad you were going to hell. Sex, anger, talking back, and adolescent autonomy were all taboo. These were subjects not to be even acknowledged, much less discussed.

As a child, my dad ate a German "poor man's diet" at home, which consisted primarily of potatoes, buttermilk, and various "old world" meats, cheeses, and fish. He once told me he remembered the pungent smell of a bucket of fish being cleaned in the kitchen, as well as the horrible smell of Limburger cheese. Later in life he would never touch these foods, armed with his lifelong war cry, "No cheese or fish for me! I _hate_ cheese and fish!!!" In retrospect, this was probably symbolic of the larger conflict he had in trying to separate emotionally from his parents.

My dad told me his mother continued to dress him as late as the 9th grade. On one occasion his mother held his face and gave him an embarrassing kiss on the lips as she sent her nearly six foot son off to high school. Dad said his father was distant and sometimes cruel, once throwing him down the basement stairs for talking back to him. Feeling guilty for overreacting, his father would then try to reconnect with him by preaching his own version of Bible stories, which always included "going to hell" as the lesson for bad or immoral behavior. My dad was socially inept, shy, and very insecure as he entered adolescence. He hated his parents' rigidity and conservatism. But he never could express it directly. Not as a child. Not as an adolescent. Not as an adult.

Dad was a great baseball pitcher for Franklin Lane High School in Brooklyn. Some years ago, I uncovered an old yearbook in Dad's basement, and saw that he was voted "best athlete" for the class of 1948. My father pitched two no-hitters his senior year in high school, including a city championship game where he doubled in the only runs to win the game. His parents never went to a single game. Dad's sister Freda, six years his junior, went to his games and collected newspaper articles about him, which I also found in Dad's yearbook. Perhaps my proudest moment as Dad's son was the first time I read those old, tarnished, newspaper clips. A "C" student in high school, baseball was his joy, his success, and his only escape from home. He was too shy to date, there was no family car, and besides, his parents didn't approve of dating in high school anyway. He was too young and impressionable.

By the end of his senior year in high school, my dad had drawn the attention of pro scouts and was drafted by the Pittsburgh Pirates. What should have been his crowning moment of glory was barely even acknowledged by his parents. Dad ultimately turned down the Pirates' offer. The poor, shy, socially awkward "C" student from Brooklyn wanted to become a doctor instead.

I often wonder what course my father's life would have taken if he had become a pro baseball player. My father's high school teammate, Robert Anton Grim, Franklin Lane's number 2 pitcher, became a professional ball player and played for the New York Yankees in the 1950's. He was the American League Rookie of the Year in 1954. I know this because Dad showed me his obituary in the newspaper's celebrity milestones in 1996, and I later looked up his name in Dad's yearbook.

Ironically, my dad the star athlete received a church scholarship to attend Westmar College, a small, religious school in rural Iowa. His parents' church gave him the scholarship. It was expected that in exchange for this money Dad would do missionary work in some far away place, like Africa, after he graduated. And so, the overprotected Brooklyn boy who did not yet know how to cook, clean, manage a budget, or wash his clothes, packed his bags for Iowa...and freedom.

Dad transferred to the University of Iowa two years later, where he enrolled in a pre-med curriculum. He struggled some at Iowa, but again, managed to pull his grades up enough to be accepted by the University of Iowa's College of Medicine. Dad met my mother at Iowa. Perhaps coincidentally, she also was from New York City, and also from a first generation German immigrant family. They married and had me while my dad was still completing medical school.

Dad went on to become an officer in the Navy, a successful private practice psychiatrist in Los Angeles, and a Professor Emeritus at Michigan State University. At Michigan State, he set up a permanent scholarship for minority and disadvantaged students who wanted to pursue a career in medicine. Although his life was marred by two rocky marriages, two divorces, and periodic drinking binges, my father had remained my champion. He had overcome so much. I always remembered my friend's wisdom. "Judge people by the obstacles they have had to overcome."

As Dad grew old, he remained a warrior. He had beaten prostate cancer in 1995, volunteering to be one of the first in Michigan to have radioactive "seeds" implanted in his prostate. He had a successful triple by-pass surgery the following year. One of the most touching memories I have of my father is of him being wheeled in a gurney down a long hospital hallway to the operating room. Lined up along one side of the hallway were about 10 of his young medical students, who lovingly touched him, kissed him, and wished him well as he was wheeled past them en route to his by-pass surgery. To me, Dad was invincible. He could overcome any obstacle. He could beat anything.

In the fall of 1999, my father was diagnosed with Alzheimer's disease. Something he couldn't beat. Something he wouldn't overcome.

4 { The Call

The call came without warning on a Friday morning in early September. Sitting restlessly in a large conference room at the Veterans' Memorial Courthouse building in Lansing, Michigan, I was waiting for my 9:00 AM staff meeting to begin. Usually these meetings were rather perfunctory. Nearly everyone that worked for the Family Court viewed Friday staff meetings as a necessary evil that we had to endure, before we could be "released" for the weekend.

For the past 15 years, I had been a staff psychologist for an innovative court program that reunited children from foster care with their biological, and previously abusive, homes. My job was full of risks, but also full of rewards. Make a mistake and you might have a dead child. Rehabilitate a family and you are a hero. Life at Family Court included a crisis just about every day. Adrenalin rushes and a hundred mile an hour pace. But at the end of the day, you felt alive. You felt human. Because you had really mattered in someone's life.

But staff meetings on Fridays were a different story. They were anti-climatic. They were filled with bureaucratic rhetoric that was not very important to those of us who worked in the trenches. Usually, I would spend staff meeting time thinking about all of the work I had done that week, and what I still had to do before I could go home. On this day, I started daydreaming about the weekend in front of me. I had to get my stereo speaker fixed, which I had blown out the weekend before listening to "Natural Mystic," off an old Bob Marley album.

Music was a big part of my life. My wife and children would vacate the house for a few hours each weekend to let me "listen" to my music. I had over 500 CD's, ranging from Bob Seger and Bruce Springsteen to Stevie Wonder, Bob Marley, Jimmy Cliff and U-2. I particularly loved reggae because of the Biblically inspired lyrics set to a hundred decibels of African rhythm and electric guitar. My family swore that I would be deaf by the time I was 50, because of my weekend habit of trying to simulate live rock concerts in our living room.

In the back of my van, the speaker was patiently waiting to be resurrected. I was preoccupied with getting it fixed right after our staff meeting so I could resume my weekend music rituals. I had worked a hard week, my 40 hours were up at 10 this morning, and I had helped a lot of stressed-out people. I had deserved my two and a half days off. I was looking forward to going to the Stereo Shoppe, getting my Klipsch-4 speaker up and working again, and then going home to exorcise myself of all the demons I had encountered during the week.

My daydream was interrupted by a pink slip of paper that was handed to me from across the room. My wife, Stacy, had called. The note was brief, but instantly worried me: "Dr. Turke. Call your wife at home immediately. Very important." It was unusual for Stacy to have a secretary interrupt me at work with any kind of message, and she knew I was in a staff meeting. What could be wrong? One of the kids got hurt? I left the room with my heart pounding and raced to a phone.

As always, I tried to sound calm, masking the internal turbulence. I was used to doing that, working for the Court.

"Hi, Stacy, what's up?"

Stacy measured her words slowly, and succinctly. "A Doctor Jahnke just called. She's a neurologist. She works in Saginaw…. Honey, it's about your dad."

Stacy continued talking, but I didn't hear her any more. I didn't have to. I already knew.

All summer long Stacy had been putting together the evidence. Dad's constant forgetting. The calls at odd hours. The uncharacteristic anxiety in Dad's voice, as if he wanted to tell me something. All those jokes about problems with his memory. His anger that his university colleagues were concerned about his performance at work; in fact they were trying to fire him. This wasn't about his drinking. This wasn't familiar ground.

Unbeknownst to any of us in the family, my dad had been going to a series of neurological and psychological examinations for the past several weeks. The university had ordered these exams, as a number of my dad's colleagues had expressed worries about him. They noticed a drop in his work performance and an inability to recall the names of familiar faces, including his students and his patients. Although I now know that these colleagues were very supportive and caring, Dad interpreted their efforts to help him as a conspiracy to get rid of him. Although Dad went through the exams reluctantly, he had refused to sign any releases to involve other members of the family. Later I would find out that Dad thought the doctors examining him were hired by a rival psychiatrist in East Lansing, believing their mission was to fire him and take over his position.

It all sounded so bizarre, so paranoid, so delusional. None of the examining doctors had called us because of "doctor-patient confidentiality." With his civil rights so bureaucratically and insensitively secured, none of his familial supports could be accessed. Dad had been suffering through what must have been overwhelming anxiety alone, every day and every night.

I could hear Stacy's voice again. "Honey, they think he has Alzheimer's disease. Dr. Jahnke wants you to call her. Honey, she really cares about your dad. She didn't honor the confidentiality because you have to know. Your dad needs you. She wants us to come up and talk to your dad this weekend. He needs to get on medication right away."

I felt a toxic mix of painful emotions. It was the first signs of a panic attack. I pushed the feelings down. Way down, as far as a person could. The Ph.D. psychologist who had spent his whole life confronting other people's denials now had some serious denial of his own going on.

"Garrett.... Garrett... Garrett! Are you there? Are you OK, honey? What do you want to do? We can be ready in an hour. Can you come home right away?"

I looked at my watch to see if it was 10:00 yet. Jesus, I looked at my watch to see if my work week was finished!

"Stacy, I'm sorry, I can't come home yet. I have to get my speaker fixed first."

5 { Unfamiliar Ground

By noon, my stereo speaker was fixed. I had somehow managed to talk to the salesman at the Stereo Shoppe without even thinking about the startling news I had received only an hour before. It's funny how denial works. It allows us to carry on when otherwise we would be saddled with so much pain or anxiety we would be unable to function. Despite 20 years of treating adults and teenagers with lots of denial, it turned out that I was no different than anyone on my caseload.

I pretended to listen to the explanation that the salesman gave me about what I had done to my speaker. Like my dad, I was a mechanical klutz. Despite all the effort the salesman was putting in to try to explain the problem to me, I just couldn't grasp it. But I played along anyway, nodding periodically as if I understood. The salesman made a small repair and pushed the reset button. The speaker was fixed in a matter of minutes, and at no cost. Too bad my dad's condition couldn't be fixed equally as efficiently.

I remember feeling happy for a moment as I loaded my newly restored speaker in the back of the van. I felt lucky I hadn't damaged it. How I could think and feel this way at the time was beyond me. I had just been told my dad had a terminal disease. I wasn't a cold, callous person. So why was I numb? Why didn't I feel?

On the way home, I tried to register the news Stacy had given me by reciting her words under my breath. "Dad has Alzheimer's disease. Dad has Alzheimer's disease. Dad has Alzheimer's disease!" The intellect understood, but my heart wouldn't react. I thought about what I knew of the disease. I knew it caused progressive memory loss. I knew it caused personality changes. I knew it robbed people of their ability to recognize their loved ones. I knew that it progressed insidiously. I knew that at the end, Alzheimer's victims lost voluntary control of basic bodily functions. I knew it exacted a devastating toll on family members. And I knew it was always fatal.

I flashed back to a visit I had with my paternal great aunt Hilda some 20 years before. She had succumbed to Alzheimer's disease. She was my favorite relative growing up. In her prime, she was so vibrant, so youthful and alive. Her personality was exemplified by her choice in cars, always a red, late model Mustang convertible. All I could remember of Aunt Hilda now was my final image of her, a mindless, feeble shell of a body wearing diapers. Would this be my dad's fate? Is this how The Champion would go out? I tried desperately to bring up some feeling, any feeling, but it wouldn't come.

When I got home, Stacy met me at the door. She hugged me, or should I say she tried to hug me. I stiffened, and made a pathetic attempt to hug her back. I turned my face away. Nothing. No feeling. The system was still shut down.

Stacy and my daughters, Shani and Miah, then age 10 and 3, were ready to go up north to see my dad. The bags were packed by the door. They were already mobilized to face the crisis. They had been waiting for me for several hours. I made them wait another hour. I had to get that goddamn speaker set back up again.

At about 2 PM, the dutiful, responsible side of my personality emerged. To an outsider, it might have looked as if my state of denial was ending, for I began to rally the troops to help my dad. I had to call my sister. I had to call my mother. I called work and said I had a family emergency and rearranged my weekend on-call coverage. It was time for me to be "the responsible one." It was time to step up to help Dad. The state of denial was ending. Or was it? I still didn't feel anything.

Growing up in my family, it fell on me to help take care of things at home. As a child, it was my job to help baby-sit my younger sisters, walk them to school, and make sure bullies wouldn't pick on them. As a teenager, when my parents started arguing more, I was the one who stepped in and tried to get them to stop. I usually did this in a diplomatic way, utilizing my dad's habit of calling for a "family meeting." Family meetings were a weekly ritual established by my dad to settle conflict amongst us kids. Ironically, as a teenager, I ended up being the one to call family meetings to settle conflict between my parents.

Now it was time for me to be the responsible one again.

The first feeling that finally showed up was anger. Not at my father, and not at the disease. Anger at my sister, Tiffanie. I had called her at work, patiently told her the news, and asked her to go up with us to talk to Dad and support him. Unlike me, she reacted strongly and emotionally, but it wasn't the response I wanted. She argued with me that Dr. Jahnke had made a mistake. She had just seen Dad the previous weekend, and he was, in her estimation, "just fine." My sister's voice had an edge to it, like "don't bother me." She minimized all the warning signs that Stacy had orally documented all summer. Tiffanie wanted a second opinion. And a third. And a fourth. As many opinions as it took to get the verdict that Dad was all right. She too saw Dad as invincible. She couldn't handle the news either. It was her version of needing to get the speaker fixed.

I didn't blow up at my sister, but I hung up the phone, furious. Furious at her, for using the same defense I had been using all morning and half the afternoon.

At 3 PM we began the drive from East Lansing to my dad's home in Bay City. It was usually a pleasant 90 minute drive that went by quickly. Today it would take an eternity. Stacy wanted to drive, empathic that I was stressed and preoccupied. She also wanted me to call Dr. Jahnke, who had left her cell phone number. I insisted on driving, stating stoically that I was "fine." I reminded Stacy that I had always loved to drive and it relaxed me.

Stacy eventually consented to me driving. Although she never said a word about it, we both knew why I wanted to drive. It had nothing to do with relaxing or collecting my thoughts. I didn't want to call Dr. Jahnke.

We made it to Flint and took the turn to the north, up I-75. As we merged onto 75, which was loaded with vacationers heading up to Michigan's lakes and north woods, I started daydreaming. I thought of the Bob Seger song, "Roll Me Away," that spoke about spontaneously hopping on a motorcycle and crossing over that mighty Mackinaw Bridge to the Upper Peninsula and symbolic freedom. Freedom from the pressures of the cities. Freedom from thousands of tedious, and occasionally suffocating life responsibilities. Freedom from the tragedies of life. As I started playing that song in my head, I drifted back to why we had come to Michigan nearly thirty years before.

We had essentially fled Los Angeles, with all of its drugs, violence, brush fires, earthquakes, and air that could choke a skunk. Despite all of the ills of LA, I remembered how angry I was at Dad for taking me out of that smog-tinged, 1971 Los Angeles culture and moving us to Michigan for a better life. In 1971, I thought Michigan was Hicksville. I was 14, and from the center of the universe, Southern California. I was proud, cool, and sophisticated. I had truly hated my dad for several years after making that seemingly autocratic decision to move our family. I didn't see the smog, the violence in our neighborhood, the drugs in my school. I just saw a father who came home one day and wanted to uproot me from my friends, my home, and the ocean I loved. From a city of 8 million, you're going to move us to a place called Traverse City, population 15,000? You've got to be kidding, Dad. You son of a bitch!

Later that summer we packed up the car and drove 2,000 miles to a quaint little town on a bay in Northern Michigan. I thought I had been transported back in time, to Hicksville, circa 1958. Although visibly miserable and depressed for at least two years following this move, I never directly talked about the trauma this move precipitated, either with my dad or my mom. The closest I had come to expressing my malcontent was flipping over the family's dining room table, fully loaded up, during dinner one evening. This drew attention to my anger, but I still couldn't talk about it. It had only served to cause the family to think, "What's wrong with him?" Later my mom confessed that she knew I was depressed and had tried to discuss the matter with my dad. But, perhaps ironically, Dad was opposed to any counseling for me or for the family. It wouldn't look good for his image as a psychiatrist who was trying to establish himself in the area.

A bump in the road brought me back to my driving. The sky was a vivid azure blue. There wasn't any thick, brown, ugly smog. There was a hawk soaring and diving high above us. I glanced toward the back seat and saw two beautiful girls sleeping. I glanced over and glimpsed my beautiful wife, looking silently out the window. She had been a lifesaver for me. As I continued playing that Bob Seger song in my head, I silently thanked my father for getting us the hell out of Los Angeles.

My reminiscing ended abruptly. "Garrett, do you want to pull over and call Dr. Jahnke? I can drive the rest of the way."

It didn't take me but a second to react. "No, I told you. I'm fine. I can call her on Monday when we get back. Or... if you want, you can call her..." Stacy's reply was more adamant than I had hoped. She knew me, and she wasn't going to fall for the avoidance. "Honey, she wanted you, us, to call her back, today."

I continued to avoid as best I could, already knowing I wasn't going to win this one. "Well, could you call her then? I don't want to stop, we're almost there."

Stacy pulled out the cell phone and started punching in the numbers. Surprisingly, within a matter of seconds she had Dad's neurologist, Dr. Jahnke, on the line. Stacy covered for my fears, as usual, and told Dr. Jahnke that we were just outside of Bay City, en route to see Dad. Dr. Jahnke had a personal interest in my dad, as he had been her clinical rotation professor years before.

Even though the small cell phone was pressed to Stacy's ear, I could hear Dr. Jahnke's soothing, reassuring voice resonating through the phone. Dr. Jahnke was personal and non-clinical. She was a real person. And I could tell she really liked Dad.

Within a few minutes, Dr. Jahnke had laid down the first prescription for us to follow. It was a lot more intense that just getting dad on some medication. It was a wake-up call that came long before I was ready to awaken.

"Honey, Dr. Jahnke said your dad needs to go on a medication called Aricept. It can't cure his Alzheimer's, but it might slow it down some. It allows the acetocholine in his brain to remain in the neuro-synapses longer before being absorbed. She said it will buy us a little time. Honey, there's a lot more we have to do. We have to make sure his will is in order. We have to make sure you or Tiffanie are legally designated as his Power of Attorney. You need to get his checkbook and finances in your name. Dr. Jahnke will help oversee and assess his competency. We have to help him retire with dignity and move him down to East Lansing to be close to his family supports. She said we have to do this as soon as we can. We have some time, but not much. Her clinic can help us with all of this; it's what they do. They have a lot of experience with this. Honey, I'm so sorry."

I didn't want to hear her, but there was no room in the van to run away. This time there was no speaker to fix. The freeway sign reminded me, cruelly. "Exit 161, 5 miles."

As we finished out those last few miles, an irrational, overwhelming, flooding anxiety came over me. The kind of anxiety that causes panic, makes your heart race, and causes that surreal, detached from reality feeling. The image that I paired with this horrible feeling was equally horrible. It was of my dad answering his front door and not recognizing who I was.

6 { The Ambush

I knew I was being irrational as I walked up Dad's entranceway. I had just seen him two weeks before, when we went up for our customary walk, swim, and barbeque, something that we tried to do at least once every few weeks in the summer. Dad thought we were coming up for more of the same. He had no idea I was about to ambush him.

Dad opened the door, smiled broadly, and welcomed us with great gusto as he always did. He had one of his usual weekend shirts on, an oversized Iowa Hawkeye football jersey, which seemed to completely envelop each one of us as we lined up in turn for Dad to hug us. Dad reached for me first. "Mmmm, my boy Garrett," he said warmly, grabbing me around the shoulders and pulling me close to his slightly stubbled face. I smelled the familiar Old Spice aftershave that I had known since I was a little boy. That smell and a hug from my dad always gave me an immediate shot of nostalgia, linking me with that secure childhood feeling you only get when you are a kid and safe with your parents.

Dad next turned to the rest of the family pulling up the rear, laden with our overnight gear and sleeping bags. "Hi Stacy," he said, also giving her a big hug that seemed to completely encompass her small frame. "I got some Angus T-bones for us to grill tonight. Would you do me the honor of helping me marinade them?"

Stacy smiled. "You betcha, Walter. I see you've gone all out for us, as usual." Stacy always put on a kind, upbeat persona in front of my dad. He truly loved her, but he never fully realized that she was the one hurt most by his alcohol-induced indiscretions. Dad's comments would get under her skin, and she was unable to easily excuse and shake them off like Tiffanie and I could. It was easy for us. We had years of practice.

Dad next turned to 10 year old Shani with another warm hug. "Hi, Shani. How's basketball?"

"Good." Shani smiled and wasted no time in bringing up her favorite activity at Dad's place. "Are we going swimming tomorrow?"

Dad was all ready for her. "You bet we are! And they'll be some whale back rides."

"Oh goody! Goody goody goody! Miah, we're going to have whaleback rides on Grampy's back!"

Last to emerge from the line was three and a half year old Miah. Dad reached down, scooped her up, and brought her close to his face. Miah was not quite ready for a bear hug from a 200 pound man, and squirmed anxiously. I could see Stacy's face tighten up in my peripheral vision.

Stacy intervened diplomatically, as she always did. "Walter, I don't think she's ready for that yet, she gets nervous when people do that. Give her some time to warm up, OK?"

Dad put Miah down gently, sensing there was some mild tension. He loved playing with young kids but had a hard time gauging their developmental stage or comfort levels when they were that young. He seemed awkward and a little unsure for a moment after he put Miah down. I was a little disappointed he didn't connect with her, but I had seen this same thing happen with Shani when she was younger. Now he was playing ball with Shani and giving her "whale back rides" in the pool. I would later feel sad that Miah would not be afforded the same opportunity.

As we entered my dad's house, I kept scanning for signs of the disease. There didn't seem to be any. The home was immaculately picked up, and the ingredients for tonight's barbeque had been laid out in a sequential, organized manner, all set to go. Dad was happy, almost jubilant, and he certainly did not seem impaired in any way. I thought for a few seconds that Tiffanie might be right. Maybe everyone's got this wrong. Maybe this Jahnke isn't that good of a neurologist. Maybe we do need another opinion.

Besides, our mission seemed poorly timed. Dad is in great spirits tonight, so why would we want to mess with this? If Dr. Jahnke is wrong, then we are going to traumatize him for nothing. And even if she were right with this goddamn diagnosis, why would I choose a night like this to deliver Judas' kiss? For God's sake, he is so happy to see us. I can't do it. I can't!

I told Stacy I would go for a walk with him in the morning. Procrastinating a few hours more couldn't hurt.

Dad had prepared his usual barbeque fare for us: expensive T-bone steaks, a canned 3-bean salad, baked beans, and a very coarsely chopped lettuce and tomato salad. He was never very good at cooking, but he could barbeque well. Although I had largely given up red meat three years before when I saw my dad's pre-bypass radiography photos, I made occasional exceptions when Dad bought those T-bone steaks. They were exquisite when Dad grilled them.

While we were barbequing outside, Dad began to tell me about a problem he had at work. This was not unusual for him, for he always seemed to value my input, and he loved talking about his job. He told me that there was a new dean on campus in East Lansing, and that he had already been up to Dad's clinic to pay him a visit. Dad seemed strangely threatened by this man, who I assumed was just making a routine site visit as the new dean. According to Dad, the new dean was very upset with him and was on a personal mission to fire him.

I would later find out that, in reality, "the new dean" represented a whole slew of worried and genuinely concerned colleagues who had collectively noticed my dad's memory lapses during the summer. The university had scheduled some neurological and psychological tests to help identify what might be going on in order to help my dad. He had missed all of their concern. Dad was convinced that a "new dean" had suddenly appeared on the scene and that he was conspiring to put him through a series of rigorous tests in order to justify firing him.

This was a new side of Dad I hadn't glimpsed before. Paranoid and delusional. It was unsettling. It surged within my stomach and threatened to erupt. I pushed it down again, just like I did earlier in the morning.

I reassured Dad as best I could. I told him that maybe we should forget about the problem for tonight and discuss it some more tomorrow, after we slept on it. I had already procrastinated on Dad's ambush, and figured I could avoid this for a few more hours also.

After dinner, we settled in for a typical evening at Dad's: a family or children's movie for Shani and Miah, followed by an old classic for the three adults. We rarely made it all the way through the adults' movie, usually falling asleep halfway through. We would wake up when the video ended, usually around midnight, when each one of us would comment on how much we liked the movie that none of us actually finished. Then we would say our goodnights and be off to bed. It was the same routine each and every time we visited Dad.

Tonight would be no different. We watched the Sound of Music with the girls, then settled in with Bogart and Bacall. We were all sound asleep midway through the second movie. At 11:45 the video ended, and true to script, we all awakened just long enough to comment on how much we liked the movie before carting ourselves off to bed.

Later that night I had a vivid, terrifying dream. It was the same dream I had when I was a kid in L.A., a couple nights after we had experienced a frightening earthquake. In that dream, I was up on the roof of our house, armed with a gun, terrified, protecting the family, scanning the horizon for some kind of impending, dreadful attack. What made the dream so scary was that I never knew what was encroaching on us from over the horizon. In my childhood version of the dream, I woke up before the dreadful event happened, then marched down to the security of my parents' bedroom, sleeping bag in tow.

In my current, adult version of the dream, I was up on a roof again. Only this time it wasn't our house in California. It was my dad's condominium roof in Bay City, Michigan. I was up there with that same gun, terrified, scanning the horizon for the impending but unseen attack. Oddly, I knew I was in a dream while I was experiencing it. I remember telling myself if I could just scream, the horrible nightmare would end and I would wake up. In the dream, I tried again and again to yell out. My mouth was open, but I couldn't get any sounds to come out.

7 { D-Day

I woke up when Stacy kept jostling my arm: "Garrett... Garrett... Garrett! You're having a bad dream. Wake up! Honey wake up! You're screaming."

As I came to, I was momentarily that scared kid again. A minute later, I was awake and back in reality. I wasn't that scared kid anymore. I was a scared adult. The dream was over, but the dread remained. The attack coming up over the horizon was real.

When morning broke, Dad was already up, showered, and dressed in khaki shorts, Iowa Hawkeye tennis shoes, and another Hawkeye t-shirt. D-Day had arrived. Dad had already eaten, and he had set the table for our breakfast. The girls were still asleep, and probably wouldn't be up for a few more hours. Dad was already itching to go on our walk. Just him and me, like the old days.

Dad lived in a set of nice condominiums that ringed an exquisitely manicured golf course, which in turn led to a stretch of woods with lots of pretty little lakes and ponds. His mission on these walks was to follow the trails back in the woods to a secret blackberry patch. Not too many people knew about it, and we sure didn't tell any one. On a good outing, we would collect several baggies full of blackberries, and later put them over ice cream. The blackberry patch was going to be our destination today.

Normally, I loved to go on these walks with Dad. Neither one of us were big talkers, but there was a sense of closeness on these walks that was precious to both of us. If I had any worries about my life or my job, this was a time to get my father's full attention and advice. Dad never responded to my worries with ambiguity or uncertainty, always confidently reassuring me that I could handle whatever the problem was, and to not make it any bigger than it actually was. He would be so confident in his reassurances that whatever insecurities I had would vanish during our walk. And, occasionally, he would jokingly remind me that we were "descendents of Genghis Kahn," and that nothing could ever defeat us. We would both laugh as if it was a joke, but I knew my father secretly meant it. And that was all it took to take my worries away.

But today, the walk was not so calming. I had a problem my dad couldn't solve for me. There would be no reassurances from him, and no advice. The shoe was on the other foot. I was on my own.

I thought about my mission. It was up to me to somehow convince Dad that he needed to be on a medication for a terminal disease he wouldn't accept he had. I thought that if I confronted him head on, I would crash right into his delusion. He would tell me that the angry new dean was manipulating me. He would say that he was just fine, and that the dean was now using me to participate in his lynching. I had to come up with something else. I had to lie, and lie convincingly.

The splash of a big fish interrupted my internal conflict. We had come to an important marker on our walk. We had come to the bridge. The bridge was a beautiful, old, covered wooden structure that spanned a slow moving creek. Beyond the bridge lay the woods and the secret blackberry patch. Normally at this point I would be wondering if we would find the blackberries ripe, if the birds had discovered them first, or the worst fate of all, finding someone else already there, picking them. But today, I wasn't thinking of blackberries at all. I was concocting a lie. A lie that would get my father on Aricept, that state-of-the-art Alzheimer's drug which, according to Dr. Jahnke, would only "buy us some more time." I wondered if I could lie with a straight face and be convincing. I had woefully little experience in this area.

"Hey, Dad, I've been having a little trouble with my memory lately. I don't know if its work or stress or that I'm getting a little older. I was at the doctor's for a regular check-up the other day and my doctor told me about getting on either these vitamins or this new drug that helps with memory. I don't know what I should do, I haven't told anybody and I was hoping you'd give me some advice."

I paused for a response, but there was just an awkward silence, so I kept going. "The doctor doesn't think anything is really wrong, but he said that this drug, I think it's called Aricept, allows the neurotransmitters in your brain to remain in the synapses longer, and I guess that helps your memory. I'm kinda thinking I should try it, so I don't have more severe memory problems when I'm older."

There, I did it. A boldface lie. I didn't die, and I didn't go to hell. I thought it was convincing. Well, it would have been more convincing if I was 65 years old instead of 43. I prayed that Dad wouldn't see through me. I looked over at him again for a response. I was taller than him by a couple inches, but it felt as if I was looking way up to him. I had become that little kid again.

Dad stroked his chin, as if he was reflecting for a moment and about to give some sage advice. "I think you should go on it, Garrett. You're getting a little older, and it might help you. I don't think it could hurt."

I couldn't believe it. Dad bought it! All that remained for me to do was lay down the final stroke of the grand fabrication.

"Ah, Dad, do you ever worry about your memory?" Now I knew he would see through me. Could I be any more transparent?

"That's funny, I've had a touch of memory problems lately myself. Maybe I should go on this drug, too. What's the name of it? Aricept? I don't think it would hurt to try it. Hey, we could go on it together!"

This was too good to be true. How could Dad be so naive to fall for this? I still couldn't believe it. It felt like a cloud had lifted over me. I switched the subject immediately, as I didn't want to risk loosing any of the ground I had just gained. Yeah, we'll talk some sports. That's always safe.

"Hey Dad, do you think the Lions will be any good this year?"

"I don't know, Son. They haven't been the same since Barry retired."

We arrived at the fork in the trail. We veered to the left, trudged through some prickly weeds, and there it was, the sacred blackberry patch. There were hundreds of big, ripe berries. We packed three large baggies full. It was the best blackberry score we had ever had.

I was so happy I practically skipped coming back to the condo. Dad seemed happy and full of energy, like he had been revitalized somehow. When we got back, Stacy met us at the door. Dad burst in first, talking a hundred miles a minute, like an excited little kid.

"Stacy, Garrett's got some memory problems but he's going to take care of it by going on Aricept. I'm going to help out by going on it too. We'll both help each other!"

The rest of the weekend was spent swimming and playing games of catch with the girls in the water. I didn't bring up the subject again. Shani got her customary "whale back rides" on her Grampy's back in the pool. Miah floated around on her little swimming ring. All was right with the world, again, at least for now.

At the end of the weekend, I asked Dad if he would consider retiring soon, stressing that he was approaching 70, and that he could build close relationships with his grandchildren if he lived nearby. I was surprised when he didn't resist this, either. He told me to set up a meeting with our family's financial advisor, Mark Peck, to see if <u>we</u> could afford it. I told him I would. I couldn't believe he had come around so quickly, even if I had tricked him. There was no resistance, no fight. I had done it. I had lied successfully for the greater good.

Two weeks later I learned that I was the one who had been tricked. One of my father's neighbors told me that Dad had confided in him. Dad told him that he was being evaluated for Alzheimer's disease and had been placed on a trial of medication. Dad knew exactly what I was doing on that walk. He had played along with my little charade to protect me from having to confront him directly. He didn't want me to feel any more pain than I had to. Although I shed some tears upon hearing the news, I finished my cry with a smile. Dad was still in there, acting as my dad. And he was still The Champion.

8 { The Clearing

My sense of victory from my walk with Dad didn't last very long. I had had an anxiety filled week at work after we returned from Bay City. There wasn't anything going on at work that was particularly stressful during the week that would account for the anxiety I was feeling. No, the anxiety was coming from another source. It was coming from all the pain, fear, and the anticipation of more pain and fear that I had stoically bottled up during the visit with Dad. It was now threatening to erupt from me like a volcano. But I wouldn't let it come out naturally. I fought it. I needed to remain strong. Strong for whom?

I did what I usually did during my life when I got stressed about something, I started cleaning the house. Although I usually was aware that my cleaning was a way of binding my anxiety, I always rationalized that the house really did need to be cleaned, and that I was the most efficient one in the family to get this done. I had two strategies for cleaning the house. One was a lot healthier than the other. The healthier version was to send the girls out to go shopping, socializing, or to the movies for the day. This version had an enormous amount of secondary gain for me besides the house just getting cleaned up. The girls would be relieved they didn't have to do this tedious chore, they would have fun on their all day outing, and they would come home happy, and to an immaculately cleaned house. I would win in this arrangement, too. I would drink a couple beers, blast my stereo system to my heart's content, be alone for a whole day, and burn out my demons. It was a perfect arrangement.

The second strategy for cleaning the house wasn't so healthy. I would be irritable and dictatorial, tell the kids and Stacy that it was "cleaning day," without any prior warning or regard for their plans, and direct them as to what part of the housecleaning chores belonged to each of them. This would create immediate friction in the home, and the resistance from three assertive, strong willed females would be formidable. Usually this strategy evoked a lot of anger. At best the girls would only reluctantly participate in the housecleaning, and the job would never be up to my impossibly high standards. This strategy didn't work, and invariably caused a lot of damage. It ended with the house being only partially cleaned, and the girls angry with me, "the tyrant." I would retreat into a martyr-esque stance that "I'm the only one around here that works hard to keep the house up." Hours later, I would come to my senses and realize that I had dumped all of my stress on the girls, that I had been unreasonable, and that I had indeed acted like a tyrant. I would then feel really guilty and apologize. In looking back on this now, this sounds a lot like how my father would act after drinking. The only difference was that I could do this without the alcohol.

On this particular Saturday, I chose the unhealthy option. I woke up, stressed about the events of the past week, surveyed the house for a few minutes, and autocratically decided it was "cleaning day." The kids and Stacy were still asleep when I had made the decision. They probably had plans of their own for the day, which might have involved something fun to do with me. But it didn't matter. The house was a mess, and I was going to be in control.

Shani and Stacy did have plans for this particular day. They promptly told me that they were not going to be cleaning that morning, but they did offer to help clean "later." "Later" was a word I didn't trust when I was in one of these funks. To me, "later" was code for "this is so low on my priority list I'll get to it when I feel like it," which could mean another day, another week, or never. I could have just gone to the healthier housecleaning option at this point. But not this day. Today I had to pick a fight.

"How come nobody helps take care of this house? It's always me that does it! How come nobody ever helps _me_?!!" After last week's ordeal in Bay City, this was exactly the wrong thing to say.

Stacy had never been passive, and despite her petite frame, she could fight back with razor sharp intensity. "We know you're hurting, but you're not going to take it out on me, or anyone else in this family! Good God, why don't you just let yourself be sad? Who gives a shit about if the house is cleaned or not? Your father has just been diagnosed with Alzheimer's disease!"

Now there was no place to hide. Stacy had stripped me of my only defenses. There was no comeback. Even if I tried to fight back, I would lose. She was right. I felt a huge sea of tears try to push up toward the surface. I could have let them come right then and there if I had only been brave enough. Instead, I turned my back. I had decided to be a coward. I angrily told Stacy that I would do the cleaning by myself. Which I did.

An hour into the cleaning, I was desperately trying to take my feelings out on the bathroom floor, but it wasn't working.

Then the phone rang. I muttered silently inside my head, "I'll be damned if I'm going to answer it, I'm busy cleaning, Stacy can get that, she's not doing anything." Looking up from the floor, I saw Stacy standing at the bathroom's doorway. Despite our fight, she had a kind, empathic look on her face. "Garrett, honey, it's for you. It's your dad."

The sadness and fear had come up from the depths. It emerged as a big lump in my throat. I could barely get out two words. "Hi Dad."

Dad's voice was upbeat. "Great news! I saw Dr. Jahnke this week. I've started taking the Aricept! I have to keep this, ah, er, ah, whatchamacallit, you know, you write on it, yeah, you know, the whatchamacallit." No more denial, Garrett. Classic Alzheimer's symptom: word retrieval problems, especially for nouns.

I instinctively helped Dad complete the sentence, something that I was going to become quite adept at. "You mean you have to complete a journal?"

"Yeah, that's it. How'd you know? I have to write in it every day to tell Dr. Jahnke if the medicine is working." Dad was so positive I couldn't believe it. Why does he sound so relieved?

I changed the subject to something safer. "Hey Dad, do you want to get together next week for the Spartan game? You could come down here this time."

"Yeah, sure, Garrett, that sounds great. I'll come down next Saturday morning." Then he closed as abruptly as the call had come in. Dad always ended a phone conversation with me the same way. "Love you, Garrett. And give my love to Stacy and the girls."

For a man that had such problems with intimacy his whole life, those closing words were so significant for him. I don't think I ever fully appreciated them, until he got sick.

I turned off the phone and laid it on the bathroom counter. I started scrubbing again. But I was only able to scrub for a second or two. The tears were all the way up. This time, I chose the healthy option. I let them flow. I was not prepared for the eruption, and it was stronger than I had anticipated. I cried. Violently. So violently my whole body shook. I tried to stop, but I couldn't pull the feelings back in.

I was unaware that 3 year old Miah had come to the bathroom door and seen me like this. She had silently crept back to her mom. I could hear her in the kitchen. "Mommy, Daddy's in the bathroom crying."

I thought, "Oh no, dear God, my daughter's seen me crying, I'm not supposed to be doing this. I'm the parent. I'm the father. Please God, please, help me get back in control." But I couldn't stop.

The next recollection I had was of Stacy coming in and holding me. She said only two words, "It's OK," and she started crying. Shani and Miah came in. I don't know how long we were down there on the floor. It was long enough to cleanse me.

For the rest of the day I felt healthy. I felt connected again, not just to my family, but also to myself. I put away the cleaning supplies and went out jogging. When I came back I took a long, hot shower and then played with my kids.

As the day wore down, I tried to convince myself I was through with the grieving. I really thought that one, long, healing cry would do it. I had made it through the worst and there would be nothing but better days ahead.

I was wrong. God had only given me a brief reprieve. I had been steered to the clearing just enough to catch my breath. I had not found my way out of the forest yet.

9 { Monday Morning

After my meltdown and cleansing cry, I made it through the weekend in surprisingly good shape. In fact, I started the workweek a bit on the cheerful side. When I came into work Monday morning for my treatment team meeting, I decided to tell everyone that my dad had been diagnosed with Alzheimer's disease. It's funny, I never had any trouble going to my program staff with my fears and worries. I couldn't always do this with my family, but I could do it rather easily with my work colleagues. They were like my surrogate family. They loved to tease and roast me in good times, but in bad times they were nothing but kind and supportive. They had seen me through several rough times in the last few years, including the death of Stacy's mom in 1994, my dad's successful battle with prostate cancer in 1995, and his triple by-pass surgery the following year. My staff was like a team of guardian angels. They always preached that family was more important than work. And they meant it. Many times before they had pushed me out of the office to take care of family business. I could count on them, and I knew I could trust them with my current situation.

Our staff at the time consisted of six caseworkers, a casework aide, and a casework supervisor. Some were older, seasoned veterans, some were young and full of enthusiasm, some were black, and some were white. Most were female. I had known all of them for over a decade, and some of them for two decades. Together we ran the Intensive Neglect Services Unit of the Family Court, a highly successful rehabilitative program that sought to return high risk children to their previously neglectful or abusive homes with intensive services, treatment, and monitoring in place.

It was not at all unusual for our cases to remain with us in the INS program for one to two years, and in many cases the clients had trouble separating from us even after that. This was unheard of for a court-sanctioned program, but all of us in the INS program knew we had a certain magic that truly saved families' lives. And we knew what that magic was. We treated our clients with the same respect we would treat our own loved ones. We would build trust in them. And then we would create a sort of foster care environment for the whole family, a safe cocoon where they could learn to treat each other better. Previously abusive parents would attach to our staff, resolve their own childhood histories of loss and abuse, and in the process, gain more empathy for their own children. It was a phenomenal process. But it was not without its trials and tribulations. The clients had a lot of initial anger, resistance and trepidation about trusting court workers in a program they were <u>ordered</u> into.

I got to work a little early that Monday morning so I could mentally rehearse what I was going to say to my staff. I put my briefcase away and looked for a legal pad to take notes on at staff meeting. I was distracted a little by the small red light that was illuminated on my desk phone. This meant that there was a message waiting for me on my voice mail. It was rarely good news when that little light was on, as most messages left for the court psychologist involved serious problems with the families we worked with. On Monday mornings, the messages often involved crises that had occurred through the weekend. I had grown accustomed to that little red light being on when I came in to work each Monday. I braced myself for the impending rush of adrenalin that would follow the recording and the expected emergencies.

I punched in the access codes and waited for that generic female voice that would tell me how many crises were waiting for me: "Dr. Garrett Turke, you have one unopened, voice mail message." Well, at least I knew it was, at worst, just one crisis. I had had days when as many as six were waiting.

But this one wasn't about work: "Hello, Dr. Turke, this is Barbara Jahnke. I'm your dad's neurologist. I talked to your wife a week ago Friday. I need to speak to you about your father's condition. It's important that we get together as soon as possible. Your father has an appointment tomorrow, Tuesday, at 11:00, here in Saginaw. I was wondering if you could come up for that."

So much for my little reprieve. So much for being the hero on the blackberry hunt.

I did talk to my staff that Monday morning. They all told me to go take care of my father, and not to worry about work. They told me they would arrange coverage for my clients and the therapy groups that I ran. I thought their reaction was a bit extreme. I was back in avoidance mode again. I told them, "For God's sake, I'm just going to be gone tomorrow." Mo, our casework supervisor, then gave me a directive. It reminded me immediately of something Stacy would do. "Garrett, your father needs you now. We'll see you in a few weeks."

That was exactly what I didn't want to hear. How can I avoid this if I can't come back to work for a few weeks?

My staff wouldn't even let me complete the staff meeting. I was pushed out the door, just like all the other family crises I had been through with them.

As I drove home I remember feeling touched by the sensitivity of my staff. I choked up and a few tears trickled down my face. I loved these people.

10 { The Appointment

It was the morning of September 21, 1999. It was a cloudy, cool day, and the first hints of fall were in the air. Some of the trees were already turning. Although I loved fall, there was always some sadness when those first cool days came. It was the inevitable sign that summer was almost gone.

My prime years with Dad were behind me. I couldn't help but think that my father would soon be gone. I thought of all the fun and loving times from my childhood with him. Jumping the waves together in the Pacific Ocean. Going to the Dodger games at Chavez Ravine Stadium in Los Angeles. Seeing Elgin Baylor, Jerry West, and Wilt Chamberlain take on the Celtics at the Forum. Clutching Dad's waist with my eyes closed on the Matterhorn Bobsled ride at Disneyland. And as a teenager, sailing around Marion Island in Grand Traverse Bay, in our little 14 foot Sunfish, on a day where we should never have been that far out in mighty Lake Michigan.

Today I was going to meet Dr. Jahnke with Dad. I had come up the night before by myself. I had had another fitful night in Dad's guest room.

I remember carrying on a trite conversation with Dad during the fifteen minute drive from my father's home in Bay City to Dr. Jahnke's office in Saginaw. But inside, I was praying. Dear God, please help my father. I don't want him to feel any pain. Please God, give me strength. I don't know if I can do this. I felt that familiar tingle down my spine when I knew I was connecting. Connecting to what I didn't exactly know. But it was greater than me and it was comforting. Some people I have talked to call this feeling the Holy Spirit. Giving it a name never mattered much to me.

We looked for the Medical Arts I Building that housed Dr. Jahnke's neurology practice. Dad saw it first. He was anxious to get to the appointment, and to be on time. I remembered what he had taught me as a child, "If you're not ten minutes early, you're late." I looked at the van's clock. Ten forty-eight. Yep, we would be ten minutes early, almost exactly. But I wasn't ready.

Then again, would there ever be enough time to be ready for something like this?

As we walked in, Dad told me how much he liked Dr. Jahnke. She had been one of his psychiatry rotation students years before, and he was proud that he had been her instructor and mentor. My dad's relationship with his students was everything to him. That was another thing I loved about my dad. In the professional arena, it was all about respect and mentoring relationships. Relationships with his students mattered to him. They were real people, not just a student number passing through his clinical rotation. Dr. Jahnke was an important person to my father. Seeing her today was more important to him than the news she would bring.

"Walter, would you come on in?' It was Dr. Jahnke's nurse, Carolyn. "Are you Walter's son, Garrett? We were hoping you could come up." We shook hands. Dad was at the top of his game. It was almost as if he was at a homecoming reunion. "This is my son, Garrett. He's my role model. He works with gang members in Lansing, trying to get them into a better life. He is the greatest." My father bragged about me every chance he could. On the surface this often embarrassed me, but it always reaffirmed that he loved me. And I knew which of those two feelings was more important.

Dr. Jahnke was an extraordinary person. When she entered the room, I understood right away why Dad liked her so much, and why Stacy was so impressed with her over the phone. "Hi, Walter! How are we doing today?" She was a cherubic woman with a large frame and a kind and compassionate face, full of energy and maternal warmth. "I'm Barbara. And you must be Garrett. Walter talks about you all the time. He really loves you, you know. I must say I love your dad, too. You know he used to be my professor some years ago."

Dr. Jahnke had already begun her physical examination of Dad. "One of the best professors I ever had. He loves his work, loves to teach, and loves his pupils. Walter, can you stand up for me, just walk to the wall over there, yes, just like that, now walk backwards for me just a bit..."

Dr. Jahnke continued with her exam, but for a moment I stopped paying attention. I was mesmerized by Dr. Jahnke's charisma. She had melted me. I didn't need to regard her as a threat. I knew within a few minutes that she would help me take care of Dad. A guardian angel had arrived just when I needed one.

"Garrett, we're going to be in this together. Walter's got a bit of a fight ahead of him, but we'll be with him every step of the way. There's a lot you'll have to learn, and very quickly. We'll help you here; it's what we do. I don't want you to ever hesitate to call me. Now Walter, I want you to put your fingers behind you're back, how many am I holding now?" I recognized the finger-agnosia test from my internship at Children's Hospital of Michigan some twenty years before.

Dr. Jahnke continued, "Garrett, my grandmother had Alzheimer's disease, I may get it myself someday, but right now everything is about helping your Dad. You know how loved you are, Walter? You've got a fine son here, and he's so responsible. You know his wife Stacy loves you too, and you have a loving daughter, Tiffanie."

"Yes, Tiffie" Dad replied. His response sounded strange to me. My father hadn't called her that since she was a little girl. Dr. Jahnke went on rapidly, like a guardian angel on a huge amount of caffeine: "Yes, they all love you, and they're all willing to help us!" Dr. Jahnke instinctively knew Dad would do better if he felt that he was a part of a team. I was already planning on making Dr. Jahnke our team's captain.

But she turned on me. "Now Garrett, you're going to be our team's captain!"

I was stunned, silent, but internally, my mind raced: What, me? The Captain? No, no, no! I want you to be the Captain. I don't think I can do this.

Dr. Jahnke interrupted my self-defeating thinking: "I'm going to teach you today what our team needs to do right now to help Walter. And after we're done with your dad's exam this morning, I'll give you some materials about what you'll need to do as power of attorney."

Power of attorney? I have to do what? No, I don't think so. I can't handle all of this. I felt my blood rush to my head, a precursor to an anxiety attack.

Dr. Jahnke continued. "Garrett, I want you to pay attention. You're a psychologist, and a great one. Walter told me. You'll know how to do this. I'm going to give your dad a test called the Mini Mental Status Examination. It's a quick test that gives us a gauge of his mental status functioning. We'll be giving it here every time you two come in. And after a while, we'll be asking you to give it to him at home. It will tell how much he's dropping off cognitively."

Now I was getting really uncomfortable. That last comment hit home with me, and with my Dad. I glanced over at him sheepishly. His face had turned beat red and his bottom lip quivered a little, like a frightened kid separating from his parents on his very first day of school. I felt horrible, because my Dad just heard the equivalent of a death sentence. His death sentence! And there was nothing I could do to overturn it. Now I wasn't so sure about the guardian angel. This seemed excruciatingly cruel to me.

Dr. Jahnke sensed I was uncomfortable. She went back to the team approach. "Now Garrett, remember, we're all in this together. You've got plenty of good times left with your Dad. And Walter, you have plenty of good times ahead with Garrett and your family. The Aricept your dad is taking now will help buy us some more time together. But we can't ignore this. Garrett, your dad has Alzheimer's disease and it's OK to talk about it."

Dr. Jahnke grabbed my father's hand warmly and continued on with her exam. My father's previously flushed face returned to normal, and he became chatty again. It was almost as if he had forgotten the death sentence already.

On the other hand, I was still pale as a ghost. I had been hoping to escape from today's appointment without having to mention or acknowledge the "A" word in front of my dad. And now, there was absolutely no place to hide or escape. Dr. Jahnke had hit me straight between the eyes.

Dr. Jahnke was ready to start administering the Mini Mental Status Exam, which consisted of 30 questions, and took only five or ten minutes to give. She started by giving me instructions. "Garrett, you'll be giving this test to Walter eventually. A normal range score is between 27 and 30 points. Most Alzheimer's patients will show a drop of about 4 to 5 points a year, and more than that if we stop loving them. It's so easy to stop loving at some point because the pain is so great for the family to bear. But you are responsible and very loving. You see, Walter told me all of this. You must promise me to see this through."

I nodded dutifully, but internally I was a wreck. I looked over at Dad. His bottom lip was quivering again. He fought back the tears, but a few managed to trickle down his face. "This... this is my son." He choked and could barely get out the words. "I'm very, very proud of him."

The test began, thank God, because I had completely frozen up. "Now Walter, what year is this?"

"Its almost 2000, you know that."

"And what month is it? "

"It's summer."

"OK, we'll give you that one. And what day is it?"

"Why it's Tuesday, of course."

"And the date?" "It's September 21st."

"What state do we live in?"

"Michigan."

"And the city you're in now?" I thought, unfair question, he doesn't live in Saginaw.

"Why we're in Saginaw."

"And the Township?" Geeze, another trick question, I don't even know that!

"Ah, I think its Saginaw Township."

"That's right Walter!" Now my Dad was beaming. He was acing the test. In fact, he had one more point than I had.

"And where are we sitting right now?"

"Why Dr. Jahnke, don't you know we're in your office at the Medical Arts I Building?"

"OK, Walter, we're about halfway done. Repeat after me. Apple, table, penny."

"Apple, table, penny. Easy"

"OK, one more time, because I'm going to ask you to recall these things later. Apple, table, penny."

"Apple, table, penny."

"OK, lets take a break for a second, we're almost finished."

At the halftime break, Dad had a perfect score of 11, even with those couple of trick questions. I thought to myself, what if there's a mistake here? Maybe Dad has some vitamin deficiency, or some concentration problem that people are mistaking for Alzheimer's. Maybe he doesn't really have Alzheimer's disease after all. I had temporarily slipped back into the land of denial.

It was time for the second half. "Now Walter, what's the name of this thing I'm wearing?"

"Why that's your watch, of course"

"And this?"

'That's your pen."

"And what's this?"

"Those are my glasses."

"Walter, would you repeat after me. No ifs, ands, or buts."

Dad was really enjoying this now, sensing his competency. "No ifs, ands, or buts."

"Great, you're doing very well!"

I was still living in the land of denial. I thought he'd show at least some impairment. Instead, he was beating me.

"So now, Walter, you remember those three words I told you earlier, that you repeated twice for me?"

"Yes."

"Could you repeat them for me please?"

"Sure. Lets see, uh, there's, uh, um...you know, the whatchamacallit, um, ah..."

I tried to feed Dad the words through telepathy. Come on Dad, its apple, table, penny. Apple, table, penny. Apple, table, penny! Come on, just get one. Come on! It's apple. Apple. Apple, damnitall! It was no use, no matter how hard I willed it, Dad came up blank. There it was again. Classic Alzheimer's symptom number one, word retrieval problems, especially for nouns.

Dr. Jahnke glanced at me. I understood her telepathy easily. Did you catch that, Garrett?

Yeah, I caught it. The test continued on, but it didn't make sense to root for Dad anymore. I just sat back and let it run its course. Dad "rebounded" at the close of the test and rattled off 12 straight points, including spelling the word "world" backwards orally. He finished the test with 27 out of 30 points, still within the normal range. My dad was very proud of himself. I felt sad, scared, and flat. I saw his impairment again right before my eyes, and there was no getting around it.

"OK, Walter, we're just about done for today. I want you to go up to the office check out counter with Carolyn. She'll get you set up with some more samples of Aricept. I've got lots of samples right now, enough to get you through to your next appointment in a couple months. Garrett, that should save you guys a couple hundred bucks. Walter, it was great seeing you again. She grabbed his hands and then wrapped her free arm around his shoulders lovingly. Dad smiled, and seemed as relaxed as a person could be, which made absolutely no sense to me.

"Come on Dad, let's get your samples and get something to eat. I'm starving." I was done. Please, God, just let me get out of here.

Dr. Jahnke looked over at me. "Actually, Garrett, now I need some time with you. Carolyn, could you help Walter get set up with his meds? Garrett and I are going to stay back for awhile."

As my father left the room, my face flushed red. I had to bite down hard to keep my lower lip from quivering.

11 { My Come to Jesus Meeting

I was sitting all alone in Dr. Jahnke's office. She had excused herself for a minute to go get some power of attorney materials for me. I was trapped. I felt increasingly claustrophobic in that little examining room, like the walls were closing in. I thought I was about to have a panic reaction.

I had not had a full blown panic attack for years, maybe even decades, but they were not unfamiliar to me. I had had a number of them in high school after we had moved to Michigan from Los Angeles. Panic attacks are one of the worst feeling states a person could ever experience. The body prepares for attack from some poorly defined or poorly understood source. The fight or flight response kicks in, but there's no real place to run to or flee. Coupled with this need for flight is a painful sense of detachment, a scary, surreal feeling that many people misinterpret as a sign of "going crazy." It is really the mind's attempt to psychologically detach from a situation that your body can't physically flee from. I suppose my anxiety reactions in high school had a lot to do with sucking in so much anger from the move, mixed with a feeling of helplessness, and the terrible sense of loneliness and isolation I had at the time. That same brutal mix of feelings had found me again in Dr. Jahnke's office.

Dr. Jahnke burst in. "Now Garrett, I know this is going to be tough, but you're gonna have to step up here. There's a lot to do. First, you are going to have to assign yourself or someone responsible to be power of attorney and ready yourself to take over all of your father's affairs. Your dad is still able to manage his affairs now, but he won't be at some point in the future. I'll be able to tell you when he's no longer competent."

I was teetering on panic, but I was the dutiful first born, so I covered it up...barely. "Dr. Jahnke, could both my sister and I be power of attorney?" I was looking for at least a little respite from the pressure. Instead, another hit between the eyes.

"Yes, technically you could, but I wouldn't recommend it. When the responsibility is shared among family members, what usually happens is that when there is conflict, no one is able to step up and make a decision."

"But my sister and I get along great, we don't have a lot of conflict."

"Garrett, I don't know quite how to put this. I don't know your sister, and I'm sure you two do get along, but there is <u>always</u> conflict in these matters. You'll have disagreements about how impaired he is, if he should be allowed to continue driving, if he needs to go to a residential facility, when to stop the life support when the time comes."

Now I was bloodied, reeling in the corner of the ring, just waiting for Dr. Jahnke's knock out punch. And it came. "Garrett, your sister is younger. You are more mature. You are used to handling pressure at your job. Your dad trusts you. It's not a question of him loving you or Tiffanie more. This is what he wants."

I couldn't respond. Dr. Jahnke didn't wait to see if I would.

"I want you to get your name on his bank accounts and investments. You'll eventually have to take over all of this. I'll be able to give you a letter when he's no longer competent, and then you'll take over completely."

I was stunned and couldn't speak.

Dr. Jahnke continued with her list of instructions. "Next, you're going to have to help him find a way to retire with dignity. Right now he's terribly angry and humiliated by this whole ordeal. He thinks people are singling him out at work and trying to get rid of him. Garrett, these are people who love your dad. They're just worried about him. Garrett, they don't think he can continue doing his job much more. He can't remember his colleague's or his patient's names. Even his new students are seeing the impairment. Garrett, he's getting lost in the building he's been working in for the past 10 years."

"Dr. Jahnke, he didn't seem that impaired today, he got a 27 on the test, I got a 29."

"Garrett, he's not that <u>visibly</u> impaired today. The disease is funny when it first starts; it kind of comes and goes. He'll have three or four pretty good days, then a bad one. Eventually, he'll have more days when he's noticeably impaired, and then he'll always seem impaired. I'm really, really sorry. But you need to know this. We don't know how much time we have."

I didn't want to ask the next question, but I did. "How much time does he have?"

"Honestly, I don't know. With some patients, the drop off comes very quickly, and they become very impaired in two or three years. With others, the drop off is more gradual, 10, sometimes even 20 years."

"Is there a chance this could be something else?"

"Yes. There are hundreds of causes for dementia, such as vitamin deficiencies, strokes, brain injury, alcohol induced, drug..." I cut her off, hoping she would throw me a crumb.

"My dad sometimes drinks moderately, well sometimes heavily." I couldn't believe I was offering this up as a hopeful sign. It sounded stupid as it came out.

"If it's alcohol induced, he would show a drop off that would then level off. From what I understand of your dad's history I don't think we'll see this. He's showing classic early signs of Alzheimer's."

"What about vitamin deficiencies, a thyroid disorder, diabetes?" I was fishing without a worm, or even a hook.

"We're going to check all that over the next few months. The odds of finding something aren't very good."

"Well how can you be sure its Alzheimer's?"

"We won't know until we do an autopsy and look at his brain. Alzheimer's patients show this characteristic pattern of plaques and tangles in the neural pathways."

Autopsy? Jesus, I was prepared for bad news, but not a post mortem exam. I tried to retain a shred of hope: "Dr. Jahnke, I read where they're doing research on mice, and in some studies they have reversed the effects of Alzheimer's with anti-inflammatory drugs."

"Garrett, they are making progress, but I'm afraid today's research will come too late for your dad. Maybe it will come in time for you and me."

Sensing I was groping for a life vest, Dr. Jahnke pulled her chair up close to me. I could feel that she was being maternal again, not clinical. "This is so hard for you, I know." She choked up a little. 'I watched my grandmother, who I loved so, go through all of this. Garrett, there's something I want to show you in the file. You're familiar with the WAIS?"

Well of course I was. The WAIS is a standardized intelligence test. I had given perhaps 300 of them in my career. An average score is between 90 and 110. Most highly educated professionals, including physicians, have scores over 120, and more typically, over 130. I guessed my father was somewhere around 130, even though he was a mechanical idiot.

Dr. Jahnke pulled out a four page neuro-psychological report, written by a Dr. Bradshaw. It was on my father, and had just been given a month or so before. "Garrett, your dad got an IQ score of 76, with multiple, severe impairments in both the verbal and visual-spatial realms."

I was stunned, and I couldn't censor myself: "Holy shit! 76? That's almost in the mentally retarded range! No, that can't be, he doesn't look that impaired."

"Garrett, your father loves you dearly. He *is* that impaired. The very intelligent people who get this dreaded disease can cover it up very well for a time. They kind of retreat into cognitive areas they are still competent in. I'm going to order some tests here, in our lab, and then order a SPECT Scan at U of M in Ann Arbor. I'll call you when they can get him in. It will probably be in about a month. The SPECT Scan will tell us what parts of the brain still have a lot of electrical activity and what parts of the brain are dying"

I had to give up. This was painfully undeniable. This couldn't be fought.

Carolyn opened the door, with my dad faithfully following, like a new puppy. "Dr. Jahnke, we're all set with Walter. He'll go give us some blood downstairs at Quest Lab. We'll see you two in 8 weeks."

We went downstairs and Dad had some blood drawn at the lab. We talked about getting some lunch at Taco Bell, as we were both starving.

My father and I walked out of the Medical Arts I Building without saying a word about the appointment. We would not talk about it for the rest of the day, or the rest of the week for that matter. We both knew the hourglass had been turned upside down.

12 { Two Weeks

On the way home, we went to Taco Bell and Dad ordered his usual, two bean burritos - without cheese of course. I laughed to myself when he put in his order, because I thought, well, here's at least one good thing about his Alzheimer's, he's eventually going to forget that he hates cheese. It's about time he gets over his stupid aversion. It was the first time I could laugh a little at the situation. I would later learn that I had to sometimes laugh at Dad's condition in order to survive it.

We wolfed down our burritos and continued on back home. I was exhausted from the morning. Dad was not. He was full of energy and excited I had taken two weeks off from work to be with him. I thought how strange it was that he could recover from such traumatic news so quickly, as if he had already forgotten about Dr. Jahnke's death sentence. Months later, I would figure out that this strange indifference to his disease was actually part of the disease process.

I had gotten better at lying, if only with Dad. I told him I had maxed out on vacation time accruing and had to take the next two weeks off. Dad had only taken the day off and was going back to work tomorrow. What was I possibly going to do over the next two weeks? I was already feeling pretty lonely and isolated. I needed my wife. I needed distraction.

When we arrived back at the condominium, there was a package waiting for us on the doorstep. Dad could hardly wait to rip it open, which he did before we even got the door unlocked. It was a movie he had ordered, "Saving Private Ryan." Dad couldn't wait to pop it in his TV player. I didn't really want to watch it, even though I hadn't seen it in the movies.

Once inside, Dad wasted no time in putting the movie in. He didn't have to pull the blinds or darken the room. The blinds were always pulled shut in my father's condo, and it was always dark in there. I never could figure out why he liked to keep his house so dark, like no one was ever home. It seemed kind of paranoid, and it would sometimes give me the creeps.

The movie was way too intense for me this afternoon. The opening scene portrayed thousands of American troops being literally sawed in half by German machine gun fire as they exited their amphibian craft and tried to secure Normandy Beach. Thousands of men had to die before a few could dig themselves in and advance on the Germans. Each wave of amphibian craft watched the line before them get sacrificed, and they knew they were next to be mowed down. I guess the scene underscored the bravery of thousands of men who were sacrificing themselves for the liberation of Europe and freedom. But it also portrayed the savagery and pointlessness of war. Coming straight from Dr. Jahnke's office, a graphic portrayal of violent, savage death was not what I needed.

Dad, by contrast, was a kid at the movies. He was riveted to his big screen TV, enthralled, and thoroughly enjoying himself. He continued to seem oblivious to his condition and the events of the morning. I buckled down and forced myself to pretend to enjoy the movie. But my eyes were not focused on the TV screen. All I could do was think about was Dad's condition and dwell on the events of the morning.

After the movie, Dad made us a nice dinner. It was all out of a can, but the effort and intent were certainly there. We talked a little about the usual benign subjects, and we called Stacy and the girls. Dad was so happy he was "on vacation" with me that I couldn't talk about anything heavy on the phone with him standing next to me. So I sucked in the pain and just played along. Stacy understood and acknowledged the charade from the other end.

We went to bed early that night. I tossed and turned again in the guest room. Dad appeared to sleep like a rock, because I could hear him snoring in the other room.

I wondered if I was going to feel this painful mix of feelings as long as Dad was sick, which now translated to the rest of his life. I prayed, and then I prayed some more. This time I wasn't praying for a miracle cure, that he was misdiagnosed, or for Dad to be protected from pain. This time I prayed for my soul to land in a place where I could feel at peace, at least for a little while. I had a lot of work to do these next two weeks. I didn't know if I would be able to concentrate enough to get the work done. More importantly, I didn't know if I had the strength to be the captain of Dad's team. I prayed and prayed and prayed until I finally fell asleep.

I don't really know how to explain it to anyone, but when I woke up the next morning the world seemed different. I was no longer mired in pain. Instead, I woke up with a sense of purpose. I knew I had to get my dad's affairs in order. Doctor Jahnke had given me a directive. Get the power of attorney, mobilize supports, keep Dad on his meds, start managing his affairs, help him retire with dignity. And most of all, don't ever stop loving him.

Dad was preparing to go off to work when I came out of the guest room. He had thoughtfully set up breakfast for me in the kitchen nook. It wasn't the breakfast an amateur chef would prepare, but it was all my dad could do. A big bowl of fruit. Every cereal box he had in the house. Two different kinds of juice. And several kinds of bread and jams from which to make my father's breakfast staple, toast and jam. It was all laid out on the counter like a poor man's smorgasbord.

Dad was in a hurry to get to work by 7:00. He was an early to bed, early to rise man and had booked his first patient at 7:30. Dad scurried out of the house by 6:50, which of course landed him at the office exactly ten minutes early. I remember being struck at how easily I separated from my dad that morning. Twenty four hours earlier, I would have been worried about leaving him, because of my own fears of loosing him, and because of my fears that he would get lost en route to work. But, strangely, this morning was different. I had let go of some of the pain and fear. Or perhaps, something else had removed the pain and fear from me.

Today wasn't going to be about feeling sorry for myself, or for Dad. I had work to do. It was time to show Dad I loved him. I was no longer the boy who needed his father to take care of him. It was now time for me to take care of Dad, unconditionally. Not just for a day, or for a week, or for a few months while he recovered from prostate cancer or by-pass surgery. This time, there would be no recovery period. The arrangement would be permanent, until his time came. I had no power to change any of it. I had to accept it and just let things be.

There were so many things to do. The obsessive compulsive side of me had taken over and I had quickly turned Dr. Jahnke's five goal directive into a list of 57 things that had to be accomplished by the end of my two weeks with him. Thoughts of what I needed to do swirled inside my head with manic flight and intensity. I could barely keep up with them in order to write them down: Call Stacy. Call my mother. Call my sister, Tiffanie. What do I do about my other sister, Dad's estranged daughter, Cindy? I put a question mark by her name. Find out everything I could about Dad's finances. Contact his attorneys. Talk to his financial planner. Look at a realtor for him. Get a hold of realty listings in East Lansing. Figure out what he needs to do to retire. Call his personnel office. Contact his doctors. Call some moving companies to estimate the move to East Lansing. See what needs to be done about change of address, and change of doctors. Review his will, and his estate affairs. Get permission from Dad to be in charge of everything. Have his attorney draw up all the papers. Get ready to take it all over, his bills, his credit cards, his investments, scheduling appointments, hell, scheduling everything. Plan his retirement. Plan the remainder of his life.

Making up the free-associated list was easy. Prioritizing what needed to be done when was a different story. My usual way of prioritizing tasks came from my years of work experience. I took my list of 57 jobs to do and split them up across 8 days. Whatever wasn't finished from a day's list of tasks would then go to the top of the list for the next day. This ensured that the most important things got accomplished. Pretty OCD, as my colleagues often joked, but this strategy had served me well. I left the evenings and weekends free to spend "quality time" with Dad. I hadn't yet come to realize that with the hour glass now turned upside down, every second with Dad was now "quality time."

I found myself struggling with the first four things that landed atop my list: Calling Stacy, my mother, and my two sisters. I should have made these calls already, but I couldn't do it. Calling these people would mean that I would have to relive yesterday all over again, painfully explaining what took place in Dr. Jahnke's office, event by event, step by step. I didn't think I could go through this even once, let alone four times.

Aside from Stacy, I expected that there would be unavoidable conflict during each of the calls. I anticipated that my mother would be detached and insensitive, and not show any compassion for a man who had left her for a younger woman some twenty years before. She would be unable to help support me because her past with my father was still festering and unresolved.

I next fantasized that my sister Tiffanie would be immersed in denial and chastise me for following Dr. Jahnke's lead and not getting a second opinion. Plus, I anticipated that Tiffanie would have a big problem with Dr. Jahnke suggesting that I be the one taking over Dad's affairs. It was overwhelming being in charge of Dad's affairs and I would have welcomed splitting the tasks to be done between the two of us. But Dr. Jahnke's advice about having only one person in control of Dad's legal and financial matters was unequivocal. She was the expert in this area, Dad wanted me in charge, and I had to respect both of their wishes.

And then there was that fourth call on my list, to my other sister Cindy, who had been out of contact with Dad for the past ten years. Do I call her? My last reasonably civil phone call with her was over seven years ago. After that, most calls to her had ended with her angrily telling me I was siding with Dad in their conflict and that she did not appreciate my efforts to bring them together. For the past seven years, I had averaged about one phone call per year to her, with each of these phone calls culminating with an emotional blow-up that felt like a nuclear fission had occurred inside my mind. Finally, I had resolved to just leave things alone and not call her for a while. The "a while" part was now going on three years.

I rationalized that I was not yet ready to make any calls. I might call Stacy tonight, yeah, I could handle that. Stacy was always very good at keeping the conversation short when I didn't want to talk, respecting my not so well disguised problems with intimacy. As for Tiffanie and my mother, I could probably handle that tomorrow or Friday. And for Cindy, forget it. There was no way I could handle that issue right now. That could continue to wait "a while."

And so, with intimacy problems in check, and with my dad at work, I decided to tackle the first non-relationship issue on his list, which happened to be Dad's finances. I felt guilty digging around in Dad's financial records, so I concocted another lie in case Dad called me or I felt compelled later on to confess I had been snooping around his house. I would tell him that I was helping him organize and clean his house because I had so much free time while he was at work. Yeah, cleaning and organizing, he would appreciate that.

I knew where Dad kept his checkbook, financial statements, and boxes of cancelled checks – all in a small desk that unfolded out of his wall unit in his bedroom. Although I hadn't technically gotten Dad's permission to go through his finances, I rationalized that this needed to be done and that he needed my help. There was no way I could accept or risk a "no" answer from him anyway. I was beginning to see him as impaired.

I was absolutely unprepared for what I found inside my father's wall unit desk. Once the family poster boy for compulsive organization and financial responsibility, Dad appeared to have randomly strewn his bank statements inside the desk unit for at least a year, maybe two. His checkbook was missing checks as if he had been writing them, yet there was no record in the ledger of what he paid out or to whom. His last notation in his checkbook ledger was from over a year ago, and I noticed that nothing had been balanced correctly for many months prior to this. Apparently, the only thing that had saved him from bouncing hundreds of checks was his substantial direct deposit paychecks and a $4,000 overdraft allotment, which he tapped into frequently according to his bank statements. Dad's checking statements showed that his monthly balance once topped $26,000 dollars, and once dipped to -$3,000 on the low end. Although his income was substantial, his bank statements showed that he sent many thousands of dollars to both the Iowa and Michigan State Medical Schools, apparently without any awareness that he was often overdrawing on his account. No wonder these schools made him a platinum level contributor.

I spent eight out of the next 12 days working on my list. It took three days alone to reconstruct his checkbook ledger from the boxes of cancelled checks. I was true to myself and spent the evenings and the four weekend days just "playing" with my dad. I called Stacy almost every night, sometimes forcing myself to talk about feelings I didn't want to rekindle. I talked to my mom three or four times and each time was surprised to find compassion in her voice, for both me and Dad, and no bitterness from the past. I called my sister Tiffanie and she said I was a hero for helping Dad the way I was. She did have some concerns about not being designated as power of attorney, but we eventually settled it by agreeing that I would be the primary POA and she would be secondary, taking over if I was unable or unavailable to perform my duties. I was surprised everyone had stepped up. I was mad at myself for having been so paranoid.

After a week, things felt like they were starting to work out. I was able to contact Dad's attorneys, his financial planner, and all of his doctors. I was again surprised how kind and helpful everyone was once I explained each time what was going on with my dad's health. Most people bent confidentiality rules if I provided some identifying information, like his social security number. All of the people that Dad had employed treated him like a human being, exuding kindness, concern, and empathy. I could tell by the reactions on the phone how well liked he was.

At the end of my two weeks with Dad, I had watched 17 movies with him, gone on 11 walks through the woods, took two sightseeing trips out of town, and went out to dinner six times. I had convinced him to retire and move to East Lansing within the next three months, and had already started the retirement process with the personnel office at his work. I told Dad that his financial planner had told me that he had enough money to retire, and that his grandchildren were counting on him to spend time with them. I had found Dad a realtor in Bay City to sell his condo. I had convinced Dad to let me share the management of his checkbook, finances, and legal affairs. Both of us knew that "share" was code for me taking control of these responsibilities.

I had also found two fifths and a gallon of scotch while organizing Dad's condo. It probably was wrong of me, but I dumped all three bottles down the toilet. Dad never said a word about where the scotch went. He would never buy another bottle of alcohol again.

We never talked about his disease the entire time I was up there. I think it was mutually understood. Or mutually avoided. Either way, we both knew what we had to do, and what had to be. It was time for me to take over. And it was time for him to let go. My relationship with him would never be the same again.

Something else happened over those two weeks. I got to be with my dad again. This wasn't like visiting him on a few select weekends, or during holidays. This was a lot more real, and a lot more powerful. We became bonded again. I learned what quality time was. And it wasn't some goddamn, overused pop psychology adage that people use to justify spending the bare minimum of time needed to marginally sustain a relationship.

Sometime toward the end of my two weeks with Dad, while he was at work, I had an epiphany of sorts. As I struggled to embrace my newfound role as caregiver, I thought out loud. "Lets see. Dad would have worked until he was 75 or 80 if he had not been stricken with Alzheimer's disease. He would have stayed up in Bay City and we would have seen him a handful of times a year. He probably would have continued to have bouts of alcohol abuse. He probably would have had a heart attack before he got a chance to retire. And he probably would have died alone, and maybe afraid."

With the onset of Alzheimer's disease, my Dad's life had been shortened significantly. I knew that I might only have him as my "recognizable" dad for another year or two. But with my dad's now impending retirement and move, and my new role as his trusted companion and caregiver, I would get back what many people never get back in their lifetime—real time to be with your parent again.

13 { Letters in a Shoebox

While driving home, I thought I could relax for a moment. I had accomplished my 57 things to do, or at least got them all organized, under control, and moving in the right direction. Well, all except item # 4 on the list.

I hadn't called Cindy yet.

Cindy was our family's unfinished business. Ten years before my dad's diagnosis, there had been a huge, incredibly painful falling out between Dad Cindy. The two had not talked in nearly a decade, and to me it seemed that they would never talk again. What made it even more horrific was that it was never very clear what specific thing had happened to cause the rift. I do know that Cindy never really felt loved by our dad. And at some point in the conflict, she asked family members to side with her against Dad. Tiffanie and I refused. My mother also refused, which might be surprising considering what my father had put her through. Mom said that she could make her own decisions about people in her life. We all tried to empathize with Cindy, but she had forced the stakes too high. The three of us, my mother, Tiffanie and me, soon found ourselves "divorced" from Cindy as well.

As usual, the "umpire" in me could see two sides to the conflict. From Cindy's perspective, she felt betrayed and victimized by my father, his drinking, and by the insensitive cruelty of comments that followed some of his binges. At the age of 35, she had made a decision not to try to chase after him anymore to attempt a resolution. In 1992, she had made a clear and seemingly permanent break from him, writing him a scathing letter that she wanted nothing more to do with him. Cindy would, from that point on, increasingly define herself as a victim of parental abuse, which, in turn, led to demands that the rest of the family acknowledge and compensate her for this. Cruel and insensitive as it sounds and perhaps was, I started calling her "the professional victim." Today, I am ashamed I once harbored such destructive thoughts about her.

My father's take on his relationship with Cindy was entirely different. There was no doubt that he loved her, and missed her. He had talked incessantly over the past decade about wanting to make peace with her. He was constantly talking about the good times we all had together when we were children, as if to convince us that none of the bad had ever happened. The "bad," had been debated within the family for years, and ranged from questions if Dad had ever explicitly abused her, to whether she was the forgotten "middle child," to did she distort her childhood to enable her to separate from Dad as an adult. Whatever actually happened was a mystery, painful, festering, and unresolved.

Dad often came to me asking what he could do to try to impart to Cindy that he loved her. He wanted to contact her, but said that she had specifically instructed him not to ever call or write her. I tried so hard to not tell Dad that I thought the situation was hopeless. So I told him to keep on writing her, but to respect her wishes by not mailing any of the letters. Instead, I told him to place the letters in a shoebox, with the hope that someday he could give them to her, and show her that he did love her all these years. My father said that he faithfully had complied with my advice, writing her letters periodically and purchasing cards for her birthday and holidays. I never saw any of them, and wondered if he had ever actually purchased a card or written anything for her.

During my two weeks with Dad I had been in every room of his house organizing things for his move. I found in a corner of his bedroom closet, high atop a shelf, a lone shoebox. I didn't fully appreciate what was in it at the time I discovered it, and expected to find a new pair of Iowa Hawkeye athletic shoes inside. I opened the box to find letters addressed to Cindy. Ten years of letters. Maybe ten years of answers to the family questions. I was tempted to solve the family's mystery by opening up the letters and reading them. But I couldn't, and so I returned the box back to its place up on the shelf. I'd like to say my sense of ethics prevented me from opening those letters, but that would be a lie.

The fact of the matter was that I was afraid to open them.

14 { Coming Home

The mid afternoon November sun was low on the horizon, foretelling the long Michigan winter that was to come. The sun pierced my eyes, and I had to squint through the streaky glass in order to see the road ahead. My dad was asleep in the passenger seat next to me, snoring away. Driving Dad's old prized car, a fire engine red, 1977 Mercedes 450 SL 2-seater, I had trouble seeing through the smeared, grimy windshield. Years of Dad's cigar smoking had left a filmy yellow-brown residue on all of the interior surfaces of his car. He had given up cigars a couple years before, but we could never get all of the smoke residue and smell out of that car. Heading down I-75, I wondered how Dad was ever able to see while driving to work.

My father's cigar smoke had been a prominent feature in my life since my childhood. It was another vice my father had picked up in the Navy, and another crutch that helped him defend against his ever-present, underlying feelings of insecurity and anxiety. My mother told me that Dad used to say that having a cigar by his side gave him a sense of power, that it helped put him at ease when he felt uncomfortable or awkward socially.

Whether it empowered him or not, Dad's cigar smoking was a constant source of conflict within our family for most of my childhood and adolescence. During my elementary school years, a lot of my friends didn't want to come over to our house or ride in the car with my dad because of the smoke. Some of the kids at school would tease me that I should cut down on my cigar smoking, because each day I arrived at school with that pungent smell reeking from my clothes. As a teenager, Dad's cigar smoking was the source of much arguing between my dad and my increasingly health conscious mother. My mother wanted him to only smoke outside the house. Eventually, Dad retreated to the sanctuary of his Mercedes to smoke his prized cigars. It would be the last place he would smoke before he quit.

And now, after all my anger, all my embarrassment, and all my worries he would someday get cancer from those damn cigars, I kind of missed that smell. I missed the familiarity. That smell was tied to my whole lifetime with my dad.

I put on a pair of my dad's sunglasses hoping it would cut down on the streaky glare coming through the windshield, but it didn't help much. I would have to wait until we got to Flint and made that turn to the west toward Lansing before I would be able to get the sun out of my face. Still, it was a good day for driving in November. Behind us was my white Chrysler minivan, with Stacy driving and the girls inside. It was packed to the ceiling with Dad's art, six decades worth of mementos, and all of his paintings and a sculpture that was too fragile or too valuable to send with the movers. The moving van had left earlier in the day. They had another stop to make and would be arriving in East Lansing tomorrow with all of Dad's furniture.

Behind the white minivan was Bay City, and all of my memories of Dad there. Also behind us was Dad's autonomy. From this day forward, he would be dependent on other people to survive. I'm not sure Dad knew all this as we headed down I-75. But today was the first day ever that he let me drive his prized Mercedes, with him in the passenger seat.

The past month had been a blur. I had come up to Bay City each weekend after our appointment with Dr. Jahnke in September. I came up to get Dad's retirement in order with his personnel department, and to help Dad pack up his house, room by room. Each weekend we did a different room. And each room represented different phases of my dad's life. These memories were all in boxes now. Things had changed. I thought that all there was to do now was to preserve memories rather than create them.

During the weekdays, my sister Tiffanie and I had been scouting out various condos for sale in East Lansing that would be close to our homes. We had had quite a debate within our family as to whether we should have Dad live with one of us or have him stay in his own place. We didn't know exactly how much time he had left being able to function semi-autonomously, but we did know if we got him his own place he might only be there for a year or two. Would it be worth all the stress and hassle of moving him in for just a year? Why even bother unpacking all his stuff? And what if the worst-case scenario occurred? He might not adjust and deteriorate rapidly. The stove would be left on. He would be up at all hours of the night. He would be confused and depressed. He might wander off and get lost.

Running with these thoughts, both Tiffanie and I entertained fantasies of Dad living with one of us. We struggled mightily with this, wanting to protect our dad from the inevitable dangers that lay in front of us. But then again, Dad never did like being dependent on someone else. Maybe Dad would have some quality time left. Dr. Jahnke had said this could be a slow process. Maybe the Alzheimer's course would slow down, or even stop for a while.

Dad had ended the debate himself. He insisted on getting his own place. There was no debate, no discussion, no argument. We respected his wishes. I think he knew we would be tremendously stressed if he lived with us. He kept reassuring us that we would be close by if he needed anything, and he would simply call us. Tiffanie and I accepted his decision without challenge. The "A" word wasn't mentioned. He was still our father. This was about respect. He still deserved his dignity, until the time came where he couldn't function on his own anymore. For God's sake, I had already talked him into retiring, moved him out of his house, selected a new place for him, and taken charge of his finances and legal affairs. All in six short weeks, and without any resistance. The least I could do was respect his wishes to have his own place. So what if he could only be there a year or two.

Tiffanie and I had found a nice condominium for Dad that was within three miles of my house and less than half a mile from the house Tiffanie and her husband Don were building. They would be moving in soon. If Dad had a problem of any sort, I could be there in about 10 or 15 minutes. Tiffanie could be there inside of a minute. We couldn't possibly get a better set up than this. God had to be smiling on us.

Dad's new condo was beautiful. It had been first owned by a wealthy accountant and his wife who used it as a summer residence in Michigan following wintering in Florida. The ceilings were high and vaulted, the rooms large, with lots of wall space. There was a completely finished, well-lit basement that offered a guest bedroom, a workshop room, a den and shower. Perfect if someone wanted to spend the night. The condominium also had all sorts of amenities, but we didn't realize that each one of these amenities was to become a liability for a man with progressive dementia. The condo was in no way "Alzheimer's proofed." We would later find this out the hard way.

Tiffanie and I had shown the condo to Dad about three weeks earlier. We knew Dad would like it. And he did. Dad fell in love with the condo the minute he saw it. He said he really was looking forward to the collegial atmosphere of East Lansing. He had been a member of the "Spartan family" for years, but he always worked out of the satellite clinic in Saginaw, which of course had none of the perks and none of the prestige of being on campus in East Lansing. Dad told us he felt at home in East Lansing, telling us that it felt like his old college days at the University of Iowa.

Underneath these comments, I think Dad was telling us that he felt like he was coming back home to his kids. He had not lived close to us for the past twenty years, since his divorce from our mother. This was not just a homecoming for Dad, it was a homecoming for Tiffanie and me. We got our Dad back. We might not have that much time left with him, but we were going to make what we had great.

We made it through Flint and our two vehicle caravan made the turn to the west toward Lansing. We would soon be home. The sun was finally out of my eyes and the glare caused by the cigar residue was not so taxing. Dad was still asleep, worn out from all of the packing the day before. The game plan involved spending the night at our house, then meeting the movers at Dad's new condo first thing in the morning. We wanted it to frame the whole thing as a celebration, not as a morbid retreat.

Dad awakened as we came in on the outskirts of East Lansing. He looked over at me and smiled. He choked up a little, like he always did when he was about to say something sincere, and heartfelt: "You're a good son, Baby Fang." Baby Fang was his nickname for me when I was an infant, when I had one front tooth poking through my upper gums. The nickname had survived in our family's oral history my whole life.

I smiled and corrected my dad. "It's Doctor Fang now, Dad."

Dad clutched my free hand and smiled. I felt a gentle shiver run own my spine. I felt like I was back home with my dad.

15 { Moving In

Dad and I surveyed his new condo together, thinking about where we would direct all the furniture when the movers arrived. They were due to come in between 8:30 and 9:00. Being his usual, compulsively organized self, Dad had already laid out the movers' tips, three stacks of six twenty dollar bills. It was a huge tip, and probably more than some of them would earn in a day. But Dad was generous like this. A job well done always earned a big reward in his book.

There was no pecking order underlying Dad's tipping scheme. It didn't matter to Dad if the worker was the owner of the moving company or some 16 year old kid they grabbed off the street to help unload. They all would get the same tip. They were all equal in my Dad's eyes. By readying the tip in advance, it was also assumed that each of the movers would do a good job. And in this little situation there was a microcosm of what Dad valued in life. People were equal. The underdog would always be given respect. He didn't give a shit if you were a manual laborer or the President. It was assumed all would work hard and cooperate. The job would get done collectively. Everyone would sweat the same. And everyone would get the same tip. These would be values I would spend my whole lifetime trying to emulate.

We set up camp in the kitchen. I had diagrammed the condo's floor plan and he mapped out where all the furniture would go. Dad was already armed with everything he needed. A hammer and a box of finishing nails. He couldn't wait to put his treasures back up on the walls.

Dad and I had discussed in advance that we wouldn't clutter up the walls of Dad's new place with <u>all</u> of his art and mementos. We had had several lengthy discussions about how this place would be different than his other homes, that we would "streamline" the condo to make the upkeep simple. We had even discussed that we would do the condo in the Japanese style, meaning very little on the walls and a general freedom from distraction. Dad loved the idea of decorating "Japanese style," and we both readily agreed to only put a fraction of his art up on the walls. And of course, he had been to the Orient three times and had many Japanese and Asian watercolors and prints to choose from. Dad was now retired, and we wanted to keep things as simple as possible to maintain. Well, I guess I wanted to keep things as simple as possible to maintain.

The movers arrived a half hour early, which Dad, of course, appreciated. It was pretty much the team that we expected, a boss-type who had two others working for him. The boss-type was rather gruff, a little crude, and all about business. He was friendly, well at least superficially, but it was clear he wanted to "get in and get out." He probably had several more deliveries to do today, even though it was Saturday. One of the helpers was a worn-out looking man in his forties or early fifties. Perhaps he was still in his late thirties if life had been unkind to him. He looked kind of down and out, as if the best in life had already passed him by, or skipped him altogether.

The other worker was a kid of 18 or 20. His beard hadn't even come in all the way yet. He could have been some high school drop out trying to restart himself, or a college kid who did this kind of work on the side. He looked bright and enthusiastic, with an optimism about him that seemed to confidently imply that his whole life was ahead of him.

True to my dad's persona, he gave each of the movers their tips in advance. I had quietly protested to Dad that this was sort of foolish, for why would they work hard if the got their rewards first? I'd like to blame this apparent lapse in judgment on my dad's Alzheimer's disease, but he was just being Dad. He figured they would work harder if they got their tips up front, plus the effort would be more sincere because they had already been paid.

I never saw such a motley crew work so hard. Dad was right there, helping them lift and move furniture. He was now a relatively wealthy man who could never lose the poor man's identity within him. By the end of the morning, not only was the job done early, but Dad had made three new friends. They were joking and laughing and sharing their histories and interests and struggles with each other. By noon, they knew all about Dad's life in New York and Los Angeles and Traverse City. And they could damn near recite the entire University of Iowa fight song.

By noon, Dad knew all about the personal histories of each worker. The boss-type's failed marriage and family and the 6 day, 18 hour a day work weeks he now had to endure. The man who I thought was about 50 was indeed just 38. He was unskilled and uneducated and needed this job to make ends meet. He had already been joking that much of his tip money would be converted to beer at the end of the day. Beer and that steak he could never seem to afford. And the young kid had indeed graduated from high school, but had to take a year off before college to earn some money, because his parents couldn't afford to send him. Dad really liked the kid, because the kid's struggle was so similar to his own.

Dad had this magic with other people. He could create bonds where you wouldn't think it would be possible. He could build a rapport with nearly anyone he met. He looked so confident and so at ease doing this. You would never know that he was still haunted by the ghosts of his upbringing, and those deeply felt insecurities that were the by-products of his childhood.

By early afternoon, the movers were on their way, probably remarking about the biggest tips they had ever received for a half-day's job. Dad and I were busy putting his Oriental art up. The girls had by then arrived, and were unloading the glasses and dishes in the kitchen. They had also brought what appeared to be a stockpile of food that would outlast any catastrophe, and were busy filling his pantry and refrigerator.

At the end of the day, Dad's place looked magnificent. It was spotless, well stocked with food, with everything very clearly labeled and easily accessible. You could hear the hum of the washer and dryer in the background. Stacy had made a nice Italian dinner. My sister Tiffanie, her husband Donald, and all of the children were over. Even my mother, some twenty years painfully divorced from our dad, came by. It sounded, smelled, and looked just like a family. Because it was a family. Dad was finally home again, and now we were home again.

After everyone had left, I helped Dad pop in a movie. It was one of his old favorites, a musical of course, South Pacific. Dad said that I looked tired and should go home to be with my family. He said that he would be fine. I obliged and packed up to leave, indicating that I would be back in the morning.

I was happy and calm as I left. Today had been a day without Alzheimer's disease, and a day without life's ugliness. Today had been about family, and coming home. I would vow to always remember, and cherish, this day.

I said a quiet prayer as I made my way to the front door. "Thank you, Lord. This day has been kind to us." A powerful shiver ran up and down my spine as I closed the door behind me.

16 { Semper Fi

As I pulled into Dad's driveway, I stopped by his mailbox and retrieved the mail that had been forgotten the day before. Although it was only the beginning of Dad's second day at the condo, he had already received a rather impressive stack of mail. Maybe it had accumulated in the mail forwarding process. I struggled momentarily going through it, debating whether it was any of my business to look at his personal matters. I even had a fleeting thought that it was against the law if I opened any of it. Then I came back to reality. I spoke out loud to myself.

"Dad has Alzheimer's, Garrett. You have to go through his mail or he's gonna screw it up. You saw what he did to his checkbook."

And with those words of advice straight out of my conscience, I began to sort his mail on the passenger seat right there in his driveway. This was going to be the way it was from here on out. Take his bills home with me, throw out the junk mail, and give him what little remained, a bulletin from the Navy or the University of Iowa, his Time magazine and TV Guide, and once in awhile a letter from an old friend who did not know Dad had been stricken with this awful disease.

Most of yesterday's mail was what I had expected; a final shut off bill from Consumers Energy for his old place, the last telephone bill, a termination of cable services billing, an insurance statement, some investment statements. There was a mountain of junk mail, most of which was thinly disguised requests for donations to causes or charities I had never heard of. I wondered how the hell anyone could receive so much junk mail from so many obscure charities.

"Exploitive bastards," I muttered to myself, thinking Dad was getting more than his share just because he was elderly. "I guess they must target this age group more than the others."

I did not yet know that Dad had fallen prey to a whole host of commercial ploys for the past two years, and that he was faithfully sending groups money whenever they sent him a plea for money. "Urgent request, only you, Walter Turke, can help us save the whales or the veterans or the redwoods or glaciers or the planet." I didn't necessarily hate their causes; I hated how they framed their requests for money. My Dad thought these were personal pleas to him, and compromised by the disease, he no longer had the insight or judgment to see that he was being taken by slick marketing strategies. He had been faithfully sending them money each time they requested it, and of course within a year's time Dad was on every goddamn mailing list in the country.

A single handwritten letter fell out from the stack of junk mail. It was from someone I never had heard Dad talk of before. The hand written return address read "Arthur Johnson, Saginaw, Michigan, USA. Semper Fi." That's funny, no street address. And what's Semper Fi? The handwriting was a little uneven, like someone older had written it. I collected the "dad-appropriate" mail, put Arthur's letter on top, and walked up to the front door.

"Good morning, Dad!"

"My son! How wonderful to see you!" Dad always seemed exceptionally excited to see me. After he got sick, his enthusiastic greetings choked me up every time. I wiped a tear from my eye, fought off a few more, and walked in.

Dad had answered the door with a hammer in his hand. I didn't have to peek beyond the foyer to glimpse into his living room. I already knew.

The condo was being transformed into The Museum. Dad had been up all night. Our beautifully manicured condominium was a mess. All of the boxes of worldly art that had been neatly tucked away in the basement had been hauled up the stairs overnight. So much for the Japanese decorum. So much for freedom from distraction. So much for my need to streamline his home. Nope. This was going to be Dad's place. Nothing was going to get in the way of that. Not his Alzheimer's disease and not his children's needs to simplify things. He was still Dad. And he was going to fight with everything he had to hang on.

Dad was in a state of hyper-kinetic excitement. I was overwhelmed. It was Sunday. I wanted a quiet day with Dad, and to go home early afternoon with everything in order, spend some time with my family, play with the kids, and get ready for the workweek. It was clear Dad had other plans.

"Ah, Dad, what happened to our Japanese decorating?"

"We're still going with it, Garrett. Just wanted to put a few more things up." Dad was completely self absorbed, and had no inkling I was concerned.

I stifled my need to speak out, but my thoughts were still clamoring. A few more things? Looks like three hundred more things! The walls were already cluttered. And they weren't very balanced. The art and prints and photos he had put up were all askew, reflective of Dad's disease.

The disease was beginning to affect Dad's neurology, and his visual spatial skills, but it hadn't taken his spirit. I put down the mail, grabbed a few prints, and handed them to Dad to hang up on the wall.

I searched for something to talk about while I dutifully helped Dad load up his walls. I thought of the letter from Arthur that Dad had received. Dad had not yet noticed the mail I had laid down, as he was caught up in his museum project. I tried to refocus his attention.

"Ah, Dad?"

"Yes, Dr. Fang?"

"Um..." I hedged a little, not wanting to pry too much. "What does Semper Fi mean?"

"It's an old Navy and Marines term. I think the Marines adopted it as their motto."

"But what does it mean?"

"Its Latin, I don't know how it translates exactly, it means something like being always faithful, always loyal. Why do you ask?"

"Well, you got a letter from someone, and he wrote Semper Fi on the return address."

My dad smiled instantly. "Arthur."

"Who's Arthur?" I had to pry now. Dad stepped down from the small ladder that he was using to hang his art.

"Arthur was one of my patients. I gave him my new address down here."

"You gave him your home address?" I was a little alarmed. In the world of therapist-patient ethics, you never crossed the line and gave patients your home address, no matter how much you cared for them, no matter how much they needed you.

"I know what you're thinking, Fang. And you're right, this isn't exactly ethical."

Dad continued. "I know, I know. But Arthur is different. He needs me. We have a special relationship."

"What do you mean, Dad?"

"Arthur's a veteran of the Korean War. He was in the Marines. That's where the Semper Fi comes in. He always signs his letters 'Semper Fi.' He is saying that he is faithful to me the same way he was faithful to the Marines."

"Faithful to you?" Now I wasn't sure what was going on.

"I have been helping care for him for years. He has schizophrenia."

I was becoming more than a little perturbed. I had a right to be, because it was now my job to look after Dad.

"Dad, are you nuts? You're retired now. You should have referred Arthur to another doctor."

"I did."

"Is he going?"

"I suppose so."

"Then what is he doing writing you?"

"I already told you, Dr. Fang. He needs me. Semper Fi." There was a rather long, awkward pause. Then Dad tried a different angle to get me to understand. "Do you remember Uncle Phil?"

Boy did I ever remember "Uncle Phil." Uncle Phil was a figure from my childhood in Los Angeles. He was not really my uncle, or my parents' uncle, or any relation to our family at all. He wasn't a friend of the family's either. Uncle Phil was one of my dad's patients.

Uncle Phil was a paranoid schizophrenic who was one of my father's first private practice patients in L.A. Phillip was actually Phillip Rosenbaum, age about 50 in 1964, the son of an eccentric San Francisco multi-millionaire. My father was actually hired by Phillip's father, during a time when Phillip was placed in a long term psychiatric ward at an old state hospital outside of Los Angeles. Phillip had been a young officer in the Navy during World War II, and suffered a psychotic break under the pressure of having to help command a battleship during wartime.

Phillip never recovered after his psychotic break. He had been deteriorating for years prior to and during his placement at the state hospital. When Phillip's father had first approached Dad, Phillip was reduced to a catatonic state, and was chained to his hospital bed. His only "treatment" was to heavily sedate him with anti-psychotic tranquilizers to keep him calm. "Calm" was code for keeping him so doped up he couldn't attack, resist, plead, challenge, run, or otherwise interfere with his "behavior management." Calm was code for keeping him damn close to being a vegetable.

My dad's first task in the "re-humanization" of Phillip (Dad's word) was to unchain him and take him out of the state hospital. My dad wasn't thinking of transferring him to another hospital. No. He was going to have Phillip's wealthy father buy his son a home in Studio City, just outside of Hollywood. Phillip was going to live there. This was more than just a radical idea back in 1964. According to my father's professional colleagues, this was absolute lunacy and unquestionably a case for malpractice. Take a chronic schizophrenic who is completely out of touch with reality and in a catatonic, non-communicative state and allow him to live in his own home? That was ridiculous. Who is this Dr. Turke, and who the hell does he think he is?

Three months later Phillip was living in his own home in Studio City. My dad had assembled an around the clock support team, a live-in caregiver from Pacoima, a male nurse, a couple of orderly types (we now call them "para-pros"), and… our family! Dad fervently believed that to help Phillip function again, he had to be treated as a "normal" person, and expected to function conventionally. Yes, Phillip would still be schizophrenic, he would still be paranoid, and he would still have to take some anti-psychotic drugs, but he would be mainstreamed, and treated with respect and dignity.

Phillip would become an adopted member of our family. My father would take him on outings with us on the weekends. Our family served as respite for the para-pro's and for Addie, his live-in caregiver. Phillip would even come to our house on Christmas in order to give the other workers a break on the holidays. It was a weird arrangement. I don't know how or why my mother put up with it. But she did. And it worked.

By 1966, Phillip was functional again. He couldn't live on his own, but he was happy, could manage his daily needs, and he could form relationships again. To us kids, he was "Uncle Phil." We went to the beach with him, miniature golfed with him, and went on trips with him. I learned to play dominoes from him. I indirectly learned a lot about the world of the mentally ill. I witnessed some psychotic episodes where he talked gibberish, and once where he took off his clothes (and his false teeth) and swam out into the Pacific Ocean. But I didn't find any of these experiences traumatic. I understood what was going on with Uncle Phil. I saw how much better he was. I had been taught by the best.

Dad didn't know it at the time, but he had assembled what is now known as a "wraparound team." Wraparound is a sophisticated service delivery system where a team of invested individuals coordinate services to provide a 24 hour, residential like structure. This allows high risk/high need individuals to remain in the community and live a reasonably normal life. The wraparound concept was first used in the 1970's and 1980's to treat developmentally disabled populations, then in the 1990's to treat mentally ill and delinquent populations.

My dad was before his time. Phillip was a wraparound case. What I didn't fully appreciate at the time was that Dad would soon become _my_ wraparound case. I had been taught by the best, and now, I would have to treat the teacher the same way the teacher had taken care of Uncle Phil.

17 { My One Hour Lunch

I glanced at the dashboard clock as I entered the freeway on-ramp. 11:57. I had snuck out of work a few minutes early in order to have enough time to see Dad over lunch. It was Monday, and I had already shifted back into work mode. All revved up and full of adrenalin, and it was not even noon yet. I had spent the morning hearing intakes for incoming cases to the INS program, which was always an emotional struggle. One case involved a woman who was sleeping (or maybe passed out) while her 4 year old son had attempted to give his two year old sister a bath. She now had second and third degree burns over the lower two-thirds of her body. Another case involved a man who had recently regained custody of his three children after being released from prison. He had been incarcerated for the past four years for nearly killing a man with a hammer after he caught him having an affair with his now ex-wife. His ex-wife had lost her parental rights due to heroin addiction, and now the Court was looking at putting the kids back home with their father. Not exactly a pleasant morning.

The afternoon was not shaping up to be a picnic either. Two high risk kids came into the detention center over the weekend; both for domestic violence against their parents, and both had been placed on suicide prevention precautions. This was so typical of the domestic violence cases. The kids who lash out violently toward their parents usually have histories of being abused and mistreated when they were younger, and when they get older the inevitable violent backlash occurs toward the previously abusive parents. The kids then sit in isolation in detention feeling terribly ambivalent about whether they were ever wanted by their parents, and a potent mix of rejection, isolation, abandonment, anger and guilt sets in. A perfect brew of dynamics to spawn suicidal thinking and acting out. The two kids that came in over the weekend were experiencing this kind of crisis. I would be seeing both of them this afternoon.

I had just over an hour to see Dad and get back to work, and I had to get clear across town to my Dad's new home in East Lansing. I didn't know if I could do it all in an hour, but I was going to try. I didn't want to go over my allotted lunch hour. Being punctual at work was very important to me, and I had a well-established track record at the Family Court for being prompt. On time, every time. A bit rigid, especially given my circumstances, but that was me. I started doing the math in my head, satisfying my OCD demons. Let's see, twenty minutes to get to Dad's if I make most of the lights, twenty minutes at Dad's for lunch, yeah that's long enough to check on him, and twenty minutes to get over to the detention center on the city's south side. Well the math worked...if I made most of the lights.

I pressed the accelerator pedal hard as I got on the freeway. Traffic was light, and before I realized it, I had pushed my speed up to nearly 80.

I pulled into Dad's driveway at 12:15. Wow, I did it in 17 minutes! That gives me an extra 3 minutes to spend with him. I laughed internally at how my compulsive mind worked. Later, I would come to realize that every additional minute with Dad actually mattered.

Dad's bills were beside me on the passenger seat. The checks were all filled out, and only required Dad's signature. As I got out of the van, I noticed that Dad's outgoing mail flag was up on his mailbox. Uh-oh. I better check. I still felt guilty snooping around with his mail, but my meddling, intruding conscience told me exactly what to do. Garrett, don't be an idiot. This is not invading his privacy. You're not going to go to hell, or to jail, for checking his mail.

I opened the box. There were five outgoing letters! My God, doesn't Dad ever sleep? When did he find time to do all this? I sorted through the outgoing stack. There was a letter to Arthur, with Dad this time writing Semper Fi on the return address. There were three letters to old friends in Traverse City. And there was a letter to George "Goober" Lindsey, Dad's old actor-acquaintance from Los Angeles, which was addressed to some P.O. Box in Hollywood. Hmmmm... Has Dad been in touch with him all these years? The last we saw him was about twenty years ago when we first moved to Michigan. Dad had arranged with Traverse City's local summer theatre to have Goober star in one of their productions.

And finally, in Dad's mailbox were three outgoing response letters to what looked like charities and scholarship funds. I was concerned about this, because of Dad's generous nature and his judgment lapses that were becoming more commonplace with his disease. These three looked legitimate. American Cancer Foundation, Veteran's Fund, University of Iowa Scholarship Fund. I thought about snatching these three response letters, but then I thought, what harm could he do? I have his checkbook, so he couldn't have enclosed any checks. Naïve and constrained by my conscience, I decided to leave those charity responses in the box. I closed up the mailbox, walked up the entranceway to Dad's front door, and rang the bell.

Dad answered as if it was a holiday and I just flew in from overseas: "My son! Wow! You're here! To see me! This is so wonderful!" He gave me one of his patented bear hugs, anointing my face with his Old Spice aftershave in the process.

"Hey, Dad, I thought I'd pop over for lunch. And I've got a few bills for us to sign."

Dad couldn't have been any happier. "That's just great. I'll get our lunch started."

Dad scurried to the kitchen, with me trailing. Within minutes he had assembled a motley combination of canned and frozen foods that he was planning to microwave. Frozen vegetarian "meat" patties, recommended by Dad's cardiologist, a can of German potato salad, a can of green beans, and a salad made up only of lettuce and a coarsely cut tomato.

"How's this, Dr. Fang?" It wasn't exactly gourmet, but it was so uniquely my dad.

"Looks great, Dad." I glanced discretely at my watch, but Dad caught me.

"Ah, Dad, I'm working today, so we'll kinda have to hurry, because I have to get back."

I immediately felt a surge of guilt envelop me. My meddling, intruding conscience was punching me inside my head. Geez, the poor guy is acting like he hasn't seen you in twenty years and you're in a hurry to get back to work! What the hell is wrong with you?

Dad bailed me out. "I understand, Fang. This will only take a few minutes." He knew the value of work and didn't seem hurt at all that I couldn't stay long.

Dad emptied the contents of the canned food's right onto my plate. Hmmm. That's odd, shouldn't this be heated? Oh well, its OK. I'm in a hurry anyway. Dad did microwave the veggie patties. Within a couple minutes they were emptied onto my plate as well.

"Lets see," Dad was fumbling for words again. "Lets see, we need, we need a, um, ah...we need a..."

This time I tried to bail him out. "A fork?"

"No, that's not it, but I guess we need forks too." Dad reached into the utensils drawer and pulled out a couple forks. Mine was coated with caked-on food, like it hadn't been washed.

"Now, lets see, we need some... whatchamacallit." Opening the refrigerator brought some relief to our word retrieval exercise. "Ah, here it is."

It was a bottle of ketchup. I thought, wow, it was as if he had a mental picture of the ketchup but just couldn't find the appropriate word to pair it with. Dad smothered his food with ketchup, rather unusual for him, but he seemed to be enjoying it. I didn't want to embarrass him by getting a new fork, so I just started using the dirty one. My conscience said it wouldn't kill me.

I gobbled down my food and glanced at my watch again. 12:32. OK, I've got about ten more minutes. I loaded my dishes into the dishwasher. I checked the china cabinet and the utensil drawer. Oh my, it looks like a lot of stuff didn't get washed.

"Hey, Dad, do you mind if I run the dishwasher?"

"Just for our few dishes?"

Time to lie again. I was getting good at it with Dad. "We'll, I just want to learn how to use your dishwasher, and this is a kind I'm not familiar with. Why don't you have a seat in the other room, we'll do the checkbook together."

As soon as Dad was in the other room, I quickly loaded up the dishwasher with the dirty glasses, plates, and utensils that were in his drawers and cabinets. It looked as if Dad hadn't washed any of his dishes after eating off of them.

"Oh, Son?" Dad hollered from the other room.

I poured in the dishwasher soap, slammed the door, and turned the dishwasher on. "Yeah, Dad?"

"We'll have to make plans to get some more cash. I'm just about out."

"OK," I replied, hurrying to get finished with the kitchen so I could get to his bills. As I walked toward our worktable in his great room, it struck me. Almost out of cash? My God, he had $800 left after the movers just two days ago, and he hasn't left the house yet.

Or has he?

I sat down next to Dad with four or five bills and their corresponding checks. "Dad, this one's for your electricity bill, could you just sign here? And this is your final cable bill from the old place. Just need you to sign this, and this one's your insurance bill..." Within minutes, Dad had dutifully signed each check, and without resistance. I thought, Man, this is easier than I thought it would be, there's no resistance at all. I sealed up the envelopes, and they were ready to go out into the mail.

"Now, Dad, you said something about needing some cash?"

"Yeah, I was thinking about driving out to the bank this afternoon to get some more money." He pulled out his wallet. I thought for sure there would be the eight hundred dollars left over from the movers inside. Dad opened up his wallet. "See, I'm just down to a, a...a small one." Dad pulled out a twenty.

I peeked inside his wallet, thinking the rest was just overlooked. I was stunned. "Dad, where did all the money go?"

"What money?"

"The money left over from the movers." My voice suddenly had urgency. I was starting to piece it together.

"I had money left over from the movers? Really? Beats me. I think all I had left is this, ah, um, you know, this um, ah... this small one."

My panic was escalating now, and was nearing crisis level. My father is more impaired than I thought! And he's now living in an unfamiliar place, an unfamiliar town, he doesn't know anyone, I've allowed him to live on his own, I have to work, I can't watch him all the time, oh my God, oh my God, OH MY GOD!!! What have I done!!

I told myself to calm down, don't panic Garrett, you're over-reacting, it's not that bad.

And as my parasympathetic nervous system tried to settle me back down, I realized where the eight hundred dollars was. It was outside, in the mailbox, in the outgoing mail, inside those goddamn charity response envelopes!

"Dad, I'll be right back," I said, trying to appear calm. "Forgot something in the van." I walked out the door, then sprinted the ten yards to the mailbox. The red outgoing mail flag was already down. The mailbox was empty. "Shit. Shit! SHIT!!! Damnitall!"

The disturbing insights came streaming in on me all at once. The panic turned to anger. The anger was quickly turning into despair. What have I done? He needs way more supervision that I thought. Cooking, money, driving, oh my God he'll get lost driving to the bank. He'll forget where he is and get lost. What if he burns himself in the shower trying to adjust the hot water? What if he leaves the stove on? And his meds? Oh no, there's nothing in place to see if he's taking them properly, if at all. Has he even been taking them?

I looked at my watch, as if it really mattered anymore. 12:43. That was all? It felt like over an hour had passed in just the last 10 minutes. As I walked back inside, I composed myself, the way I always did at work. I compartmentalized and rationalized. OK, there's not a lot I can do right this minute. You've got to get to work, you've got two kids on suicide watch to see. OK, how do I buy some time with Dad, so he doesn't leave the house this afternoon? OK. Let's set him up with a couple movies, I'll go to work, I'll tell him I'll come back over after work and we'll have dinner. I'll tell him not to go anywhere because I don't know exactly when I'll be coming back. Yeah, that might work.

Please God, please. Please give me the strength to get through this, please God, please keep my daddy safe. I hadn't thought of my father as "daddy" since I was little. Funny how it re-emerged at this moment.

I slowed my pace as I entered back into the condo. Calm and compartmentalized. "Hey Dad, found what I was looking for. I've got to be getting back to work in a few minutes. Hey, why don't we go out for dinner tonight?"

Dad walked up to me, all excited and enthusiastic. "Really? Dinner with you, tonight?"

"Yeah, and I'll have the girls meet us."

"Wow. That will be fun! And we can get some more money on the way?"

"Sure we can, Dad."

It was Uncle Phil all over again. It was the beginning of the wraparound. Only this time I was the teacher, and Dad was the patient.

As I was preparing to leave, I pulled out two long movies from Dad's massive video collection. I had selected two more of his favorites, Bogart's "Casablanca," and Rogers and Hammerstein's "Sound of Music."

"These are nice and long," I mumbled to myself, "that'll take up the afternoon." Dad stopped me as I was taking the movies off the shelf. "I don't need to watch those. I'll just watch these two right here." He pointed to the "South Pacific" and "Guys and Dolls" videos that were already on his coffee table. I recognized them as the two videos I had set Dad up with a couple nights before.

"I haven't seen these two in a long while."

"Ah, Dad? You just watched those two the other night; I left with you watching South Pacific."

"No, Son, I think you're mistaken. I haven't watched either one of these in years."

I swallowed the lump in my throat, said my goodbyes, and got another Old Spice laden bear hug. "See you tonight, Dad."

"I'm looking forward to it, Dr. Fang. See you after work."

18 { Setting up the Wraparound

The next two weeks passed without major incident. I had developed a ritual of seeing Dad each day for lunch, then also stopping by on my way home from work to help him make dinner and to set him up with a movie for the evening. Even though this ritual became quickly ingrained into our daily routines, Dad would call me constantly at work to ask if I was coming over that day.

Superficially, Dad seemed to be functioning fairly well on his own, but I never really knew what he was doing to occupy his time during the day. Although I was constantly worried he would drive off and get lost in an unfamiliar town, his two cars laid dormant in the garage. I knew this because I checked the odometer each time I was over, much like my parents used to check the odometer on the family car when I was left home alone as a teenager.

Each noontime I also checked Dad's mail, sorting his bills and offering to take out his outgoing mail for him. While I always respected the privacy of his personal letters, I felt more comfortable opening up the "charity" response letters. And sure enough, sometimes there was cash in them. I had learned in less than a week never to let Dad have access to more than 40 or 60 dollars cash at a time. His charity response letters would typically have 20 or 40 dollars in them, sometimes with a handwritten note scrawled inside: "Sorry, this is all I have to give this time. Will send more next time. Your friend, Walter." I would open these response letters, take out the cash, then recycle it back to Dad telling him I had stopped off at the bank for him and had brought some money. I still felt a little bad lying to him, but I was getting used to it. It's for the greater good, I would tell myself, and my conscience would temporarily back off.

Dad's "Museum" appeared to have been largely completed during these two weeks, although it was hard to ignore the presence of his disease when his wall hangings and art were all crooked, unbalanced, and askew. He kept taking sections of the museum down, reorganizing it, and then putting it back up, oblivious that he was doing this repeatedly. He seemed to be enjoying this process, and I guess it kept him busy.

During the day, Dad seemed content living off canned and frozen foods. While I got plenty of fresh vegetables and fruits during our grocery shopping trips, most of it lay wilting and untouched in the refrigerator and counter tops by the week's end. The closest Dad had come to fresh fruit was polishing off two packages of Fig Newtons each week.

Stacy and the girls had been incredibly understanding throughout the course of the past few weeks. I had come home tired and stressed at about 7 o'clock each night. Still early enough to play and socialize with the kids and to have some time with Stacy, although they were done eating dinner by the time I got home. I actually ate two dinners each night, one over at Dad's (he wouldn't allow me to sit idly and watch him eat), and one at home, as Stacy thoughtfully had left a plate out for me. I would eat the first dinner out of respect for Dad's feelings. I would eat the second dinner out of stress. I did not expend much thought anticipating the far-reaching consequences of this, but six months later I wound find myself a bit pudgy, twenty pounds heavier, and my blood pressure inching up into the high borderline range.

I obsessed over how to structure my dad's life for virtually every waking hour of each day during the week. I called everyone I could think of that could help structure Dad's time and routine, which I discovered was not that many. All of Dad's friends were either in Bay City, at his old job in Saginaw, or in Traverse City. I quickly realized that aside from our family, Dad didn't have anybody to look after him in East Lansing. I had become so absorbed in spending time with Dad again that I had completely ignored the host of friends that Dad had left behind "up north." Surely he missed them, but he never let on that he did.

I had called for a "wraparound assessment meeting" with Stacy, my sister Tiffanie, her husband Donald, and my mother Rosemarie, who despite the divorce, still found enough unscarred love in her heart to volunteer to help. I also invited Dad's neurologist, Dr. Jahnke, who obviously couldn't come, but who nonetheless volunteered to be on Dad's wraparound team. That was all we had, five people and a phone consultant, to cover 168 hours in a week. The delinquents who got wraparound at work and needed less monitoring typically had teams of eight or ten. But five was all we had initially, and five was what we went with.

The wraparound meeting was set up on a Saturday morning at my house. My family thought it was kind of ridiculous when I started the meeting like a psychologist at work, with a wipeboard, flipchart, colored markers, and a calendar book.

"Oh Garrett, you don't have to be so formal, we don't need all that," my sister laughed, with my mother chortling in. Her response was a very normal thing anyone might feel or say in such a contrived situation. Yet I was offended by this. My sister and my mother still did not think Dad was all that impaired. They were accepting that he had been diagnosed with Alzheimer's, but not fully accepting that he actually had it yet. Neither of them had been able to help Dad get ready for the move, and they had not seen the impairments to the extent that I did. I thought they perceived me as "paranoid," overly protective, and over-reacting, and I responded defensively.

My sister was quick to chime in, "You're making this way too complicated. Dad's doing fine, I just saw him last night. We don't have that much time today to do all of this."

Great. Tiffanie and Mom want to leave the meeting before we even get started. This may or may not have been actually true, but it is how I interpreted their comments.

I could hear my mom under her breath, "He's always got to be so controlling, just like Walt was."

I felt the anger rising up inside of me. Doesn't anyone see the value in this? I knew from work what would happen if we didn't structure this thing tightly. Everyone would be enthusiastic for a few days, then get lazy with the wraparound, and then the structure would drop off. And if the structure dropped off, the results would be disastrous for Dad.

I tried my best to regain my composure. I wanted to say to my mom, Look, I've been the one spending all my goddamn free time making sure Dad is OK, none of you are taking this seriously enough to do anything pro-active, and you have the gall to call me controlling!

What actually came out was, "I'm trying to set this up for the day when Dad can't fully take care of himself anymore; it's for the future." That quieted my mom for the moment, although I wasn't so sure it was effective. But Stacy grabbed my hand, and Donald looked at me sympathetically.

Donald broke up the awkward moment. "What do you want us to do, Gart?"

"Gart" was what Donald called me affectionately, a nickname he had conjured up during one of our many fishing expeditions. I could have hugged him. He and Stacy understood.

"Well, here's what I think we should do," I felt my anger subside, as I was shifting into work mode. It was as if I was making a presentation to a class. "We've got to structure virtually all of Dad's time, from the time he gets up in the morning to the moment he goes to bed at night. We have to make sure he's eating properly and washing himself. We need to make sure he's taking his meds. Tiff, I'm really worried he's not taking his meds. Have you ever seen him take his Aricept?"

"Well, he says he's been taking it, I don't really know for sure."

My mother then chimed in, "I was talking to your Aunt Eleanor, who as you know is a nurse. She works with elderly patients now; some of them are like your father. She said to unplug the stove, turn down his water heater thermostat, and take his car keys."

I said, "Good point, Mom." Maybe I had been the one who was overreacting and hypersensitive. Maybe Mom was trying to help.

My mind took a moment to process my mom's points. I could see unplugging the stove, we'll just tell him it's broken and we've called in to get it fixed. And turning down the water heater thermostat? Yeah, we can do that. But take his car keys? My God, that's like a death sentence. Dad will never go for that. His prized Mercedes? Dad's identity is wrapped up in that car.

By mid morning we had devised what I thought was a pretty tight wraparound plan. We would Alzheimer's-proof the house. Unplug the stove, turn down the water heater, tape the heater/air conditioner thermostat, disconnect the burglar alarm, and take control of all of his meds. Tiffanie would come over each morning on the way to work, I would come over at lunch, and I would come by at dinnertime again on my way home. Tiff would make him breakfast and administer his meds in the morning, I would see to his lunch at noon, and intercept his mail. At 5:30, I would make him something to eat, do his laundry, and run the dishwasher before I left. My mom would come over every other afternoon to get him some exercise, look at old family pictures, and maybe watch a movie. Donald was to be our "rover back," an old football term for a position that floated to wherever the need was. He could take a break from work mid afternoon when we couldn't, and he volunteered to come by occasionally on weekends to give me a break.

The wraparound plan seemed pretty tight, except that we had long stretches in the mornings and some afternoons with no coverage. But it was better than no wraparound at all, and it was probably the best we could do with a five person team.

Tiff and I thought long and hard about taking his car keys. This was the most logical place to start his restrictions. We could just take them and pretend that he had lost them, and tell him each day we were planning to replace them. That might work, albeit awkwardly, and Dad would have been stuck but safe within the house. And everyone else on the road would have been safe also. But we couldn't do it. This was too cruel. Dad loved his cars, and he loved his freedom.

Tiffanie offered me a way out: "He's not that bad yet, Garrett. I was just in the car with him yesterday." I believed her only because I wanted to. We compromised by agreeing to put a compass in both of Dad's cars, drawing a map of East Lansing and taping it to his dashboard, and putting a list of emergency numbers in the glove box in case he got lost. We talked about getting him a cell phone.

Talk about naïve! Dad was never good with directions, had never used a compass in his life, and he had no idea what a cell phone was. But the emergency car plan was enough to insulate us with some more denial, at least for a little while.

We thought we had covered it all. We thought Dad would be safe for the future. This would be our illusion. An illusion still cloaked in a massive amount of denial.

Dad, as always, was in a cheerful mood when he returned home with Tiffanie. We made our plans for the afternoon. I set him up with a movie and told him I would be back at dinnertime. The wraparound had begun.

The time I had bought with Dad's wraparound would be relatively short-lived. But every day, every hour, every minute was so precious now. I knew we had done the right thing.

My family was never one for family prayers, and today was no exception. I wanted to call my family to prayer but I felt awkward and uncomfortable. It was a feeling akin to having to sing an unexpected solo in front of the class. And so I said a silent prayer as we all filed out the front door.

Dear God, thank you for all the times my father took care of me. Please help me know how take care of him now. Stacy noticed the tears in my eyes. I looked up, too choked to speak.

"You don't have to say anything, honey. I already know."

Later that night as I prepared to go to bed, I found a sealed card on my pillow. On the envelope was a drawn heart, in that fancy, sensitive handwriting that only women can do.

I started to cry before I opened it. Because I already knew what was inside. It would be a card that I would never throw away, a card that would always be on my nightstand, a card that I would keep forever.

"My dearest Garrett. I know what pain you are going through. I will be there for you. I am always yours. Forever, Stacy."

From that day forward, I would read that card whenever I thought I couldn't bear any more pain. God on one side and Stacy on the other. I knew I would be safe.

19 { Charade

It was closing in on December. The drab November landscape was now replaced by the first beautiful mantle of winter snow. It had become bitter cold outside, but if you lived in Michigan, you got used to it. "The wraparound" had been going for a month now, and I was amazed that everyone had bought into the concept. It didn't always work as efficiently as my compulsive mind had hoped, but it was working. Dad was still happy. And he was still safe.

Dad had had a nice Thanksgiving at my house with my mom and Stacy's side of the family. He had only lasted an hour and a half at the house, claiming that he was tired and had to go. He left at halftime of the Lions' football game, acting and seemingly believing as if it was the end of the game. We didn't correct him. I was sure that all the stimulation and commotion that Thanksgiving brought was a bit too much for him. I would learn through the course of Dad's disease that maintaining a predictable, consistent schedule was critical in keeping Alzheimer's patients calm and oriented. Anything outside of their normal routine could be very anxiety provoking and potentially diminish their hold on reality.

Dad's early exit at this year's Thanksgiving would be a sign of things to come. He still didn't look very impaired to the casual observer, but I could now clearly see his failings. Food would be left out on his counters that would spoil. He wouldn't shave or keep his hygiene up unless prompted. He had to re-learn how to use his TV remote almost every day. Any money I gave him would come up missing. He had lots of word retrieval problems for common objects and appliances. He had "forgotten" the name for his microwave oven and for the stove. His brain plugged in descriptors in place of the forgotten noun. The microwave was the "white thingamajig on top," and he now referred to his stove as "the flattop." The warning signs were all around me now. Try as I might, I couldn't miss them anymore.

Our family continued to build upon the wraparound structure. We saw that the few hours of structure a day we could provide Dad eventually wouldn't be enough to keep him safe. My mother responded to this insight by trying to drag me to a local Alzheimer's Association meeting. "Drag" was the correct description. I told myself that I already knew about what needed to be done for Dad's care, and that any advice doled out at the meeting would be redundant. Under this rather pretentious, arrogant façade, however, I secretly knew what I was avoiding. I didn't want to go to the meeting because of my fears of intimacy and self disclosure before a group. I didn't want to have to face my fears of Dad's disease and his mortality. I didn't want my façade of competency and being in control threatened.

Besides, I still wasn't completely comfortable acknowledging my dad's disease in front of people I didn't know. There was still a shame and a stigma attached to having my dad afflicted with Alzheimer's, and I was still putting a lot of effort into trying to make him look "normal" to the outside world.

And so, while I played this little charade of avoidance, Stacy and my mom made an appointment and scheduled our attendance at the next meeting.

My fears of self disclosure in a group were so hypocritical. I thought of all the work, all the programs I had built in my twenty five years as a psychologist. The foundation of everything I had built and espoused to others was predicated on self disclosure. All of the programs I had built at work for neglect and delinquency families had support groups at their core. I always figured that people would tend to respect the input of others that were in the same boat, rather than some contrived response that came out of a paid therapist's mouth.

While I preached the need for support groups at work, I had been bullheaded when it came to going to a support group myself.

There were only about five families at the Alzheimer's association meeting, but they were all in the same predicament our family was in. All of the people in attendance either had a parent or a spouse with early stage Alzheimer's disease. Ironically, after weeks of worrying about the meeting, I found myself relaxing within moments of entering the room and sitting down. Mom apparently was right. I did belong here, at least on this night.

The meeting turned out to be a lifesaver. Not only did I learn that there were others out there struggling just like us, but I also found out we were doing a damn good job with the wraparound-like structure we had set up for Dad. We were way ahead of the other families in terms of providing care. In fact, the other families were in awe of the structure and check and balance care-giving system we had organized for Dad. I was able to offer advice for the other families, bringing in some of my wraparound "expertise."

While receiving accolades felt good and reduced my anxiety about the support group, I was nonetheless lacking in a key insight. What I had done at the Alzheimer's Association meeting was put myself in the role of teaching other folks. Being a teacher was my strength and my familiar role, but it also allowed me to escape from my own self disclosure. I had cleverly, perhaps even unconsciously, covered up my weakness and my fears at the meeting. I was the proud, confident wraparound instructor leading the way. The charade covered up the scared, vulnerable son who was having profound trouble facing his fears of losing his dad.

If I hadn't been so encapsulated in denial, my fears of intimacy and vulnerability would have been readily exposed by the direction the meeting took in the second hour. While our family was very advanced in the area of providing coordinated care-giving and structure, the other families at the meeting were seemingly way ahead of us in another area. They were actively talking about the painful and all consuming emotional effects of the disease. I heard some agonizing stories of how their mothers or fathers or spouses were coming to grips with their disease. Their loved ones were frightened and anxiety ridden and angry and depressed. These caregivers talked about the disease openly with their afflicted loved one, despite their grief and the emotional fallout. In fact, the "emotional fallout" was portrayed as a good thing, as if it was some sort of cathartic preparation for coming to grips with the disease's inevitable, insidious, and terminal course.

Our family was doing none of this. Dad was happy, upbeat, seemingly relaxed, friendly, and incredibly kind. In fact, Stacy and I had had many talks over the fall that Dad's overall mood, disposition, and outlook had become a lot more positive since he was stricken with the disease. He seemed increasingly oblivious to having a terminal disease that was robbing his memories and stealing his identity. At least we thought he was oblivious to his affliction. We didn't really know, because we had never brought the subject up with him. We just kept telling ourselves that we didn't want to disturb Dad's apparent blissful state.

Were we all in denial? Afraid to face the reality? Afraid to feel the grief, the loss, the pain? I am still not really sure. I certainly knew Dad was sick, and I was becoming increasingly vigilant about the dangers his impairment brought. But to openly discuss his terminal disease with him was something I just couldn't do. Why take someone who is happy albeit oblivious to his circumstances and elicit pain, fear and anxiety for the sake of "dealing with it." What benefit would that bring my Dad? I couldn't do it. I wouldn't do it. I convinced myself it was better to play this charade with Dad in order to keep him happy.

I ended up going to the Alzheimer's Association group meeting just once, hardly what you would call an investment. I went back to my old strategy of telling myself I was just too busy to attend very often, but if I needed help I now knew where I could go. It really disappointed my mom, who wanted our family and wraparound team to attend regularly.

The Alzheimer's Association meeting did produce two rather vital referrals, for which I really was and still am grateful. One was an organization called Safe Return, a national Alzheimer's identification database that provides medical alert identity bracelets for Alzheimer's patients. If the individual gets lost or disoriented, there is an 800 number on the bracelet that alerts the authorities and aids in returning the individual to their family, care facility, or other safe environment.

The second referral to come out of the Alzheimer's Association meeting was a geriatric community center program in East Lansing called the Active Living For Adults (ALFA) Center. This was a program that served brain injured, cognitively disabled and early stage dementia patients like my dad. The program met every other day for about six hours per day, arranged for transportation via a SpecTran bus, and had an invested, enthusiastic staff of four, including a geriatric nurse. The program involved exercise, activity groups, reminiscing, watching old movies and playing board games. And they served a nice lunch in the middle of the daily program.

The ALFA Center seemed to be a perfect fit for Dad. He needed more structure. He needed more supervision and care giving during the day. He needed more social activities. He needed friends. And most importantly for my dad, he needed to be needed.

It was the unanimous consensus of our family and wraparound team to have Dad go to the ALFA Center. The problem wasn't if he should go, but rather how we would get Dad to invest in going to the ALFA Center without resistance. I would have to play out another charade with him. A charade that I thought might have to last for the rest of his life.

I knew that what was a charade for me might become a delusion for Dad. I told myself it was for the greater good.

20 { Welcome to Your New Job

The ALFA program entered our lives at just the right time. The every other day format of the program could fill in the gaps during the days when we had no wraparound coverage for Dad. It also gave me a break from racing out each lunch to intercept Dad's mail.

I had taken it upon myself to bring Dad to the ALFA Center for his introductory session with the program's director. I told my family that I would find some way to get him to invest in the program. My family knew I was good at persuading people, and in particular, persuading Dad when no one else could. What my family probably didn't know or appreciate was that I was about to plant a false belief system in my dad's thinking. It would be a delusion that in my view would help him adapt and buy in to the ALFA Center.

I had told Dad that I was taking him to a community activity center to make some new friends. Dad thought he was going to join some kind of club. When we entered the building, Dad immediately noticed that all of the "members" were intellectually impaired. His first words were telling:

"Boy, Garrett, I don't think this will be all that fun for me. These people look pretty disturbed. What do they have, Alzheimer's?"

Oh-oh. I thought to myself. Dad's on to me. But he wasn't. He really had seemed to have forgotten that he had the disease. It was really strange. Dad was as impaired as many of these people, yet he didn't see it.

I had to think quickly. The "you're going to join a social club" approach wasn't going to fly.

"Ah, I'm sorry, Dad, you must have misunderstood. Dad, you're here to help the staff."

Dad seemed curious, so I just played it up a little more. "Um, I hope it wasn't presumptuous of me but since you've been a little bored being retired, I thought you might want to work here."

Then I had an epiphany. "Dad, they need a part time psychiatrist. They want you."

My Dad's face lit up. "They want...me?"

"Yep. They sure do. And they're going to pay you." Why I said that I will never know. It was a bold faced lie right in the first few seconds of entering the ALFA Center. It just popped out of my mouth with no forethought or apparent self control.

"They're going to pay me? Really? To help with the staff? Really? That's so wonderful."

My increasingly critical conscience stepped in. OK, now you've done it, Garrett. You should have quit while you were ahead with the "help the staff" part. Pay him? Why'd you say that? You imbecile! You're building lies you won't be able to pull back out from!

Dad continued, now with peppy excitement and enthusiasm. "Pay me? Wow! This is unbelievable! When will I get my checks, and how much is my salary?"

Now my conscience was railing on me. Oh my God, how could you manipulate him this way! You ass! Now you've really done it! Think of something, quick!

But instead of reeling in the lie, I embellished it even more. "They're going to pay you $500 every Friday. Not bad for a part time, every other day job, Dad! And, they're going to drive you here each day you have to work. They want you that bad."

"Wow, that's so incredible. This is great, Dr. Fang. You're the best! Now, lets get this straight. You will also be working here, with me?"

"Um, why yes! But only some days. I'll be consulting with you!" Dad was so happy by now that he practically skipped into our appointment inside the director's office.

I had to now face my lies with Margie, the program's director. How am I going to rectify this with her, with Dad sitting right there?

Margie was a maternal type in her late 50's or early 60's, sharp as a tack, with soft, kind eyes. I had spoken to her on the phone several times prior to coming. She was another guardian angel, doing work that brought her neither wealth nor prestige, with a sense of purpose that was fueled solely by altruism, love, and empathy for people she didn't even know initially. I immediately felt that I had betrayed her by concocting such a ridiculous set of lies to manipulate my dad.

"Ah, Margie, could I see you for just a minute, out in the hall?"

Margie looked perplexed but accompanied me outside the office. "Ah, Margie, I feel kind of ashamed telling you this, ah, but the only way I could get Dad to buy into coming here was to tell him he was going to be one of the staff here. He noticed the other patients here were impaired and didn't seem to get that he…"

Margie cut me off. "It's alright, Garrett, you don't have to explain. I can see that you love your Dad. You're just trying to shelter him."

Margie continued, in a soothing, maternal sort of way. "You know, I guess we could sit down and explain to Walter that he is as impaired as everyone else here. But what purpose would that serve? He'd just get needlessly anxious and frightened, maybe mad and agitated. And then, some moments later, he would have forgotten all about what we said. So what would we do then? Tell him all over again, and give him another round of fear and anxiety? And again and again, each time he forgot? I don't think so. You did the right thing. The important part is for your Dad to feel wanted. He needs to feel loved and to still be connected. Besides, we could use a good psychiatrist around here anyway."

I was beginning to feel validated for protecting Dad the way I did. But my conscience wasn't quite yet ready to let me off the hook.

"I told him he was going to get paid."

Margie cut me off again. "So what? Let him think that. It's just a little white lie. Tell him the money gets direct deposited and act all excited on payday. You're controlling all his finances anyway, aren't you?"

I nodded.

"So he'll never know. Now let's get back inside with your Dad"

A half hour later Dad was the ALFA Center's first geriatric psychiatrist. Dad was ecstatic. He couldn't wait to start. I assumed he would start the following week.

"So, we'll be seeing you next Monday?" I asked Margie, just expecting a simple affirmative.

Margie took hold of my dad's hand. She still had that reassuring, maternal posture and tone. "Well, Garrett, I was thinking that since your Dad is off to such a good start here, we'd let him start working with the patients right away. How about if he stayed here for the rest of the day?"

My eyes immediately met Dad's. We were both caught off guard, and both more than a bit anxious. I thought to myself. Leave him here? But he just met you, and he doesn't know anyone here.

Margie, the mind reading guardian angel, intercepted my thoughts again. "You're dad is doing great, and we need our psychiatrist today. We'll arrange for a ride home for him, I'll set it up with Spec Tran. How about if you meet him at home at 4:00, he'll be glad to see you after an afternoon at work."

What could I say? This is already all scripted out. Margie was right, of course, but I didn't feel ready.

Dad sensed my anxiety, but still managed to get out the right words. "I'll see you later, Dr. Fang, I guess it isn't your day to work yet."

I managed to get out the right response, but mine came out choppy, because I choked up trying to spit out the words. "See you.... after... after work, Dad."

I took my dad's free hand and then patted him on the back. His lower lip was trembling. It reminded me instantly of one of my first childhood memories, when my mom said goodbye to me on my first day of kindergarten.

I let go of my father's hand, turned, and walked out the main entrance door. I looked composed, but inside I was churning. I had learned an important lesson this day. I couldn't control everything, and I would have to rely on others to help. I also learned that there were angels out there, surrounding me, and surrounding my dad.

I was waiting for Dad at his condo when the Spec Tran bus dropped him off that afternoon. He was like an excited little kid coming home from his first day at school. In his hand was a notebook, and a pen Margie had given him.

"Whatcha got there, Dad?"

He smiled, and exclaimed proudly, "Oh, not too much, just some notes that I will be keeping about my patients' progress."

Dad had found his purpose again, despite his disease. It was wonderful to see him connecting with others again. The disease was attacking him, but it couldn't take that part of my dad out. He was still The Champion.

21 { The End of the Innocence

It was two weeks before Christmas, and three weeks before the start of the new millennium. People were excited about Christmas, and the year 2000. Prince's "1999" was resurrected on the airways, and many people were planning huge parties to celebrate. But a lot of people were worried about "Y-2K."

I didn't get a chance to participate in the preparation for the millennium celebration or the Y-2K hysteria. I didn't give a shit about Y-2K. I wasn't excited about the new millennium. And for the first time in my memory, it didn't feel like Christmas to me. All I cared about was maintaining my Dad's wraparound. Life outside the wraparound was rapidly becoming a tired black and white movie that I was reenacting every day and every night. I was still a good, conscientious psychologist at work and a faithful, dependable father and husband at home. I still found time to play with my kids and make love to my wife. But something was happening to me, slowly, almost imperceptibly. I was walling off my feelings.

It was time to go up and see Dr. Jahnke again. Carolyn, her ever-present sidekick nurse, had left an appointment reminder on my voice mail the day before. Included in the brief, routine message was something unexpected. "Yes, Garrett, this is Carolyn over at Dr. Jahnke's office. Your dad is scheduled to come up this Friday at 11:30 for his regular appointment. And, oh yes, Garrett. Dr. Jahnke would like you to take your dad to a SPECT Scan appointment at the U of M hospital on December 20. You'll need to take the day off, as it will take you most of the day. Dr. Jahnke will explain when she sees you on Friday. Hope all is going OK. See you then."

Friday came quickly. I got to work at 6:30 in the morning so I could leave at 10:00 without using any sick or leave time. My OCD was still working just fine.

When I got to Dad's place 15 minutes early, he was already waiting outside, all excited about the trip. To my father, these visits to Dr. Jahnke's office were never about his neurological status or cognitive functioning or coming to grips with Alzheimer's disease. Nope. They were like some kind of odd reunion tour where Dad would reconnect proudly with a former student and fellow doctor.

Dad still had his driver's license, but rarely drove anymore except for an occasional trip to the grocery store, or to Tiffanie's or my house. He knew how to get to the bank, however, which worried me. What should have worried me more was Dad getting disoriented on the road and running through red lights or going the wrong way on a one-way street. Increasingly, on these longer trips to see Dr. Jahnke, Dad was more than happy to have me drive his car. It was another sign that he was getting less sure of himself, and more dependent on me.

After a week of neatly suppressing and compartmentalizing my anxiety, I was starting to worry about what the SPECT Scan was all about. Dad, sitting next to me, was his usual exuberant, oblivious self, talking about whatever popped into his mind. I wasn't fully cognizant of this yet, but it was another "side-effect" of his disease, the diminishing capacity to censor his thoughts or anticipate the social consequences of his uninhibited speech. Dad was brimming with old memories today, reminiscing about his childhood in New York, his athletic experiences at Franklin Lane High School, his college pranks with his friends, and our life in Los Angeles. It started out as a fun, joyful trip down long term memory lane.

Initially, Dad's stories were fascinating, sometimes funny, and took my mind off the SPECT Scan. I learned about gang wars in Brooklyn. About life as an immigrant's son. About his sister, Freda. About his relationship with his parents. I got to know about a whole host of characters who were my father's childhood, adolescent, and college friends. My favorite character was a college kid Dad knew in Iowa, who my dad nicknamed the "webbed tentacle." I could only imagine what that meant, and I didn't ask for clarification. The webbed tentacle was Edward Lemanski, and apparently he and my dad were quite the practical jokesters in college. Dad told me about a time where Ed had embarrassed my father in the locker room, and so in retaliation Dad took heating balm and placed it inside Ed's jock strap cup, which apparently immobilized Ed for most of the rest of the day. Dad was absolutely full of himself telling me these stories, and, unaware of what was to come, I innocently egged him on to tell me more.

As we took the turn to the north onto I-75, the "what was to come" came. I was completely blindsided. Dad had moved beyond his college days at Iowa and was now in 1960's Los Angeles.

"Those were some great times in L.A., Fang. Remember all those hippy clothes, those Nehru jackets, and the tie-dye shirts?"

"Yep. I sure do. Remember that head shop we went to in Hollywood? We'd get those love beads; I think you got an Egyptian ankh symbol there. We sure came across a lot of weird and interesting people out in LA. You and mom went to a lot of parties I remember."

"Yeah, your mom and me." Dad sounded a little deflated. He didn't like to talk much about her after the divorce. But he perked up again. "Did I ever tell you about the time your mom and I smoked pot at one of the parties? I thought it was kind of fun. But your mom became boring on it, she just went to sleep."

"No, you didn't tell me that, Dad." I felt a little disappointed in knowing this, as I had always believed my parents were above the rampant drug experimentation scene in Los Angeles. But I quickly rationalized this to myself. Hey, if that's the worst of it, that wasn't so bad. Everyone's at least tried some pot, so what's the big deal? I had come from a culture in LA where there were problems at my junior high school with 13 year olds taking LSD in class. No, I guess Dad and Mom experimenting with a little weed wasn't much of a big deal.

"Yeah, those were some times, Dr. Fang. Rosemarie couldn't always handle the Los Angeles pace. I liked it. She was kind of boring to be with sometimes."

I didn't like where this was going. I was becoming terribly uncomfortable.

But it was too late. Dad was already going again. "Yeah, Rosemarie." He grimaced a little. "She didn't like the fast life."

Then dad's face suddenly brightened. "Did you know I had some girlfriends out there?"

My heart dropped. I had heard from various sources, including my mom, that Dad was suspected of having affairs. No one ever actually directly told me, I had just heard bits and pieces of evidence. My mom would accidentally let something slip out, and there were some rumors I overheard. I remembered Cindy sometimes mentioned it when I was still talking to her. I guess I could have put it together if I wanted to, but I didn't want to face it. After all, he was The Champion. He was my hero.

But now, the evidence was beyond any doubt. Dad had shot himself, point blank between the eyes. There was no way I could miss it. And I didn't. The boyhood image of my dad as hero was now being crushed beneath a cascading avalanche of previously suppressed evidence.

Dad was beaming next to me, completely unaware of my distress. Oh my God, he's reliving one of his affairs right now! "Fang, do you remember our good friends, Debra and Ray?"

I wanted to tell Dad, "Shut the hell up, this is hurting me, you asshole!" But nothing came out.

"Yeah, Debra." Dad now had a big smile on his face. It was like Dad had become some 16 year old about to tell his sexual exploits to his buddy in the locker room. "She was a good one. You know we made love in the bathroom once when we were all out to dinner at a restaurant? Yeah, Rosemarie and Ray were right there, at the table. I went to the bathroom first, then Debra said she had to go a few minutes later, and then we had sex together in the men's room."

Dad seemed all excited. I was mortified. Who is this person next to me?

I recognized the beginnings of an anxiety attack. That sudden loss of connectedness to the world, and that strange, scary feeling of depersonalization and detachment. And then the accompanying knock-out punch. A surge of heart pounding, get me the hell out of here fear. But nowhere to go. Trapped inside the car going to a doctor's appointment with someone who is totally dependent on me. No room for escape. I can't bail out here. I can't afford to feel panic and fall apart! Where the hell is that goddamn parasympathetic nervous system response? Come on, calm down, calm down, and push the fear back down. I'll panic later. Compose yourself!

I started to pray, please God, just a little of your strength to draw from, please God, I just need to calm down and I'll take it from there. And I calmed back down. At least to the point where I could function. Thank you Lord. Thank you.

Apparently Dad didn't get the call. He was still ramping up. "Yes, that Debra sure was exciting. And I had another girlfriend, too. What was her name? Who's-is-whatses...Oh well, she used to meet me down in San Diego. I would tell Rosemarie I was going to a conference, and meet her down there. We would stay at a hotel that had a floating bar in the middle of the pool. I would go down on her. You know what that means, Dr. Fang?"

"And then there was Teri in Traverse City. Boy was she ever...."

I had heard enough. I was screaming inside. The Hero. The Champion. Crushed. Destroyed beyond recognition.

22 { 30 Out of 30

"Now, Walter," Dr. Jahnke's soft, kind eyes met my dad's. "I want you to repeat the three words I told you earlier."

"OK, but you know this is the one I don't like. Lets see... well, you said, 'apple,' then, ah, um, it's long and flat..." Dad's eyes searched the room for a clue. He found it, and a big smile emerged on his face. "Why Dr. Jahnke, you know it's "table!" It was so hard not to like my dad. Even after he just shredded me with 30 years of transgressions.

"Walter, you're doing very well today. Now what was that other word I asked you to remember? "

"Well, it's... you know... a small one."

Come on Dad, you can do it! My anger was fading, at least for the moment, and I couldn't help but pull for him. My thoughts were now broadcasted out loud. "Come on, Dad, you can do it. What's the name of the small one?"

Dad paused for a moment, then beamed. "Penny! Its penny! Penny, penny, penny!!!" Dad acted like he had just won the World Series. He stood up and did a little impromptu jig around the office. Even Dr. Jahnke high-fived him. The test went on, but the remaining items were easy for Dad. Fold a piece of paper in half, drop it, then pick it back up. The test closed with copying some geometric shapes and writing a sentence. Dad wrote, "To Dr. Jahnke, my close friend and the best doctor in the world. I look forward to seeing you again. Love, your friend forever, Walter."

Dad was wrapping up his fraternity club meeting. And he made Dr. Jahnke tear up. How could you hate him? Moments before I thought he was a bastard. Now he was The Champion again. I stuffed all of his bastard qualities away in the walled off part of my brain, and became The Champion's son again. Love is more powerful than hate. Always.

"Walter, you got a perfect score today, 30 out of 30. I think you can thank your son Garrett over there. His wraparound seems to be working. That and taking your Aricept regularly. Dr. Jahnke came over to me and put her arm around my shoulders. This was no ordinary doctor. This was an angel disguised as a doctor. She looked me dead in the eyes, "Now don't forget, Garrett, never stop loving him. We have all made our mistakes in life, and all we have to do to heal is offer forgiveness. <u>Never</u> stop loving him, it's our promise to him." A shiver ran up and then back down my spine. How did she know to say that?

I was overwhelmed, but I was elated. Dad's perfect 30 and Dr. Jahnke's kind, almost prophetic words had resurrected my soul from the depths. But I was greedy. I began to think about Dad's score. Wow, he got a perfect score this time. Even better than before. Maybe he doesn't have Alzheimer's after all. Maybe Tiffanie was right. He is just fine. Maybe it was just some vitamin deficiency or a thyroid problem, or one of the other curable forms of dementia-like symptoms. Back in the land of denial. Well, who could blame me for trying?

My pleasant little fantasy was interrupted by Dr. Jahnke. She was thumbing through Dad's chart. Lets see, your Dad's lab work came back, everything looks fine here, except... well it appears he has a vitamin B deficiency."

Vitamin B deficiency? My mind was fully awake, and searching its dementia research department for information. Vitamin B deficiency is common in the elderly and a deficiency of B12 can bring on Alzheimer's-like symptoms that can be corrected with treatment. Maybe I wasn't lost in the land of denial after all. I had to speak, but I kept my elation in check in front of the all-knowing angel. "Dr, Jahnke, could this be the reason for his memory loss?" Dad turned beet red, for amidst my excitement I momentarily forgot he was in the room.

"Yes, it's possible, but it's highly unlikely. Your dad still is showing the classic early symptoms of early Alzheimer's disease." Dad's lower lip was quivering now. Dammitall! We should have had this conversation somewhere else, without him. I returned to my conversation with Dr. Jahnke, seizing the "it's possible" part, and ignoring the caveat. I guess I needed hope at that moment. I also needed more time with my dad. I wanted the hourglass stopped. I needed time to integrate the bad stuff I heard on the trip up. I needed time to be angry and time to forgive. For despite all of Dad's indiscretions, moral weakness and apparent character flaws, the good part of my dad remained within him. He was still my dad, and I was still his son.

"Now, Garrett, Carolyn here is going to take Walter out to get some more samples of Aricept. That will save you a few hundred dollars. You'll meet up with your dad in the lobby." Dad trotted off with Carolyn. He had already forgotten all about our talk of vitamin B deficiency, of Alzheimer's disease, and memory loss.

"Now, Garrett, about this SPECT Scan I set up for your dad on the 20th. I want you and Tiffanie to go down to U of M hospital and make this as easy on your dad as possible. It's like an MRI. They'll hook all sorts of wires to your Dad and he'll enter this tube-like structure and they'll take pictures of his brain. It will show us which parts of his brain still show electrical activity, that's good, and which parts are beginning to atrophy."

Atrophy? I started to feel surging anxiety again. Atrophy means tissue dormancy and then tissue death that comes from inactivity. This doesn't sound like a curable vitamin deficiency at all! This is another version of the death sentence! My mind raced, and then composed itself with a rousing reappearance of my friend denial. Well, if it's a vitamin deficiency then we won't be finding much of his brain dead or dying. Yeah, it will just confirm that he doesn't have Alzheimer's. He'll beat this too, just like he did his heart disease and his prostrate cancer, and his upbringing in the New York slums, and....

Dr. Jahnke again interrupted my thoughts, thankfully, because I was approaching full-blown mania. "So here's a map to the hospital, and the time of the appointment, 10 o'clock. You probably want to get there a couple hours early because you'll have to go through all this insurance processing. It will cost a few thousand dollars, but your father's retirement insurance and his Medicare should cover most of it. Now, for the vitamin deficiency, I'm going to prescribe this mega vitamin B complex tab that he'll need to take for a couple months. We'll see him again in about 8 weeks to see how his levels are. Maybe we'll see some improvement by then." Dr. Jahnke meant improvement in his blood levels. I heard it as "remission of his dementia symptoms."

I met up with Dad in the lobby. He was sitting there, smiling and joking with another one of Dr. Jahnke's patients, who was waiting for his appointment. Dad had already built enough rapport with this man to shake his hand and pat him on the back as we were leaving.

Love is stronger than hate. Always.

23 { Holding Hands

As soon as we got back on the freeway, Dad was at it again. Free wheeling thoughts and dialogue that lacked any semblance of a restraint system. Dad started talking about his second wife Teri, an ill fated, tumultuous five year relationship that was rumored to have started before my parents were divorced. This was particularly embarrassing to us kids and humiliating to my mother. If you had an affair you could remain pretty much anonymous in a city of 8 million in Los Angeles. That didn't hold true in Traverse City, Michigan.

I decided not to just passively listen and suck in another lethal dosage of anger and emotional conflict as I had on the ride up. If Dad had to release these demons of the past, I was going to be in control of it. Teri didn't matter to me. That relationship was known and it was all over town during my adolescence. I could pull up images of my mother crying and the acts of betrayal by my father on my own. No, if Dad's brain was set on dumping out demons from the past, I would choose which demons would be dumped.

What mattered to me was my sister Cindy. And the unopened letters in that shoebox. The letters, still unopened, had been carefully hidden away in a file cabinet in my basement. I purposely locked the file cabinet and put them in a rarely frequented place so I wouldn't be reminded the letters were there. But I didn't really think I could ever open them even if they had been within ready access. They were not meant for me. They were meant for my sister. I hadn't seen her for nearly eight years now, but I knew that someday I would give them to her.

As we came through Flint and made the now all too familiar turn to the west toward Lansing, I mentally reviewed the falling out that had occurred between Cindy and our dad nearly ten years before. Her sudden break from Dad occurred shortly after she moved from Michigan to Maine with her husband. No one knew exactly what had happened between Dad and her.

Cindy and Dad appeared to have been emotionally close prior to her marriage. But soon after, their relationship became strained, and following a trip Dad made to Maine, Cindy severed ties.

The questions brought about by the falling out were numerous and plagued our family for years. Dad's drinking and obnoxious comments were certainly a big factor in the falling out. But there was an undercurrent that something else had occurred. Was Cindy betrayed by my father? Did she need to be angry with him in order to separate emotionally from him? Was she physically or sexually abused by him? Or did Cindy suffer some other trauma that was not known to our family? The answers to these questions haunted us.

But now, unexpectedly and right in front of me, I had a chance to unlock some of the mystery. It was as if Dad had taken truth serum today. He was lucid and expansive, and seemed capable of sharing everything from the past. I could ask him anything today. What to do, what to do, what to do? I could easily punt this one to another day. But would there be another day? Would Dad ever be this lucid and honest again? Would the truth serum wear off forevermore after today?

I knew there was a good chance I was going to receive bad news if I opened up Dad's issue with Cindy. After all, all the other disclosures of the day had been appalling, and extraordinarily painful. But I could perhaps get some answers. I was terrified, because if the news that came back was bad, I would be trapped in a horrible bind. What if Dad had abused her, sexually abused her maybe, and I would then be forced to sever my relationship with him? And how the hell was I supposed to do that when he is completely dependent on me?

I figured I was about 45 minutes from home, and even with the worst news I could make it home and be in Stacy's arms before the panic decompensated me. And I knew I could trust Stacy. I would always be safe with her.

I readied myself for the inquisition. Dad's inquisition.

"Ah, Dad, could we not talk about Teri anymore, I mean I already know everything about what happened there."

"Why certainly, Garrett. What do you want to talk about?"

I thought the expanding lump in my throat was going to choke off my windpipe. "I'd like to talk about Cindy" Oh, dear Jesus, I think I made a mistake. I've started it, the effects of the truth serum are still present, and it's too late to turn back now. I readied for the first painful blow.

"Cindy? Who's Cindy?"

Well, here's my chance to be cowardly and pull back. I really wanted to retreat, but again, something stronger than me pushed out the words.

"I mean, I wanted to talk about Cindy, you know, my other sister, your oldest daughter?"

My Dad's face instantly grew sad. I continued. "Cindy. You know, she lives in Maine now, with her husband, the spider-man." Spider-man was a nickname Dad had given to Cindy's husband Steve, as he was of wiry build, full of energy, and liked to climb things. Like an ADHD kid inside an adult's body.

"Yeah Dad, the spider-man. You know we haven't seen her, ah, I mean Cindy, in nearly ten years."

"I know. I'm very sad about that. You know I've been writing her but I can't mail it to her. She doesn't want to get anything from me, so I have to honor that." Dad teared up, and this time tears came down his face. I now thought I had made a terrible mistake. I was not only going to get bad news, but I was going to devastate Dad, and in an hour, leave him alone at his house. Dad could handle his Alzheimer's news because it never got transferred to long term memory. The pain with Cindy only existed in long term memory. Dad suffered with it there, inside the only intact part of his brain.

Dad reached out to catch my free right hand. The tears were flowing. His speech was unsteady, and reflected the effects of a trembling body. "Garrett, I love her."

"I know you do, Dad. What happened?" I gripped his hand tightly. It was a show of support, but also a show that I meant business.

"Some very bad things happened."

Dad was crying now. I was beginning to tear up.

"I was too hard on her. I was harder on her than you and Tiffanie. She says I hit her with the belt, which I did. I am so ashamed."

"Dad, you hit me with a belt a few times too." I don't know why I said this, as it could have been interpreted as an avenue to let him off the hook.

"She said it was abusive, which it was."

"Dad, everyone got hit with the belt back then. All of my friends did when they did something really wrong. We didn't think it was abusive."

"I know you don't think it was abusive, and I thank God for that. But she does. And I should have known that."

"How could you have known that?"

"Because it happened to me, by my father. He whipped me while I was on the steps going to the basement, and he threw me down." Dad was in a full-blown cry by now. I had seen him tear up many times, choke on his words many times, but never let out an unrestrained cry. Not until now.

Dad wasn't done. "I…I…I whipped Cindy on the basement steps like my father did to me. I don't think she loves me anymore. I'm so ashamed."

I wanted to comfort him. I was going to comfort him. But I wasn't finished yet. My voice grew loud and forceful. "Dad, did you sexually abuse Cindy?"

My Dad's face grew white. He was mortified and perplexed by the question. You could see it made absolutely no sense to him. He was still crying.

Dad was shaking as he gripped my free hand.

"Is that, is that what everyone thinks? May God strike me, may God damn me to eternity if I am lying. I never did anything like that. I would never do that, to anyone. I despise people who do that. You hear me, I despise that! May God damn me to hell if I am being untruthful."

24 { December 20th

December 20th came soon enough. Tiffanie and I had taken the day off from work and we picked Dad up in my van. Dad was in his usual, jovial mood. The trauma of the talk about Cindy was not affecting him. I'd like to say it had become a distant memory for him. The fact of the matter was that it had become no memory for him. Aside from his long term memories from about pre-1990, I was learning that I only had the moment with Dad. His entire world was the immediate present. Almost nothing from the present lasted in his mind more than a few minutes, and almost nothing from the present made it into long term memory.

We arrived at the University of Michigan hospital at 7:45 AM and checked in. Although Tiffanie and I were prepared by Dr. Jahnke for the insurance processing part of the experience, I was struck by how cold and impersonal the medical world had often become. Here you have a patient with a terminal disease, who has to have a major procedure done that will have considerable impact on how the rest of his life will be played out. Here you have a patient who is almost certainly going to be extremely anxious, as is his family. And all the fucking preparation, all the orientation, all the dialogue and conversation and resources when you arrive at the hospital has to do with money and insurance coverage. Two hours of forms and waivers and address of financial and insurance concerns and exactly two and a half minutes of emotional preparation before the procedure began. Nice job, system.

Dad was strapped into a gurney in a small room with a gigantic machine that had a tube-like cavity. The SPECT Scan, short for Spectrum Scanning Imagery, was a formidable machine that seemed capable of swallowing a person whole. Dad was soon wired with electrodes all about his head. He looked like some sort of creature out of a 1950's grade B horror movie. But Dad was in the company of doctors, and so this was just another type of frat club meeting for him. He was cheerful and upbeat, and actually seemed to be enjoying the attention from the techs that were preparing him for the procedure. In fact, within a few minutes Dad had loosened up the previously emotionally flat techs so that they were having a friendly chat with him. Dad truly was the king of the rapport builders.

The cavity part of the machine gobbled up Dad's head. I don't know how long he was in there, but to Tiffanie and me it felt like an eternity. Dad tolerated the whole experience well. He should have come out of the monster's cavity with a claustrophobia attack, but instead he came out smiling and excited, as if he had just gotten off a Disneyworld ride.

I asked the attending tech if he could informally share any of the results relatively soon. He gave the usual, expected answer, "Well, I'd like to, but you'll need to wait for the radiologist."

Four excruciating hours later, our boredom was broken in the unit waiting room. "Walter Turke, the radiologist will see you now." Oh great, they are planning on giving the news to Dad himself, the Alzheimer's patient who can't transfer anything to longer term memory. Don't they read the frickin' chart? I had made it clear to everyone on arrival that he had severe memory problems and to be sensitive to his impairment.

The radiology unit truly was planning on seeing Dad alone. Dad didn't help matters by telling us in front of the nurse that he could see the doctor by himself. Tiffanie and I had to explain again who we were, that our dad had significant memory impairment, possibly Alzheimer's disease, that we were his caregivers, and that he wouldn't be able to recount the doctor's feedback to us on his own. Another unnecessary, awkward, painful moment for my dad, as this had to all happen in front of him. His face turned beet red, but as expected, a few minutes later he had forgotten everything that had happened.

Tiffanie and I were finally granted access and the three of us were shown to a small, sterile, conference room. We were told that the radiologist would be in shortly with the photographs of Dad's brain. Tiffanie and I were no longer bored. We were terrified, and anxious as hell. Meanwhile, Dad was cheerfully chatting away. He did keep asking why we were here. We kept telling him the same pat answers, "Oh, we're just finishing up with your doctor's appointment. The doctor will be in with your script, and then we will be off."

A quick knock on the door and the radiologist burst in. He was a nice-looking, younger man in his early thirties. But he was all about business, and obviously in a hurry. There would be no time for rapport building. The king of the rapport builders extended his hand and tried to elicit some friendly conversation. The young, managed care trained radiologist had no time for that. "Yes, well, Mr. Turke… "

I politely corrected him, "it's Dr. Turke, actually." Dad was still a doctor, and worthy of the respect that came with that.

"Yes, well, Mr. Turke, you had a SPECT Scan done this morning and I'm here to show you the results." He unrolled the radiography, which looked like a giant black and white photograph in the shape of a skull, with varying areas of light and dark shading across different regions of the brain.

"You see these areas here, these lobes are much lighter showing a great deal of electrical activity. That means your brain tissue is still active and healthy in these regions."

OK, OK. Even if this guy has no bedside manners, this news sounds good so far. Hey, maybe it is a vitamin deficiency after all.

The radiologist continued. "But you see over here, and again here, and again over here, these regions of your brain are shadowy. They would be lighter if there was healthy tissue and electrical activity. This shows the parts of the brain that are dying, and there is very little electrical activity going on there. I'm sure Dr. Jahnke will explain this to you more when you see her. I will leave a copy of the imaging for you to keep."

The radiologist was ready to leave. That was it? Come in like a bull in a china shop, deliver a deathblow to a 69 year old man, traumatize his children, and then exit with no time to debrief? No sensitive talk? No waiting to see how we would handle the news? What kind of inhuman system is this? Doctor Jahnke wouldn't have handled it this way! Doctor Jahnke wouldn't have put up having her patient treated this way!

Tiffanie and I had questions, but we sure as hell weren't going to ask this guy to answer them. Tiffanie and I were stunned. Dad had already gone through his less than a minute phase of face turning red with his bottom lip quivering. He had already fully recovered, oblivious to it all. Tiffanie and I weren't so lucky. The radiologist's sentence was playing over and over in our heads, like an old fashioned record that was stuck: "This shows you the parts of the brain that are dying, there is very little electrical activity going on there."

So much for the vitamin deficiency theory. This was irrefutable evidence. Huge sections of his brain were dying. We could see it in black and white, over and over again. As many times as we needed to.

We left the hospital exhausted and defeated. Well, Tiffanie and I were exhausted and defeated. Dad was rambling on about how wonderful it was to have his two children with him, together. Tiffanie and I needed to cry, but it wasn't the place. I think we were too tired to cry, anyway.

Dad slept on the way home. Tiffanie and I barely spoke. We were both still listening to that broken record inside our heads.

Five days after Dad's SPECT Scan was Christmas. I would be stunned and traumatized by the results of the SPECT Scan for weeks. It never felt like Christmas that year. I wondered if it would ever feel like Christmas again.

25 { The 45 Minute Day

The winter was almost over. Already the first flowers of spring were poking their heads up through the crusty remnants of snow and the brown grass that had been matted down by months of snow and freezing rain. It had been three long months since that SPECT Scan appointment had sealed Dad's fate. Three long months for me to integrate all of Dad's indiscretions into my new internal image of him. A more realistic image of him. And three long months of doing wraparound care. I was getting increasingly depressed. Not sad, not anxious, not fearful. Depressed. I was losing interest in things I used to enjoy. Traveling. Photography. Going out to concerts and shows. I was still exercising and spending time with my family, but there were always time pressures now. Dad's wraparound was gobbling up more and more time.

Despite our Herculean efforts, Dad wasn't getting any better. Not that I consciously expected him to. But deep within the reservoirs of my unconscious, I think I did expect him to improve. If we were shelling out all this energy, if we have set up such a tremendous wraparound system, well of course Dad would show some improvement. At the very least, we should be preventing him from getting worse. It was textbook magical thinking. And despite all of my education and experience, it was still, even at this stage, textbook denial. The SPECT Scan results should have ended the struggle. But I was still trying to fight it. Don Quixote still thrusting his lance at the windmill. Something had to give. I was convinced it would be me.

In three months time, Dad had lost his ability to care for himself without someone else's prompting and organization. He was having trouble remembering how to use the microwave and the TV and the phone. He couldn't adjust his thermostat anymore, and he was losing his ability to judge temperature. I'd come into a house that was either freezing cold with Dad wearing a heavy jacket, or a house that was 90 degrees. Dad's food would spoil and he would forget to eat. When he did fix himself something to eat it might be a whole package of Fig Newtons or a jam sandwich. And he would constantly rearrange his furniture and wall hangings, with each new look being a bit more bizarre and unbalanced than the previous one. It was clearly a losing battle. So what if his Mini Mental Status Exam scores were still normal. You could see the disease was winning.

I had purchased Dad an erasable wipeboard and hung it in his front entrance hallway where he would see it each day. Upon it I wrote each day's date and wraparound schedule. Tiff or Don over for breakfast at 7:30. Garrett over for lunch at 12:15. Rosemarie over for a walk at 2:30. Garrett over for dinner at 5:30. Each day was nearly the same, except for the days Dad went to the ALFA Center to treat his "patients."

From Dad's perspective, everything was going great. Things had settled into a nice daily and weekly routine for him. He was happy the way his life was going, ecstatic each time he saw us kids and his grandkids, and he remained extraordinarily cheerful, seemingly oblivious to his condition. His ALFA notebook was filled with odd but touching little tidbits about the other ALFA Center participants. "Rob is a pharmacist, originally from Chicago, seems a little depressed. Needs more exercise and more social activities." "Mary lost her husband two years ago. Seems depressed. Needs supportive psychotherapy and group therapy." "Fred is a father of three. Misses his kids, who live in Arizona. He needs our understanding." Dad was on it. You just couldn't hold him down, disease or no disease.

Superficially, Dad's wraparound team was going well, too. In addition to the five family members, Dr. Jahnke, and the ALFA Center, we had added Dad's neighbors on both sides of his condo to the wraparound team. Frank and Jeffrey, a wealthy gay couple, were on one side, and Rob and his disabled wife Liz were on the other. They didn't have much of an active role other than knowing my dad's condition, and checking in on him once in awhile when we couldn't structure his time. Frank and Jeffrey would have Dad over for dinner or a barbeque once in awhile. Dad's neighbors provided me with a great sense of relief and security. I now had several people in immediate proximity to Dad who could be mobilized within minutes or even seconds if there was a problem.

Dad still had his driver's license. He wasn't using either of his cars much anymore, and seemed to have lost interest in driving. Dad's family physician wanted Tiffanie and me to petition the Secretary of State office to revoke his driver's license. That was certain to be another traumatic blow for Dad, and probably a humiliating experience to boot. Tiff and I couldn't do it, not just yet. We settled for taking his car keys, both to the Mercedes and Chrysler, hoping he wouldn't notice. He didn't.

I received a wealth of compliments for coordinating Dad's care in such an invested, caring and elaborate way. Many people called me a hero of sorts. The compliments were always welcomed and seemed sincere. I am sure they were intended to give me hope and to pick me up. But for me, increasingly, life inside the wraparound was not so marvelous. It wasn't working as well as it appeared to the outside world. It was taking more and more out of me, and draining me of my ability to care for others who I loved. Like my wife. Like my kids. Like my mother.

It took huge amounts of energy to keep the wraparound running smoothly day-in and day-out. People got sick, things came up, and vacations, social plans, and school activities all got in the way. All understandable, all to be expected, all part of life. But Dad's needs were so great that you couldn't go without "coverage" when something came up and the regular wraparound care wasn't available. Dad's needs never took a vacation or a day off. And, try as I might to compensate with more and more wraparound structure, Dad's condition was worsening, and his needs were growing.

I took it upon myself to fill in gaps in the wraparound coverage when others couldn't be available. The ALFA Center was closed for a holiday break and so I took time off from work to be with Dad. Tiff had a sick kid and I would fill her shift. Mom wanted to take a painting class and so I covered the next three Thursdays. Everyone else seemed so much less rigid than me. They wanted to adjust to life. They wanted to have a life. I sometimes felt I was even being chastised by my family that I was taking my role and duties too seriously. They were maintaining their lifestyles and I should too. I guess they were trying to help me by keeping me in some semblance of balance. But at Dad's expense? I didn't know if I could do it. I equated taking care of myself with neglecting Dad.

In an effort to keep up with Dad's growing needs, I tried, single-handedly, to coordinate all of his household and daily living needs into as short of an amount of time as possible each day. I figured that way I could still spend time with my family, friends, and loved ones. I called this intense, ratcheted up effort, "the 45 minute day."

The "45 minute day" was so named for two reasons. One, I tried to cram a whole day's worth of chores into a 45 minute period. Two, after just 45 minutes with Dad, he would estimate that I had been there, toiling away to help him, for the entire day. At the end of the 45 minutes, he would often try to close with me by saying, "Well, Garrett, we had another nice long day together. I'm beat, I think I'll finish this movie and go to bed." He would then try to push me out the door to go home to my family.

The 45 minute day was either logistical brilliance or an indication that my obsessive compulsive traits had run amok. I would arrive at Dad's about 5:30 after work. First stop: gather up his laundry and throw it in the washer. His clothes never got really dirty, so I could get by with the short, 20 minute cycle. While that was going, select a microwave dinner for him out of the freezer, and cut up some fresh vegetables or fruit. While that was being microwaved for 6 minutes, start his shower, help him get out of his clothes, and lather him up in the shower. Next, give him a shave and clip his finger or toenails if they needed it. Then give him his meds and vitamins. At about this time the microwave would start its incessant beeping, indicating his meal was ready. I would help Dad change into his pajamas while his dinner cooled a little. Then sit him down to eat, talk for a few minutes of the events of the day, and wait for the washer buzzer to ring. Once that happened, transfer the load to the dryer and resume chatting with Dad over dinner. Once Dad finished, collect all the dishes up from the day, and put them in the dishwasher. The dishwasher was rarely full, but if I didn't run it, Dad would keep removing the dirty dishes and continue to eat off of them. Then settle Dad in around the living room table to sign a check or two for bills, and maybe read a letter together that came in from one of his friends, or from Arthur. Next get Dad into the bathroom to brush and floss his teeth. Then plug in a long movie that he could watch before going to bed. After watching the movie with him for ten minutes, the dryer would buzz. The laundry was ready to be folded and hung. I completed this, and laid out Dad's clothes for the next day in his bedroom. Then I went back and watched 5 minutes of the movie. I would feign a few yawns, Dad would notice, and he would send me home, telling me sympathetically that I had had a long day with him and that I needed to go get some rest.

I did this ritualized routine everyday. At first, it would take me several hours to do these chores. But after a few weeks, by multi-tasking, I had figured out a way to do them in about 45 minutes.

From the outside looking in, the wraparound was a marvelous super-support structure. From the inside looking out, I was feeling trapped, lonely, disconnected, and now, increasingly depressed. Doing the same routine day in and day out might be helping Dad, but it was killing me. Is this how I would be spending virtually all my days for the next year? For the next 5 years? How am I going to find the energy to continue working? And to be the family man I wanted to be?

I prayed each night to help show me a way out of this trap I had inadvertently built for myself. When nothing changed, I prayed harder. Days and weeks passed, and I was still depressed. Stacy wanted me to go into therapy, and to get on some medication. I was beginning to resign myself to the fact that I was going to be depressed indefinitely. Maybe always.

Then I had an epiphany. It came to me in the middle of the night. I awoke to a voice that came from within my head: *"Quit fighting this. You can't beat this. This is so much bigger than you. Your Dad's time is coming. Enjoy your time you have left with him. This is why he is here with you..."* These were not random thoughts. This was not a worried rumination within my head. This was not my spirit trying to fumble its way through darkness. This was a directive.

I slept like a log after this "awakening." The next morning I woke up happy and cheerful for the first time in months. It was Saturday. I hurried downstairs and grabbed some paper and a pen. It was time to make plans for the Farewell Tour.

26 { Booking the Farewell Tour

I recoiled a bit when Stacy first put her arms around me. I didn't like to be bothered, much less touched, when I was deep in thought. This was especially true first thing in the morning. But that didn't matter much to Stacy. She hugged me anyway, wanting me to know she loved me. "What cha working on there, honey?" I looked up, a little annoyed I had been disturbed. But when I saw her big brown "bambi" eyes, I stopped what I was doing. She could always melt me.

"I'm going to be coming out of this funk I've been in."

"Oh? You've been in a funk now, have you?" She knew damn well I had been struggling emotionally. She smiled a big, brown-eyed smile. "How are you going to pull out of it? Have you decided to go talk to someone?"

"Nope!" I said proudly, as if I thought therapy was something to be ashamed of. "I've decided to go on a bunch of trips. Actually, we're going to go on a bunch of trips. I'm going to be getting back into my photography, do some traveling, head back up north to see some old friends and haunts."

"That sounds...ah... great, honey." I could hear the "that's not very realistic" undertones that were beneath her words. Then the anticipated caveat: "But who's going to watch your dad? Tiffanie?"

"Nope."

"Your mom?"

"No, not her, either." Now it was my turn to smile. It was becoming a playful game of cat and mouse.

"Well I know you're not going to leave him alone. Who will watch him, then?"

"I will." I flashed a big broad smile. A happy smile, my first in months.

"You will. Ah ha, I see...while you, we, will be going on all these trips?"

Stacy was now sarcastic.

"Of course!" I was building to a crescendo.

"How is that going to be possible?" Stacy was now direct, and increasingly serious.

"Why Dad will be coming with us, of course." I handed Stacy the piece of paper on which I had been making the list. She started reading it aloud.

"Visit Culps, Millikens, Hayes, Welches in Traverse City. These are his old friends, huh?"

"Yep."

Stacy continued reading, "Get tickets to see Sarah Brightman at the Wharton Center. Are you serious?"

"I saw it in the paper today. Tickets go on sale Thursday. Let's try and get seats in the front row. Dad loves her."

"Garrett, you've got a trip to Northern Michigan on here for a photo shoot. You think your Dad can handle that?"

"Sure do. He's gonna have to, because I'm going. "

"And sailing in Grand Traverse Bay?"

"Yeah, Ron Culp said we could come up any time and go sailing. He's got a thirty foot sail boat."

"You think he really meant it? I mean, with your dad's Alzheimer's?"

"Yeah. He said, anytime. Well, this is anytime."

"Let's see, you've also got a tour of Traverse City and Leelanau County."

"His two favorite places. He loves Lake Michigan. The orchards and the dunes."

"And a color tour of the Irish Hills this fall?"

"Yeah, I was thinking the same place we went to last year."

"And a Michigan State Football game?"

"They're playing Iowa this year for Homecoming. I can get tickets from my friends at work."

"You're really serious?"

"Do I look like I'm kidding?"

"Does Tiff know about this?"

"Nope. Just you. I just thought about all this last night. Actually I was told to do this. Think we can handle it?"

"You were told to do this?"

I didn't want to explain, because I didn't really understand it myself. So I muted it a little.

"Well, it was sort of like my conscience told me."

Stacy hesitated, and my self imposed mania deflated almost instantaneously. "I don't know if your Dad can handle all of this, honey. I know the girls and I could probably only do some of this. Some of this you're gonna have to do on your own with him. But honey, I really don't think he can..."

I wouldn't let her finish the sentence. I looked into her eyes. Tears were welling up in mine. "Stacy, this is probably going to be my last year with him. What else can I do? The same routine each and every day for the rest of his life? That will kill my spirit. It almost did already."

I tried to fight back the tears, but it was no use. It was time to cry. And I did. Finally. The SPECT Scan and Dad's affairs and his indiscretions and Cindy and the wraparound. All that pressure converging on a single moment in time. It was time to start letting it go. The voice inside me reminded me I didn't have to be in control all the time. *This is bigger than you, Garrett.* So I let go.

After ten minutes of sobbing like a frightened six year old, Stacy finally let go of me. As I recomposed myself, Stacy went off into the kitchen. I could hear her from around the corner. "I'm going to make you some tea. That will help relax you."

A few minutes later Stacy returned with the tea. She put her arm around me and smiled some more. "You know, before your dad got sick we were talking about taking the kids down to Disneyworld. I was thinking of calling right now and booking it for spring break."

I looked up at her, perplexed, and still sniffling a bit. "Next month? What about Dad?"

"Why he'll be coming with us, of course. You know he loves Disney as much as any kid. Think you can handle it? Well, you're gonna have to, because we're going."

And, after that, I began to pull myself out of my funk. Yeah, it might have helped if I had seen a counselor or got on some medication. But in the end, all I needed was Stacy's arms and an answered prayer.

27 { First Stop: Disneyworld

Dad was already awake. I had been awake most of the night because of Dad's incessant snoring. He had a horrible snoring problem that would not only keep whoever was in the room awake, but also I think anyone within a ten mile radius of him. Dad's snoring overnight had rekindled a twenty year-old memory of mine. I couldn't stop thinking about it.

When I helped Dad drive to Arizona during his move in 1981, his snoring kept me awake for the first three nights of our transcontinental journey. Dad's snoring was one of the most brutal forms of torture that a person could inflict upon another. He could sleep 15 or 20 minutes just fine without a sound, then erupt like a volcano, jarring anyone in the room with him. Then he would mellow again, I'd drift back to sleep, and just as things were peaceful and relaxed, the volcano would go off again.

Some twenty tears later, and after Dad was diagnosed with Alzheimer's, I did some research on sleep apnea and recognized Dad's symptoms. Today there is a known correlation between sleep apnea, reduced oxygen to the brain, and predisposing dementia. It was too late for a sleep apnea study and corrective surgery to increase Dad's oxygen consumption. Dad already had Alzheimer's disease. I was beginning to accept that his disease was here to stay.

Stacy had pulled it off. We were away from all the problems and worries for a week. Dad, the kids, and Stacy and I were in heaven. The only problem was that Dad needed to be watched continuously. We knew this going in of course, and I had volunteered to take the lion's share of the responsibility of watching him. This would become a moot point anyway, because Dad refused to ever leave my side.

On this, our first morning at Disney, Dad was showered, dressed and raring to go before 6:00 AM. He came over to the bed and nudged me, whispering that it was time to get up and start our day. He seemed to be having one of his more lucid days, as he remembered where he was and did the shower-shave-dress sequence all on his own without any prompting. These more lucid days were becoming less and less frequent, and I was learning to treasure them.

Our family had plans to hit the Magic Kingdom at 10:00, but Dad's early rising forced me to come up with ideas to occupy Dad's time so the girls could get some more time to sleep. A cruel fate for the one who had been kept up all night by the perpetual snoring machine. Barely conscious, I managed to drag myself into the shower in an attempt to wake myself up. I put on some shorts and a green and white Michigan State University Spartans t-shirt, just like Dad was wearing. MSU was in the NCAA Basketball Final Four this week, with both the semifinal and final games taking place in Tampa, just a stone's throw from Disneyworld. Dad and I were big fans of this particular Spartan team, led by their fierce point guard, Mateen Cleeves.

I had already noticed that Disneyworld was swarming with fans of the University of Florida Gators, one of the other final four teams. I joked with Dad that we were in hostile, enemy country being from Michigan State. I immediately realized I screwed up when I said that, as Dad might take such a comment quite literally and begin to search for his Navy Officer's uniform and get ready for battle. But he took it in a lighthearted way this time, and stated, "Oh, not to worry. I think they'll take the championship, they're the best team." OK, thank God, today he gets it. So far so good.

We decided to kill some time by going down to the nearby cafeteria to get some coffee. Although it was barely 6:30, there was already a long line in front of the self-serve coffee dispensing machine. Dad and I grabbed a couple of complimentary Disney jumbo mugs and took our place in line amongst the other caffeine addicts. There was a row of sugar packets, creamer, and other condiments before we got to the coffee dispenser. I grabbed some sugar and creamer packets and emptied them in the bottom of my mug. Dad attempted to do the same. I hadn't noticed this, but Dad grabbed packets of salt instead of the sugar and was emptying them into his mug. I heard some rather unsophisticated types behind us start to laugh, but I hadn't yet figured out why. They had noticed that Dad was pouring salt into his coffee mug.

Dad arrived at the coffee dispenser first. He was confused by it. He pressed about four different buttons, all of them wrong, and had a mixture of tea, hot chocolate and hot water circulating with the salt in his mug. Once

I noticed what he was doing, I felt very bad that I had neglected him, albeit only for a moment. I stepped in to help him, but my first move also resulted in pushing a wrong button. I could feel the unsophisticated types behind us getting inpatient.

Then I heard the words. Fighting words. "Looks like we've got dumb and dumber up ahead of us, Son."

I turned with a rage I had not felt since the fourth grade, which was the last fistfight I had had in my life. Prior to the fifth grade, I had had three substantial fistfights. Each one against a different neighborhood bully. Each one an episode where I erupted after being picked on for days, weeks, months, until I just couldn't take it any more. And each fight ended with me pummeling the instigator until he was crying, bloodied, or running away. The last fight in the fourth grade ended with me standing on the bully's chest, his nose streaming blood, as if I had proudly conquered him. My mother came out and I was the one who got in trouble. She didn't want to hear that it was the instigator's fault and he had got what was coming to him. I guess I should have felt remorse, but I didn't. I took my punishment from Mom, pretended to be sorry, but was secretly proud of myself. The instigator never talked to me again. He would cross the street whenever he saw me coming. I would cherish this incident as a personal victory against the forces of evil my entire life.

I had prided myself in being a diplomatic, non-fighting peacemaker ever since this incident. But today might be different. The guy behind me had delivered a low blow to my dad, when he was down. I reeled around, ready to defend Dad's honor.

There he was, the 50-something, pot-bellied instigator and his twenty something, pot-bellied son. Both of them were wearing Florida Gator shirts.

The older, larger unsophisticated one smiled a hostile, instigating smile. I immediately recognized it from my childhood. "Ready to get your asses kicked?" I thought he and his son were getting ready to fire off a couple punches at us. He was actually referring to the possibility of an MSU-Florida showdown in the finals. I was still stuck on his dumb and dumber comment from the previous minute.

I glared angrily at the person behind me. I wanted to say, "Are you <u>trying</u> to act like a moron, or were you just born that way?" But I didn't.

Physiologically, I was ready to fight. Sleep deprivation will do that, but instead, I just turned my back on them and returned to attending to my father. I had some thoughts that I was being way too passive, which bothered me. But my identity was tied to being the peacemaker, so I turned the other cheek and let it go. I wasn't going to wreck our vacation by getting into it with these two ignorant SOB's. Meanwhile, Dad had dumped his coffee and was filling it correctly this time. He was completely oblivious to the conflict that was percolating behind us. He turned to me innocently. "All set, Doctor?"

"All set, Dad."

"Then we're off! Let's walk around a bit before we pick up the girls, OK?"

"Right-O, Dad." That wasn't part of my vernacular. I was starting to pick up Dad's slang words because I hung around him so much now. And with that, we just left the two bullies standing there. But for the rest of the trip, those two kind of lingered uncomfortably in my consciousness. I had really wanted to bloody their noses and step on top of them. The two of them made me realize that not everyone in the world would be kind and understanding toward Dad as he progressed through this dreaded disease. Some would be cruel, some would be insensitive, some would be ignorant, and some would be exploitive.

The week at Disney turned out to be truly magical. Everyone had tremendous fun. Dad sang his way through the It's a Small World ride. We went on the Flying Dumbos and Space Mountain. We talked to the Disney characters and got their autographs. We went to the MGM studios where Dad cried when he saw mementos of his childhood movie stars. And he absolutely loved the recreated movie set of 1940's New York, which spanned a whole block. Dad said it felt just like being back home in Brooklyn.

Dad was a happy little kid for a whole week. His only frustration was not being able to go on the Pirates of the Caribbean ride, which was closed for renovation. Although I told Dad the ride was closed, it never registered into his longer term memory, and every hour or two he became obsessed with going on the ride. I learned to just go on a hunt to find the ride with him when he got into one of these obsessive states. I would purposely walk him in a direction opposite from the ride until he forgot what we were looking for. After a few days of this, I decided to just make up a little white lie, telling Dad how much fun he and I had had on the Pirates ride, and describing the ride in great detail. Miraculously, this stuck in his memory as "fact." When we returned to Stacy and the girls, Dad was so convincing of the fun he had on the ride that the girls thought that Pirates of the Caribbean had re-opened.

During the last night of our stay at Disney, Michigan State was playing Florida for the national championship. I was almost fanatical about this game, because it had become more than a basketball game for me. It was Garrett and Walter against the two bullies who were in line behind us at the coffee dispenser. Our family watched the championship game sitting atop a king-sized bed in the hotel room. The game was really close in the first half, but Mateen drilled three clutch 3-pointers and the Spartans had the lead at halftime. Dad said immediately after the halftime buzzer sounded, "they've got this game won." I reminded him it was only halftime. He said, "I know, but they've got this game won, no one can beat Cleaves tonight." He was right.

We might have just been sitting on a bed in a hotel room in Orlando, but we cheered and stomped and danced like we were in the streets of East Lansing.

The next morning Dad and I got up early again. We proudly put on our Michigan State t-shirts and made our way through the gardens en route to the cafeteria. We stood in line at the coffee dispenser. I looked around for the two bullies, ready to exact my revenge. But they were nowhere to be found. Instead there were two other Florida Gator fans behind us in line. One extended his hand to Dad. He had a thick Southern accent. "Nice game. Those Spartans could have beaten any pro team last night." Dad smiled, shook his hand warmly, and then pulled me forward with his other hand.

"This is my son. I am very, very proud to have watched the game with him." Dad choked up like he always did. And I wiped away some more tears from my eyes.

28 { Sorting the Mail

The crusty remains of an early spring snowstorm crunched beneath the van tires as we pulled into Dad's driveway. Our adventure in Disneyworld was over. I had already dropped the girls off along with our luggage at our house, and now all that remained was to bring Dad home. "All that remained," however, involved a bit more than just dropping him off. I had to re-orient him to his condo and his wraparound routine. A surge of dread swept over me as we parked in the driveway. I didn't want this vacation to end.

Dad was anxious to be home. Although the week had been enormously successful and great fun, it was obvious that he was physically spent. I was pretty tired myself. Although the trip was a blast, it had been hard work tagging along with Dad, around the clock, for over a week.

I had called our wraparound team from the Detroit airport. I needed a break from Dad, even if it was just going to be for a day or two. The team was already two steps ahead of me. Tiffanie, her husband Don, and my mom had already decided to structure Dad for the weekend so I could recuperate a bit. This was a huge relief, for the thought of immediately ratcheting back up for Dad's wraparound care was overwhelming me.

The contrast between being on vacation for over a week and coming back to the daily grind of Dad's care and work elicited a sad, lonely, depressive feeling within me. This always happened when I came back from a long vacation, even before Dad got sick. It was amplified this time, however, because it had been so very long since I had had a vacation, and because I knew Dad's situation ultimately would not have a happy ending. Some more sand had passed through the hourglass.

I parked the van, took Dad's suitcase out of the back hatch, and helped Dad step out of the passenger seat. Dad fumbled with his keys trying to unlock the front door, and I had to help him insert the key correctly. The calming smell of a freshly cleaned house hit us as soon as we opened the door. The wraparound team, namely my sister, brother-in-law, and mother, had thoroughly cleaned the condo while we were away. The carpets were vacuumed, the hardwood floors polished, all the laundry done, and there was a big pot of Moroccan eggplant stew, courtesy of my mom, awaiting us in the refrigerator. I expected a lot of work opening that door, and it had all been done for me. Thank God for my family.

A huge pile of mail awaited us on the dining room table. True to my "work first, play later" upbringing, I decided to get the mail done before Dad and I settled in for the evening. I threw in a load of Dad's laundry that was left over from Disney, put his suitcase away, and descended on the mail. It was incredible how much had accumulated in just one week. Aside from the expected mountain of junk mail, some bills, and the ongoing flood of donation requests, there were a number of personal letters. Also buried in the pile was a driver's license renewal from the Secretary of State office. I should have been prepared for it, knowing Dad's birthday was approaching. I wasn't.

The driver's license renewal instantly amplified my post vacation funk. It was one of the areas I hadn't dealt with. Dad rarely drove anymore, but he still had his driver's license. I had his keys, and he would rarely even ask where they were. I still sometimes asked if he wanted to drive, but he increasingly deferred any and all driving to Tiffanie and me. It worried us that Dad still had an extra set of car keys somewhere in the house. Although I looked for them periodically, I could never find them. I figured Dad would never be able to find them, either.

Inside Dad's garage sat the last reminders of Dad's freedom and independence. He had loved his two prized cars, the forest green Chrysler sedan he used to drive to work and for his daily errands, and his treasured 1977, fire engine red Mercedes 450 SL convertible roadster, which, despite 247,000 miles, had no rust and still ran like a top. Dad especially cherished that car, and before he got sick would only take it out on sunny days and special occasions. I had mixed feelings about the Mercedes, because I associated it with Dad's midlife crisis, his narcissism, the divorce from my mom, and his affair with Teri during his breakup with my mom. To me, that car represented everything bad about my dad. I would cringe every time Dad took me for a ride in it.

I distracted Dad and hid the driver's license renewal form in my pocket without him seeing it. I knew it meant trouble. Dad shouldn't be driving anymore, and it was irresponsible of me to allow him to keep his license. It was too dangerous. I could hear the words of his family physician ringing in my ears. "Garrett, he could get confused out there and kill somebody." Mom had relentlessly echoed those same words. They were right, of course. I knew what had to be done. I couldn't put my head in the sand anymore.

Dad and I went through the remaining mail. There was so much junk mail I had to bring the kitchen garbage container over to use as a dumpster. I nearly filled it with the generic requests for money that had come to Dad's house. The volumes of exploitive mail made me think of another neglected area. Dad shouldn't be receiving mail anymore through standard mailbox delivery. That was also too dangerous. He should have a P.O. Box that only I had access to. That way I wouldn't have to rush out to intercept Dad's mail every day.

Near the bottom of the gigantic stack of mail were a number of personal letters and a post card. The post card was from a couple my dad and mom knew in Traverse City. They were retired now, and wintered on the Gulf Coast. The postcard read that they would be returning to Traverse City soon for the spring and summer, and that they would love to see Dad. There was another letter with a return address in Traverse City. It was from my father's old friend, Ron, who was a social worker therapist my dad had set up a private practice with many years ago. Ron wanted Dad to come up and visit this summer and go sailing with him. He had been asking Dad to go sailing with him for years, but they had never actually got around to doing it. I knew immediately this would be the year they didn't just talk about it. I would see to it. It was their last chance.

And finally, there were three letters from Arthur. I was intrigued. Wow, three letters in just over a week. I wondered what was going on with him. Each was very short, just a few lines asking about how Dad was and what he was up to. Each note had some antique looking post cards enclosed about the Navy or Marine Corps, and some patriotic stickers or patches. It was a little unusual, but touching. And each note ended with "Your friend, Arthur. Semper Fi." Always faithful.

For the first time, I thought about how Dad's disease would affect Arthur. Pretty soon Dad wouldn't be able to write very well. Pretty soon, Dad would not be able to offer him any meaningful advice or direction. Pretty soon, Dad might not even remember who Arthur was.

Arthur seemed so attached to Dad, even if their relationship now was just through correspondence. Did he live alone? Was he married? How was he managing without Dad? Arthur didn't know Dad was sick. What should I do? Tell him Dad has Alzheimer's, that he is terminally ill? That would devastate him. Hell, it might cause a psychiatric regression in him. What is the right thing to do here? In the past, I had always gone to my father with these sorts of dilemmas and questions. But I couldn't do that anymore. Now what do I do?

Dad and I finished with the mail. I made us some coffee and found a pad of paper. I then began doing what I always did to try to break out of a post vacation funk. I started planning the next vacation. First, I made a list of fun, short-term things to do with Dad, and then I made a longer term list of plans for the summer. On the short list went the Sarah Brightman concert next weekend, Stacy's decision to take Dad to see the "Guys and Dolls" musical at the Michigan State Wharton Center, and a couple movies I had wanted to see with Dad.

On the summer list went trips to Traverse City and Lake Michigan, including visits to all of Dad's old friends and haunts, a sailing outing with Ron, and a photography shoot that Dad would accompany me on.

Dad was ecstatic with our plans. He was so excited that he got out a map of the state and asked me to start plotting our proposed travels. He searched for his Guys and Dolls movie. And he proudly showed me his Sarah Brighman collection, which included five CD's, two videos, and a program from her London Phantom of the Opera tour. Hmmm...maybe Dad did meet her in London after all.

After sorting the mail, making up our plans list, and performing the 45 minute day, I was beat. I yawned and made up my usual excuse to leave. Dad said he was beat, too, and indicated he was going to watch Guys and Dolls and then go to bed. I reassured Dad that Tiff, Don and my mother would be over "later," code for "the rest of the weekend." I then wrote down the weekend wraparound schedule on the wipeboard.

As I made my way to the door, Dad called to me from the living room, where he had begun watching Guys and Dolls.

"Oh, Dr. Fang?"

"Yes, Dad."

"About our, you know, the... the thing we were writing on, you know it has to do with the, ah, um, plans for the, ah..."

"You mean the summer vacation list?"

"Yes. That's it. The vacation list for you and me. I was just thinking."

"Yes?" I turned, and began walking back toward the living room.

"I was just thinking. Is our friend Arthur on our list? He needs us right now. There is so much he is..."

I cut Dad off, not wanting to pursue the subject anymore. "Uh, yeah, Dad, I'm on top of it." I didn't know what to say or do. <u>Our</u> friend? On <u>our</u> list? Dad, he's your patient. This is totally unethical. Don't suck me into this. But my words reflected none of that. I just said something to fill the void.

"Yeah, don't worry, I'm working on it, Dad."

"My son! You are the greatest!"

And with that, I closed the door. I smiled as I got into the van. I'm the greatest? Wow, that makes me feel good. I'll remember that forever.

Now what to do about Arthur...

29 { The Lynching

Three weeks had passed, and Dad and I had settled back into the familiar. Two weeks prior, we had had a wonderful time as a family going to see Sarah Brightman, with seats in the second row. I didn't know she had been married to Andrew Lloyd Webber, and I really enjoyed the medley of familiar songs that came with that. Last weekend, Stacy and Dad had gone on a "date" to see Guys and Dolls. Dad wore a suit, and acted as if Stacy was his royal escort. All was well, at least on the surface of things. The wraparound structure was still working. Dad was enjoying his "job" at the ALFA Center. Tiffanie was coming out each morning to fix breakfast and give him his meds. I was still coming out twice nearly every day, at noon to eat lunch and intercept his mail, and again at 5:30 or 6:00 to do the "45 minute day." And my mom still came over every other afternoon for a walk and to reminisce about bygone days.

I was more accepting of Dad's disease now. Instead of praying for a miracle or a misdiagnosis, I was now praying that I would have as much quality time with him as was possible. The intense feelings of sadness and loss were suppressed for now, although it was easy to conjure up tears by thinking of any one of a number of my childhood memories with him.

I was also able to suppress the short bursts of hatred I was beginning to sometimes feel toward him. These feelings were always short lived and transient, but they were intensely disturbing to me. I was having trouble accepting all of the marital indiscretions Dad had told me six months before, during that dreadful car ride up to Dr. Jahnke's office. Marital indiscretions? Wow, that's a pretty innocuous sounding word. Sounds like a sanitized way of compartmentalizing my feelings and minimizing them. How about, "You wrecked our family you mother-fucking, insensitive, womanizing son of a bitch!!"

These bursts of hatred didn't jive well with my image of Dad as The Champion. It worried me that I wouldn't be able to resolve the quandary this put me in. So I would close the door on these feelings each time they emerged, after allowing myself to feel them for just a few seconds. I told myself I had enough to do just caring for Dad. I didn't have time to deal with this. I'll deal with this later. A lot later. Like when he's dead. It certainly seemed a lot easier caring for Dad as The Champion. Caring for Dad the bastard wouldn't be as easy. I thought maybe it might not even be possible.

But today I had a job to do. It was a Thursday morning, and I had taken today and tomorrow off from work. Tomorrow Dad and I would be heading up north, to see his old friends Paul and Delphine, who had returned to the Traverse City area after wintering along the Gulf Coast. We had set up a lunch date at Old Mission Peninsula north of Traverse City, at a classy restaurant adjacent to an art gallery were Paul had a series of his most recent watercolors on display. It would be great fun to see these two tomorrow, and Dad and I were anxious and excited in anticipation. But today Tiffanie and I had something else planned for Dad. Today was the day of Dad's driver's license exam. Today was the day of his lynching.

I had written two agonizing letters to Dad's family physician and to the Secretary of State's Office right after we had returned from Disney. In it I explained Dad's condition, the inevitable, terminal, insidious course of his disease, and that, in my opinion, he was no longer fit to drive. It nearly killed me to drop those letters in the mailbox. But the thought of Dad killing someone else on the road trumped my selfish desire to further procrastinate on something that just had to be done.

Dad had a 9:00 AM driving test at the Secretary of State's office across town. He thought this was just going to be a routine driver's license renewal, after which Tiff and I would take him out for breakfast. He had no idea it had all been arranged.

It was raining and rather dark outside that morning. Dad insisted that he drive. As far as we could tell, he hadn't driven in many months. We had possession of one set of keys, and the other set was believed lost somewhere inside Dad's condo.

"Ah, Dad, it's raining pretty hard and it's kind of dark outside. Want me or Tiff to drive instead?" This kind of offer had resulted in Dad deferring the driving to us 100% of the time over the past six months. And besides, he always hated driving in bad weather. But not today. Not this time. Damn it!

"Thanks, Dr. Fang, but I can handle it." Dad walked eagerly toward the driver's side of the car.

"But it's raining really hard." Tiff was just short of pleading with him.

"So what? That's why we have ... you know, they go back and forth on the windows. You know, window flippers. Besides, I'm the one who has to take a driving test, not you or Garrett."

And with that, Tiffanie and I dutifully climbed into the car, Tiff in the passenger seat and me in the back. Tiffanie and I exchanged worried looks. This was against our better judgment. But he was still our father, and we had to still respect that.

It was a scene from Disney's "Mr. Toad's Wild Ride" getting to the Secretary of State's office. It started in the driveway, with Dad confused as to what gear to put the car in to back out into the street. Next, he turned on the radio, fan, lights, flashers – all failed efforts to get the windshield wipers started. Next, he was confused about which way to turn the wheels to back out into the street. I was already a basket case before we had gone 20 feet.

Tiff and I should have ended the sham right then and there. But we didn't. We just passively sat there, knowing Dad was risking our lives.

We made it to the end of the street with a herky-jerky stop. Dad then turned right onto the main road, with its 55 MPH speed limit. Forget making the 12 mile trek across town safely. I was already envisioning two crashes occurring before we got to the next intersection. The first would be at the 20 MPH blind curve coming up in about 30 seconds. If we survived that, the crash would occur when Dad misinterpreted the lights at the busy Park Lake-Saginaw Avenue intersection and sent us careening into the busy highway.

Dad brought his speed up quickly. My eyes fixed on the speedometer. Fifty, fifty five, sixty miles per hour. Dad had absolutely no awareness he was having any trouble with his driving. I tried to raise his consciousness.

"Ah, Dad? You might want to slow down coming up here. It's a 20 MPH curve. See the sign?" Dad put his foot lightly on the brake, then rode it. The Chrysler Cirrus squealed as it rounded the curve at 46 MPH. We survived. But there was no time to relax. Dad was going to have another chance to kill us in another 30 seconds. I could see the Park Lake-Saginaw intersection coming up ahead.

"Dad. The intersection we want to turn at is coming up ahead. You'll need to slow way down. I mean way down, Dad. We've gotta turn right." Dad could sense the agitation in my voice.

"Relax, Fang, everything is fine. You always worry too much."

Tiff came to my rescue. "Garrett's right. It's a tricky intersection, Dad. Its real busy, so slow way down, OK?" Her voice was a lot more gentle, more soothing, than mine.

Dad did slow down. I could see the intersection up ahead. Oh, Thank God, the light's still green. We can make this right turn, and then it's a straight shot across town on Saginaw.

The light turned yellow as we approached the intersection. Oh-oh. Dad sped up, then slowed down, I thought to stop, then sped up again as the light became red. He was confused what the colors meant.

I screamed out, "Dad, stop! Stop! Stop!!! He hit the brakes hard and we screeched. Before we could stop we were already part way into the intersection. "Dad, turn right, turn right!!"

Dad made the turn. The car advancing from behind honked us. "Son of a bitch! What's he so upset about?" Dad had no idea he had almost wiped us out in the intersection.

We white knuckled it across town for twenty minutes on Saginaw Street. I saw my life flash before me at each intersection. Tiff had taken over as co-pilot and was doing a much better job at it than I had. She kept her voice calm and talked him through the whole way. I shut up in the back seat, white as a ghost, my heart racing out of control like a runaway train. I watched anxiously as Tiff successfully guided Dad to a safe landing at the Secretary of State Office.

Tiff had to remind Dad how to put the car back in park before shutting off the engine. Dad was as relaxed as he could be. "Well, that was a relatively easy drive, now wasn't it?"

Tiff and Dad sat down inside the Secretary of State Office lobby, while I took a number and waited to be checked in at the front desk. It was already crowded at 9 in the morning. Fortunately, I had sent the letter and had called the office the day before. They were all prepped, and would take Dad in right away for his driving exam. They assured me they would handle the situation sensitively. Why Dad even needed to take an actual driving test and written exam was beyond me. It was just policy. Everyone, except Dad, knew that within the hour Dad would be stripped of his driving license forever.

Finally, my number came up. "Hi, I'm here to check in my father, Walter Turke, for a driving test and exam." The clerk started pulling his identification up from the computer.

"I called yesterday to let your office know that he has Alzheimer's disease and that the family and his physician feel his license should be terminated."

No response. Oh well, she at least heard me. It's already pretty hectic in here. "Whoever I spoke to also said they would get my father in quickly because of his condition." Still no response.

Finally the clerk looked up from the computer. "Walter Turke? Just have a seat over there? We'll call your name shortly."

We checked in to a smaller, more self-contained waiting area. This looked like an area where they pooled people who were scheduled to take the driving exam. Already seated was a young teenaged guy looking very anxious and worried, an elderly woman who appeared much more intact than Dad, and three people who did not appear to speak English. We took a seat next to the anxious looking teenager.

I leaned over to Tiff, and whispered, "Don't worry, Dad will get right in, I called yesterday to prep everyone."

We watched the elderly lady, the nervous teenager, the Middle Eastern couple, and the Korean or Chinese man all go before us. After 45 minutes of waiting, Dad was becoming inpatient.

"Well, we might as well go home and come back another day. It's pretty clear they don't care about us." Dad was now starting to get angry.

Finally, a tall, stone faced, 50-ish man came out of the office and approached us. He neither smiled nor extended his hand, my father's two prerequisites for developing a good rapport with someone. The man's face was alcoholic-red, he was overweight and sweating, and he looked like he was on the verge of a heart attack. He exuded no warmth whatsoever. "Mr. Turke?"

I immediately corrected him as to the appropriate Turke protocol, "It's Doctor Turke, actually."

"Yes, OK, Doctor Turke then. Come with me. The two of you can stay here"

"We're his children. Did you get my letter?" I approached him individually and discretely. "He has Alzheimer's disease. We need to go with him."

The alcoholic-red, stone faced man showed no expression. Damnitall, you could at least pretend to be a little more sensitive.

"Yes, very well, you can come in, but this is my meeting with him, you two will have to keep quiet."

We stepped into the stone faced man's office. He had my letter on the table in front of him, right out in the open, where Dad could see it. "Mr. Turke, I'd like you to take this written exam first." I recognized it as the standard, fifteen or so item, multiple-choice drivers' license renewal test. My father had probably taken at least 10 or 12 of these in his life, the last one being four years ago, before he got sick. I thought, well, Dad will probably pass this, but he'll never make it through the driving test.

Tiff and I both choked up watching Dad try to complete the written test. It was brutal. Dad apparently had forgotten what a multiple-choice test even was, and how to take it. He ignored the checkboxes and started writing what I guess he thought were the right answers in the test margins. I was helpless. Tiff was helpless. Dad's face was getting red.

The man whose face was always red shook his head disapprovingly and started filling out some other form. Just another impaired senior to be discarded. You bastard! Treating my father, treating anyone, this way. Your turn will be next, your alcohol abuse will send you into dementia some day. Fuck you, evil man. Fuck you! Can't you see my dad is drowning right in front of you! The words would never reach my vocal cords. I just sat there, feebly, as Dad "finished" the test.

The stone faced man took Dad's test and with a decisive red pen marked every item on Dad's test wrong. My Dad's lower lip trembled.

"Yes, Mr. Turke, based on the results of your test we won't need a driving test exam today. Can I have your driver's license? "

Dad reluctantly reached into his wallet. He found his license, but couldn't figure how to remove it from the transparent wallet sleeve it was kept in. I helped Dad remove it and gave it to the evaluator. He took out a single-hole punch from his drawer and tagged the corner.

"Mr. Turke, this is the end of your authorization to drive a car in the State of Michigan. I have a letter here from your Doctor and one from your son, stating you have a terminal disease, Alzheimer's dementia. They don't feel you are safe to drive anymore and neither does the State of Michigan. We can get you a free State ID today, it will look like a drivers license but it is only an ID card for you to verify who you are. This hole I punched in the corner of your license here invalidates it. Now if you would just step outside my office and go up to the front desk we'll get you your State ID."

I said nothing. Tiff said nothing. Dad said nothing. He looked me straight in the eyes. His eyes were swelled up with tears and his lip was trembling. I didn't really know what Dad was thinking. Maybe he was just confused. But I interpreted Dad's look personally. I interpreted it as, "How could you betray me, Son?" I didn't mean to, I had planned against it. But in the end it felt like just that. I had indeed betrayed him.

Dad would never drive again. His last vestige of freedom and autonomy had been stripped. He had been humiliated in the process. And now, there was no recourse. No way to make things right. It was too late. The lynching was over. All that remained was to cut him down and take off the noose.

We waited in the "State ID" line for what seemed like an eternity. No one said a word.

When we got to the front of the line we were met by an African American woman in her 40's with a big, friendly smile. She looked surreal and out of place in the office. "So, honey, you'll need a State ID card today?'

Dad looked up and into her warm eyes. He stammered as he spoke. He was not confused at all. "I don't have a license anymore. I'm in good company, though." As he said this, Dad pointed toward the back of the office. There was a portrait of President Reagan on the office wall. "He and I, we're in this together."

The woman grabbed Dad's hand and said, "We're all in God's hands, my child." She snapped Dad's picture and glanced over at Tiff and me. "God bless you two. He is watching over you also."

Tiff drove us back home with Dad in the passenger seat. We had all been traumatized. I stared out the window. The feelings of intense sadness and loss were back.

30 { Overdose

The beautiful spring morning couldn't rescue me from the despair brought on by the loss of Dad's drivers' license. But Dad was a different story. True to his disease, Dad had forgotten all about the traumatic events at the Secretary of State Office by the time he had been returned home. Unfortunately, I was not so lucky. I had been up all night ruminating about how some people could be so cruel toward Dad. He was vulnerable now, and I was starting to realize that I couldn't count on everyone in his path to treat him kindly.

Dad was waiting for me on the edge of the street when I pulled into his driveway with the van. It was a typical late spring morning in Michigan, chilly at 8 AM, but the strong May sun would push the temperature up into the 70's later in the afternoon. Today was the day we would begin the next leg of our farewell tour. We had plans to be in Traverse City by noon, and to have lunch at La Bella Galleria Tavern with Dad's old friends Paul and Delphine. We would then spend the weekend doing what Dad loved, driving along Lake Michigan, and visiting old haunts. I had brought my cameras. The cherry blossoms were in bloom. I was also going to do what I loved.

Dad was dressed in shorts and an Iowa Hawkeye t-shirt that I had laid out the night before, but he didn't have on a sweater or jacket to repel the 35 degree chill. He was shivering and his hands shaking when I arrived. I didn't know that he had been standing outside waiting for me for nearly two hours. Another symptom had crept up on me when I wasn't looking. Dad was loosing his understanding of time.

"There you are, Dr. Fang!" Dad's shivering countenance transformed as he beamed at the sight of my van pulling in.

"You look all set to go, Dad." I got out of the van and put my right arm around his back, giving him a pat in the process. He was ice cold. "You look a little chilly, let's go inside and get you a jacket. You've been waiting out here long?"

"Not too long. I've been out here since… since…" He looked at his watch for a clue, but none came. "Ah…well it was still dark out when I came out."

Still dark out? That was two hours ago! Oh my Lord! He's been out here looking for me for that long? I thought instantly of all the other times in the past couple months where Dad was waiting for me in the driveway, pacing, when I arrived to pick him up. I always assumed he was just a few minutes early, as was Dad's habit before he got sick. I saw his earliness as a sign that he was still organized and conscientious of time. Now I anxiously wondered if each time I picked him up he had been waiting for hours out in the cold.

I opened the door with my key and found Dad's lightweight jacket where I had laid it out the night before. "Here Dad, lets put this on. It will be warm out later, but right now it's still pretty cold. Let's make some coffee to warm us up for a minute. We've got to take our meds, too."

Dad didn't use a coffee brewer. He was an instant coffee man since the 1960's. I opened the kitchen cabinet. The instant Maxwell House Coffee jar was only a quarter full. That's funny, I thought. I just bought coffee a few days ago when we went shopping. It couldn't possibly be almost gone already. "Hey Dad, where's that new jar of coffee we just bought?"

Dad looked at me incredulously as I scooped two teaspoons of instant coffee into his mug. "Why my son, you're using it right now."

What? He's gone through a 12 ounce jar in three days? "Dad, ah, how much coffee have you been drinking lately?"

"Not too much. You know, I just have a cup in the morning."

A mountainside of boulders cascaded down on top of me. Oh my God! Dad's making himself coffee every morning, drinking it, forgetting he already had a cup, and then making more. And again and again, over and over, 5, 10, 15…20 cups a morning.

I poured Dad's coffee down the drain. His hands were shaking. I had thought it was from the cold. Now I thought it was from the caffeine. I felt like I had been negligent. I had let him down again. I had to consciously tell myself that I couldn't control everything. But, in a battle between reason and my self-deprecating conscience, it would be no contest.

Damn it all! I had been so careful with hiding and dispensing his meds so he wouldn't overdose. I had made sure there was never any alcohol in the house. But it never dawned on me he could poison himself with caffeine.

I thought about what other foods or liquids there were in the house that he might misuse. I did a quick mental checklist of all the items we purchased at the grocery store a few days before. Coffee, bread, jam, margarine, fruit, cut veggies, frozen dinners. Seems like we're OK. I never heard of anyone overdosing on strawberries or broccoli before. Lets see... milk, Q tips, toilet paper, mouthwash, dental floss... Mouthwash? Wait a second. That has alcohol in it.

I ran toward the bathroom. "Just a minute, Dad, just going to get some vitamins." Vitamins? Dad could overdose on those, too. Good God, they're just laying out on the bathroom counter.

I entered the bathroom expecting the worst. And the worst was what I found. The giant, economy sized bottle of mouthwash, purchased just three days before, was half gone. Dad was rinsing his mouth that many times? Well, that was the hopeful hypothesis.

"Hey, Dad, could you come here?"

Dad trotted in like a cute puppy searching for his master. "Did you find the, ah, the.. ah, um, the whatchamacallits you were looking for?"

"Yeah, Dad. We're all set on the vitamins. Hey, while you're here, don't forget to brush your teeth."

"Oh yeah, you're right. Geez, I almost forgot." I watched Dad perform his morning ritual. He still brushed his teeth well, something instilled by a whole host of dentists who were concerned about his genetically poor teeth. Dad reached for the floss when he finished, and proceeded to floss his teeth equally well.

Then the mouthwash. A nice big mouthful, swishing it around, yes that's it, swish swish swish, now spit.... Dad blew the last step. After swishing for a good thirty seconds, there was a big gulp and the 30-proof mouthwash was in his stomach. Not only was Dad speeding every morning, he was also getting drunk.

"Well, Son. Ready to shove off?"

"Anchors away, Dad."

As we exited the condo and locked it up for the weekend, I fixed upon one thought. I would have to hurry the farewell tour.

31 { The Demon Intruder

I picked up Dad's small, weekend suitcase I had packed for him and put it atop the second row of seats in the van. I had to squeeze it in amidst the eight large, framed landscape photos I had also packed back there.

Photography was what I loved to do before Dad got sick. I loved it because it was like having all my hobbies and interests rolled into one. It required travel to beautiful and interesting places, composition skills borrowed from my other love, oil and acrylic painting, and matting and framing skills, which required a mixture of artistic color balancing and technical skill. This was the side of my brain inherited from my mother the artist. It was less developed than my psychologist brain, but I always knew a wealth of talent lay deep within my right cerebral hemisphere, waiting to be tapped.

I had discovered my artistic talent in the early 1980's, when I began experimenting with acrylic and oil painting after just a couple lessons from my mother. I was surprised how easily and naturally painting came to me. My first "masterpiece" was an abstract portrait of reggae superstar Bob Marley, which still graces my home. I painted it in a self absorbed, manic-like state in under 24 hours, staying up all night in the process to finish it. It was like I was possessed by some spirit while doing it. Many people have asked me who the artist is and where I bought it, to which I would proudly feign modesty and say, "see my signature down there?" No one expects a psychologist to also be an artist, I guess. And much less a psychologist who paints an image of a dreadlocked Rastafarian.

By the end of the 1980's, I had produced a series of paintings, most of which I had given to friends. I had also done a series of acrylics on subjects and themes I had brought back on film from my trips to West Africa. I had been to West Africa several times before Dad got sick, inspired by Mr. Marley's music and my African Studies minor at Michigan State back in the late 1970's. West African culture had left an indelible mark on my brain, and on my development as a person. Respect for the elderly. The community raising of children. The spiritual interdependence of all things. The group is more important than the individual. And a value I admired most, your ancestors continue to live as long as you remember them. I didn't fully know it yet, but I was about to witness each of these traditional West African values manifest themselves in my dad's care giving.

With my psychologist career in full swing in the 1990's, and with a family to raise, I no longer had the time to paint. But I soon discovered I could revisit the artistic, painting side of my brain by taking photographs. To me, each photograph was a painting. I found I could get almost the same intrinsic reward out of photography as I could with a canvas and brush. Only photography was quicker. Way quicker. And I was able to do it even with all my career and my family responsibilities. I had it all in a nice balance. That is, until Dad got sick.

I had amassed quite a photography portfolio when Dad was first diagnosed with Alzheimer's disease. I had fantasized for years that once I had enough photos in my portfolio, I would form a business and market them at art shows and in galleries. Although friends, family, and my graphic design director brother-in-law all had told me my photographs were very marketable, I always fell short of making that first step to sell them. I was hesitant to apply for an art show, or to bring them for review to a gallery owner. My confidence just wasn't there. While I was busy procrastinating and hesitating, over 200 transparencies of images laid dormant in my basement photography office, along with nearly 100 images I had matted and framed.

Dad's disease had made me realize how precious time was. And so, on this our first leg of the farewell tour, I decided to get a little selfish. We were going to meet his friends, Paul and Delphine, at a restaurant that had a prestigious fine art gallery attached. Paul was a well-established artist whose most recent watercolor series was on exhibit there. Paul knew the owner, Verna, who was a sculptor by specialty.

I had built up some courage the previous weekend and had phoned Paul, under the guise of confirming our lunch date. But what I really wanted was to ask him if he would take a look at my photographs and critique them. I was secretly hoping that if he said yes, maybe he'd have Verna take a look at them as well. After all, we would be right there, in the gallery, anyway. It was a great little plan, albeit slightly manipulative. And when Paul said he would be happy to look at my images, I was ecstatic.

I selected what I thought were my best 8 images to bring up with us. I was hoping that maybe, with some luck, one or two might be good enough to be selected by Verna to show in her La Bella Galleria.

Although visibly tired, Dad was his usual happy, positive self in the van. The caffeine overdose from earlier in the morning was wearing off. He too felt the relief of going up north. Although I had to remind him multiple times of just who we were going to see, he was anxious to see his old friends, even if it was just for a long lunch.

I was excited for Dad. He had been cut off from his friends who lived in Bay City and Traverse City since he made his move down to East Lansing. This was very much a homecoming for him.

As we made our way into the fringe of the northern Michigan woods, Dad drifted off to sleep. I glanced over and looked at his peaceful countenance. You would never know he had a terminal disease by looking at him. He looked healthy. And happy. And at peace.

For the moment, I felt happy, too. I knew I was doing the right thing by taking him up to see his old friends. I tried to make a pact with my conscience not to get too down on things this weekend. Try to have some fun with Dad. Let's leave his disease out of it, at least for the weekend.

Taking a break and escaping from the pain and stress of Dad's diagnosis made sense. I looked out toward the highway in front of me all the way to the horizon. Yes, I think I can leave the stress behind. Even if it's just for the weekend. I popped in one of my favorite Jimmy Cliff CD's, 1973's Struggling Man. The first three songs immediately connected with me this morning. "Struggling Man," "When You're Young," "Better Days Are Coming." "Better Days" hit home and I played it twice, turning it up the second time. Dad didn't mind. He used to do the same thing with his music.

I sang along with Jimmy Cliff. "Better days are coming, by and by. Don't you get down hearted, don't you cry. A change will come, we'll have fun. Better days are coming, by and by." The tropical, uplifting reggae beat brought me up. I felt like I could stay there, at least for today, maybe for the weekend if I was lucky.

Within minutes an unwelcome intruder shattered my little bit of happiness. I thought it was my conscience again. It came upon me right out of the blue. But this time it wasn't back to soothe or reassure me. These thoughts were not generated from love. It was like some demon had suddenly invaded my soul. It felt like it was talking to me. No, it felt like it was interrogating me.

Garrett, how can you let yourself be at peace with this? This man, your father sitting next to you here, admitted to you not too long ago that he was having affairs while married to your mother. And you already know how cruel he could be when he was drinking that scotch. You know it led to your parents splitting up. You saw what it did to your mother. You can still remember her crying, can't you? Can't you? And the falling out with your sister. That didn't happen by chance, now did it? No, your Dad, the one you call The Champion over there, he had something to do with that too, didn't he? Didn't he? And you just continue to drive along your merry way, supporting him, making him feel all comfortable, all loved. He doesn't deserve it, now does he? I think I deserve an answer. No, you already know the answer, don't you?

I tried to fight off the demon intruder. As cruel as the internal apparition was, it had some points. Had some points? What is this, a high school debate? Dad damaged people's lives, my family member's lives, maybe permanently. How the hell am I going to resolve this? It's evil, it's ugly, but it's the truth. It's pretty clear I can't suppress this. I can't procrastinate. I can't choose to deal with it later, like when he's dead. It, my conscience, or whatever the hell it is, won't let me. Why is this a burden I must bear? I didn't ask for this. I didn't do anything wrong. I just wanted to be at peace.

I had worked myself up into a state of agony. And suddenly, I felt all alone on that highway. I felt strangely detached from the person sleeping next to me. I wanted so badly to love him as The Champion. But now, I was beginning to realize, I also wanted to kill him.

My anxiety was escalating. I thought about calling Stacy with my cell phone. But what would that do? I'm a hundred miles away from her and counting. I'm stuck with this. I can't bail. Dad has to be confronted on how much he hurt us. It has to be done. I have to do it for my mother and my sister, for all of us, really. No, I can't do that. He's sick, he has Alzheimer's. He doesn't even remember he told you about his affairs. I just can't do it... Yes, you have to do it! You won't be able to live with yourself otherwise. You have to do it while he's still somewhat intact mentally or it won't mean anything. You'll have to do it soon! No, I can't. I won't! I shouldn't have to do it at all. He's sick, he's down, this would be unnecessary cruelty. Don't do it! He's turning to me for support. Crush him now and he'll have nowhere to go.

I did the only thing I could do. This was too big for one human being. This might be too big for human beings, period. And so I prayed. Hard. With as much concentration as I possibly could. I've got to make a connection. Please help me find another clearing.

The fourth cut on the Jimmy Cliff CD punctuated my distress. "Sooner or later, you're gonna have to stand up strong. Sooner or later, when your back's against that wall. Sooner or later, you'll have to be the one you are, or you just might find, that you're out of time, and it's just too late...."

By the end of the song, the demon intruder had vanished as quickly as it had attacked. My mind cleared and I was again focused upon the horizon. I would like to say that I had a revelation. But no words from above came to answer my prayer. Instead, a soothing feeling enveloped me. I felt it. A chill, a tingle, rippled down my spine and spread out from there. Connected again. I was reminded that I was not alone. I had forgotten this, albeit for just a moment. I had made myself feel isolated when I wasn't even alone.

32 { Eagles Nest Way

10:45 AM. We were ahead of schedule, as usual, as we came into the Northern Michigan resort town of Traverse City. I got the expected nostalgic feeling as we entered town. This happened every single time I visited Traverse City. I had to relive the loneliness I felt when we moved there from Los Angeles. I had to relive my parents arguing and my dad's drinking. I had to relive Dad's affair with Teri. And I had to relive the beginnings of my father's emotional conflict with my sister Cindy. But Traverse City also brought back a whole host of good memories. Summer days at Lake Michigan. Sailing our 14 foot Sunfish sailboat around the bay. Hiking adventures in the woods. Fishing. My first girlfriends. I felt this powerful mix of feelings every trip "up north." It was always bittersweet.

Traverse City was one of Michigan's west coast jewels, one of a number of gorgeous small towns that hugged Lake Michigan's shoreline. Most people outside the Great Lakes have no idea that the western Lake Michigan shoreline looks like pristine ocean front, complete with clear, turquoise-blue water, wide, white-sand beaches, high sand dunes, and periodically, waves high enough to boogie board and body surf. In recent years, full board surfing had taken hold, with 6 and 8 foot boards that had three tail rudders to stabilize the board against erratic lake waves that could sometimes reach 10 feet high. These high waves occurred occasionally in the summer but often in the fall, so it was not uncommon to see wet suited surfers out there on 45 degree days. Crazy.

I loved the Lake Michigan shore because it often reminded me of my childhood visits to the Pacific Ocean outside Los Angeles. Only Lake Michigan had fresh water, was way cleaner, and had no Portuguese Man-O-War jelly fish to sting you. I had been stung across my entire upper torso by a 3 foot diameter colony of Man-O-Wars when I was 10, and was afraid to enter the ocean waters again until I was 12. No such dangers awaited in the waters of Lake Michigan. It was like the ocean without the side effects.

Traverse City was in all of its glory on this sunny day in mid May. The cherry and apple blossoms were in full bloom, and the rolling hills of terraced orchards was like an impressionist painting of pink and white splashes that faded off into the dreamy waters of Lake Michigan in virtually every direction. Dad just stared off into the distance with a pleasant smile upon his face. He too had his share of positive and negative memories of this place.

Our destination, La Bella Galleria and Tavern, was near the end of the peninsula. It was one of the few Traverse City galleries that were open year-round, and it drew a sophisticated, wealthy clientele that came from all of the country. My heart quickened as we made our way along the hilly road that led us down the peninsula. I was actually becoming rather anxious in light of my possible meeting with Verna, the gallery's owner. Oh, how sweet it would be if even one of my images were selected for inclusion in the gallery!

I spent a few minutes mentally reviewing the images I brought. There were scenes from every season in Northern Michigan. A close up of white dune grass against an azure blue backdrop of sky and Lake Michigan. Fall's crimson and orange leaves reflected in the water along the lakeshore. Glistening trees covered with ice and snow from one of Michigan's notorious ice storms that culminated with a foot of snow over the ice. And my favorite: A striking photo of 10-15 foot waves conjured up by a November Lake Michigan gale, the same kind of November gale that downed the gigantic ore carrier Edmund Fitzgerald in Lake Superior, and inspired the famous Gordon Lightfoot song. And then there were the Kauai scenes I had also brought along, taken during our 1994 trip to Kauai. I had some beautiful shots from atop the Napali trail, looking down into the valley where Jurasic Park was filmed. And there was my crowning glory, a shot of 20 to 30 foot waves rolling into Kauai's South shore at Poipu, compliments of a category 3 hurricane that passed just south of the island during our stay. I hoped that Verna would take just one or two of these images, but I couldn't select any particular one as the likely favorite. I loved them all. They each represented a time in my life when I felt free.

My daydream was interrupted by a road sign that Paul had told me to look for. "Old Mission Lighthouse, 2 miles." Soon the gallery would be coming up on the left. I slowed down, and asked Dad to help look. We saw a large white building that looked like a converted farmhouse on the left. And next we saw the sign, La Bella Galleria, welcoming us. I put on my blinker and pulled into the parking lot. My heart was pounding so fast I could hardly stand it. But this wasn't the same kind of heart palpitations I had become accustomed to when worrying about, or reacting to, Dad. These palpitations were all about meeting Verna and my chances of getting some of my images in the Gallery. I wasn't thinking about my Dad or his friends or his disease at all. This was only about me. Although it was kind of selfish, I hadn't had the luxury of feeling or being absorbed in my own needs in a long time. And it felt good.

We had arrived in the gallery's parking lot at 11:25, five minutes before the gallery and restaurant opened, and a good half hour before we were to meet Paul and Delphine for lunch. The parking lot was empty except for us and one other car, a Lincoln Continental, which had Wisconsin plates on it. Dad and I, with our tradition of being compulsively early, got out of the van and strolled toward the front entrance, expecting the door to be open already. A sophisticated-looking, middle aged couple got out of the Lincoln and also proceeded toward the entranceway. There was a nice, newly planted flower garden along the entrance walkway. When the entrance door wasn't open, the four of us started killing time by admiring the fledgling garden.

The woman from Wisconsin spoke first. "Wow, these flowers really look nice for so early in the season."

I answered next. "Yeah, they really look like someone planted them with a lot of care. Beautiful."

I expected Dad to chime in. He loved flower gardens, and each spring and summer spent an inordinate amount of time outside gardening. But Dad didn't respond as expected. He did an Alzheimer's-induced, Dr. Jekyll and Mr. Hyde flip instead.

"Goddamn it! They knew we were coming, and now we are stuck out here waiting. How come they're so goddamned late! They should have opened up the doors a long time ago. Can't they see us standing out here? They're <u>always</u> so late." Dad looked furious, right out of the blue.

I glanced at my watch. It was only 11:32. They were officially only a couple minutes late opening up. Dad was reacting as if he had been waiting for hours. In his world, maybe he had.

"They always open up late?" The wealthy Wisconsin man sounded a little concerned.

Dad answered, not knowing what he was talking about but acting like he did. "Yep. Every time I've been here they're always late. And the service is terrible."

I whispered to Dad, angrily. "Dad, stop it! They're just a couple minutes late, and you've never been here before in your entire life. I can see them in there vacuuming, I'm sure it will be just a couple minutes."

It was almost too late. The Wisconsin couple had been contaminated by Dad's fabricated criticisms. "Dear, maybe we should go somewhere else to eat."

Dad couldn't wait to get the next word in. We had moved way past embarrassment. "Yeah, Son, maybe we should, too. These bastards are so inconsiderate."

That was it. I was reaching the snapping point. Dad was destroying my first glorified moments at the gallery. I pictured him swearing inside the gallery and Verna telling us to get the hell out of her establishment. Dad's Alzheimer's disease was kicking in again. Only this time I didn't care. I didn't have any empathy. I wasn't even thinking of his Alzheimer's disease. I was thinking of two things and two things only. Me, and my images. This was supposed to be my moment.

Instead of being the kind, loyal, dutiful son, caring for his Alzheimer's afflicted father, I snapped. I grabbed his arm angrily. "Dad, could you come with me for a minute?" I smiled an awkward smile toward the Wisconsin couple.

"Sure, Son." Dad didn't have a clue that I was upset, much less unraveling.

I got Dad back into the van, barely able to control my emotions. I started the engine and drove across the street, down a hilly country road, where I pulled over. I grabbed Dad's hand forcefully. There was no forethought, no planning, no censuring, and no impulse control. Just release. And not just release from the frustration of the past 10 minutes. It was a release of the past 30 years.

"Goddamn it, Dad! You screwed up my life, you screwed up our family, and now you're going to screw up my chance to get into a gallery for the first time in my life. Who the hell do you think you are?"

I was out of control. "I've been waiting for this moment for several years.

Well, you're not going to mess this up now, Dad. This is my chance. I'll lock you in the goddamn van if I have to! Do you hear me? Do you hear me??" I gripped his hand tight. "Do you hear me, Dad?!!"

I felt enormous guilt as soon as I stopped spewing venom. The kind, dutiful son had lost it. Dad was confused and quivering next to me. His hand shook as I loosened my grip. Oh sweet God, what have I done? I just hit him harder than all those insensitive people I had been trying to protect him from the past few months. And I gave him more than he deserved for being rude at the gallery. About 30 years more than he deserved. He had gotten what he deserved for being unfaithful to my mother and for wrecking our family and for ripping me out of Los Angeles as a teenager. It had been a long time coming. And it came out completely spontaneously, at what seemed like the wrong time and the wrong place.

I tried to compose myself. "Are you ready to go into the gallery, now, Dad?" Dad was humbled. He seemed like he was on the verge of tears. But I'm not sure he even got my point. Maybe it didn't matter. I felt enormous guilt. A totally self permeating, eat you down to your soul guilt.

"Yes, sure, Son. Lets go in." Ten seconds later, Dad didn't even seem shaken anymore. The moment had passed and he had already recovered. Now I was the one whose hands were shaking. I was worried that my demon would soon find its way back.

We drove back to the gallery parking lot. It was open now, and there were suddenly a lot of cars in the lot. The sophisticated Wisconsin couple was inside. I thought to myself, Thank God we didn't scare them off. But I sure hope they don't see us.

Inside the restaurant, Paul and Delphine were waiting. I recognized them instantly, even though it might have been 15 or more years since I had seen them. Paul was a very robust, edgy-but-funny man with a deep voice and long burly beard, while Delphine was a tall, slender beauty who was still very attractive even as she approached sixty. They were my parent's friends up in Traverse City before their divorce, and they had known us kids during our adolescence. Paul and Delphine were one of the few couples who didn't choose sides during my parent's divorce, and they had maintained an independent friendship with both my mom and dad after their break-up. Paul and Delphine stood up and hugged Dad and me eagerly when we approached.

The lunch went fabulously. There was lots of talk about the old days, pre-divorce of course, and a lot of funny stories from the past. Dad was soon laughing boisterously, and you would have never known he was impaired. His disease was still like that then, one minute he could be obviously impaired and very vulnerable, the next he could fool anyone and appear completely normal and intact.

I wish I could have recalled some of the stories from the lunch. But the fact of the matter was that I was completely preoccupied. I should have been preoccupied with guilt from blowing up at Dad, but that wasn't it. I was completely self absorbed with getting my images into the gallery. I wasn't even thinking about Paul critiquing them. I was way past that. I was thinking of what I was going to say to Verna to try to sell my images to her. This still wasn't about Dad's reunion with his old friends. It had reverted to me again. I guess I should have caught myself and readjusted my priorities, but that afternoon I couldn't do it. It had felt so good just thinking about me for a change, and I wasn't going to let go of that so easily.

An hour and a half later, lunch was over, including the hot fudge sundae that Dad had ordered himself for dessert. Three years ago I would have stopped him from having such a dessert on account of his heart disease, but what did it matter now? That was one positive by-product of his affliction, suddenly things that could kill him in another 5 to 10 years, like hot fudge sundaes, just didn't matter much anymore. As we strolled toward the door, which also had an adjacent entranceway to the art gallery, Paul asked if we wanted to see his latest watercolor series on display. Before I could say "sure," Delphine interrupted.

"Paul, you've been so busy talking about yourself that you forgot that Garrett wanted you to look at some of _his_ art."

"Oh, right, dear. I'm so sorry, Garrett. There I go again, just thinking about myself. Delphine's always reminding me of that."

Still lacking any trace of true humility, I went right into feigned modesty. It was part of my pre-conceived sales pitch. "Well, I don't know if you'd be all that interested, but I've got a few pieces out in the van. Should I get them out?"

Paul seemed a little cautious. I took that as a bad sign. "Ah, well, maybe we could just look at them over at the van. Let me go get Barb from the gallery."

I was immediately dejected. Why can't I bring them into the gallery? And who's Barb? I thought the owner's name was Verna? While we waited for Paul, I asked Delphine, "Who is Barb? Isn't the owner's name Verna?"

Delphine smiled. "Verna owns the gallery, but she's not in today. Barb's the assistant manager." I felt even more deflated. Delphine continued, "Oh, and I think I should tell you, Garrett. Verna makes all the decisions. She's into fine art, and might not consider photography fine art per se. Paul said she's never accepted a photographer into her gallery before."

Now I wasn't just deflated. I was free-falling and expecting a fatal splat onto the pavement. I thought to myself. Verna's not even here. She's never accepted a photographer, and I'm not even an amateur! I've never even sold a single piece! I'm cooked. Oh, I'm so embarrassed. My work isn't going to be nearly good enough for a place like this. They'll know that as soon as they see it. I knew it! This is so embarrassing!

Paul came out of the entranceway accompanied by a tall, middle aged woman who was immaculately dressed in a sophisticated suit. Paul introduced us. I pulled open the van slider door and took out my first framed image, a 3' by 4' framed image of golden Lake Michigan Dune Grass sparkling against a deep blue, polarized sky and lakeshore. I rested the image atop my shoes because it was so heavy.

Barb was the first to speak, "Oh my, this is stunning! Not what I expected at all! It's so simple, but the composition, its...its like a painting! You can feel the wind blowing just looking at it, can't you! Wow! The contrast with the sky is striking."

Whoa, just what my attention-starved ego needed to hear.

"Lets see some more!" Barb asked eagerly.

Delphine was my sales manager, God bless her. "Barb, these are very striking. I think we should get them inside for a better look, to see how they look up against the walls."

"That would be fine. Garrett, how many did you bring?"

I didn't want to appear full of myself, which I was. "Well, I've got eight actually, but we don't have to..."

Barb didn't let me finish. "You can bring them all in. I'll send some people out to help you."

And one by one, the eight images were brought into the gallery. A magnificent gallery with gigantic walls, huge sculpture, fancy blown glass, oils and watercolors. This was the big time.

My Dad was helping to bring them all in, holding doors and directing traffic. He was my old dad again, making friends with everyone and beaming with pride. Soon, a small crowd of gallery goers were standing around my images. Dad was so proud. He did his usual choked up, tearful introduction. "My son, Garrett over here, took these. And I was with him when he took each one!" Well, that part wasn't exactly true. He hadn't been with me while taking any of them. But today, he believed that he was, and I just let it go.

After the admirers dispersed a little, Barb approached me off to the side. "Garrett, I really like these. But I don't know if Paul told you, Verna doesn't consider photography to be fine art, and she's never accepted a photographer's work here. She'll be in tomorrow at 11. Could I leave them here overnight, and you could come by tomorrow, say after lunch some time?"

"Sure."

"If you don't mind, could I ask you how much you might want for each of these? Remember, there's a forty percent commission. That's pretty typical for a gallery up here."

I don't know what possessed me, but what came out of my mouth was pure, unadulterated bullshit. "Well, these are my most popular images, so I was thinking about 350 dollars or so."

"That's about what I was thinking for them. At least, we're on the same page. Well then, until tomorrow?"

"Until tomorrow. We'll come by about 1:30."

Paul and Delphine had scurried Dad off to the opposite side of the gallery to give Barb and me some more privacy. Dad was admiring Paul's most recent watercolors when I got back over there.

"Well, how'd it go?" my business manager Delphine asked. A broad smile came over her face. "Is she going to keep a few for Verna to look at?"

"She wants to keep all of them overnight, I guess that's a good sign." I pretended to be more interested in Paul's paintings, but I was screaming with joy on the inside. Delphine saw through the bullshit. "Oh Garrett, you don't have to appear so interested in Paul's work. He's done hundreds of paintings and he'll do hundreds more. This is great for you! I'm so happy for you!"

Paul came over and gave me a pat on the back. "Maybe you'll be the first photographer to get something up in here."

We exchanged some warm good-byes and promised to see each other again. Although most people would make an obligatory offer to see an old friend again after such a reunion, Paul and Delphine actually meant it, and expected it. Dad hugged each of them and then they hugged me. Paul closed by saying, "Now you go down and say hi to your mom from us. Tell her we expect her up here soon."

"I'll do that, Paul." We turned and headed for the door. Within a minute Dad and I were on the road again, heading back down the peninsula toward our hotel in Traverse City. The van no longer rattled as there was no more art in the rear seats. I loved the quiet ride as it kept reminding me of my victory. As we headed back, I jammed the brakes hard in order to make a sudden turn. A high bluff, laden with pink and white cherry blossoms, was off to our left. There was a road that went to the top of the bluff.

"Hey Dad, want to do some photography with me?"

"Of course, Dr. Fang, that's why we're here. I was there for all your other shots, remember?"

"You sure were, Dad. Lets do some more. I bet if we get to the top of the bluff we'll have a nice vista of the lake with all the blossoms below." We climbed the bluff, but the sun wasn't at a good angle to light the blossoms the way I wanted. So we headed up over the ridge and down the other side. In a valley that lay below was an old apple orchard, also in bloom, with a bright yellow carpet of dandelions at the base. There was an interesting-looking two-track road cutting through the orchard, presumably made by a tractor. It was dead silent, incredibly beautiful, and not a soul or dwelling in sight.

"Dad, lets get a shot down in here. Look how still it is, and how the yellow dandelions contrast with the white blossoms. I'm going to make that two-track road the subject of the composition."

I could hear Dad in the background. "Got your shot, Dr. Fang? This is the most beautiful place on earth. And we're here together."

I rattled off about fifteen shots, each with a slightly different aperture and shutter speed to insure at least one shot would come out perfectly.

"Hey Dad, I got it! Now just let me get over here, at this angle, just a couple more shots and then we can go. OK, Dad?"

Dad didn't answer. I didn't think anything of it at first. "OK, Dad?" Still no answer.

I peered through the viewfinder. I snapped the shot and kept composing. "Dad?"

Just then what seemed like a huge winged shadow moved right over the ground I was standing on. It was so big it blocked out the light and startled me. I heard the flapping of wings as the shadow moved across my path.

I looked up anxiously but didn't see anything at first. "Dad! What was that?" For a second, it was Garrett the little boy running to his daddy again. I turned and saw Dad following something in the sky.

My eyes finally caught it. A bald eagle. A huge, great, magnificent bald eagle. I had always wanted to see one in the wild. I ran back to Dad. We stood there, completely silent, mesmerized, for a good three minutes while it circled us. There was no Alzheimer's disease at that moment. There was no divorce, no affairs, no worries, no anger, no sorrow, no sadness. There was no time. Everything had stopped. Everything stood still. Except for that eagle.

Dad was the first to break the silence. "Aren't you going to take its picture?"

"No, Dad. This moment is just for us. I want to remember it just this way."

We continued to watch the eagle circle, occasionally dipping down to the tree line. "Oh, Dad? I'm sorry I yelled at you outside the gallery. I was pretty uptight about them looking at my images."

"You yelled at me? Why I don't recall." Dad apparently had already forgotten what had happened.

But then he put his arm around my back. His lips trembled and his eyes teared up, like they always did when he was touched or about to say something meaningful. "Oh, Son?"

"Yes, Dad?"

"If there was ever anything I did, I mean ever in my whole life that hurt you, I'm truly sorry."

"I know you are, Dad." And with that we watched the eagle go up and over the ridge. I packed up the camera equipment and put it in the back of the van. We headed back down the bluff toward the main road, all the while looking for another glimpse of the eagle. But we never saw it again. As we got to the bottom of the bluff, I checked the street sign to mark it in my state map. I always did this whenever I took a shot that I thought might be an "award winner." But the name of this particular street never needed to be written down, because I will never forget it.

"Eagles Nest Way."

We made it back to Traverse City, had a nice dinner, and watched an old movie on TV before going to bed. Dad snored all night, as usual, but I was able to keep my murderous thoughts to a minimum this time.

The next day we set out for a nice morning drive along the Lake Michigan shoreline, stopping for some cinnamon buns and fritters at a roadside market. Then we headed back out on the peninsula and toward the gallery. We arrived at the gallery too early again, and so we headed back up Eagles Nest Way looking for that majestic bald eagle. But we didn't see it this time. I have made my way up to Old Mission Peninsula many times since, sometimes with my family, sometimes alone, once or twice again with Dad. But I would never see that eagle again. Maybe that's how God intended it to be, that one moment with my Dad, permanently fixed in my mind, for all eternity. Beautiful.

It was 1:30 and time to meet Verna. She wasn't in the gallery when we walked in, but my photographs were all grouped together and lined up against one of the walls. I thought that they were all placed there for me to pick up and take home.

The demon tried to come back. Nice try, Garrett, but this weekend was all about your Dad, not you. It was rather arrogant and selfish of you to put your needs first. There might be another time for your photos, but it's not now. Now get over your disappointment, put on a good front, and get ready to pack your photographs back into the van. It's time to go back to being the caregiver. You can be a photographer later, like a lot later, when your Dad has passed.

Dad was over by my images, admiring them. I went over to retrieve him. When I got there, I noticed each one had a little sticker on top of the frame, marked $350. I thought that Barb probably put them on there to let Verna know what I was asking.

"Are you Garrett?" came a voice from across the room. "Hi, I'm Verna, I'm the owner of the gallery." Like Barb, she was a pretty, well-kept, middle aged woman who was stylishly dressed.

This time I had not prepared any bullshit response. I was nervous. Real nervous. "Yes, hi, ah, I'm Garrett, and this is my father, Walter." Dad smiled warmly and melted Verna instantly. Damn! Every time. How does he do it?

"My son the psychologist is also a great photographer."

"I can see that, you must be very proud of him."

"He's my, he's my…My son!"

"You are very lucky to have him for a son. Well Garrett, I'm sure Barb already told you I normally don't even consider photography for the gallery, but in your case, well these are so beautiful, I'd like to keep them."

I didn't appreciate the magnitude of what she was saying, for what she said was outside the realm of the possible. "Great, Verna! Which one do you want to keep up here?"

"I would like to keep all of them, if that's OK."

"You want to keep all of them?" I could see the fireworks going off in my mind.

"Yes. You told Barb you wanted 350 for each, I think that's reasonable, but you know we'll take 40% from that, so you will get about 210 dollars each, if they sell. Is that all right with you?"

"That would be fine with me." I was flabbergasted. I couldn't believe it. My images? In this gallery? Up on these walls?

"Oh, and Garrett? Could you put together a little bio on yourself, with your picture on it, so I can tell my clients about you and your work? And I'll need some cards."

I would spend the next forty minutes in the gallery with Verna and my Dad, me cataloguing my art on her inventory sheets, Dad talking to Verna and Barb about his life and our trips together. Not everything in Dad's recollection was exactly true, but it didn't matter. Verna sensed that Dad had some impairment after a while, and I discretely told her had Alzheimer's disease.

I learned a great many things about life that weekend. I learned that my father didn't have to be a saint for me to love him. I could hate some of the things he did, but I didn't have to hate him. I learned that to forgive someone didn't always require a lot of talking or thinking or analyzing. All that was required for redemption was love and forgiveness. It was a feeling, a spiritual feeling, and it didn't require a lot of cognitive processing. Love and forgiveness could occur silently and without effort, and sometimes without preconceived intention. And I learned that if you practice love and forgiveness, good things would come naturally, without forcing them or trying to script them out. These would be lessons I would keep forever, and keep close to my heart.

I would see Verna a number of times in subsequent years bringing my art up to the gallery. Each time she and Barb would ask about my father. And each time I would drive to the top of Eagles Nest Way. I never saw that eagle again.

33 { Saving for a Rainy Day

We made it back downstate in a little over 3 hours, both exhausted from our 24 hour whirlwind excursion up north. The farewell tour was off to a great start. First Disneyworld, then the Sara Brightman concert, and now our first trip up north. I realized the farewell tour didn't have to feel so morbid. I didn't have to be preoccupied with "this will probably be the last time we ever do this together," or "Dad will never be able to do that again in his life." Instead, the farewell tour could actually be fun. Not just fun for Dad. Fun for both of us. How I framed it inside my mind was my choice.

I had already been planning the next leg of our farewell tour during the ride back. Dad had handled twenty fours hours away from home quite well. Everything went fine, except for that little 10 minute Dr. Jekyll and Mr. Hyde episode outside the gallery. And when I thought about it, my 10 minute meltdown afterwards was equally as bad. Who really was Mr. Hyde here? Chalk it up to Alzheimer's disease and stress and move on. The rest of the trip had been fantastic. On the ride back home, I began to jokingly refer to Dad and me as the "dynamic duo." I couldn't wait until our next adventure.

The next leg of the farewell tour was going to be a sailing trip with Dad's old friend and business colleague, Ron Culp. Ron was semi-retired and had a large sailboat moored in West Grand Traverse Bay. He had maintained contact with Dad after Dad left Traverse City, and had always asked Dad if he wanted to go sailing. But they never had gotten around to it. Well, now they would get around to it. I would see to it. My plan was to call Ron as soon as I got Dad settled back in his condo.

We pulled into the driveway and bumped the curb a little. Again, no rattling. Again, the reminder that there were no framed images in the back of the van. I couldn't wait to tell Stacy, the kids, my mother, my neighbors, my work colleagues, hell, I wouldn't mind taking out a newspaper ad and announcing it to the whole world. My first trip to a gallery with my art and I hit a grand slam!

I made us a quick micro-waved dinner, cheerfully performed the "45 minute day," and settled Dad in. Tonight's movie was "Camelot," starring one of my Dad's heroes, Richard Harris. I felt a joy that I hadn't felt in a long time that night. Stacy and I had some wine, we made a great dinner, and we played "Catch Phrase" with the kids. It wasn't a huge or extravagant party. But it was one of the best parties ever for me. Not only did I remember what it was like to re-connect with my family, I remembered what it felt like to reconnect with me.

The next day, Sunday, around 7 PM, I sat down with Dad's bills. I paid his cable bill, his mortgage, his utility bill, and his phone bill. I tossed all the donation request letters. And I kept the letter from Arthur, with its "Semper Fi" return address, for Dad to open tomorrow. All that remained to do was go through the three letters from his bank and to balance his checkbook from his bank statement.

I opened the first of the three bank letters expecting it to be advertising on a new type of loan, or an announcement that the bank was going through yet another merger. It was neither. It was an overdraft notice.

I thought out loud. "That's funny, there must be some mistake, Dad's got over $5,000 in his account, plus overdraft protection."

I opened his checkbook and saw $5,243 in his ledger. Oh my God, this is a huge problem! There must be some sort of mistake here. Maybe the bank is in error, or maybe one of his automatic deposits got screwed up. I felt a surge of panic travel up from my stomach.

I opened up the next bank letter. Oh-oh, another overdraft notice, and this one's for his last mortgage payment! I was now feeling very anxious. That caregiver responsibility dread that I had managed to escape the past two days was back. I opened up the third bank letter. Yep. Another overdraft notice, this one for his homeowners' insurance bill. Oh my God, how many other checks are there out there that are going to bounce?!! I opened up the checkbook ledger. There were six or seven checks still out there that hadn't been cashed or cleared yet.

"Stacy!!"

"Yes, Garrett. What's such a disaster that you have to call me at the top of your lungs?"

I had the bank statement out. But I couldn't find anything wrong. All of his automatic deposits had gone through. And the $700 I took out in cash every other Friday to cover groceries, his prescriptions, and miscellaneous expenses was listed in predictable sequence. I couldn't figure it out.

"Stacy, could you look at Dad's bank statement here? He's somehow bounced three checks. There's got to be a mistake from the bank. He's got plenty of money in his account, like $5,000. I don't understand it, this shows a negative balance of $2,000. See, here are his direct deposits, here's the $700 I take out every two weeks, here's all the checks that are accounted for…"

Stacy the technical whiz was busy scanning. "What's this?"

"That's the $700 I take out every other Friday for groceries and his prescriptions. I usually pay cash for it when I go grocery shopping. You know, his scripts are like $800 a month now."

"No, that's not what I mean. Look, this isn't a seven hundred dollar withdrawal; this is a seven thousand dollar withdrawal. And it wasn't withdrawn on a Friday. This was taken out on a Tuesday."

"Well it's a bank error then."

"Or your dad went to the bank two weeks ago."

"That's impossible. He doesn't drive anymore, and I have his keys. This is just a bank error."

"You have one set of keys."

"Yep, the other set is lost somewhere."

"Or he's hiding them."

"I've searched the whole house. They're lost. He's not capable of hiding them."

"Garrett, I think you better call Tiff and go over to his condo. I bet your Dad's got $7,000 somewhere in the house. I can't go with you; I've got to get the girls ready for school tomorrow."

"Shit! Shit! Shit shit shit!!!" I was just coming off a nice weekend, I was finally starting to feel better, I've got to go to work tomorrow; I don't want to do this! I'm going to call Tiffanie and make her do it! I'm sick of all this shit. I thought I could have a good weekend for a change, but no, the great caregiver has to go out on a Sunday night and ransack his father's house. Damn it all. Damn it all to hell.

"Garrett. I'll call Tiff. You head on over."

Tiff was already at Dad's house when I arrived. Tiffanie didn't really believe Dad could have withdrawn $7000 on his own, either. This had to be a bank error. There were too many steps for dad to sequence correctly to get to the bank and withdraw money. He hadn't driven in months, to our knowledge, except for that ill-fated drive to the Secretary of State last Thursday. And besides, the bank knows he has Alzheimer's and that I'm managing his money. Well at least the managers know. Wouldn't they have called me if he showed up trying to withdraw that much?

Tiff and I did what we usually did when we had to snoop around Dad's house for something. She distracted him and kept him occupied while I searched. Within minutes, Tiff had made him a snack and popped in a movie. While they were talking, I started my scavenger hunt for the money.

I went through his entire office room. Nothing. Every cabinet and drawer in the kitchen. Nothing. It was now 8:50 and getting dark outside. I started to fret that I would be at this all night, and would be a wreck tomorrow at work. Keep pushing, Garrett. No time to worry. OK, next, the bathroom. Nothing. Utility closet. Nothing. I was beginning to dread I would find nothing upstairs and would have to look downstairs in the basement, which was huge, and still a mess from the move and Dad's continual efforts to reconstruct the museum.

On to his bedroom. I know I won't find anything here. I've searched this room lots of times already looking for his keys. No chance of finding anything there. I went through every shelf on his bedroom wall unit, took apart his closet, and scoured his bathroom. Nothing. This has got to be a bank error. Well, just these two nightstands and then I guess I'll have to start going through the basement. Damn it all.

The first nightstand was easy. There was nothing in it. The second nightstand had some books in it. Probably nothing here, either. I lifted the stack of books out to find a cigar box underneath. Dad had scores of these boxes from his years of cigar smoking. I lifted the cigar box out of the dresser. There was an air of anxious apprehension as I opened up the box.

Inside were his missing car keys, his Navy officers' "bars," and a stack of money. I quickly counted it. It was mostly in hundreds. One thousand...two thousand....three thousand...four thousand...four thousand, three hundred and fifty dollars. Although there wasn't seven thousand dollars there, I knew what had happened. There was no bank error. Stacy was right.

I probably shouldn't have done this, but I emerged from Dad's bedroom with a fist full of hundred dollar bills. "Dad, I was cleaning in your bedroom and I found some money."

Tiff looked very relieved. "Dad, where did you get this?"

Dad looked anxious and guilty, just as he used to look when Tiffanie and I would catch him drinking. "Well, you know, I needed a little cash on hand."

"A little cash? Dad, there's over four thousand dollars here!"

"Well, you never know when you'll need it. I was saving it for a rainy day."

"Dad, you bounced at least three important checks, you overdrew your account by over 2,000 dollars!"

"I did? Really? Well, you can be damned sure I'll never do that ever again." And there it was again, Dad's pledge to stop forever. Just like with his drinking.

"Dad, we think there might be another two or three thousand dollars around here someplace. Any idea where? We've got to get this money back to your bank account tomorrow."

"How much more? Two thousand? No, that can't be. I don't have any more. Maybe I spent a little here and there."

"Spent it? Where? You haven't been driving, how could you spend it?"

"Well, I see you found my car keys."

Tiffanie continued to distract Dad, and within minutes he had completely forgotten I had found his secret stash. I pocketed his car keys, put the money in an envelope for deposit tomorrow, and snuck back to the van through the garage. I locked the money in the van's safe, along with the car keys. I was stunned that despite his impairment, he could still manage to outwit us. It was so bizarre, he seemed so affected by the disease, but seemed to still be able to consciously compensate for it.

The next day I called my administrative supervisor and told her what had happened. Mo told me to just take the day off and take care of what I had to do. I went to the bank at 9:30, deposited the 4,350 dollars, and instructed the manager to never authorize any withdrawal to my father without first notifying me. It would be a moot point, because I now possessed his last set of car keys that had been missing for nearly a year. I would make sure he would never have the opportunity to drive again.

After I finished with the bank, I went next door to the post office and took out a PO Box in my and Dad's name. I filled out a change of address form to divert all future mail to the PO Box. When I got home, I called Dr. Jahnke and told her to please draft a formal letter declaring Dad incompetent to manage his personal and financial affairs. I then called his attorney and asked him to please review Dad's last will and testament to make sure there were not any changes or revisions that had to be made before he was formally declared incompetent.

More sand had passed through the hourglass. I couldn't dawdle with the farewell tour.

I cried, hard, for about half an hour, and then I was all right again. Then I called Ron Culp and set up the sailing trip for next month.

Tiff, Stacy, my mother and I have searched Dad's house many times looking for the remaining 2,700 dollars. We have never found it.

34 { Namaste

A month passed. Dad and I were back in a stable, predictable routine again, and his wraparound was going well. He was enjoying himself at the ALFA Center, which was now expanded to 4 days per week. Each day the Spec Tran bus would come to bring him to "work" and then take him back home at the end of his "shift". Dad continued to take notes on his patients at the Center, and still believed he was the clinical director overseeing their care. And each Friday, before Dad and I went shopping, I would lie to him that his paycheck from the ALFA Center had been direct-deposited into his account.

My mother, Rosemarie, continued to come out two times per week to see Dad. They would reminisce about the past, which they both seemed to greatly enjoy. The "reminiscing therapy" took many forms. Sometimes Mom and Dad went for walks through the condominium neighborhood. Sometimes they would go out for a ride. Sometimes they would watch a movie or listen to some nostalgic music. And sometimes they would go through some old home movies or photographs. Dad loved it, but, strangely, so did Mom.

It was healing for me to see my parents getting along again after all these years, even though the circumstances were so difficult. I still choke up thinking about how my mom was able to step outside of her own personal pain and history with my dad and contribute lovingly to his care. Occasionally I would ask her why she wanted to continue her involvement with Dad. "Mom, don't you relive all your pain with him every time you see him?" or "Mom, you don't have to do this anymore if you don't want to, he treated you so badly, it must be so painful to look back in time with him." I would always give her an "out" if she didn't want to care for him anymore. I guess I thought she was doing this more out of obligation to help Tiffanie and me. She wasn't.

I had struggled for many months trying to figure out why my mom was so eager to help Dad. She had every right to abandon him.

Why would Mom hang on and continue to support him? She must have so much denial. Or, she is still so dependent on him. Or even, wow, what a masochistic relationship. My psychologist brain thought in terms of deficits and pathologies, of unresolved issues from childhood. The answers to my questions about Mom could only be found in understanding some sick dynamic still going on between my parents. Or in some festering wound from her childhood. It nagged at me, relentlessly.

My mom had a horrible childhood that she rarely talked about. Perhaps this is why she was drawn to my father in the first place, as they both had similar histories of feeling misplaced, isolated, and perhaps at times, unloved. Like my dad, my mother's family came from Germany, and had fled Europe in the late 1920's by immigrating to the United States. My mom's parents met in New York, and were married in 1929. My mom, the older of two daughters, was born in New York City in 1930. Unlike Dad's family, my mom and her parents went back to Germany in the mid 1930's, for what was supposed to be a visit to see relatives, and perhaps to try to arrange for other extended family members to come to America. They got trapped instead. Mom's parents had not yet applied for American citizenship, and the Hitler regime wouldn't let them return to America after their visit. Only my mother, then age four, having been born in the Bronx and being a U.S. citizen by birth, could be authorized to return to the U.S.

Unable to leave, my mom and her parents stayed in Germany through the rise of the Third Reich. Mom's sister, Eleanor, was born in Germany in 1936. She was named proudly and perhaps defiantly for Eleanor Roosevelt.

Mom told me once what happened to her and her family during the rise of the "Deutsches Reich" and the onset of World War II. I am sure the events were so painful, so traumatic that she could only muster enough chutzpah to talk about this once with me. She could recall the German military occupation. The brainwashing of the German people and the German children. The Hitler Youth camps the children were forced to attend. How they were taught to hate anyone who wasn't Aryan. How people feared for their lives if they didn't submit to the doctrine. How terrifying it was to maintain an opposing stand to the Nazis when Hitler's paranoid tentacles were everywhere inside German culture and society.

Mom had a number of Jewish childhood friends and playmates. One day the German soldiers arrived and carted them all away. They were told they were going on a vacation. My mother never saw them again.

In 1944, my mother's father was drafted into the German Army. He was deployed and ultimately captured by the Russians. He was held in a frigid Russian prison camp for one year near the Chinese border, where he nearly died. He was released after the war, and had to make his way across Europe without resources to return home. He arrived back in Germany emaciated and mentally ill. He would recover physically, but never emotionally.

My mom recalled the bombing of Dresden when the Allies arrived to liberate Europe from Nazi rule. Her recollections were not one of freedom and liberation. Her memories were of a city on fire, screaming, and the smell of burning human flesh.

It is no wonder she could only talk of this once.

In 1946, my mother's father took her to the American Consulate in Berlin. She was the only family member with American citizenship. She would be the only one who could return to the United States. My mom, Rosemarie Ingaborg Katarina Lengsfeld, a pretty girl of 15, would have to immigrate to America on her own.

One day, I will write my mother's story. For I cannot do it justice here.

For years, my mom had a piece of glossy ceramic hung at the entranceway to her home. It is still there to this day. On this simple piece of ceramic was etched, in beautiful calligraphy, a strange word. "Namaste." I didn't know what it meant, and for a long time I never bothered to ask. But on this piece of ceramic was the answer to my question about why Mom chose to continue caring for my dad.

Some time after Dad got sick, I asked Mom, finally, what Namaste meant. She said that Namaste is an ancient, Sanskrit-derived word that is a cornerstone of the Hindu faith. She said it meant, essentially, "always look for the good in others."

The answer to my nagging question about why my mom continued to care for my dad had been before me all along. I just didn't recognize it. And now I understand. It wasn't about co-dependency or masochism or unresolved childhood issues. It was much bigger than any of that, and much simpler. It was about love and forgiveness. It was about Namaste.

Mom didn't feel pain in caring for my dad because she wasn't looking for it. Despite all of the trauma in her life, she had taught herself to only look for the good.

Namaste.

35 { Come About

Dad was smiling as he steadied the sailboat's rudder. The wind was blowing across our faces as the 30 foot sailboat began to pick up speed. Dad had his Navy baseball cap on, and he squinted a bit as the bright July sun splashed across his face.

It was a glorious day on Traverse City's Grand Traverse Bay, that beautiful, finger shaped Lake Michigan bay that jutted into Michigan's northwest coast. We had come up for the weekend to see my Dad's old private practice colleague, Ron Culp. It was another leg on the farewell tour. Ron and Dad had been great friends a couple decades before, and had managed to stay in touch and to stay friends through my parents' divorce, Dad's move to Arizona, and his return to Michigan. Like my father, Ron was approaching 70 and had recently retired. Like my father, he too had been an officer in the military. Ron was a major in the Army, an equivalent rank to my father's position as lieutenant commander in the Navy. The two would always joke as if they were fierce rivals, Army vs. Navy, but they were always the best of friends.

Ron was indebted to my father because they had built a highly successful clinical practice together. Back in the 1970's, it was unheard of for a social worker to be in private practice, much less a private practice with a MD psychiatrist. Back then, social workers had none of the prestige or third party payment privileges that the then more esteemed psychiatrists had, and they were often considered the bottom rung on the mental health ladder. Many psychiatrists had enough trouble accepting parity with the Ph.D. psychologists, much less the "lowly" social workers. But my father saw Ron's superb therapy skills and his undying respect for patient care, and invited him into his practice. This was a radical concept back in the mid 1970's, and caused quite a stir in the community. But my father, always the champion of the underdog, didn't care what the community thought, or what the proper protocol was for psychiatrist-social worker relations.

Within a decade of his association with Dad, Ron had built a highly successful career with my dad. The 30 foot sailboat we were riding in was one of Ron's fruits for a lifetime of hard work in this practice. He wasted no time in telling me that he was forever indebted to my father for helping make it all happen.

Ron was gently directing Dad to "come about," meaning change the course of our zigzag tack, as we crossed the west arm of the bay. He pulled the main sail in and instructed me to duck as the boon swung around to the other side of the boat. As Ron let out the sail again, he struck up a conversation with me about my parents' divorce, and my sister Cindy's estrangement from the family. Ron knew of all the skeletons in our family's closet, thanks to my mom. They too had stayed in touch through the years.

"So, Garrett, how is your mom doing these days? I just saw her a couple months ago when she was up here visiting some of your parents' old friends. She told me about the situation with your sister. You know, I can remember when all of you were kids, you, Cindy, and little Tiffie. Tragic. You are all such nice kids. I wish there was something I could do to help."

I was stunned at Ron's directness, not to mention that the line of conversation had caught me completely off guard. I thought to myself, damn it Ron, today is supposed to be about Dad, the two of you getting back together, finally going sailing together after all these years of talk, and you're opening up yet another wound. I'm having enough trouble saying goodbye to Dad, taking him around to all of his old friends for what might be the last time, and now you're throwing this shit at me. It was Cindy's choice to divorce from the family, not mine.

Ron persisted, as he couldn't hear any of my thoughts. "Ah Garrett, it's probably none of my business, but how long are you going to let this go on with your sister?"

My thoughts were now screaming inside my head. Good God, Ron, now you're putting me in charge of all this? This was Cindy's and Dad's doing, not mine. I don't know, maybe she was abused or mistreated or neglected but not by me. This is between her and Dad. And now you're putting me in charge of it? For God's sake, why does everyone just assume I'm going to be the responsible one? I'm tired of all this shit! Don't I <u>ever</u> get a break from this? Who props me up?

As usual, what actually came out of my mouth didn't even come remotely close to what I was really thinking or feeling. "Thanks for being so concerned about us, Ron. Frankly, I don't really know what to do about Cindy. It's been a long time, and she's made it pretty clear she doesn't want any contact with..."

I already knew that what I was saying was a politically correct, sugar coated, chicken shit, pansy-assed lie. I knew exactly what had to be done. Dad's time was running out. Dad and Cindy needed to reconcile their differences. It had been almost ten years now. Pretty soon, Dad wouldn't remember who Cindy was. Pretty soon, it would be too late. Forever too late.

Ron cut me off. He didn't have time to beat around the bush. He already had rapport and my respect. I was on a boat in the middle of a huge bay. I couldn't go anywhere to get away. I couldn't bail or change the subject. No wonder Dad liked him so as a therapist. Ron was aiming for his target, and zeroing in. And the target was me.

"Garrett. This may sound a bit arrogant of me, but this kind of falling out happens all the time in families. It's usually about feelings, not about something physical that may or may not have happened. I know your Dad, and I know your family. This thing with Cindy is killing your Dad, whether it shows on his face or not. Someone's going to have to try to bring her back into the family." And with that, Ron Culp, the wise old therapist sage, released his arrow straight for my heart. He wasn't aiming for my mom, or my sister Tiffanie, or some third party to intervene with Cindy. The arrow was meant for me, and it landed right on its mark. Bull's eye.

"Garrett, your Dad has Alzheimer's disease. I know about this one. My father had it. Now that I'm 70, I worry if I'm going to get it. You have some time left with your dad. He still looks pretty good; he still knows who people are. I see what you are doing, by reconnecting him with all the people he loves. You are doing this without any regard for your own stress. I know this, I can see it. It's a beautiful thing you are doing. Your mom has told me about everything you have done, and are doing. But..." Ron slowed the tempo down, as he searched for the right words. "But... if you are going to reconnect him with all the people he loves, you better include Cindy."

I couldn't speak. There was a huge lump filling my windpipe.

Then Ron offered his prophetic words. I didn't know it at the time, but they would turn out to be true. "Garrett, you will someday be in contact with

Cindy. When it happens, don't blow it." And with that, Ron was done. He smiled and put his arm around my shoulder for a minute. Although I hadn't seen him in years, it felt like he was my second father.

Ron looked back at Dad. "Come about!" Dad moved the rudder all the way to the right, the main sail came in, we ducked as the boon passed over our heads, and Ron let the sail out again on the port side. The sailboat turned, the wind caught the sail, and we felt like we were flying across the top of the water.

We spent six hours that afternoon out on the boat. Ron let Dad commandeer the ship the entire time we were out. I was his deck hand. Ron was on the ship's radio all afternoon, communicating with other retired sailors who were traversing Grand Traverse Bay.

Ron beamed with pride on the radio. "Hey everyone, guess who I have commanding my ship today. It's Walter Turke, my old partner. It's a beautiful day and we're having a great time out here."

The radio crackled all afternoon. "Ron, you say hi to Doc Turke for me! Let him know we all miss him and hope to see more of him out here!"

At 3 PM a large sailboat passed us, parallel to the starboard side. Two people, too far away for me to recognize or distinguish, waved from the boat's deck. "Hi, Walter!!!"

Dad's bottom lip quivered and he smiled broadly. "They're...they're... they're my friends. All here." Tears filled my dad's eyes. He turned toward the passing boat and tipped his Navy cap.

We sailed until we got tired. We went to a nice restaurant next to the marina, and then went to Ron's house for a few beers. We looked at some old photographs Ron had from the 1970's. I took a picture of Ron and my dad.

As we drove back to our hotel, I felt proud of myself. The great sailing adventure had been accomplished. I had vowed to Ron that we would return to do it again. But we never would. There wasn't enough sand left in the hourglass.

As I drove along Grand Traverse Parkway, Ron's words from earlier in the day interrupted my thoughts.

"You will someday be in contact with Cindy. When it happens, don't blow it."

36 { The Photograph

Already a week had passed after Dad and I returned from the sailing adventure with Ron. I had the photograph I took of Ron and Dad developed, and it had come out beautifully. Both had their arms around each other and were smiling like best friends do. I liked the 3x5 so much that I immediately had it blown up to an 8x10.

I took the enlarged photograph over to Dad's to show him. He was so touched he choked up, fighting back a tear or two, like always. I offered to put it in a nice frame for him. But Dad, enthralled with the image, didn't have time for that. He found a few map pins and immediately placed the photograph in a position of prominence on his living room wall. It was now part of the museum.

Today was cleaning day at Dad's condo. I was already a little bit behind, which was unusual for me. Tiffanie was due over in a couple hours to take Dad to the movies, and I wanted to be done by then. I set Dad up in his office to write some letters to old friends who had written him, and I started doing the housework that had to be done. In the past, Dad had kept an immaculately clean house. Everything was tidy, and everything had its place. His home looked as if he never really lived in it, because he cleaned it almost every day.

Dad's Alzheimer's disease had done a number on Dad's obsessive compulsive cleaning habits. The floors were now usually sticky with food residue that Dad dropped while eating, the counters smeared with jam and covered with toast crumbs. His bathroom toilets got moldy quickly, as he frequently forgot to flush. And his carpets were pretty soiled in spots, the victim of spilled drinks he brought into the living room, or the sticky food residue that he had tracked in from the kitchen dining area.

Dad's house still didn't really look that bad, but these conditions would have been intolerable to Dad when he was well. I did my best every couple of weeks to restore the house to the pristine conditions my Dad used to like, but it was a losing battle.

Dad offered to help me clean. I knew that would only slow me down, so I made up some excuse to do it myself. And so, quite dutifully and divorced from any real feelings, I did Dad's laundry, vacuumed the entire first floor, washed his foyer and kitchen floors, and spot cleaned his carpet in the areas he trafficked. I emptied out his dishwasher and scrubbed down his kitchen counter tops. Then I tackled the bathrooms. After about two hours, I was finished, at about the same time Dad's letter writing was wrapping up. Soon Tiffanie would be here to take Dad out for a while. I started to pack up my things, collecting them by the front door.

Dad emerged from his home office, where he had been written at least four letters to his friends during the past couple hours. Although his speech increasingly bore the mark of the Alzheimer's disease, his writing had not declined in the least. Always a good writer, his letters were still fluid, cohesive, and very much alive. Reading them, one would never know he was impaired.

"Oh, Son, before you go…"

"Yeah, Dad?"

"Before you go, so, ah, when's our next trip?"

"Next trip?" I hadn't thought that far out, in fact I thought we might be done for the summer.

"Yeah, our next trip!" Dad approached me like a lonely puppy, his eyes suddenly gleaming at the thought of our next adventure.

"Um, yeah." I fumbled, completely caught off guard. "What did you have in mind? It's your turn to choose."

"You know, we're supposed to see, oh, what's his name now, geez, I was just writing, ah, you know, he lives way up…"

Dad's Alzheimer's was back, front and center.

"Yeah, he lives, well you know already, its way up."

"Traverse City?"

"No, no, no. Not that far up! You know it, Garrett." Dad was picturing it on a map in his mind, but he couldn't retrieve the words.

"I'm not sure, Dad. Is it a place, or someone we know?"

"Oh for God's sake Garrett, it's both. A person and a place. And you know it! It's, you already know, you go way up."

"Bay City?"

"Yeah! Well no, that's close, but not quite."

Now we were playing twenty questions.

"OK Dad, it's close to Bay City, and one of our friends." Despite Dad's disease, I was starting to enjoy the game. "Is it Midland?"

"No, no , that's not it. It's ah, close…"

"Is it Saginaw?"

"That's it!!!" Dad reacted as if he just won the Lotto. "I knew you'd get it, Dr. Fang!"

"So it's our friend, Dr. Jahnke."

"No! Well yes, she's our friend too, but this is our other friend in Saginaw."

"It's our other friend in Saginaw? Who's that? All right Dad, I give up."

Dad was starting to get really frustrated. And while the culprit was his word retrieval difficulties stemming from his Alzheimer's disease, I was about to get the blame.

"You can't give up, for God's sake, Garrett!" Then a light bulb went on inside Dad's head. He had an alternate strategy. "Ah ha!" Dad beamed and marched confidently back into his office. He emerged a second or two later holding an addressed, sealed envelope. Dad handed it to me, and I glanced at the address he had written.

"Arthur!" I exclaimed.

"That's it, now you've got it! It's about time! Geez, Son, I was starting to worry about you! You can't remember anything today. Yes, of course it's our friend, Arthur. Semper Fi! We need to go see him."

I tried to reason with Dad, but it was a losing battle against his Alzheimer's disease. "Dad, Arthur is your old patient. I don't even know who he is. I've never met him It's not appropriate for me to see him."

"Old patient? You never met him? What on earth are you talking about? Arthur has been a friend of ours for years. Come on now, quit joking with me.

You know him well!"

"He was your patient, Dad."

"He was never a patient. For God's sake, Dr. Fang! What's wrong with you today? He was, he is, our friend. He's been writing us, as you know, almost every week. We should go see him!"

Dad's reality had broken down. Up to this point, I thought he had just memory and word retrieval problems. This was a contact with reality problem. This was a delusion. I had read where Alzheimer's patients developed delusions as their disease progressed. It's an adaptive mechanism where they fill in voids in their memories so that events and relationships still make sense to them. But this couldn't be happening to Dad. Not this soon. I thought I had a long ways to go before we would see a breakdown in his reality contact.

I decided to test his reality a little bit further. I was scared to do this, not knowing what I would find. "Hey, Dad? Do you remember when you were married to Rosemarie?"

Dad's eyes grew huge. It was utter disbelief, as if I was playing a twisted joke on him. "Married to Rosemarie? Me? Oh, let's not start that again! I was never married to her."

"Yes you were, Dad. You were married in 1954 and got divorced in 1981."

"That's not very funny, Dr. Fang. I don't know if I even like Rosemarie. Yes, yes, she comes over once in awhile and it's sort of fun, but...married to her? That's the most ridiculous thing I've ever heard. She's so much older than me. Now maybe if you said she was my aunt or my grandmother..."

I was startled. Dad wasn't joking with me. In fact, he was starting to get upset with me. He thinks Rosemarie is his grandmother? Feeling uncomfortable and more than a little creeped out, I decided to change the subject. "So, Dad. Do you remember when you used to smoke cigars?"

"Why I never smoked cigars. I've never smoked in my entire life! What has gotten into you today, Garrett?"

I next glanced at a picture of Dad and Hayden Fry that was part of his museum presentation. "And Dad, do you remember your friend Hayden?" I was stretching this already, as Hayden Fry was at best a peripheral acquaintance to Dad, the two of them having met a few times on University of Iowa alumni cruises. Hayden politely wrote back to Dad a few times, probably out of a sense of obligation. Dad had framed Coach Fry's brief, obligatory notes on his "wall of fame" in the living room.

"Hayden. Hayden Fry." Dad carefully took the photograph off the wall, admiring it. "My friend? Well, Garrett, you're wrong there."

Thank God, I thought to myself. At least he knows he wasn't ever really friends with Coach Fry.

Dad continued. "Hayden Fry wasn't exactly my friend..."

"I know, Dad. You met him ..."

Dad interrupted my interruption. "He was my coach!"

"Your coach?"

"Yes, yes, yes. You know this already. He was my coach when I played for Iowa."

"You played for Iowa?"

"Garrett, please. You know all this. Of course I played for Iowa. Why do you think I have all that Hawkeye football gear all around the house?"

"I thought those were just mementos you bought from the Hawkeye Student Store?"

"Mementos?" Dad chuckled sarcastically. Now he was really getting annoyed with me. "Son, don't insult me. All of these things are from my football years at Iowa."

I quit. Nothing left to do but play along. "So, Dad. What was your biggest game?"

"Why the Rose Bowl, of course."

"The Rose Bowl?" I fought back a genuine laugh. "You played in the Rose Bowl?"

"Yep. Against USC." It was now hopeless to try to talk sense to him.

"Wow! That was a really big game. Weren't you nervous in front of all those people?"

Dad was eating this up. "A little... Who wouldn't be in a big game like that? But it never slowed me up."

"So, ah Dad, what position did you play?"

"Halfback. What is wrong with you? Don't you remember anything today? I got two touchdowns in that game. You've seen the newspaper articles I have. We won, 14 to 10. Garrett, why do you keep asking about all these things you already know about?"

Dad put the Hayden Fry photograph back upon the wall. He was no longer fantasizing about being a celebrity star. He was living it.

One last test. "So Dad, Coach Fry is retired now, he's about 70 I think. I thought Hayden was about the same age as you." I thought that maybe if Dad did the math, he'd see that his thinking didn't make any sense.

"Same age as me? You must be joking. He was my coach, Fang. He's much older than me. He must be Rosemarie's age."

Now the clincher. "So, ah, Dad. How old are you again? I mean, how old are you right now?"

Dad paused, as if he was doing the math in his head. "Well, lets see, I would be...I would be about... 36. Yep I'm 36 right now." Dad was dead serious.

It was time to go. I thought about waiting for Tiff and telling her about Dad's latest symptoms. But I didn't call her. I told myself I didn't want to ruin her trip to the movies with Dad.

Although all my things were packed up by the front door, for some reason I went back into the living room. I went back to that picture of Ron and my father, which Dad had placed in a position of honor the middle of his living room wall. It was my turn to look at the picture, mesmerized, frozen in time. I said a prayer for my father while standing there. "Dear God, please keep him close to you now." I knew Dad was slipping further away from me. He was worsening right before my very eyes.

From that day on, I would stand before that photograph for a moment or two virtually every time I entered Dad's home. It came to have great significance as a memory for me. And, as was the case for most memories that were formed during the course of Dad's disease, it would be bitter sweet. That image would forever remind me of the great farewell tour of the spring and summer of 2000. But that image would also come to signal the end of the early stages of Dad's disease process, when he was still "normal," still intact, still lucid, most of the time.

I didn't know it yet, but that picture of Ron and Dad would be the last photograph ever taken of my dad where he still looked normal. Every single picture of Dad that would follow would capture a certain vacancy in his eyes, where he looked disconnected and distant. I would come to treasure that last "intact" photograph with Ron, because that is how I would like to remember my dad.

37 { Jack and Lois

I was tired. I didn't know if I had it in me. But Dad had insisted that we have one more trip before the summer wound down. He wanted to see Arthur, his former patient who had been writing Dad regularly and faithfully. I knew Arthur would not let go, as evidenced by the mountain of mail Dad received from him. Dad would not let go either.

Dad kept each and every letter Arthur had written in a file cabinet in his office. Arthur wrote him every week, and occasionally, several times in a week. Dad would show me some of the letters. The ones I saw were never very long, but they were always touching. They would always end the same way. "Thank you for all you've done to help me. Stay in touch. Semper Fi. Arthur."

I wasn't ready to just drive up and see Arthur. I still thought that would be extremely inappropriate considering the doctor-patient ethics involved. I couldn't do it. Maybe, however, I could write him. But the only appropriate reason to write him would be to tell him the truth, that Dad had a terminal disease that was robbing him of his identity and memory. That Dad soon wouldn't be able to write him intelligible letters, and maintain an appropriate role with him. That soon, maybe Dad wouldn't even remember him. This would be devastating to Arthur. From what little I knew of Arthur's mental condition, I also thought the truth about Dad might decompensate him, in a psychiatric sense, like hurdle him into some major psychotic or depressive episode.

I didn't know what, if any supports Arthur had. I didn't know if he lived alone or had a wife or had family in the area. The only way I might find out would be to read all of the letters. And, as much as I wanted to, I couldn't do it, for the same reason I couldn't read Dad's letters to Cindy. I had to respect the boundaries. I had to respect their privacy. I had to respect the confidentiality and the ethics involved.

And so, on a sunny, mild Friday morning in late August, Dad was expecting the final leg of the farewell tour, a trip up to Saginaw to see his best friend Arthur. As I helped Dad into the van, I knew I would have to spin yet another set of lies. I had an alternate weekend planned.

As we pulled out of the driveway and headed up Park Lake Road toward the freeway, I took a deep breath, squelched my guilt, and lied again to my father.

"Ah, Dad?"

"Yes my son."

"I have good news and I have bad news. First the bad news. I talked to our friend Arthur and he said this weekend isn't a good time to visit. He wants to see us, but it's just that this week isn't a good time for him."

"Oh, is his wife sick again?" Dad sounded genuinely concerned.

I just played along, not knowing the significance of what Dad knew. At least I now knew Arthur had a wife, and that was comforting to me.

"Yeah, I guess that was it. His wife isn't feeling well."

"Well, I certainly understand, and will tell him so in my next letter. Strong man, that Arthur. So where are we going, then?"

"Ah, that's the good news. Back up to Traverse City. We're going to see our old neighbors, Jack and Lois, on Lin-dale Drive. Remember them? We're going to bring them lunch. I brought them your favorite, Lebanese food from Woody's Oasis, it's in a cooler in the back. Then, in the evening, we're gonna have a night on the town, just me and you. And then, the next morning, I've called all your old friends and they're all going to meet us at the Omelet Shoppe for breakfast. Ron and Karen, and your old friend John, and his wife Elnora, oh and I let Paul and Delphine know too."

Dad lit up like an old fashion pin-ball machine. I was starting to relax a little, as for once the agenda I had just laid out to Dad was actually all true.

"All that this weekend? For me? Dr. Fang, you are treating me like a king! I don't deserve it! Son, you are the greatest." Dad grabbed my arm, and his bottom lip quivered a bit.

I blushed. I had really connected with Dad again. I had had more real connectedness, more of these touching moments, in the year following his diagnosis than I had had in a lifetime of knowing him previously.

I put my left blinker on and merged onto the freeway. We were now heading "up north," toward symbolic freedom, and away from all my problems and worries. I punched in my favorite "going up north" CD, Bob Seger's Greatest hits, with my favorite song, "Roll Me Away." Dad fell asleep and I was alone for a while with the music and my thoughts.

Dad slept all the way up. I wondered if he had been up all night. I didn't realize it then, but I was witnessing another disease symptom emerge in Dad: the tendency to drift off into sleep whenever he was not being actively stimulated or aroused. I don't know exactly what the biological mechanism is, but with Alzheimer's patients, it is as if the brain shuts off and goes into a hibernation mode when it is not being actively stimulated.

"Hey Dad, wake up, we're almost there. We had come about half way down the Grand Traverse Peninsula, and I was counting off the streets as we approached our old neighborhood. "McKinley Road, Gray Road, next it will be our old street..."

When we got to Lin-dale Drive, I barely recognized it. What used to be a nice, quiet dirt road with only a few medium sized homes on it was now all built up and developed. The cherry orchard that enveloped the neighborhood was long gone, replaced now with concrete, more subdivision streets, and huge mansions that looked very out of place on the bluffs overlooking Grand Traverse Bay. I felt uneasy. My expected nostalgia was shattered. I had seen this kind of "growth" before, in Los Angeles. Damn it all. Can't anyone leave paradise alone?

Our destination, the home of Jack and Lois Hayes, was just around the bend at the top of the hill. They were Mom and Dad's old friends from nearly three decades before. Jack was a high-powered attorney from the Detroit area who had moved to the Traverse City area to escape the "rat race." Jack had always been a loyal family friend despite my parents' divorce and moves. He had stayed peripherally in touch with my mother all these years, often inquiring about Dad, and also, about me. Jack had always taken an interest in me and had come to my wedding in 1985. I had not seen him since.

Jack's wife, Lois, had suffered a stroke recently and was significantly cognitively and physically debilitated. Jack had told me when I called that she was very depressed in the wake of her stroke and wouldn't eat or participate in her rehab regimen. Jack was worried she was giving up her will to live. My phone call to him ended up being more like a therapy session.

But I didn't mind. Jack had been kind to us all these years and it was now my turn to reciprocate.

We pulled excitedly into Jack and Lois' driveway. The house hadn't changed much from the outside, and I was immediately catapulted back to age 14. Standing at the front door, I remembered my most vivid childhood experience with Jack. Well, I didn't exactly experience it, but I had heard about it enough times so that it seemed like a memory.

There was a certain party so many years ago that us kids weren't supposed to know about. The neighborhood adults, then in their late 30's/early 40's, got drunk one night and decided to go skinny-dipping in the bay, in the dark. Everyone had a great time, except Jack, who slipped and slid down an embankment trying to get down to the water. In the nude. On his rear end. Right through a huge patch of poison ivy!

I don't know for sure who betrayed the secret of what happened that night, but I think it was Dad who blabbed the story to me. Poor Jack was immobilized for weeks. I was sure Dad was going to resurrect the story at lunch, Alzheimer's disease or not.

The front door opened and it was Jack. He had aged well, and looked good physically. Same old round, pleasant face. Same old warm smile and handshake. Unmistakably Jack. I felt right at home in his presence.

We entered the home, lugging our lunch in the trusty blue cooler that was now the staple of the farewell tour. We went up a small set of stairs that connected floors of their beautiful, split level home. We came into a cozy living room that had a fabulous view of Marion Island. There, lying upon the couch was Lois, who was looking frail and sort of withdrawn. Dad wasted no time going into therapist mode, in which exuded incredible warmth and sincerity. If it was an act, you'd never know it.

"Why Lois, it is so good to see you after all these years. I know you've had some rough times of late, but we're here to build you back up. You're far too good a person to keep down for very long. You've got that beautiful smile inside you, ready to emerge again. Here. We've brought you some Middle Eastern food from my favorite place, Woody's, it's a Lebanese place in East Lansing, where I now live with Garrett."

Jack interrupted. "It's no use, Walter. We can't get her to eat anything. She's eaten almost nothing the past three days. Her doctor is very worried about her, as am I." Jack sounded dejected, if not outright defeated. He had been trying, unsuccessfully, to get her to eat for days.

Lois spoke up, responding to Dad, and sounding considerably more healthy and upbeat than her husband. "Why Jack, how nice it is for Walter and Garrett to come visit us all this way. And they brought Lebanese! We haven't had Lebanese food since we lived in Detroit. I love kibbee."

"Right here, Lois." Dad pulled out a container of kibbee balls. We apparently had brought just the right thing.

We had a wonderful lunch. Hummus and tabouli and spinach pie and grape leaves and falafel. It was a veritable feast. Everyone was talkative. Lois came out of her shell. Jack talked a lot about how much fun he had at my wedding 15 years ago. And he paid me the highest of compliments. "Hey Garrett, I saw your work down at Verna's Gallery. Exquisite and stunning. I didn't know you were a pro-photographer as well as a great psychologist."

I responded by blushing and smiling. I always wanted to be known as something other than a psychologist.

Dad talked about the old times they had together, including, of course, the time Jack slid down the ravine naked, through the poison ivy. Lois laughed uncontrollably replaying that story. I laughed uncontrollably as well, pretending that I had heard it for the first time. After all, us kids weren't supposed to have known anything about that night.

Nearly three hours later, the Lebanese food, which we thought was enough for several meals, was completely gone. We ran out of stories and everyone started to look a little tired. And so we said our goodbyes and vowed to see each other again soon. Jack would phone me days later reporting that Lois had started eating and walking about again after our visit and Dad's "therapy." She got better for a time and was able to leave the house and go out sometimes with Jack. Stacy, the kids and I had dinner with them during one of our weekend getaways to Traverse City.

Lois had another stroke some months after my family's visit and passed away. The lunch with Dad and me would be remembered as one of the last bright spots of her life.

As we drove off from Jack and Lois' home, I felt thankful I still had my dad with me. Yeah, he may be impaired. Yeah, his time left is marked. And yeah, I'm stressed out most of the time. But he is still here, and here with me.

38 { The Great Wallet Caper

Thirty minutes after leaving our three hour lunch with Jack and Lois, Dad and I pulled into the parking lot of the Cherryland Resort hotel, which sits at the foot of East Grand Traverse Bay. It was still a beautiful late summer afternoon, and Dad and I decided to check in, take a shower, then go for a walk downtown. Neither one of us could stomach the thought of more food, so we nixed the dinner out idea in favor of a nice walk. Dad was quite an exercise buff in his prime, and he loved to go on "walks," which usually turned out to be several mile hikes.

As Dad got ready for his shower, I noticed a new, ritualized kind of behavior I had not seen before. He opened up his shaving bag and laid out all his items to get ready for the evening. He then arranged them in a line on his bed, in the sequence he thought he would be using them. He talked himself through the sequence, correcting himself if he discovered he made an error in the proper order. What I was witnessing was an adaptive mechanism he had unconsciously come up with to cope with his Alzheimer's disease.

"Lets see. We've got the wallet and keys, belt, handkerchief, then the razor, toothbrush, shaving cream…No that's not right, the toothbrush comes last. So it's the razor, shaving cream, Old Spice aftershave. That's right! Then nail clippers, Q Tips, and meds. Then the toothbrush for later. Got it." He then went through the sequence again, silently, pointing to each item in turn with his index finger. After Dad showered, he went to the front of the line of items on his bed, and performed the tasks in sequence. It was sort of what I had been doing with him during the "45 minute day."

When it was my turn to shower, I noticed that I emptied my pockets and laid out all my things on the bed just like Dad did. I guess the 45 minute day was rubbing off on me a little, too.

An hour later, we were both ready to go. We put on our tennis shoes and prepared to walk off the 3,000 calories of Lebanese food we had consumed at lunch. Dad was raring to go in the wake of his nap and shower. I wondered how far Dad could walk safely at age 70. He talked as if he was ready to hike 4 or 5 miles, all over town. After all, in his mind he was still a young man of 36.

We set out on Front Street, the main drag through town, and stopped in just about every little store and gallery along the way. Dad made a point to tell the managers or owners in each gallery that I was a famous photographer and that they should display my work. It was embarrassing, like always, but I knew he was proud of me and that he loved me. And that trumped the embarrassment every time.

We walked all the way through downtown, and up Union Street. A mile or so up Union we passed an old restaurant we used to go to, which spawned a few nostalgic stories. But then, approaching on the right was a building I had not prepared myself for. It was Dad's old private practice office. Only I never associated it with his private practice. I associated it with my parents' separation.

After my father met Teri, he separated from my mother in order to cultivate his relationship with her. I remembered the day he moved out on us and took his clothes and a few pieces of furniture to his private practice office. He set his office up as a sort of makeshift apartment. It had a shower and a small kitchenette area, and Dad "lived" there for some months before finally divorcing Mom and moving in with Teri. I would go to the office to visit Dad whenever I was up from college, often with my sister Tiffanie.

Passing by the office now, I was feeling the ghosts of twenty years ago. Dad noticed how preoccupied I was, but didn't know why. He apparently didn't remember his office apartment.

"Dr. Fang, what's wrong?"

"Oh nothing, just a little tired, I guess."

"Well then, we should start heading back. I'm starting to get a little tired myself."

"Maybe we could stop by someplace and get a couple sandwiches. We could take them back to the room and watch an old movie."

"Great idea, Dr. Fang. Wow this has been a fun day!"

And so we meandered our way back through town. Dad chirped all the way back about seeing his old friends Jack and Lois. I was surprised he even remembered that he saw them today. I smiled and nodded as if I was having a great time. But my head was still back in that office.

I tried to disconnect. Come on, Garrett, stop it. That's over and done with. But I couldn't. I kept picturing myself as a 20 year old with my little sister in tow, climbing up the stairs to get to Dad's office. I remembered that I felt sorry for Dad then, knowing that his fling with Teri wasn't going to last. I already knew back then that the only thing that would last from Dad's indiscretions was the break-up of our family.

We bought a couple Italian subs, which Dad loved, and I went to pull out my wallet to pay. I mumbled to myself in a barely audible tone.

"That's funny, I must have forgotten my wallet." I patted myself down; covering all the pockets in my shorts, before I realized my wallet wasn't on me.

"Here, Dr. Fang, I've got it." Dad pulled out his old, overstuffed wallet and handed the cashier a twenty.

"Hmmm. I wonder what I did with my wallet. I thought I had it with me."

"You worry too much, Garrett. You probably left it in the... ah, the ah, the whatchamacallit, the ah..."

"The hotel?'

"Yes that, or in the car. Don't worry, it will turn up when we get back."

We hurried back. I told Dad we had to get back to catch a movie on TV. But I was really starting to worry about the wallet. I couldn't remember seeing it after I had paid the cashier at Woody's in East Lansing.

We made it back to the hotel parking lot. The first place I searched was the van. Nothing. Oh well, I didn't expect to find it there anyway. It's probably upstairs in the hotel room. Oh yeah, I emptied all my pockets out on the bed before I took a shower. Now I remember! The wallet must still be on the bed, or maybe I didn't see it because it fell onto the floor. I relaxed immediately, for I knew I had left it in the room.

We entered the room and my eyes made a beeline to the bed. That's funny, there's nothing on it. I went over to the side of the bed and looked on the floor along side it. Nothing. Under the bed, nothing. Now I was starting to worry. I had over $400 in the wallet, not to mention at least four credit cards, not to mention my social security and insurance cards.

I looked in the bathroom, under the furniture, all through my luggage, even inside the closet. Nothing.

A wave of panic started coming over me. My wallet was stolen! Or was it at Woody's in East Lansing? Or maybe it fell out of my pocket during our walk. I fixated on the worst possible scenario: My wallet was stolen, the $400 dollars is now gone, and someone is out there, running up all my credit cards, including my Visa with its $10,000 spending limit.

Then the obvious struck me. Dad's got it. "Hey Dad, are you sure you didn't pick up my wallet by mistake?"

"Now why would I do that, Son? Of course I didn't take your wallet."

"Oh, I didn't mean on purpose. Just maybe you picked it up accidentally, thinking it was yours." Then I did something I shouldn't have. I walked over to Dad, and without asking, started frisking him, from head to toe.

"Hey, wait a minute, what are you doing?" Dad pulled his arm back, as if he was cocking it to strike me. Another Alzheimer's symptom I would be seeing more of. For a split second, I wasn't his son Garrett. I was an unfamiliar stranger, who was accosting him.

"Get off of me, what are you doing here?" Dad shoved my arms back angrily. He was all riled up. I backed off, with submissive posture, after I couldn't find anything on him that felt like my wallet. All I had found that was remotely close was his wallet, in his back pocket.

"Sorry, Dad, I guess I got carried away. I thought you had picked up my wallet by mistake." I immediately felt bad for what I did. For a split second, I had not treated him like my Dad. I had treated him insensitively, like he was some kind of detainee suspected of carrying contraband.

"Geez, I thought you were going to rob me."

I laughed, albeit anxiously. Dad didn't. He was serious.

I went back to my original catastrophic hypothesis. "Well, I guess my wallet's either back at Woody's, or it's been stolen. Shit."

I fought back another surge of panic and opened up the phone book. I called everyone I could think of. Woody's in East Lansing. Jack and Lois. The hotel manager. Even the Traverse City Police Department. All blanks. Then Dad and I got back in the van, drove downtown, and retraced all of our steps, including every gallery and shop we had been to. Nothing. The wallet was gone. I was virtually convinced I had left it in the hotel, and some maid had found it and walked off with it. Damn it.

We drove back to the hotel. I did the only thing left to do that I could think of. I called Stacy.

"Hi Stacy." I didn't take the time for niceties, opting for the unnecessary drama instead. "We have a problem up here. My wallet's been stolen."

"You've been robbed? Are you alright?"

"We're fine. Well, we weren't exactly robbed. I mean I can't find my wallet. I've looked everywhere. All through the hotel, where we've been, Jack and Lois' house. I even called the police. It's gone."

Stacy, always calm and always smart, went right to the quick. "I bet your Dad's got it on him. Did you search him?"

"Yeah I searched him." I didn't confess that that was one of the last explanations I thought of.

"Did you search him carefully? I mean, have him empty all his pockets?"

"Yeah, I did all that already." Well that wasn't exactly true, I didn't have him empty his pockets. The frisking incident was bad enough, but there was no second wallet on him.

"You sure you searched him carefully? I'm sure he's got it on him." Stacy actually sounded confident. I snapped back at her angrily.

"I already told you he doesn't have it. It's been stolen!"

"Then you're going to have to call all your credit card companies and cancel all your cards. Like immediately."

"I know, only I can't. I don't have any of the account numbers or customer service numbers up here. You're gonna have to go through our file cabinets and get those numbers off the billing statements". Now Stacy was getting hot. The thought of spending the next four hours with a host of customer service reps was not very appealing.

"Garrett, I'll get the numbers for you but you'll have to call."

"I can't Stacy, I've got Dad. Could you call?"

Four and a half hours later, at 11:20 PM, Stacy called back. It was done. All of my credit cards were cancelled, with replacement cards to be sent out in the mail. All I had to do was call the companies back with a password to activate the new accounts. Stacy had saved the day again. I was appreciative. She was still hot.

"Garrett, honey, I still think that wallet's on your Dad." Stacy wouldn't let go of her hypothesis. We said goodnight, although I was annoyed at what I thought was her pestering.

"True Grit," the old John Wayne movie we had been watching on TBS, was over and it was time for bed. I watched Dad do his ritual again, laying things out on the bathroom counter while he got into the medical scrubs he used as pajamas. I could hear him recite as he laid the various items out. "Lets see. Keys, wallet, wallet, comb, meds, razor, shaving cream, toothbrush…"

Wait a minute. Keys, wallet, wallet? Huh? Wallet wallet? I jumped off the bed and ran into the bathroom. There, on the counter, next to each other, were two wallets. Dad's and mine! I opened up the wallet and found $400 in twenties. That and all my credit cards. All of them cancelled and now unusable. By Stacy. Over the past four and a half hours. Late on a Saturday night. I didn't have the courage to call her back.

Dad looked as surprised as I did. "Fang, we've done it! We've found the wallet!" He acted as if he had no idea how it had got to the counter top, and in sequence with all of his things.

"Oh what a great day this is! Your wallet, Dr. Fang, your wallet! Right here!" Dad was practically dancing with joy. I wanted to punch him. Until my conscience reminded me that this was the work of Dad's Alzheimer's disease, not Dad himself.

I later was able to deduce that Dad had placed both wallets in his back pocket when I was showering earlier that afternoon. When I frisked him, I thought I had found only one, over-stuffed wallet.

We had had enough excitement for the day and went to bed. I was so relieved I fell asleep quickly. I had a dream that night that Stacy had put me in a home for Alzheimer's patients. I didn't have to dream the nightmare for very long, however, because Dad's fitful snoring kept waking me up. Finally, at about 2AM, Dad's snoring stopped, and, exhausted, I fell into a deep sleep. What I didn't realize was that Dad's snoring had stopped because, unbeknownst to me, he had gotten up. At 2:17 AM, I was awakened by the sound of our hotel door opening. It was stopped by the chain lock.

I leaped out of bed, still half asleep. "Dad! There's a man in our room!" The rapid rush of adrenalin brought me to full alert within seconds. I could see only a shadowy figure by the door. I looked over at Dad's bed. It was empty.

"Dad, is that you?"

The shadowy figure whispered back, sounding anxious. It was Dad. He was fully dressed, and both of our overnight bags were packed up and next to him. He was very confused. "I've got to get back home. I'm going out to the car and drive home. You can stay here if you want."

"Dad, it's the middle of the night and we're in a hotel room in Traverse City."

"We are?" Dad's whispering voice trembled. He was very anxious.

"Yeah, we are. Remember we came up here for the weekend? We're seeing your old friends. We'll be getting up soon, it will be morning. We'll have breakfast and then go home. We'll go home together."

Dad started to calm down. "Dad, it won't be much longer until its light outside. Now come on back to your bed. Its gonna be alright. Here, just take your shoes and socks off and lay down. I'll cover you up." It was like I was tucking a six year old back into bed after a nightmare.

Dad was compliant, his anxiety seemed to abate, and I thought he was becoming more lucid and oriented again. I thought wrong.

"Son?" Dad said, while settling back into his bed.

"Yes, Dad?" I was back in my bed, desperate to get some sleep.

"We'll be leaving for home real early then?"

"Yeah, Dad. Right after we see all your friends at the Omelet Shoppe. Why are you in such a hurry? This is going to be fun."

"Well, I have to get back home to see my girlfriend."

"You have a girlfriend, Dad?"

"Oh yes. She comes over almost every day."

I thought he was talking about Rosemarie, my mother and Dad's ex wife.

"You mean Rosemarie?" I smiled, feeling that Dad was still attached to her.

"No, no, no! Not Rosemarie. Are you crazy? She's my grandmother. I'm talking about the young one, with the blond hair. What's her name, ah...you know, the pretty one..."

I was terrified to say it, but I did. "Tiffanie?"

Dad replied, ever so matter of factly. "Yep. That's her. Tiffanie. My girlfriend. I've got to get back to see her."

Dad drifted off to sleep, and within minutes was snoring away. I didn't sleep anymore for the rest of the night.

The next morning came, like it always did and always would. The sun was up and streaming through the blinds when I opened my eyes. Dad was already up, shaving in the bathroom. He seemed lucid, organized, well rested, cheerful, and fairly normal again. I was exhausted, emotionally spent, angry, and scared. I wanted to race back downstate, right into Stacy's arms. I wanted to be the one who was being taken care of.

We had a wonderful breakfast at the Omelet Shoppe. Most of Dad's friends, who I had invited, were there. They all exchanged stories about the past, including the skinny dipping story where Jack got poison ivy all over his genitals. Dad laughed and joked right along with everybody. At the end of the breakfast, my Dad's old friend John, who was a retired physician, pulled me aside. He said, in all seriousness, "Garrett, your Dad doesn't look impaired at all. Are you sure the Alzheimer's diagnosis is correct?"

All I could reply was a curt, "Yes, John." I didn't have anything left in me to explain what had been happening.

The farewell tour was over.

39 { Slipping

A cold morning rain was knocking down the orange and yellow leaves from the trees outside the house. I peered through the window as the wind driven rain splattered against the glass. I was alone today. Stacy had taken the girls out shopping, and then they would have lunch and go catch a movie. They wanted me to go. I had wanted to go. But I couldn't. It was my day to be with Dad.

The inertia I was feeling this morning wasn't like me. Normally I was a bit on the hyperactive side, anxious to get up and go, anxious to do as many things as I could possibly do in the time available. But today I didn't feel like doing anything. I didn't have any energy. I didn't have any drive. I could pass the morning just staring out the window from the living room couch.

I needed to escape. But there was nowhere to escape to. I had built this elaborate wraparound structure to catch my father, with me at the hub. Now I was a spider caught in my own web. I felt trapped, and unable to free myself.

The fall had brought a new feeling, a new impulse, and a harbinger of things to come. At first I wasn't sure if the impulse was a fear or a wish. I thought it had initially cropped up as a stray thought, a random impulse I could quickly dismiss. But it kept cropping up, again and again, until I couldn't suppress it anymore.

I was beginning to wish that Dad was dead.

The rain splashing against the window reminded me that I probably needed to cry. For the past month I had been really very depressed. I was preoccupied with all the things I had to do to take care of Dad. The previous six months had been easier, with all of the distractions of the farewell tour. Now those distractions were gone. Dad was slipping fast. And so was I.

I tried to force myself to cry by thinking of particularly sad things about Dad, or some of my cherished memories from the past. But no tears would come this morning. Nothing to cleanse my soul.

Two hours passed with me staring out that window. Finally, the rain stopped. A few patches of blue sky appeared, allowing the sun to come through and illuminate the sparkling water drops that covered everything. It was already 11, and I should have been at Dad's already. I forced myself to leave my perch on the couch and found the phone lying on the kitchen counter.

"Hey, Dad, it's Garrett. Feel like going out on a color tour and picking up a few pumpkins?" My voice lacked its usual enthusiasm and vigor. I didn't have the energy to fake it today.

"Sure, Son. I'm all ready to go. Hey are you all right, you sound a little down?"

"Yeah, Dad, I'm fine. Maybe I'm coming down with a cold or something." The usual lie, designed to protect Dad's feelings, had once again found its way out of my mouth. What I could have said was, Dad, I'm really depressed. I don't see my family very much because of you and your goddamn disease. You know, the disease we never talk about? The one that's changing you into another person right in front of my very eyes? The disease that's eating up all of my free time? The disease that creates perpetual stress that is only going to keep worsening? Yeah Dad, I am a little down.

The tone underlying my thoughts was no longer one of sadness and loss and empathy and let's mobilize for The Champion. I was becoming resentful and bitter and angry. Who the hell is this person I'm caring for? He's not really my dad anymore. I'm sacrificing myself for someone who's becoming a person I don't even recognize.

Of course, every angry, bitter, resentful thought I had was matched by an equally powerful barrage of guilt. My conscience was brutal in the counterattack. How the hell can you feel that way toward your father? After all, it is your duty to take care of him.

"Son, are you there?" Dad interrupted the war inside my head.

"Sorry, Dad. I got distracted."

"Honestly Son, I sometimes worry about your memory. Are you sure you're OK?"

"I'm fine, Dad. See you in a few minutes."

And with the lies in place and the feelings submerged, I headed out on the road again. I picked Dad up, and we headed southeast, toward the Chelsea area, home of actor Jeff Daniels and the beautiful Irish Hills. I was hoping that the fall colors would lift me out of this depression I had been in. My plan was to make this a pretty short trip, a couple hours or so, and to pick up a few pumpkins at some farmhouse along the way. I could surprise the girls with them and we could carve them up tonight.

Although it was supposed to rain all day, the skies had partially cleared, at least for the time being. We got off the freeway and headed down Dexter Trail, a pretty country road that would wind through the hills and farmlands of southeast Michigan. It was absolutely beautiful. A brilliant azure blue sky punctuated by huge, billowing clouds. Everything was wet because of the rain, which made the colors "pop" and the leaves sparkle. Normally, this type of sightseeing trip would pull me out of whatever funk I was in. But not today. I was mired in my depression. It scared me that I couldn't shake it.

Dad loved the drive. At every turn he "Oohed and ahhed." He was having a great time. Meanwhile, I thought about how unfair things were. Dad's the one with the dread disease, but he seems the most oblivious to it. His every need is met, he gets to have great trips and adventures, with people waiting on him at his every turn. I'm a healthy, relatively young man, great kids, great wife, used to be happy all the time, and now I'm miserable, with things only expected to worsen. Where has my life gone?

My conscience admonished me. Quit being such a martyr. This is life. This isn't God's fault. This isn't anyone's fault. Suck it up and do the right thing.

As we started to wind our way back home, Dad reminded me that we still had to pick up some pumpkins, which I immediately thought was rather ironic given his memory and word retrieval problems.

About 10 miles outside of East Lansing, we came to an old farmhouse alongside the road. The house looked kind of deserted, like no one was home, but out front was a large, old-fashioned wagon filled with pumpkins. Atop the huge pile of pumpkins was a stuffed scarecrow the size of a real man. It was dressed in blue jeans, a flannel shirt, and a straw hat that perched upon a pumpkin head. It was kind of cute and kind of eerie at the same time. The scarecrow was holding a sign that read, "Pumpkins for sale, $3 each, please leave money in the can." This was not at all unusual in rural Michigan. People put their produce out and you paid on the honor system.

Dad and I hopped out of the van and walked over to the wagon to pick out a few pumpkins. I had selected four, put a twenty in the scarecrow's can to cover two more for Dad, and started loading them into the van. After loading the last one, I noticed Dad was still over by the wagon. He looked like he was talking, and was gesturing with his hands. I wasn't sure, but he looked like he was angry.

I yelled over to him. "Hey Dad, I already paid. Just grab a couple pumpkins and come on over."

"I can't. I'm waiting for some assistance from the guy over here. And I'll tell you, I'm getting pretty fed up waiting."

Huh? There must be someone on the other side of the wagon I couldn't see. I walked over to Dad, expecting to do damage control with someone, but I didn't see anyone else over there.

"Dad, come on, it's getting late. Just grab a couple pumpkins. I already paid."

"Oh you already paid? OK then." Dad picked out two medium sized pumpkins and we walked back to the van.

Dad looked upset. "Son of a bitch," he muttered. "Couldn't get off his fat ass to help us. How rude can someone be? I don't think he deserves our business."

"Dad, who are you talking about? There's no one there."

Dad looked back over his shoulder. "Why there he is, Garrett. Sitting atop the wagon with his big, fat ass and his ugly, pumpkin head. Son of a bitch is he rude."

I felt like a scared little kid riding back with Dad. I had the creeps. Dad's personality change had sent me reeling into some kind of surreal, anxiety induced, dissociative state. A nightmare I couldn't wake up from. Fortunately, Dad eventually fell asleep. When we arrived at his condo, I put his pumpkins on the stoop and hurried him inside. Dad wanted to know if I wanted to watch a bunch of movies and stay overnight. I just wanted to get home and back to some sense of normality.

I performed the 45 minute day but I was just going through the motions. I was very anxious and still feeling eerily detached. Where did my father go?

In a short period of time he had changed. His persona had changed. He didn't feel like my dad anymore. This person was someone else.

I finished my duties and put Dad in front of the TV for the evening. I was worried if it was safe to leave someone so tenuously in touch with reality by himself. But on this evening I didn't care. I just wanted to get the hell out of there.

When I got home, it was going on 7PM and getting dark. It had clouded over and the rain had started again. I got the remaining pumpkins out of the van's hatch and put them out on the front steps to surprise the kids. But I came home to an empty house. On the kitchen counter was a note from Stacy. "The girls and I have gone to the Y. We waited for you but assumed you were still with your Dad. Dinner's in the fridge. See you around 8:30. Love, Stacy, Shani and Miah."

I went over to the living room couch and watched the wind blown rain splash up against the windows. Most of the trees' colorful leaves had been knocked off by the squalls. I looked at the four pumpkins I had put on the front steps and started crying.

I cried for a number of reasons that night. I missed my wife. I missed my kids. They were starting to do things without me because they assumed I would instead be with Dad. I cried because I was overwhelmed with worries and problems. I cried because Dad was turning into someone else, right before me. I cried because I was beginning to feel as much anger toward Dad as I was sympathy for him. And I cried because there was no end to the stress in sight.

40 { The Prelude

It was November again. The second November after Dad's diagnosis. The holidays were fast approaching, and I dreaded it. I kept thinking of how painful last Christmas was, and I anticipated more of the same this year. I just wished the whole holiday season would pass right by me. Magically and without any pain.

What made matters worse about Dad was that I couldn't fully grieve the loss. Dad was, well at least technically, still here, and he needed to be cared for. The finality of death wasn't there. It was like the pain of death without any ending point. It was like a wound that would never close and heal. Stacy would tell me that Dad's condition was worse than death. I was in some sort of purgatory with my dad. And that he was occasionally "with it" made it tougher. On his more lucid days, it was like Dad came back to life. Each time he was "back" it was like a miracle. And I would pray and pray and pray that he would be back to stay. But the lucid days never lasted. Dad would invariably go back to the Alzheimer's victim. And he would always revert into a person I didn't recognize or know.

Stacy was the only one that I thought understood. She was usually the only one I would ever let my guard down around. And that didn't happen very often anymore, because I wouldn't let it. I didn't have room to feel any more pain.

Stacy understood what pain was. Some six years before, she had lost her mother. Joyce had entered the hospital with back spasms. They were pretty severe, she was in a lot of pain, but it certainly wasn't anything that someone died from. While in the hospital, Joyce had a routine IV shunt put in her arm. The IV "rolled," the site got infected, and a cyst developed under the skin. Stacy had noticed the infection and had alerted the nursing staff and Joyce's primary doctor immediately. But no one seemed to take it that seriously except Stacy. The infection festered for four days before the hospital staff and primary doctor decided to treat it with an antibiotic. By then it was too late. The infection had entered her blood stream and had found its way to Joyce's heart.

When Joyce went into cardiac arrest it was already too late to save her. The bacteria had eaten away much of her heart muscle and two of her heart valves. She died on the operating table, a victim of medical neglect, from an infection that was fully preventable, and then initially fully treatable. Stacy had to say goodbye to her mother on a hospital gurney that was soaked in blood. I still cannot think of anything more horrible than that.

It took Stacy five full years to get back to some semblance of normal after her mother passed. And now, Stacy was telling me that my trauma with Dad was worse than the loss of her mother? Oh my Lord, if it took Stacy 5 years to recover from a "finalized" death, how long would it take me to recover from Dad's "partial" death? Stacy was right. This was worse than a death. This was purgatory.

Stacy wanted me to go into therapy. I wanted to stick my head in the sand. Even though I was a therapist, and well versed in dealing with people's aversions to getting help, I thought of every ridiculous reason in the world not to get help. I'm too busy caring for Dad. Seeing a therapist will take even more time away from my family. And of course, the arrogant, I'm <u>Doctor</u> Turke, the great child therapist for the Family Court. How will it look if I go for treatment? Stacy thought I didn't want to look weak, or at least vulnerable to other people. But none of those were the real reasons I avoided going into therapy. It was a secret I was afraid to tell.

The real reason I wouldn't go get some help was that I was afraid of my old ghosts. Did Dad abuse my sister? Do I need to contact her now? And what about all of Dad's affairs? And his drinking? Maybe he isn't The Champion I had made him out to be all these years. I was afraid of opening it all up. And not to someone else. I was afraid of opening it all up to myself.

It had been a while since I talked with God. Sure, I had prayed a lot in recent weeks. I had been praying all along. But my depression hadn't alleviated one iota. Although my faith hadn't been shaken, I was beginning to wonder if I was asking God for the right answers. I had been praying for selfish reasons. Dear God, give me a miracle. Make Dad's lucid days stay. Please, dear God, take this pain away from me. Just let me hide from this. Me, me, me. Those prayers didn't seem to have a return address. I had wondered if God had forgotten me.

Then the epiphany: Maybe I should stop fighting this, like I was able to do during the farewell tour. Maybe the lesson is not about removing my pain. Maybe the lesson is about submission. Maybe the lesson is about letting go. Maybe I didn't have to be in charge of all this.

And for the first time in several months, I felt that old, familiar shiver run up and down my spine. I had connected again.

I was still depressed. I was still afraid. But now I knew exactly what I had to do.

41 { Saying Goodbye to the Father I Knew

The leaves were all down and the grass had turned brown in advance of the long winter ahead. It hadn't snowed substantially yet but you could feel it in the air on this day. A cold front was moving in from Canada and the dreary light rain that was falling would soon turn to snow.

I didn't know what prompted me on this morning to do what I had to do. I certainly didn't feel like it. In fact, I dreaded it. The thought of it had been hanging in my conscience for weeks, waking me up almost every night and haunting me during the day. I didn't know if I would be brave enough. I didn't know if I had enough strength. I had talked to Tiffanie and we agreed that it was the right thing to do. Only Tiffanie said she couldn't do it. She said she wasn't feeling strong enough.

It was time to say goodbye.

It was time to say goodbye to the father I knew while he was still with us. I couldn't just let him drift away without talking to him about our lives together. I knew it was going to be brutal. The pain was already unbearable just thinking about it. I imagined it would be ten fold worse when I actually did it.

I had told Tiffanie I was going to talk to Dad this weekend. I kind of wanted her to do it with me, for support, but both of us knew that this was a private thing that each of us had to do alone. Tiffanie wasn't ready to do it yet. And while I warned her that we didn't have much time left with Dad, I understood that she wasn't ready. Besides, it was inevitable that this had to be done alone. I was the one who was ready, it was my turn, and I would go first. There was no way around it.

I told Stacy when she got up that I had to go say goodbye to Dad. She knew exactly what that meant, without any explanation. She cried and couldn't say anything. She just hugged me. I never asked her how she felt. I knew she not only felt some of my pain, but also the loss of her mother again.

I had no idea how I was going to do this. I had rehearsed the whole thing countless times in my mind. I had several versions. One was angry and damning. "You could have been a great father but you blew it with your drinking, the divorce and all of your goddamn affairs. And now one of my sisters is gone because of it."

Another version was taken from the land of denial. "You were a great dad. Lets walk through all of our memories together, the trips to the beach, our sailing adventures in Grand Traverse Bay, all those Dodger and Laker games we went to in Los Angeles. Wow, we had a great life together, Dad" That version would be easier, but I would probably be forever haunted that I didn't step up to the plate.

And then there was the third version, the most truthful one, which integrated all of the feelings together, the good and the bad, the beautiful and the ugly. That version was going to be the most painful, as I would have to feel the anger and the sadness and the separation and the loss all in one toxic mix. That was the version that was the most real. That was the version I was most afraid of.

I got in the van without really knowing what I was going to do. I didn't even call Dad to let him know I was coming. It was 8:45 AM. I knew he would already be up, and probably watching some old movie on TV.

During the 13 minute drive over, I rehearsed the three versions in my head. It only served to make me more confused and more nervous. When I got to Dad's street I didn't put on my blinker, and I didn't slow down. I just kept going. I couldn't do it.

I drove to a nearby lake and parked the van at a roadside park. I stared out over the misty water. The rain was starting to mix with snow. I prayed. I prayed for God to tell me which version to use. What an idiot.

I sat there without any answer for a good thirty minutes, apparently waiting for a decision from God. Nothing. No thoughts, no tingling sensation up the spine, no words in my head, just more and more anxiety. I thought about turning around and going back home. I wasn't ready yet, apparently. Maybe I was weak. Maybe I couldn't face all of my demons and ghosts from the past. I felt my depression like a knife in my back. I was getting scared. I couldn't have felt any more alone.

I put the van in reverse and turned around. I was soon traveling south, down Park Lake Road. I would pass Dad's street in a few minutes, keep going, and head on back home. I was going to fail. I hoped Stacy would understand. I knew Tiffanie would.

When I got to Dad's street, I heard a voice. It wasn't my voice, but it came from out of my mouth. *"Garrett, this is the time. Slow down, make the turn, you don't need any script. Just do it. It will be all right. You'll see."* And as I made the turn, I felt the tingle up my spine that I had tried to conjure up earlier. I had connected again. I knew it would be all right. I was not going to have to do this alone.

I rang the doorbell and Dad answered it immediately, almost as if he had been poised in the foyer awaiting my arrival. "My son!" Dad reacted like he always did, as if I had been overseas for the last five years. "Wow! I can't believe it! You're here! All this way to see me! Come on in, let's have some, ah, you know, we'll have some..."

I finished his sentence. I had grown adept at that over the past year. "Lets have some breakfast together."

"Exactly what I was thinking. Boy, Dr. Fang, it's almost like you can read my mind!"

"Should we go to Denny's?"

"Oh boy would I like that." Dad was becoming excited. And he was making sense. I had caught him on a good day. I couldn't turn back now.

We drove to Denny's and Dad ordered his usual, oatmeal with fruit and toast. We had a cute twenty-ish waitress who seemed kind of tired and distant. Dad noticed this and, true to form, asked her empathically if she had had a long shift.

"No, actually I just got here. I was up late, studying for my MCAT."

Dad perked up, recognizing instantly he was talking to a pre-med student. "You're going to become a doctor?" Dad pointed proudly to himself. "University of Iowa, 1956. And this is my son, Garrett. He is a great psychologist who works with gang members."

It was embarrassing, as always, but maybe only to me. Dad had done it again. Within a few seconds the waitress had completely warmed up and was chatty with us. Well, chatty with Dad.

Our meals came and I searched for the right moment to bring up what I had come here for. But it didn't feel right in the restaurant. And so I waited for our breakfast to be over.

Leaving the restaurant, I began to think that maybe we could have the talk in the van. I could drive him home in a round about way, through the Rose Lake natural area, and we could talk there without any distractions.

"Hey, Dad? Mind if we take the scenic route back? I kind of feel like a nice drive."

"Sure, that will give us time to talk. I've got some, ah, some ...ah, whatchamacallit, some things I want to tell you."

Time to talk? He wants to talk to me? Wait a minute, I'm the one that needs to say good-bye. I'm finally ready to do it. And now he wants to talk to me?

I knew I couldn't wait until we got to Rose Lake. He might forget everything by then. I closed the passenger side door, making sure Dad's fingers were out of the way. I started the van, backed up, and headed down Grand River Avenue. I wasted no time getting the conversation started.

"What's on your mind, Dad?"

"Well, it's actually been on my mind a long time. I don't know how to ah, say this, so I'll just say it and I hope you will understand. All those very kind things you did for me, ah I mean with me, well for and with me, this summer. And before that. Well, you know, our whole lives together. You've always shown me that you love me, and well, you know I didn't feel that I was loved so much as a child, and so, you've helped me know that I can be loved, too. Even when I really didn't deserve it."

"Wow, Dad." I didn't know what to say, but it didn't matter. Dad had grabbed my free arm forcefully.

"No, wait! I'm not done with it. That's not all of it."

I glanced over at Dad. He was starting to cry. Not the choked up, teary-eyed sentence or two that I was accustomed to. He was actually crying.

"Son, this is so hard for me to say, but I've made a lot of mistakes and I've hurt a lot of people. Like your mother and your sister, ah, not Tiffie. You know, the other one. Cindy. And maybe you, too. And when I'm gone, I don't want anyone to think I wasn't sorry for what I did to everyone, and I sure hope you can forgive me and that you don't hate me."

"Dad, I don't hate you. You did make some pretty bad mistakes. You did hurt me, and you hurt us. But I'm not angry any more. I'm really not. You were right. You are loved. And love is stronger than any hurt. I actually didn't know that until this past year."

"I love you, Son, and I always will."

"I love you, Dad, and I always will. I'll always be holding your hand, like we did jumping the waves when I was seven."

Dad clutched my free hand and didn't let go. We then drove on through the Rose Lake Natural Area. The wet snow was sticking to the trees. It was no longer a dreary day. It was beautiful outside now.

The talk was over. It wasn't as long as I thought it would be. It wasn't as sad as I thought it would be. It didn't turn out to be my talk with Dad. It didn't turn out to be Dad's talk with me. It was our talk.

Thank you, Lord.

42 { The Return of the Webbed Tentacle

P.O. Box 485 was so full I had trouble pulling all the mail out. I only checked Dad's mail on Fridays, and I was always amazed at how much mail he received over the course of just a week. Unfortunately, most of the box's contents were meaningless junk mail and requests for money. Although I wanted to just dump the whole lot, I had to sort through it carefully to make sure I didn't throw anything important out. It made me angry to see how much junk mail my father received, as he received approximately ten times the donation requests that I received at my house. I wondered what triggered that. Was it his age, or was it that he had sent so much money out in the mail before I took over that he was branded "sucker" on a thousand computer registries?

I cradled an armful of Dad's mail and set up camp next to one of the post office's recycling bins, ready to reduce my three pound pile to a few legitimate letters or bills. This week, there were two letters from Dad's patient turned friend turned Navy buddy Arthur, two bills, a property tax statement, and a letter that was postmarked Ottumwa, Iowa. I glanced at that letter and noticed the return address was from a man named Edward Lamanski. The letter had been forwarded twice from Dad's prior addresses. Hmmmm...Edward Lamanski. I've heard that name before. Ed Lamanski. Lamanski. Where do I know that name? I knew Dad had talked about him somewhere before.

I threw out the rest of the junk mail and walked gingerly out to the van. I headed out to Dad's to take care of the few bills with him, then I could take him grocery shopping for the week. On the way out, I challenged myself to remember who Ed Lamanski was. I know Dad has talked about him before, but where? The name sounds so familiar. Who is he?

As I turned down Park Lake Road, it dawned on me. Ed Lamanski! Dad's old college buddy from Iowa. Ed Lamanski. Ed Lamanski, the one Dad had nicknamed, "The Webbed Tentacle," which always sounded to me like a comic book character. I pressed down on the accelerator. I couldn't wait to get this letter to Dad.

I rang the doorbell excitedly. Dad was apparently asleep in front of the TV again, and I took the liberty of unlocking the front door with my key. "Dad! Dad! Wake up! You got a letter from The Webbed Tentacle, wake up!" Dad shot up out of his Herman Miller chair. He had an excited, but perplexed look on his face.

'The Webbed Tentacle? From Iowa?" Dad was having one of his lucid moments again. "No, it can't be. Why, why I haven't heard from him since, since...I think since I was in college." Dad told me the old, familiar story again. His long term memory was still amazingly intact. Ed Lamanski was indeed The Webbed Tentacle, the one who tied Dad up in the locker room and then dumped him, naked, way out on an Iowa country road somewhere. Dad had to hitchhike back to campus in the nude. Dad retaliated by placing Ben Gay heating balm inside Ed's jockstrap. Although I never thought this was particularly funny, Dad roared every time he replayed the story. I had heard the story re-enacted countless times since I was a boy. Dad always concluded the story the same way. "Damn you, Webbed Tentacle!" It sounded just like a comic book ending.

I was never quite sure what caused Ed to be called The Webbed Tentacle, but I had my ideas. I wondered if being called The Webbed Tentacle was what drove Ed to exact revenge upon Dad. Yep. I'm sure of it. That would only make sense.

I hurried Dad to open the envelope. It was a simple greeting card, with a short, handwritten message.

"Dear Walter.

It's been nearly 50 years since we've seen each other. I found your name on our college alumni registry. I'm a salesman now and still live in Iowa. I hope this finds you well. I understand that there is going to be a class reunion coming up next spring. I wondered if you were going to go. Maybe we could see each other again? Please write back if you get this.

Sincerely, Ed."

Dad was all excited. The letter was like a time machine that brought him back to his college years at Iowa, and his delayed adolescence. Dad was already making plans to go to the reunion. Only his Alzheimer's disease had already caused some fundamental misinterpretations in Ed's letter.

"Dr. Fang, you and I need to go to this. When is it? It's coming up soon. We've got to get ready. My oh my, The Webbed Tentacle's putting on a big party just for us. I wonder what he's up to. I like him, but you know he's up to something. We won't be able to trust him." Dad laughed. "Damn you, Webbed Tentacle!"

I knew that if I removed the letter from Dad's home he would forget about it and the issue would be over. While the Webbed Tentacle lived intact in Dad's long term memory, today's letter would never be registered in his short term memory, the part of Dad's brain that was most affected by his Alzheimer's disease. I could just end the whole thing by taking the letter with me.

I was really torn. Part of me wanted to just ignore and forget the whole thing. Part of me wanted to inform Ed of Dad's condition, and to let him know that at Dad's current rate of decline, there was no way he could attend the reunion next spring. And part of me really wanted Dad to go to that reunion, no matter how unrealistic that might be.

I performed the 45 minute day with Dad. I noticed when it was time to shower that he seemed confused for a minute about what to do with a washcloth. Although I had grown accustomed to having to prompt Dad to do the proper sequence of self care skills, this was the first time he seemed confused about how to do a simple task like washing. I pantomimed to Dad how to use the washcloth and it came back to him. Within a few seconds he was fine. But I had already noted on my internal mental checklist that he had lost some more functioning.

I put Dad in front of the TV with a nice long video, Evita. Dad was engrossed in the movie, and I left him there, humming to the music, thoroughly contented.

When I got home there was a nice dinner waiting for me at the table. The girls had eaten two hours before, at the normal dinnertime. I felt more anger toward Dad.

After I ate, I sat down with the Webbed Tentacle's letter that I had snatched from Dad's study on my way out of his house. I had decided to write Ed back, and to be honest with him about Dad's disease and condition. I didn't know it at the time, but my letter to Ed was about to become the prototype for many letters to come, including Arthur's.

"Dear Ed,

My father just received your letter earlier today. Sorry it has taken so long, but your letter had to be forwarded twice in order to reach us. My Dad has lots of great memories of you and him during your college years. He lights up every time he recalls those days, and he recalls your friendship fondly. Sadly, I must tell you that Dad has been stricken with Alzheimer's disease. He is in the early stages still, but he has become noticeably impaired in recent months. His short term memory and his speech are most affected now. It's too early to tell for sure, but I don't think he'll be able to handle the class reunion next June. I will keep the date posted, however, and we'll see as the time draws closer.

It was wonderful for Dad to hear from you. I am sorry to return such bad news to you. Please know that Dad is happy and that our family is coordinating a lot of care for him. You will always live in his long term memories as one of the happiest times of his life.

Enclosed is Dad's address, and my address and phone as well. Dad loves to write, his writing doesn't seem to be that affected yet from the disease, and he might not seem impaired at all in his letters.

Thank you so much for thinking of my father.

Sincerely, Garrett Turke, Walter's son."

I normally would have teared up or cried after writing such a letter. But after my goodbye talk with Dad, I didn't feel so sad. This is just something that had to be done. I was ready for duty again.

I sealed and stamped the envelope, put it in the mailbox, and then curled up on the couch in front of my stereo. I put on Bob Marley's Legend CD and cranked up "Jammin". The girls yelled at me, as always, to turn it down. But I didn't hear them. I was already a million miles away in some surreal sanctuary Marley called Zion.

Two weeks later, on the day before Thanksgiving, I got a letter in the mail from Iowa. It was from Ed Lamanski. At first I thought Ed had got the addresses mixed up and that the letter was for Dad. But the letter was addressed to me, and so I opened it.

It was a simple greeting card, with a simple, handwritten message inside.

"*Dear Garrett,*

I received your touching and heartfelt letter the other day. I understand what it is like to be a caregiver. It is my experience that the caregivers are usually the ones that are the most neglected, the most under recognized, the most under supported. The caregivers are such special people. They are God's people. They are doing God's work.

Garrett, you are doing God's work. I don't know how many times you hear this, or if you ever hear this, but thank you.

Please stay in touch.

Warmest regards to you, your family, and your father. Ed."

43 { Engine Failure

It was the last Saturday in November. Thanksgiving had come and gone, and I had survived. I had attempted to have Dad over to join Stacy's family and my mother for Thanksgiving dinner, but Dad couldn't handle it. He looked confused and was overwhelmed with the number of people there. I had to take him home after about half an hour. It was OK, everyone understood, but my Thanksgiving evening was spent performing the 45 minute day and plopping in a movie for Dad.

It was time to face the inevitable. Dad's needs were changing again, and I felt it was time to call for another wraparound meeting with our team of family caregivers. I was worried that Dad would soon become unsafe to continue living at home, at least by himself. Part of me wanted to make a pitch that we should start looking at residential care for him. I had no idea what kind of facility to look at. The only experience I had with residential facilities were the ones that the Family Court sent our delinquent kids to. And I thought some of those placements were dehumanizing. They could break a person's spirit. And that was the last thing I wanted to see happen to my dad.

I opened the door anxiously, looking for the arrival of my mother, my sister Tiffanie, and her husband Don. As I stared down the cul-de-sac, I was worried how this meeting would go. I had been neglectful of our wraparound over the past few months. Dad was in much worse shape than the rest of the team knew. I hadn't told Tiffanie about his delusion that she was becoming his girlfriend, instead of his daughter. I hadn't told my mother that Dad now referred to her as his omie, or grandmother. And I hadn't told anyone that he was sometimes forgetting how to do simple tasks, like washing himself with a washcloth.

My mother was the first to arrive. She parked her blue Ford Taurus in our driveway, and emerged with two full garbage bags. I studied her for a moment as she hadn't noticed me standing at the door. She looked fit and trim, her face far younger than her 70 years. I wondered how she had weathered all the traumas in her life and still managed to look that good.

"Why good morning, Garrett. I didn't see you standing there in the doorway. Say, I was wondering if you could open the garage, I've brought some recyclables for your bins and some fresh, juicy compost for your garden."

Good old Mom. She never threw anything out. Organic compost. Cans. Bottles. Bags. Boxes. Used wrapping paper. Bows. Ribbons. Paper. Everything. And it all made its way, in some shape or form, back to my house. Maybe it was a vestige from her years during the Great Depression or her refugee years during World War II. Or maybe she was just way ahead of her time.

"Say, could you give me a hand? Why don't you take this bag of compost back to the garden?" She lifted a big, clear plastic bag full of two week's worth of fruit and vegetable scraps that she had kept in a pail under her sink. The putrid contents were now thoroughly rotten, mostly liquefied, and way beyond funky. I was afraid to open the bag.

"Your garden will just love that stuff. Nice and juicy, isn't it?"

"Yeah Mom, the garden will just love it. Nice and juicy." Mom didn't hear my sarcastic, barely audible reply.

As I walked back up to the front of the house, Tiff and Don pulled into the driveway. They looked a little rushed as they got out of their Grand Prix.

I invited everyone inside and sat them down in the living room. Before I even opened my mouth, I was worried that I hadn't done a very good job preparing them. I had told everyone that I just wanted to update them as to how our support system was going. That was far from the truth. They had no idea about what I was about to dump on them.

True to form and reflective of my insecurity, I went into formal psychologist mode. "Well, hello, everyone. Thanks for coming. I know everyone is so busy these days. Tiff and Don, you guys are busy building your new house, Mom, you're busy with the Montessori school. I know everyone has such little free time so I'm really appreciative you took time to be here."

Everyone except Don looked a little annoyed with me. Although the entire team was probably thinking it, Tiff was the first to say it. "Garrett, why do you always act so formal? Just say it. We don't have that much time today. Dad's been doing great. Why do we need this meeting?"

Bitch. That's what I thought to myself. Tiff didn't deserve it, and my conscience immediately railed on me. Your sister asked a perfectly legitimate question, especially since you haven't been telling anyone about everything going on with your dad. This isn't Tiff's fault at all. Good thing she didn't hear it.

"Well, you all know that we've got Dad pretty well structured..."

Mom interrupted me. "Yeah, he's doing great. I just saw him yesterday. You could hardly tell anything's wrong with him. He really seems to be enjoying his walks with me. And we're going through all the old family photos. I think we should make an album of them for him, we can color-copy them at Kinkos. We can do that for Christmas."

"Well, I know that all of you think that Dad's doing great, and he is doing great in a lot of ways. We're doing a really good job with him. Dad's happy, and he really enjoys the time we're spending with him. But I've been worried lately."

"Oh Garrett, you always worry so much. Relax, he's doing just fine." Tiff made what I was about to say even harder. I felt like she had already made her mind up about Dad's condition, and now I was going to have to argue to get my point through.

I heard my mother whisper, just like she did in the last wraparound meeting. "He's just like his father. Walt would worry about everything, too."

Thank God Donald was there. He saw that I was struggling, and he seemed to respect what I was saying.

"What's wrong, Gart? You wouldn't have called this meeting if nothing was wrong."

With this opening, I just blurted it out. The more tactful approach wasn't working anyway, because of my contrived formality. "Dad's really slipping. He doesn't always know where he is, he's getting really disoriented when he's out of his routine, he thinks Mom is his grandmother and Tiff, you are becoming his girlfriend. The ALFA Center director, Margie, called me this week and said he's trying to leave the building some days, and they're really struggling to keep him there. I'm worried he's going to walk off somewhere and get lost. I know we're doing all we can, but I think he needs more. His MMSE scores at Dr. Jahnke's office have fallen suddenly into the impaired range. I think its time we need to start looking at a residential facility."

Well, that was a mistake. Your family has been busting their butts to take care of him, and now you dump all this shit on them all at once. They've had no preparation for this, and you've insulted Tiff and Mom. They're not going to believe you.

And I was right. "I'm his girlfriend? Garrett, I think that you're the one that's beginning to lose it. He's fine. You called us all here to tell us this? I just saw him yesterday. He doesn't think I'm his girlfriend. That's crazy. Why are you doing this to me? "

"I was just trying to let everyone..."

Tiff interrupted my explanation. "And Mom is his grandmother? That's ridiculous. Come on, he knows who Mom is. You're the one who's tripping here."

Tiff wasn't through. "If you're worried, why don't you get Dr. Jahnke to just increase his medication? And those tests, what do they really tell you anyway? I don't believe in those stupid psychological tests. You and I sometimes miss some of the items when we take Dad in. Dad was just having a bad day."

Mom did her best to play peacemaker. "Well, Garrett, maybe that's how he's going to be in the future. Maybe you're just trying to prepare us now. As for me, he knows who I am. I can feel that he does. I think he tries to tell me he's sorry for what happened in the past."

Now I was starting to get ticked. "He is sorry for what happened, he just told me. But I'm telling you guys, he's starting to get really confused. He couldn't even remember how to use a wash cloth the other day."

Tiff readied the knock-out punch. "Now I know you're losing it. God, Garrett, he talks to me, I see him everyday, and he's just fine. You can barely tell anything's wrong. My friends don't see anything wrong with him when he's over. You're always so negative."

"And dramatic! Just like Walt used to be." Mom seemingly couldn't wait to drop that one on me. Damn it all, why would I make this up? And just like my father? I've never had an affair in my life, I've never been unfaithful to anyone in my family, I don't bounce my family from home to home, I've had the same job for 16 years, and I've never been divorced, and I've never screwed my wife out of money. Jesus Christ, I'm the most stable one in the family! But none of those thoughts ever reached my lips. I had chosen a more passive route. This wasn't going well, and I was thinking about just giving up. Screw it.

Stacy, the voice of reason in the family, tried to right the ship. "Well, I know people weren't really prepared for this today, but I have noticed that Walter is really slipping the past few months. He does look more confused. Most of the time he's OK, but sometimes he's not. Garrett is over there all the time, he sees him more than anyone else, I think he has more chances to see Walter when he's not doing so well. Garrett's as freaked out about this as anyone, but I can tell you he's not trying to be dramatic. He's just really worried about him. He's worried we're not going to be able to support Walter the way he needs to be supported."

Mom responded, somewhat defensively, "We're doing everything we can."

Stacy finished her point. "That's not what Garrett's saying. Everyone is doing the best they can. It's, it's...it's just not enough anymore. My husband is over there almost every single day, sometimes twice in a day, a few times three times in a day. Jesus God, he's taken your father, your ex-husband all over the state to see all of his old friends this summer. He hardly sees his kids, he hardly sees me, and it's killing him. It's killing him! All he's saying is that Walter might need more care, more care than any of us can provide him with."

Stacy's speech was soul stirring, but unfortunately, only for me.

Tiff was unmoved. "Well, I don't know how much more I can give. We have a new house that's being built. You know that. I can't stop working on that now."

So was my mother. "And I'm giving him two, sometimes three afternoons a week now. I have my work at the school, I have my own life. You should be thankful I'm giving Walter this time."

Total engine failure. Plane in flames and going down.

We all talked some more and Stacy asked if anyone wanted coffee. We rode out another hour but nothing changed. Tiff and Mom didn't see Dad's condition as being as severe as I did, and there was nothing I could do to change that. Maybe they were right. Maybe I was being overly dramatic. Maybe my secret, vacillating wish to be rid of caring for Dad was beginning to color my perception of his status.

I would have accepted that explanation except for one thing. Stacy thought I was right on the mark.

Everyone left by noon. Tiff and Don went to their new house site to see how the construction was coming. Mom went home to prepare for her next lesson at the Montessori school. Life went on.

Two days later, I mustered up enough courage to call a local residential care facility that serves Alzheimer's patients. I actually had three facilities on my list to call, but I could only build up enough courage and energy to call one. I talked to one of the nurses at this particular facility. She was very nice, and listened thoughtfully to my description of Dad's symptoms and the eroding course I thought he was on.

To this day I can clearly recall her concluding sentences. "What you are saying is really common for Alzheimer's patients and their families. From what you describe, your father is about a year away from going into residential care. If I were you, I'd check around to see what kinds of waiting lists there are at the facilities in the area. Find a care facility that feels comfortable to you, and your family. And then don't hesitate to get him on the wait list. You can expect to pay about fifty to sixty thousand dollars a year for his care. All the facilities are about the same, cost wise. If you have any questions, please feel free to call me again."

I told Stacy what the nurse said.

I didn't tell anyone else.

44 { The Christmas Present

It was a beautiful winter morning as Dad and I pulled out of the driveway. The first snows of the year were now beginning to accumulate on the ground, ending the month of drab November brown. It was December now and everything was white. Christmas was approaching and Santa Claus was coming to town.

Dad and I were heading up north to Traverse City for the day. I had received my first Christmas present a few days before in the mail. It was an innocent looking letter from Verna at La Bella Galleria, where I continued to have my photography on display and for sale. Inside the letter was a brief note from Verna, and a check for $840. Four of my large, framed landscapes had sold! I folded the check and put it in my wallet for safekeeping, but I kept taking it out to stare at it. I wanted to see that it was real. It wasn't a dream.

Verna's note was also inspiring.

"Dear Garrett,

As you can see, your work is really selling up here. Lots of people have come in and are drawn to your prints. Please come up with some more images! Oh yes, the couple who bought your winter scene were from Norway. They are living right now at Interlochen Arts Academy. They want to know where and how you photographed that shot. The wife was nearly crying, she said it reminded her of her childhood back home. Here's their address. Could you call or write them? Hope to see you soon.

Fondly, Verna. P.S. How's your dad doing? Burb and I hope he'll come up with you.

I had folded Verna's note up and had also placed it in my wallet for safekeeping. I kept taking that out of my wallet to look at it also. I couldn't believe it. I had actually sold some of my work. I'm not just a psychologist after all. I'm not just a caregiver. I'm an artist at La Bella Galleria! I had finally had broken out of my box.

The time on the way up went by quickly. Four hours and eleven minutes later we rolled into the gallery's parking lot. I woke Dad up and told him we were there. He asked me where we were, as he had already forgotten. I told him we were dropping off some of my photographs at La Bella Galleria. He looked confused for a minute, then said with a smile, "You think we can look for that....that big, you know the great big winged..."

"You mean the bald eagle we saw on Eagles Nest Way? I was so glad Dad remembered.

I opened the van's hatch and brought out five more 3 x 4 foot landscapes, all from northern Michigan. My favorite was a simple field of sunflowers against a polarized blue sky. Dad loved that one too, and had a copy at his house. He said the sunflowers reminded him of his favorite artist, Vincent Van Gogh. Dad had done a biographical study and slide show of Van Gogh and put on a presentation each year to his professional colleagues. The slide show was synced to Don McClean's Vincent (Starry Starry Night). I now tear up every time I hear that song.

We entered the gallery with three of the photographs, and Barb came out to take the other two. Barb and Verna loved the images and said she would keep all of them. As was the case the first time I had brought my work to the gallery, a small assembly of patrons gathered around me as I took the images out of their protective sleeves. I felt like some famous artist who was in demand! It was such a good feeling. I felt released from the box I had barricaded myself in the past couple years. I didn't know how long the feeling would last, but I didn't care. This was my day.

As I chatted with some of the gallery patrons, I saw Barb and Verna talking away with my dad in an opposite corner. Dad was very animated and excited looking, pantomiming and expressing himself with his hands. I overheard him saying something about the eagle we had seen the last time we were up. I thanked God he could remember that, for it would always be one of the most special and powerful moments of my life with Dad.

Verna eventually came over to me. "I just love talking to your Dad. He is so full of life. He was telling me about that eagle you guys saw last time, up on the ridge. Did you really see it? "

"Yep. We sure did. I don't know why, the camera was all set up, but I didn't photograph it."

"That's because it was meant for just you and your Dad." Verna smiled. She was a kind soul. "So, I'm sorry, but I have to get going. As you can see, it's busy around here, with the Holidays and all. Do you have any plans for a photography shoot next year?"

And then, something inexplicable happened. The words that came out of my mouth were completely unexpected. I couldn't believe I was hearing them as they came out. Were they even my words? I hadn't thought about any of this, well at least not consciously.

"Verna, the next time you see me I'm going to bring you a series of prints from Italy."

"Garrett, you're going to Italy?"

"Yes. I'm going to take Stacy and the girls." What? Where is this coming from? I had given this absolutely no thought until this very moment.

"Well then, Garrett, I'll look forward to seeing those. Barb and I want you to know how touched we are that you take care of your dad the way that you do. You are a wonderful son."

I was so choked up I couldn't say anything, so I just shook her hand.

Dad had meandered over in the meantime. "So, anchors away?"

"Yes, but in a minute, Dad. First, I think we need to buy something from the gallery. There's a beautiful purple blown glass vase over there. I was thinking of buying that as a Christmas present." I showed Dad the vase. He saw the price sticker on it. "Its two hundred, seventy dollars."

"Yeah, I figured it would be expensive. But I really like it."

Dad, being his usual generous self, offered to pay for it, without even asking who it was for.

"I'll let you pay half, if you insist. Aren't you going to ask who it's for?"

"Great. It will be from both of us."

"Dad, you still haven't asked who it's for."

"Well, aren't you going to tell me?'

"Dad, this is going to be the year that I'm going to do the some things I've always wanted or needed to do. I'm not going to hold back anymore. I'm going to take the girls to Italy. And we're going to buy this Christmas present for someone that is special to both of us."

"Who is that, Dr. Fang?"

"Cindy."

Dad teared up. "We're going to send her a, a... a...?"

"Yes, we're going to send her a Christmas present. From the two of us. And we are going to see her again someday. I'm going to see to it."

"That's so wonderful." Dad cradled the vase lovingly, and brought it over to Verna at the register.

Dad choked up again. "This is for Cin...Cin... oh well my daughter. We haven't seen her in a long, long, long time."

Verna placed the delicate vase lovingly inside a box and cushioned it with tissue paper. "Merry Christmas, Walter. And Garrett, you tell your family hi. They're gonna love Italy. Make sure you go to Sienna, if you can."

And with that, we were on our way back to the van, five images lighter and with a promise for the new year. It was not going to be a year that would be remembered for grief, no matter what the future held for Dad. I had made a decision. I was going to contact Cindy. And my family was going to go to Italy.

45 { A Christmas Call

I awakened to a completely dark and still world. Within seconds, however, the clock radio went off. 6 AM. Johnny Mathis' version of "Sleigh Ride" had just begun. Before I could be taken back to 1966, Stacy reached over and kissed me. "Merry Christmas, honey."

"Merry Christmas, pretty girl. Let's just lay here a while, it's so still and peaceful."

"Sorry, honey. Its already 6. We've gotta get up before the kids beat us to it."

And with that, we shot out of bed. Stacy hit the shower first, while I went downstairs to plant the evidence. The girls were still sleeping soundly in their bedrooms as I passed by. They had been up late the night before awaiting their annual call from "Santa," a role well-played by Stacy's father, Terry. He would call about 10 o'clock each Christmas Eve ever since Shani was a little kid.

Shani, the precocious child of the family, had figured out there was no Santa before her fifth birthday. She had noticed that the Easter Bunny at the mall was really a man dressed in costume. Shani deduced almost immediately that all the other childhood mythical beings weren't real either, including the Tooth Fairy, Big Bird, Sparty, the Michigan State mascot, and then most tragically, Santa Claus. She cornered us one day and badgered us until we confessed. It was a terrible blow for us parents.

At least Shani still played along every year after Miah was born. Miah was four now, typically the perfect age for Christmas magic. Eight hours before, she was so nervous on the phone with Santa that she couldn't speak. But she listened intently to his every word. And Miah's green, bambi-shaped eyes grew huge when Santa let out a rousing, guttural "Ho ho ho!!"

I tiptoed gingerly down the stairs. I had a lot to do before the kids woke up. Downstairs, by the fireplace, was the glass of milk and the three cookies

Miah had left for Santa. And, of course, a handful of carrots left out for the reindeer.

I did what I always did each Christmas morning. I ate the cookies sloppily so they left some crumbs on the plate. Next, I poured the milk down the sink and returned the empty, milk-filmed glass to Santa's plate. And last but not least, I took the handful of carrots out to the front porch, where I chewed them up and spit out a trail of carrot particles in the snow. Yep. Santa and his reindeer had been here last night all right.

When I got back inside, Stacy had come down and was already doing what she did every Christmas morning, making hot, buttery cinnamon buns. She used the same recipe her mother had used every Christmas. And while the cinnamon buns were baking and filling the air with a heavenly aroma, I popped open a bottle of champagne. Stacy and I were not heavy drinkers, and we never drank in the morning. Except on Christmas, when we mixed orange juice and champagne to make mimosas.

We heard a door open and close upstairs, followed by a tiny voice. Miah had gotten up. "Shani, Shani, wake up. Wake up! We have to see if Santa Claus came."

Then we heard Shani, 11 years old going on 40. "Of course Santa came, Miah. You just talked to him last night. You know he always keeps his promises. Just a minute, I'll go down with you."

And within moments, the two were coming down stairs, hand in hand. That didn't happen any other day of the year, as normally the girls jabbed at each other when they first got up. But not today. Not on Christmas.

Miah's eyes were ready to pop out of her head when she saw the family room filled with presents. But before we could open any of them, Stacy and I had to perform the ritual. Shani was now adept at playing along with the ritual, an encouraging sign for the next generation.

Stacy went first. "Look Miah, the cookies and milk, they're, they're..."

"All gone!" said the tiny voice.

And while Miah stood mesmerized in front of the empty plate and glass, Shani and I went to the front door. Shani, the apprentice, beat me to the punch.

"Miah. Miah! Come quick! Come quick!"

"What is it, Shani?" said the tiny voice. Miah trotted over to her at the front door.

"Look! There, in the snow."

"The reindeer ate up all my carrots. Good boys!" The tiny voice sounded very excited.

"I'm sure they were very hungry," Shani said. "There's nothing left but these little pieces."

We reassembled in the family room and let the girls open their presents from Santa first. Within 15 minutes, the room looked like a ravenous pack of wolves had torn through all the boxes. I then started scooping up all the torn wrappings and ribbons and put them in a garbage bag. Stacy stopped me.

"Garrett, honey, don't forget, your mother asked us to fold up the pieces of wrapping paper and keep all of the ribbons."

"Whatever for?" I asked, teasing, already anticipating the answer.

"So she can reuse them, of course."

I felt a twinge of anger that I really didn't want to feel on Christmas. Mom always had a plan to re-use everything, and I didn't want to spend Christmas morning doing one of her recycling jobs. I looked at Stacy, looked at the pile of wrapping paper remains in front of me, looked back at Stacy, smiled deviously, then grabbed the pile of wrapping paper and bows and smashed them into the garbage bag.

"Oops, guess I forgot!"

Stacy smiled. And with that, the twinge of anger was gone.

"Hey, Garrett. The cinnamon buns are almost ready. Why don't you go over and get your Dad?"

"But he's gonna come over later, when Mom comes over, at 10, that was the plan, remember?"

Stacy persisted. "You and your plans. Well I'm changing the plan right now. It's Christmas morning, honey. Go on, go get your dad. He's not due at Tiff and Don's until 2 o'clock anyway."

"Maybe I should call him first."

"No, don't do that, just go on over there and surprise him. Come on, honey, it's Christmas."

Stacy smiled as I grabbed the van keys and headed out through the garage. It was exquisitely beautiful outside this morning. A light dusting of snow overnight had cleaned up the snow banks lining he streets. The sun was now peaking out and illuminating all the sparkling fresh crystals. There wasn't a soul on the road the entire way to Dad's condo.

Dad was poking his head out the front door, fully dressed with his winter coat on, when I arrived.

"Geez Garrett, I thought you'd never get here."

"Dad, we were going to see you at ten, remember?"

"I know, and it's past ten right now!" It was no use. Dad's disease had taken over again. He didn't have a clue what time it was. But he knew it was Christmas.

"Merry Christmas, Baby Fang!" Dad smiled lovingly. And for a few seconds, it was Christmas morning back in 1966. I could picture our old house in Los Angeles, our Christmas tree, and that prized electric football game that I had wanted so badly. There was one box under the tree that was the game's size, but I couldn't tell for sure. I had tried to peek under the wrapping paper by making a small tear in the corner, but my clever mother had outwitted me. She had double wrapped the box.

I had also received a beautiful, metallic blue 10-speed bike that Christmas. That was really nice, especially with the speedometer, and I'm sure that my parents believed that would be my favorite present. But what I really wanted was that game. Over and over for the entire month of December, I imagined myself opening that box and finding the coveted "NFL Live Action Electric Football" game inside. And on Christmas morning, 1966, the box that I thought contained that wonderful game was indeed the box of my dreams. I played that game all winter, each and every Saturday with my friends and each and every Sunday with my dad. There was no greater human activity on earth.

Dad interrupted my daydream with a big hug. "Mmmmm, my baby fang." Dad brushed his stubbled face up against mine. The familiar smell of Old Spice aftershave transferred to my face. I was still in 1966.

"Merry Christmas, Dad. Looks like you're ready to go." It was time to go back to 2000.

"Boy am I ever. Anchors away?"

"Anchors away, Dad." And with that, Dad climbed into the mini van and we were off.

When we arrived home, the girls met us at the door, anxiously waiting for us. This morning was not going to be some dutiful or obligatory Alzheimer's check in. No. The girls needed my dad there to make Christmas complete. And that made me feel good. Christmas was already shaping up to be a great day.

"Hi Grampy. Merry Christmas!" Shani was the first to approach and hug him.

Miah tried to follow suit, but she was still way too shy. Stacy scooped her up and walked over to Dad. "Merry Christmas, from all of us, Walter. Why don't you have some hot cinnamon buns with us? We made them just for you."

Dad loved the cinnamon buns, as we all did, and we opened some more presents. The kids continued on like wolves on a feeding frenzy, but Stacy made them slow down and pace themselves. After the two little wolves were saturated, Dad encouraged Stacy to open her presents from me.

I pushed a great big box in front of Stacy. Inside, were the three little Italian travel books I had purchased for her. They barely filled up a quarter of the box, but I had cleverly filled the box with kitchen utensils to give the box extra bulk and weight. She would have no idea that I was hiding something small inside.

"So Garrett, this box is so heavy I can barely lift it. What'd you put in there? Two of my pans are missing!"

Darn it! How does she always know! Stacy opened up the top of the box, and sure enough, removed the two large kitchen pots I had wrapped inside.

"Now, what did you really get me? Hmmm... ah, here it is. Wow, a beautiful picture book on the Amalfi Coast."

"Where's that, Mommy?" said the tiny voice.

"It's in southern Italy, Miah," said the 11 year old going on 40. Shani's voice had a touch of "don't you know where that is?" in it, as if Miah at age 4 was supposed to already know her Italian geography.

Stacy entered the conversation, happily strolling through the pictures. "It's so beautiful; I always wanted to go there. Positano and Sorrento, and Naples."

"Look, Mom, there's more." Shani nudged her on.

Stacy dug into the box deeper. "Oh, here's another book."

Stacy pulled out the second book. "Oh look, a picture book on Rome and Tuscany. Rome, the Eternal City, I always wanted to go to Trevi Fountain, and the Coliseum, the Forum, the Pantheon, I could go on and on. And Tuscany, I need to go there someday to expand on my Italian recipes." Stacy thumbed through the photographs almost nostalgically, as if she had been there before. Stacy acted as if she was a reincarnated Italian. My mother actually believed that to be true.

Stacy continued to search the box. "So what else do you have stashed away in here?" She pulled out what had the shape of a wine bottle wrapped in tissue. "Oh, a bottle of Tuscan Chianti. Nice choice, Garrett. We can have this with dinner. Well, shouldn't we be getting to some of your presents?"

"You're not done yet." I tipped the box so she could see her last present from me.

"Oh. There's one more book, here." Stacy tore the wrapping off, exposing the cover. It was the Frommer's 2001 Guide to Italy. Stacy was silent. She knew I had a flair for being dramatic, especially on birthdays and Christmas.

"Go ahead, open it." Stacy was still silent.

"Go on, Stacy, open up the cover." Now the girls were excited. They had not been clued in, because I was afraid Miah would blab.

Stacy opened the cover and a card fell out. It was from me. "Stacy, you are the love of my life. Thank you for always standing by me, no matter what life has thrown at us. Merry Christmas!" I had signed it as I signed all of Stacy's cards, with a simple red, hand drawn heart next to my signature.

A handmade coupon was also inside the card. "Good For 4 Tickets to Italy in April."

Stacy looked at me and stared. She was like that when she was surprised.

I tried to break the silence. "Book it!"

Stacy started to cry. She still couldn't say anything. So I said it again.

"Book it, Stacy. I checked the Internet. Tickets to Rome are only about $400 each in April. Book it. You can do it today."

"You mean we're going to Italy? All of us?"

"Yep."

"But how? How are we going to pay for it?"

And that was the best surprise of all. I pantomimed "just a minute," and pulled out my wallet in front of her. I took out the check I received from Verna's gallery nearly a month ago. Stacy could see it was from the gallery.

"Oh honey, you sold one of your images!"

Now it was my turn to play coy. "Nope."

"Then what's the check for?"

"I didn't sell one." I then reached into my wallet and pulled out two more checks. The holidays at La Bella Galleria had been good to me.

"I didn't sell one. I sold six!" Two more checks had come in the mail this week. I now had $1,260 in sales from just the past month. And one of the Court's judges had just purchased my other copy of "Hurricane Watch," giving me a grand total of 1,560 dollars. I was so excited I could hardly stand it!

Now it was Dad's turn. He handed Stacy a card that was addressed to all of us. He had another one in his pocket addressed to Tiffanie's family. Dad had tears in his eyes. "I want you to use this in Rome."

Stacy opened the envelope. It was a check for $2,000. Dad had insisted on giving everyone in the family a $500 cash gift for Christmas. I had to approve, sign, and log the check in Dad's register, but I didn't know he was going to designate it to be spent on the Italy trip.

Dad stammered his way through what I guess was his way of saying thank you to all of us. "I want to tell…. I want to tell all of you, well thanks to each of you for all that you've done, I mean everything, having me over, those trips, dinners, you know, everything, Christmas today…" His bottom lip trembled, and his eyes teared up, like they always did when something touched him.

"Walter, this is too much money." Stacy did what she always did when she thought a gift was too extravagant. She tried to give it back. But Dad pushed her hand holding the check back toward her. "No. This is for you and your family. You'll be in Rome soon and you'll need it. I've been to Rome many times. It's you, Stacy. It's your city."

Stacy interjected, anxiously looking over at me. "But what about Walter's...."

I cut her off, anticipating the rest of her sentence. All my time with Dad made me good at that. "I already talked with Tiffanie. Everything will be fine while we're gone."

Now everyone was tearing up, Stacy, Dad, the girls, me. Finally, the reality caught up with Stacy. She squealed with delight, her voice turning into a singsong celebration. "We're going to Ro-aam, we're going to Ro-aam, and A-mal-fi and Tus-can-ee-ey too! We have to buy a no- ote- book to put my recipes in! The ne-ew ones I'm going to get from It-al-ly! We're going to Ro-aam, and Flor-ence to-o, to see Michael- An-gel-o!" Mi-ah's go-ing with me and Sha-ni and Gar-ret to-oo!" I hadn't seen Stacy this happy in over 6 years. It was the first time I felt she came all the way back from her mom's death.

We opened a few more presents, including mine, but everything was rather anticlimactic after the Italy trip present. Soon the doorbell rang.

Mom had a beaming smile on her face as I opened the door. I'm ashamed to say that I scanned her for evidence that she brought more recyclables and compost. I was relieved when the big bag she was holding was full of the kids' presents and not used milk jugs and cans. Mom came in full of energy, like she always did. "Merry Christmas, everybody! Mmmm... something smells good in here!"

"Merry Christmas, Mom!"

"Mmmm, Stacy, smells like your cinnamon rolls! Maybe I'll have one later, wow they smell good!

Mom sat down next to my dad. She tried to make conversation with him, but he was more interested in joking around with the kids. Finally he said something meaningful to her. "It's a great day! Garrett's taking his family to Stacy's favorite place, it's called, it's called, it's a far-away place that's really old! I helped him sell a whole bunch of his... his... er... ah.. his watchamacallits, his ah...paintings, and now they are going!"

Mom smiled, but didn't really react. At first, I don't think Mom understood anything he was trying to say, or if she did, she didn't really believe him. I hadn't clued Mom in either.

"Say, Garrett," began my mother, oblivious to Dad's pantomiming. "Are you saving the wrapping paper for me, like I asked?"

Shit. Here we go. Fortunately, I had rehearsed this scenario already in my mind, as it was predictable. "Ooops, Mom. I forgot. We've been throwing it away."

Mom went to the garbage bag and saw all the crumpled up paper. Oh-oh, here it comes, brace yourself.

Mom's voice sounded very disappointed, and to me, judgmental. "Oh no, I was going to use all that for my origami lessons at the school."

Bull's eye, Mom. Guilt on Christmas Day.

I didn't want to feel upset at Christmas, and I didn't want to be upset at my mother. I tried to convince myself that she didn't mean any harm, it just came across that way, with my mom's German accent, and the German to English translation problems, and, frankly, every other rationalization I could think of.

Even Dad, Alzheimer's disease and all, could feel the sudden surge of tension and tried to lighten it with an apparent joke. Dad's Alzheimer's disease had taken its toll on his sense of humor, as he rarely could abstract anymore. But today he returned to form, if only for a moment. He went over to the garbage bag, pulled out a few handfuls of crinkled up wrapping paper, and exclaimed, "Looks like Kris Krinkle was here!"

Everyone rolled over with laughter. Impaired or not, Dad had made the joke of the day, and he knew it. Even Mom had to laugh. Dad was so self-absorbed in his own wit he giggled periodically for the next hour, even after he seemingly forgot his own joke. He had saved the day, and he knew it.

We finished opening the remaining presents that we had saved for Mom's arrival. Mom, as usual, gave some of the best gifts. She never went out and shopped impulsively, like I tended to do. She always bought educational gifts, and they were always thoughtfully reflective of the recipients' interests and personalities. They would be presents that the recipients wouldn't tire of after a few days, or a few weeks.

After exchanging presents, Shani and Miah put on their favorite Christmas movie, "A Christmas Story." I too, loved that movie, especially the part where Ralphy beat up the neighborhood bully. As the kids engrossed themselves in the movie, the adults tried to make small talk with my mom. Then, Mom did the thing that she always did on Christmas. The thing that I always dreaded. It usually came at the end of our Christmas get together, but today it came early.

"Say everyone, why don't we call all the relatives?"

Even though this was the right thing to do, and a tradition of my mother's, I never liked doing this on Christmas. Calling the relatives meant work. It was never relaxing to me, and I always anticipated that some sort of conflict would merge from the phone calls. I was overreacting of course, the calls usually went fine, but I had had enough bad experiences calling "the relatives" in my life to keep the fear and anxiety alive.

I went to get the phone, dutifully respecting my mother's wishes, and expected the first call to go to my aunt and uncle in Connecticut. Only Mom threw a curve ball at me this time.

"Why don't we call your sister, Cindy? Walter, you know who Cindy is, our other daughter?"

Dad looked very anxious. I immediately went into protective, defensive mode as a wave of anxiety enveloped my body.

"Mom, I really don't feel that today..."

Dad interrupted me. "Cindy? The one we got the ah, the ah, that purple thingamajig...the purple..."

I helped finish the sentence, as was now my duty with Dad. "The purple vase. Mom, do we have to call her? I mean I'd like to talk to her and all, but it always ends in an argument, and well, maybe we should call her another day. It's gonna ruin Christmas. I don't think she wants to talk to me, I know she doesn't want to talk to..."

I was operating on three year old information, which was the last time I talked to Cindy.

I was trying to squirm my way out of this one, but it was too late. Mom would have none of it.

"Quit putting negativity out there in the universe! Come on now, someone has to break the ice. It's Christmas, what better time to call? I'll make the call and do all of the talking. You just say hi. I'll even pay for it if you don't want to."

I felt the twinge of anger return. That last line was uncalled for, Mom, I thought to myself. But the thought wouldn't reach my lips. I was starting to feel an anxiety attack coming on.

"I'm telling you, Mom, this will turn into a fight." I was already replaying my last conversation with Cindy, from three years ago, which concluded with, "Don't call me ever again, I'll call you when I'm ready." Well, folks, I'm not ready. What more do I have to say?

Mom persisted. "Look, somebody's got to do this. I can just start dialing now. Come on, what could it hurt?"

I guess Mom was right. The words of Ron Culp started to creep back into my mind, like some sort of psychotherapist prophesy. "Someday, you'll have the opportunity to talk to Cindy again. And when you do, don't blow it." Well, I guess that someday just arrived. I didn't plan it, I didn't feel ready, but here it came anyway. On Christmas Day.

"OK, Mom, you call her. I'll just say a word or two. "

Mom dialed the number immediately, before I could change my mind. Stacy rubbed me back sympathetically. Dad looked confused. The kids were a million miles away inside their movie.

Cindy answered the phone. I had been cowardly hoping that we would just get her answering machine. I could hear her voice through the receiver. She sounded the same as three years ago, ten years ago, twenty years ago.

Mom said all the usual, expected niceties. "How's your Christmas going? How're the kids? What are you doing at work these days?" Then the real reason for the call. Way before I was expecting it. "Well, Cindy, there's someone here who is anxious to talk to you. Garry's right here and I'm putting him on."

Before I could flee the room or otherwise stick my head in the sand, Mom had thrust the phone in my face. The pool of anxiety that had been sitting in my stomach raced up my torso and transformed into a massive lump in my throat. "Hello...Cindy?"

"Yes...Garry?" There were only three people in the world that still called me Garry. My mom, my barber Bob (who 15 years before didn't get my name right and I never bothered to correct him), and Cindy. Garry was the name I used in early elementary school after my peers kept making fun of "Garrett." I grew tired of "Garrett is a parrot whose mother was a carrot and whose father was a ferret." I thought I'd just go with the more common and acceptable, Garry.

"Hey, Cindy. It's been awhile."

"Yes it has. How have you been?"

"OK. Are you having a good Christmas?"

"Yes. You?"

"Yes."

The conversation couldn't have been any more trite, and safe. We danced around a bit, each one afraid to say anything that might be construed as the least bit inflammatory.

Cindy was the first to take a chance. "I got your presents. The vase, it's beautiful, and the photograph you sent. Was that Lake Michigan, up north?"

"Yes, I took that at the beach in Empire during a gale. Those are 10 foot waves."

"That's one of my favorite beaches in Michigan! I just love that photo." Then, unexpectedly, Cindy opened the door. It was the first time that door had opened in almost a decade. "I'm putting that photograph up on one of my walls that's just for you. I hope you will send me others and I can fill the wall someday."

And for the first time in years, I felt touched by my sister again. I thought the relationship was dead. I thought the feelings were dead. I had even told myself a couple times that my sister was dead to me. But today, in a three minute conversation, the feelings came streaming back. I had missed her.

I wanted to put Dad on the phone but I was afraid to. Dad seemed hesitant, too. He looked confused and pensive. I was going to give the phone back to Mom but Cindy interjected. "Is Dad there?"

"Yes."

"Tell him I said Merry Christmas. And that I like the vase. I don't need to talk to him."

Well, that solves my dilemma. She doesn't want to talk to him. But, before I could acknowledge that, Cindy added, "You know we've been writing each other. Mom told me he has Alzheimer's disease. Are you sure? Because his letter wasn't impaired at all."

Letter? Dad's been writing her? I pushed the conversation down a very scary path. "I didn't know he was writing you."

"Well, yeah, I wrote him, Mom gave me his address, and he's written me back. His letter was very well written, he was very lucid, it makes me wonder if he's really that impaired."

I was mute. Stunned. Cindy continued, "Well, we'll talk some more, later. When you're ready and when I'm more ready. But you should know that Dad and I understand each other now. He gave me all I need to know in his letter, and I think I want to leave it that way. I don't need to ever see him again."

What? Never see him again? But it's my job to reconnect you two again! To make peace. What kind of peace is this? Never see him again? The sand is pouring through the hourglass. His time is marked. You need to walk with him hand in hand. What do you mean you're never going to see him again?

But, with all of my censors on, none of these thoughts were ever spoken. There was too much at stake between Cindy and me.

I was devastated. This was not how the story was supposed to end. I stepped up to the plate, like I was supposed to, and Cindy's choosing to not see him ever again? I was too late.

Cindy wanted to wrap up. "Well, Garry, have a Merry Christmas. I hope we can talk again. I really loved that photograph. There's more room on my wall."

I faked the rest of the conversation. "Yes, well Cindy, have a great Christmas, and send our best to the kids. I'll talk to you again."

I wanted to say "I love you" but I wasn't brave enough. I hadn't said that to her in nearly 10 years.

I faked the rest of Christmas Day. I had to. Mom and Dad left to go spend the rest of the day with Tiffanie's family. Stacy spent the afternoon designing an itinerary for our trip to Italy. The girls were busy playing with their gifts. By 6 o'clock they had watched "A Christmas Story" three times.

We had a nice Christmas dinner. Stacy had made a Turkey with all Italian side dishes, including homemade meatballs rolled in bread crumbs. After dinner, Stacy sat down next to me. She knew what was on my mind.

Stacy looked right into my eyes. "You did the right thing, Garrett."

"No I didn't. I failed. Cindy doesn't want to see Dad ever again. He'll die without ever seeing her again."

"But they made peace, honey. You said Cindy said it clearly."

"What kind of peace was that? I failed, I was too late." I put my head onto Stacy's shoulder and started to cry. I tried to hold it back, and did. Not on Christmas. Not in front of the kids.

Stacy, as always, was persistent. "You didn't fail, and I'll tell you why. The phone call wasn't about your dad reconnecting and making peace with Cindy. They already took care of their business, whatever it was. She told you. The phone call was about *you* reconnecting with Cindy. And you did that. You didn't blow it."

I excused myself to the upstairs bedroom. Stacy went with me. It was now time to cry.

After a half hour or so I came downstairs with Stacy. I had been cleansed, and I felt all right again.

The third play of "A Christmas Story" was ending. I popped in "Miracle on 34th Street," and got down on the floor to play with my kids.

46 { Buon Giorno, Italia

"Buon giorno, Signora. Buon giorno Signore. Come sta?" The Hotel Britannia clerk smiled as she momentarily looked up from her paperwork to welcome us to the hotel's continental breakfast. She was a strikingly beautiful, twenty something woman with big, brown, bambi-shaped eyes, just like Stacy's.

"Buon giorno, Senora! Bene, grazi. E lei?" Stacy replied in almost perfect Italian. There was now little doubt that Stacy was a reincarnated Italian. After a seven hour flight with a pocket Italian primer, and only a few hours listening to the Roman citizens, she had already picked up a more than a handful of phrases. More impressively, however, Stacy was already picking up the Italian inflexion and rhythm, something I would be struggling with the whole trip.

I looked at the calendar at the clerk's desk. 26 Marzo. I couldn't believe we were in Italy. And in Rome, the Eternal City! Three thousand years old and five thousand miles away from Michigan. Five thousand miles away from my dad. And five thousand miles away from all the worries and fears and hurt and sorrow I had accumulated over the past two years since Dad's diagnosis. I had left the entire wraparound super-care structure behind, along with my grief, in my sister Tiffanie's hands. She said she was up for the challenge, and encouraged us to have a great trip, but I could tell she was very nervous when we left. She had never performed the 45 minute day, at least in its entirety, and now she would have to oversee Dad's care and routine everyday for nearly two weeks.

The winter had flown by preparing for Italy. Dad turned into one of our biggest cheerleaders for the trip, although his disease process continued to slowly worsen. Throughout most of the winter, he thought that each day was the day we were leaving for our trip. That perception must have been exhausting, not to mention extremely anxiety arousing for him.

We stepped through the lobby of our downtown hotel and toward the small, but stunning breakfast dining room. Shani and Miah trailed us, Miah cradling her stuffed dog that had been renamed "Lupe," or "canine," once we landed in Italy. Shani, the precocious almost 12 year old, was used to commanding the attention of others when we traveled. But not on this trip. This trip belonged to 5 year old Miah. Italians adore young children, and wherever we went in Italy, strangers would come up to Miah, pat her on the head, and call out, "La bella bambina!" or "the beautiful little girl!" And today was no exception.

The beautiful hotel clerk, upon seeing Miah, stepped down from her desk, produced a chocolate bar for her, and exclaimed, "Ah. La bella bambina! Mi chiamo Gabriella. Come si chiama?"

Stacy would help her out. "Miah, Signora Gabriella is asking you what your name is. Say "Mi chiamo, Miah."

The tiny voice replied, "Mi chiamo, Miah."

"Ah, si, Miah. Signorina Miah. Bella!"

We sat down amidst the busy little dining room patrons, many of who appeared to be businessmen who were preparing for the day's work. In front of us was a huge, fresco mural depicting what appeared to be the history of Rome. It was a very old hotel, and we wondered how old that mural was.

During breakfast, Stacy poured over a map of the city with Shani. Miah, as usual, ate just a little and started playing with her food. I thought about Dad and his care for a second and wondered why I wasn't feeling guilty for leaving him. The lack of guilt surprised and perplexed me. While I knew Stacy and the girls would have a magical time in Italy, I truly thought that I would just be there, going through the motions, constantly having to put up with feeling preoccupied and guilty about leaving Dad. But so far, so good. Just some fleeting thoughts of Dad and no guilt. It was like God had given me a reprieve. I didn't second guess my freedom, either. I knew I had earned it. And I knew that Dad knew I had earned it.

We finished our breakfast and headed out for our tour of the city. Stacy had selected a hotel that was very centrally located. She had planned and organized the trip entirely on the internet. We would spend the first three and a half days in Rome, then take the bullet train to Florence, go to all the museums there, see Michelangelo's David, and then take the train down to

Naples, where we would hook up with a driver named "Giovanni." Giovanni was a driver once used by a couple we knew back in Michigan, and Stacy had hired him after being impressed with him on the phone. He spoke English well. The first half of our trip was designed to be at a frenetic pace, to absorb as much sightseeing as possible, while the second half was designed to be more relaxing in Italy's subtropical Amalfi Coast. Our entire trip would span nearly two weeks. We were determined to stretch out every day as long as possible.

We had left Detroit, 26 degrees, in a heavy early spring snowstorm. When we arrived in Rome, it was late spring, sunny, and in the middle 70's. Everything was in full bloom, and the lemon and orange trees had fruit on them. It reminded me of California, and some of the fragrances in the air were smells I hadn't experienced since we left Los Angeles nearly thirty years ago. It was wonderful to be away. It was wonderful to be in Italy. It was wonderful to be free again.

I tried to remember the last time I felt this free. The memory I pulled up was the first day of summer vacation when I was 10. What a tremendous sensation to feel like a kid without a worry in the world. It was a shame that life would eventually rob all of us of that kind of innocence.

We walked the streets of Rome all day and never seemed to tire. The next day we took the bus to some of the sites that were too far to walk. We went to all the places Stacy had mapped out and had read about. She knew more about some of the sites than the tour guides did. And she was frequently so touched, so overcome with awe that she just stopped and cried. By the third day we had conquered the city. The Pantheon, the Forum, The Aqueduct, Trevi Fountain, the Spanish Steps, St. Peters Basilica, the Sistine Chapel. Republican Rome. Imperial Rome. Christian Rome. Medieval Rome. Renaissance Rome. Baroque Rome. Modern Rome. Centuries and centuries of history.

Stacy told me the city's eras were built next to and on top of each other. Very little was ever torn down or destroyed. When we were there a shoe store was expanding, and they removed a wall to make room for the expansion. The contractors discovered a 1,500 year old mosaic during the construction process. The store and the surrounding area had to be closed while the archaeologists unearthed and protected the find. Incredible!

I had my camera out the whole time, fantasizing about the L'images d'Italia show I was going to put on at Verna's Gallery. And everywhere we went, people came up to Miah and exclaimed "La bella bambina!" with such enthusiasm that we felt regal. Well, everyone except Shani. After so many years of being an only child and commanding everyone's exclusive attention, things were starting to balance out. And, while annoying for Shani, this turned out to be extremely important for Miah's self esteem.

Day three was also an adventure. We took a tour bus to the Vatican and got into St. Peter's Basilica, then, in true Turke traveling style, ditched the tour group and set out on our own. We saw the majestic basilica, the Vatican Gardens, and Michelangelo's incredible mural, the Final Judgment, at the Sistine Chapel. In the Sistine Chappell we saw three poorly disguised American Secret Service Agents, and then saw Barbara Bush and her twin granddaughter's walk in behind them. That night we returned to shop the streets of Rome, and I treated Stacy to an entire Italian outfit, complete with a black leather jacket and some very expensive Italian boots. I topped off the outfit with a bottle of Roma perfume.

We had incredible food in Rome. For lunch, we usually had fresh bread and cheese. At dinner we went all out, with many different kinds of pizza (none similar to any that we've ever had in America), pesto, and Stacy's favorite dish, potato gnocchi. The most interesting pizza had an extremely thin crust with a full course of vegetables on top of it, with asparagus, peas, eggplant, mushrooms, and artichokes in pie-wheel shaped sections. That was topped with fried eggs in the middle. It wasn't our favorite, but it certainly was the most unusual. And each dinner we had lots of red wine, typically house wine, "vino de la cassa," which Stacy could fluently roll off her tongue. Shani looked at us as if we were becoming alcoholics. But we were in Rome, didn't have to drive anywhere, and we were free. We didn't have a care in the world. It was about time.

Before we left Rome, we walked back to Trevi fountain to make a wish. We each threw a coin into the water. Later we asked each other what we had wished for. None of us wished for fame. Nor did we wish for fortune. We didn't wish for a miracle of any kind. Even for my Dad. We all wished for the same thing. And that was to simply return to Rome again as a family. I had gotten my family back.

On day four we took the bullet train to Florence. On the train, I thought of Dad for the first time in days. I tried to make myself feel guilty for a minute, but stopped myself. This is our trip, Garrett, don't wreck it. And that was the last time I thought of Dad the entire trip.

Florence was a very expensive place, even more so than Rome, and to conserve money Stacy booked us a two star hotel downtown. The hotel was billed as a quaint, traditional European hotel that catered to eco-tourists who wanted to save money. When we got there, we found a hotel that was very spartan in its accommodations, filled with high school students from other countries, no heat, no screens on the windows, and a rickety turn of the century elevator. What the hotel did have, however, was location, location, location! It was directly across the street from the Cathedral di Santa Maria, more commonly known as Il Duomo. Built in the 13th through 15th centuries, the Duomo was spectacularly lit up at night. Even though our room was damp and cold, that view was to die for each night.

Florence was fantastic. By day we visited Florence's world famous museums, of which the Uffizi Gallery was the most spectacular. The Uffizi houses Michelangelo's stunning statue "David," carved out of a 17 foot block of marble in the early 1500's. This statue, widely regarded as the most spectacular sculpture in the history of the world, was worth the entire trip to Italy completely in its own right. Stacy sat down at the foot of the sculpture and cried. I was at first embarrassed, but then I noticed other people were doing the same thing. Even Shani and Miah, who you would think would be bored in a museum, stood mesmerized before the incredibly detailed, life-like sculpture. Stacy and the girls stood before David at least an hour. I didn't bother or pester them. Stacy told me later it was one of the most powerful experiences of her entire life. To this day she will still tear up talking about it.

My most powerful experience in Florence happened completely spontaneously and unexpectedly. On our last night in Florence it was crystal clear, so clear you could see the Milky Way amongst the stars. Stacy and the girls were exhausted, even though there seemed like a million French, Spanish, German, and Italian students rampaging noisily through the hotel. The girls managed somehow to sleep through this. At about 11 or 11:30, I couldn't take the noise any more, grabbed my camera and tri-pod, and headed for the roof. There were some tables and wait service up there during the day, but I figured it would probably be empty now on such a chilly night.

When I got up there, I was out of breath from the nine flights of stairs I had climbed with the 40 pound camera bag and the nearly equally heavy tri-pod. I took the stairs because I didn't trust the hundred year old elevator, especially with all those rowdy students banging around the place. But what I found up on the twelfth floor was worth the hike. It was completely empty on the roof. I could see the whole city lit up, with that beautiful illuminated Duomo less than a hundred yards across the street. Absolutely beautiful. I had lots of film. I set the tri-pod up. I wanted to capture one of the most beautiful sights I had ever seen in my life. I knew I would be up there for hours.

I used both of my cameras, the Mamiya medium format and the Nikon F-4, interchanging them on the tri-pod every 15 minutes or so. And within twenty minutes I was in some surreal place. I was still snapping photographs, but I had transcended time. I could have been in the 16th century or I could have been in the 21st. The Milky Way was illuminated above me and the Duomo was illuminated next to me. Time stood still. I was alone, but I didn't feel alone. I felt extraordinarily happy. No, ecstatically happy. And not because I felt free again. And not because I loved my wife. And not because I loved my children. Just because I was alive, and amidst such beauty.

I was prepared to spend the entire night up there. I didn't want the feeling to ever end.

The quiet of the night was soon shattered by a group of teenagers who had found their way to the roof. I thought to myself, shit. I was just having this spiritual awakening and now these rowdy students, the same ones I tried to escape from, are going to wreck everything. Oh well, such is life. I should have expected it.

The students noticed what I was doing and respectfully sat down all the way across the rooftop. They were speaking a language I couldn't quite pick out. It sort of sounded like Italian and it sort of sounded like Spanish. But it was neither. I would later find out they were Portuguese.

Although I thought they would bother me, they never did. I resumed looking through the camera lens and soon was transported back to my surreal, transcendent state. A few minutes later, while still looking through the lens, I heard the most beautiful flamenco-style guitar, beautiful soothing voices, and rhythmic hand clapping. They were singing Portuguese folk songs. Beautiful, melodic songs. I didn't understand the words, but I didn't need to. A perfect accompaniment for the feeling I was being bathed in.

The Portuguese students sang for the next two hours. I snapped my shutters for the next two hours. They were in harmony. I was in harmony. They were at complete peace with themselves. I was at complete peace with myself.

I was filled with a joy I had not felt in a very long time. I was glad to be alive again.

47 { Bella Vista

The bullet train passed a sign that said "Napoli, 10 km." We came down a rugged mountainside that hugged a beautiful turquoise-blue, Mediterranean bay. Soon we would be in Naples, where we would meet Giovanni, our driver for the next week of our fantasy Italian tour. Giovanni was to take us to Sorrento, and then to our hotel at a little village called Massa Lubrense.

The train sped down toward the coast and I grew excited. We were coming into Naples, the largest city in southern Italy and the subject of several famous romantic songs and movies. Poorer and less industrialized than Rome and northern Italy, southern Italy was reported to be much different than the north. The architecture was more Greek and even Arab influenced, the people more classically Mediterranean and sometimes Arab in their features, the food more vegetable and olive oil based, and the culture even more expressive and emotional. Outside of the cities, the pace of southern Italy was slower, much slower, and the weather warmer. I couldn't wait to get off the train.

The train slowed as we came through the suburbs and then crept as we entered into the downtown station. I had heard that downtown Naples was dirty and could be dangerous, so I had a trace of apprehension as we came to a stop. We pulled out our bags, Miah grabbed her stuffed Lupe, and we started to make our way down the crowded aisle in the middle of the train.

The expected happened, again, as it always did in Italy. "Bella bambina, bella bambina!" And soon Miah's head was being patted by some elder Italian woman, whose 80 years of life were chiseled regally across her face. They were all grandmothers in Italy. Miah's grandmothers.

"Americano?"

I smiled, not knowing exactly what to say. Stacy, of course, did. The reincarnated Italian was by now confident in her basic command of the language. "Si, Americano. Mi chiamo Stacy. Come sta?"

"Molto benne, grazie. Mi chiamo Francesca."

Stacy looked down and prodded Miah, her junior incarnate. "Mi chiamo Miah" said the tiny voice.

The elder woman smiled and we pushed through the line. Italians can get by with almost no personal body space, and we had to learn that no harm was meant by the close nudging and pushing. "Ah, si. La bella bambina. Che belezza!"

"Grazie." Stacy and I smiled. Shani didn't.

"Andiamo. Ciao, Signora. Ciao, bella Signorina."

Stacy bent down to the junior incarnate. "Miah, say goodbye. Say ciao."

"Ciao," said the tiny voice.

"Arrivaderci," said the elder grandmother.

Shani and I rolled our eyes at each other. We couldn't compete with Stacy's Italian. My Italian was embarrassing. I was reduced to only a few words I knew I could pronounce, namely buon giorno, grazie, and ciao. If I couldn't respond with one of those three words, I was cooked.

We pushed and bumped our way through the line, our bags knocking against people's backs and buttocks. This would be rude in America. But not here.

We emerged from the train and a handsome, forty something man with graying hair and warm eyes hurried toward Stacy. He took her hand as he spoke. In America this would be perceived as a threat, or a come-on. But not here.

"Ah, Signora Stacy? Hello! I am Giovanni!"

"Giovanni, it's so nice to meet you after talking on the phone! Come sta!"

"Buono, buono!"

I came up quickly, feeling a tad jealous. "Hi Giovanni!"

"You must be Garrett. Welcome to Napoli."

"How did you know it was us, I mean there are so many people coming off the train?"

Giovanni laughed. "You can always tell, the Americans at least. Look at all your camera equipment. I can tell, well at least I can with you. Now Stacy, she's different. She looks Italian. Tell me, are your people Italian?"

"No, they're Jewish, Russian Jewish, actually."

"Ah, Jewish!" Giovanni smiled and grabbed her hand again. My very best customers have been the Jewish Americans. So generous, and so thoughtful."

I was sure Giovanni was playing us. Charming and smooth, already setting the stage to milk us out of every dime we had. Pretty paranoid, Garrett. Bad side effect from growing up in Los Angeles.

Even recognizing my paranoia, I still wasn't sure about Giovanni. And this thing about holding Stacy's hand, I'm not sure I'm going to like that. My paranoid self would think this way about Giovanni for the next hour or two, but then I would change my mind. I didn't know it just yet, but Giovanni was about to become our friend. And he was about to change our lives.

Giovanni approached our children. "Ah Signorina Shani. Come sta?"

"Bene. It's nice to meet you." Shani was friendly, but a little reserved and wary of the emotionality we were seeing. Just like me.

And then Giovanni's eyes shifted over to Miah. And with one great big, fell swoop, he scooped her up and held her as high in the air as he could. Before Stacy could intervene and say, "She doesn't like that," it was too late. But this time Miah didn't seem uncomfortable. Giovanni had melted her.

"Ah, la bella bambina! Miah. And her pet Lupe!" He took Lupe and nuzzled the stuffed silver-blue dog into Miah's face.

Miah smiled, then giggled. Melted.

"Come! We have much to see and do! Italia is waiting for us!" Shani and Stacy went for the suitcases. "No! No! Scuzi, Signora. Scuzi, signorina. Garrett and I will take these. Come! My car is just over there."

Giovanni scurried us to a sleek, immaculately clean "D" series Mercedes. Wow. We would be touring southern Italia in style.

"Maybe the three Signorinas could sit in back, there's plenty of room, while Garrett and I discuss our plans in front." Giovanni peered over the back seat and extended his arm to pat Lupe. "Hello, hello, Lupe. Bella Miah? Would you and Lupe and your sister Shani like to get some ice cream? It's called gelato here."

Miah nodded excitedly.

"Good. Strawberries are in season and they will be making strawberry gelato. We'll go to a place I know on the waterfront. But first, let's get out of here."

Giovanni accelerated extremely quickly and made a U-turn that made my head spin. We sped through the narrow downtown streets and soon were on a grand boulevard that hugged the waterfront. The city was not nearly as affluent as Rome or Florence, but it still had the bustling emotionality that seemed to characterize everything Italian.

"Garrett, so, this is your first trip to Italia?"

"Yes. I'm so excited to be here."

"Stacy told me on the phone that you love to take the photographs. I see you have a very large camera bag. You must have an awfully big camera."

Shit. I had tried so hard to find a generic looking backpack that wouldn't be an instant give away that I had expensive camera equipment. Am I that obvious? Do I look that much like a tourist? And then there's Stacy behind me, practicing her Italian in the back seat. She not only looks Italian, she acts it, she passes for it, she blends right in. This is cruel. I'm supposed to be the experienced traveler here, seven countries in Asia, three times in Africa, Jamaica once, not to mention Canada and Mexico a bunch of times. Damn it!

I regained my focus. "Well, there's actually two cameras in there."

"Oh, two cameras? Very impressive."

"Yeah, I have a Nikon F-4 and a Mamiya medium format."

"Oh, you have the 645? That's a nice one. And I know the F-4, too. Which one you like better?"

"The 645 medium format. Because it's more simple, less automated, it's more like an art using it." Hey, maybe this Giovanni guy is all right after all. He seems to know his "camera speak."

Giovanni leaned over the seat to whisper to me. No one noticed in the back seat, because Stacy was conducting an Italian lesson with the girls. "Garrett. We will show Stacy and the girls a wonderful time. They will see all the sights, and they will learn all about our culture. But you and me, we'll have a different mission. Si, si, mi amico. You will see all the sights too. But you see, my new friend, I used to be a photographer years ago. And you already know Italia is a beautiful place. I will take you to places very few non

Italians know about, some places that are never photographed by people outside my country. And you know, the lighting is very important, the sun must be hidden or low and just right to take the beautiful image. I will make sure you have lots of beautiful images from my country. And when you get home, you can send me your best one from Italia, and your best one from your home country for my bedroom. My wife and I, we just re... how you say, remodel it, and it needs some pieces of art. Capisce?"

"Ah, ah, si."

"Oh and one more thing, Signore Garrett. We must work on your Italian. You see, your wife, Signora Stacy, is shaming you! We cannot let this happen." Giovanni smiled, and extended his hand to make a pact. It was a strong, firm handshake. The kind my dad taught me signaled someone you could trust.

I didn't know what to make of Giovanni. He was so forward, so self assured, so smooth, but yet he seemed so sincere. And intuitive as to what our needs and personalities were. In America there would be no doubt he was a smooth con. But here, I couldn't make that assumption. The Italians were forward and confident, but the people I had met so far were also absolutely trustworthy. And I had no reason to believe that Giovanni was any different.

Giovanni pulled into a roadside stand and ordered four strawberry gelato. I took out some money to pay but Giovanni pushed my hand away. "My treat."

"Thank you, Giovanni."

"No, no, no! Our pact! Our pact! You say, 'mille grazie' meaning, 'thank you very much.' And I say, 'Prego!' or, 'You're welcome.' Capisce?"

"Millay Grat- zee"

Giovanni laughed. "You'll get better." And I started to relax a little.

We finished our ice cream, er, ah, gelato, and were soon on the expressway heading south of the city. When we came into the southern suburbs we saw a gigantic volcanic mountain off in the distance to our northeast.

"Ah, it's a clear sky today. That's Vesuvius in the background. You often cannot see it because of the haze. But today you can. You know the story already. In 79 AD it erupted, covering a whole city, Pompeii, in ash and lava. We'll be seeing Pompeii in a few days. The eruption killed thousands of people. Most people think they were killed by the lava or the gas, but that is not correct. Do you know what killed them?"

Everyone paused, as we all just assumed the lava or gas killed everyone.

I offered a weak response. "The heat?"

"No, no, not that. The people were foolish. They heard the beginnings of the eruptions and had time to get out, but they didn't. Did you know no animals were found in the remains? They all were smart enough to get out."

"So what killed everyone, if it wasn't the heat, the lava, or the gas?"

"All of the people, they suffocated first. You see, an explosion and fire of that great size takes all the oxygen out of the air for many, many kilometers. When the people realized it was time to escape there was no oxygen left. The people, they just dropped from exhaustion and then they suffocated. It was too bad for them. Then, later, the ash and lava came, and it covered everything."

Giovanni had a flair for making everything interesting. We got off the freeway and soon were on a narrow, winding road that hugged the Mediterranean shoreline. The coast was beautifully cut with numerous fjord-like inlets and rugged cliffs that dropped off right into the sea. I thought to myself, Oh my God, this is going to be the best photo shoot of my life.

Giovanni read my mind. "This would be a great place to take a photo, no? The sun is just right now, it's still morning and not too high. Here. I pull you over for a shoot."

I thought the words before I could say them. Pull us over? Here? We're on a three thousand foot cliff with no guard rail, two tiny lanes that would barely pass for one in America and you're going 80 kilometers per hour, lets see, that's 50 mph. OK, let's spin out of control and go over the edge of the cliff. And if that doesn't kill us, I'm certain to get hit by a car taking the photograph...

"Giovanni, we don't have to do this just yet, we're all tired, you must be tired, I'm sure there'll be other..."

"No no no. Ma che! Non faccio lo stupido! This is not a problem!" Giovanni decelerated as quickly as he had gained speed, and we pulled off the road on the edge of some cliff. I thought if this was any car but a Mercedes we'd all be dead. Half the car was still hanging out in the right lane, however, with cars beeping their horns and whizzing by.

The view was gorgeous, but I was pretty sure that this was going to be the last photo I ever took. I opened the door and saw the cliff's edge.

"Careful, mi amico, the cliff is right there."

No shit, Giovanni. I opened the door and had about one foot leeway before I would fall to my death.

"Go on, go on, the sun is just right now. Take your time. Don't let us rush your masterpiece!"

I hugged the car as I got out and set up the tri-pod in front of the car. Giovanni stepped out also, and was enjoying the view while propped against the hood of the car. Although he wore an expensive suit, he looked totally calm, totally relaxed, all of the time.

I looked through the lens to compose my shot. The vista was even more spectacular through the lens, as I had my 80 – 200mm zoom lens attached. I could see the beautiful little villages dotting the coastline as far as the lens could see, the horizon peppered with glistening white and gold domes that identified all the five and six hundred year old churches and cathedrals that each little village seemed to have. I snapped the shutter, once, twice, five, twenty-five, forty-five times in all directions.

"Bella vista, no?" I could hear Giovanni as I was finally finished and took the camera off the tri-pod.

"Bel-la vista!" I got the pronunciation almost right, but it didn't roll off my lips, like Stacy could do. I sure didn't know what that meant, but I wanted to please Giovanni.

Giovanni smiled. "You do not know the meaning of that, do you?"

"Sure I do," I smiled coyly. It means "Good image."

Stacy chimed in from the back seat. "Nice try. It means, 'beautiful view.'"

"Shameful!" Giovanni shook his head playfully. He took the tri-pod and put his free arm around my shoulder. "We must fix your Italian immediately. We will have lessons for you everyday." Giovanni laughed. You could tell he was enjoying us already. I relaxed some more. Maybe he wasn't a con after all.

We drove down the side of the mountain and suddenly were in a wealthy, bustling, sophisticated little town. All of the people were well dressed, and it seemed like all of them were talking loudly on cell phones. It looked and sounded like an organized chaos, with all the activity, the car horns, the beautiful clothes, the cell phones, and the lunchtime smells.

"Welcome to Sorrento!"

Stacy was ecstatic. "Sorrento. I've dreamed about this place my whole life. Sorrento! Shani, look at all these shops. Oh my, are we going to have some fun here! Think of the purses and shoes we are going to buy."

Giovanni pulled the car to the curb abruptly.

"More photo shots for Garrett?" Stacy inquired.

"No, Senora Stacy. Time for you to stretch your feet a little. Just for a little while, and then we'll have some lunch."

Stacy and Shani were growing excited. The thought of shopping for Italian shoes could fuel them for days at a time. "So, we'll meet you back here in fifteen or twenty minutes?"

Giovanni laughed. Senora Stacy, you are not in America anymore, this is Italia. Slow down, take your time. See you in two or three hours."

"Are you guys coming, I mean, shopping with us?"

Giovanni let out a loud, guttural laugh. "Senora, we don't want to kill your husband, do we? Three hours of shopping will kill him! No, we will go off on our own." Giovanni popped the trunk with his remote. "Signor Garrett, go get your camera and tri-pod."

"Magnifico!" I thought I had made this word up, but it actually was correct Italian. And I had said it with proper Italian inflexion and enthusiasm.

"Ah, mi amico, I see there is hope for you now. Lets' go! Andiamo!"

"Andiamo!"

Giovanni took the tri-pod from me and began to escort me down some narrow cobblestone alley toward the waterfront. He looked back over his shoulder toward Stacy.

"Oh, Senora Stacy. Try to put everything on your card. It's safer that way, and you'll get the best exchange."

Giovanni pulled his head in toward mine and whispered, as if he was confiding privileged information. "The women, Garrett, they just love to shop. What is this thing they have with shoes? My wife, she must have thirty pairs."

"I don't know, Giovanni. But it's not just an Italian thing."

Three hours and seventeen minutes later Giovanni and I returned from our hike. I had been dressed for it, like an American tourist, while Giovanni had made the trek in a fine Italian suit and dress shoes. He didn't seem to mind one bit. In my pocket were five rolls of exposed film, 180 shots that I had taken in three hours. Giovanni had taken me through the back streets of Sorrento, and I had lots of shots of narrow streets with beautiful pots, vases, and hanging baskets on the patios and balconies. Wisteria was blooming everywhere, with their purple grape like flowers hanging down from the vines. We had been on the veranda of some wealthy estate, where I had got some more great shots of the rugged coastline, this time looking up into the cliffs instead of down. We had been along the beach. We had seen some magnificent old churches. I had been in photography heaven for over three hours.

The girls were patiently waiting in the warm Mediterranean sun when we arrived back at Giovanni's car. They each had shopping bags full of shoes and blouses. We had been with Giovanni only a handful of hours and already the experience was completely magical. He was a perfect fit for our family. And I finally let go of my paranoia.

We went to a nice restaurant. When we got there, Giovanni kept using the word "fresco" when talking to the waitress. I asked Stacy what that meant, and she said "fresh, the way he's using it I think he's telling the waitress we would like fresh vegetable dishes that are in season." I was in awe of the reincarnated Italian.

We sat down, and Giovanni, without asking us, ordered vino for the four of us. That's right, eleven year old Shani was old enough to have wine in Italy! We discretely told her to politely pass on the wine. She wanted no part of it, anyway.

The wine came in a big pitcher. "Vino de la casa!" Stacy rolled off with perfect inflexion.

Giovanni poured the wine and raised his glass for a toast. "This is to the Turkes on their first trip to Italia! And before your adventure with Giovanni begins, you must promise me one thing, that you will come back again and again to Italia."

Stacy teared up. It was as if she had returned home.

The lunch was spectacular. Colorful and bountiful. Fresh asparagus, artichokes, pesto, mushrooms, garlic, pasta, seafood, and an assortment of fruit. And two "bowls" of wine, as Giovanni called them. Stacy and I were somewhat drunk when the meal ended. But it didn't matter. We didn't have to drive, and we didn't have a worry in the world. I had left Michigan seven days ago. It might as well have been 7 years ago, or 7 centuries ago for that matter.

We left Sorrento and drove along the rocky coast. "You see the real Italia here. You see how beautiful she is." Giovanni was so proud of his homeland. The sun was low on the horizon now, and glistening over the Mediterranean.

"Soon we will be in Massa Lubrense, which is the village next to mine. I will pick you up at 8:30 every morning, we will have great adventures, have a nice lunch, then I will bring you back to the hotel every evening about six or seven. They will have a nice dinner and some wine for you each night. They have a beautiful antipasto each night, and it all comes with your room free. So. I am thinking you might like one day on the Isle of Capri, where the Emperor Tiberius used to vacation, there you will see the rich Italians, maybe, how you say, your American movie stars, and the Grotto D'Azure, the Blue Grotto. And I think we will have one day to see Positano, very, very beautiful there. And of course a day at Pompeii, and a day where we go to this pizza place in the mountains where they make Limoncello, Stacy you know, the lemon liquor that is famous to this region. And I'm thinking a day or two where we go wherever you want to go, maybe to Sicily or to Paestum, where the Greek ruins are. You know the Greek ruins in Italia are better preserved than they are in Greece? The Romans, when they conquered the Mediterranean region, destroyed the Greek temples and architecture everywhere except in Italia. There also have been less tourist pressures here, and they are very careful to preserve them."

Stacy and my eyes grew huge. We were already having the trip of a lifetime, and this was beyond what we were even able to imagine. Selfishly, I did a quick mental calculation of how many rolls of film I had left. I was going to go crazy down here with Giovanni. I had started with 40 rolls and had about 25 left. Stacy thought I was crazy to bring that much. But I would arrive back in Michigan having used every roll but one.

Giovanni pulled into the circular driveway of the Bella Vista Hotel, owned by the Francischiello family. Built into the cliffs overlooking the Mediterranean, it had a spectacular view. Giovanni quickly summoned some hotel staff to get our bags, and soon he was escorting us inside the hotel. It was a beautiful, but unpretentious, family-owned hotel. The hotel staff, seemingly all of them, raced up to greet us. The most maternal looking one, probably the mother in the family, came up to Stacy and me. "La famiglia Turke, si?"

"Si si, signora," said Stacy. "Mi chiamo Stacy."

"Mi chiamo Garrett." I was growing more confident.

"Mi chiamo Shani."

Miah didn't get a chance to speak. "La bella bambina, bella bella bella bambina!!" She reached over to Miah and hugged her. What is it with these people? Shani and I glanced at each other and rolled our eyes once again. Miah had a smug little grin on her face.

Giovanni led the hotel staff to our room. They put our bags up against the wall of our huge, rectangular shaped room. Giovanni tipped the wait staff and they left. Giovanni had a huge grin on his face as he walked over to the windows. The curtains were closed, and Giovanni wanted Stacy positioned properly before he opened them.

"Signora, this is one of their best rooms, and I will show you why." He pulled open the curtains, exposing an incredible sunset view of the Isle of Capri. The sunset was glistening red and maroon off the white limestone cliffs that flanked the island.

"Every night you will see this, and every morning the sunrise will reflect a blue color off the island. You like it? Well, I will see you in the morning, at around 8:30. Bella sera."

Stacy started crying. Shani and Miah were staring out the window at the mesmerizing view.

I was already on the balcony setting up my tri-pod.

48 { For Giovanni

The early morning sun was coming up over the horizon, splashing its rays onto the two thousand foot limestone cliffs that flanked the east side of Capri. I centered my tri-pod in the middle of the balcony and looked through the lens to compose my shot. As I focused the lens, I saw a beautiful white domed villa hugging a nearby cliff in the foreground, with Capri across the bay in the background. The island's cliff's were a bluish purple color and glistening, just as Giovanni had described. "La bella vista," I whispered to myself, and I snapped off twelve shots, each at a different focal length.

It was Thursday, and nearing the end of our trip. We had been with Giovanni for the past five days, with three more to go. Normally I would begin to feel twinges of sadness as a vacation started to draw to a close. But not on this one. Giovanni had made each day seem like it had a week's worth of activities in it, without racing or pressuring us. The last three days still held many adventures to come. I had been totally rejuvenated here.

Giovanni had made this place seem like a second home to us. And each day, Stacy would talk to Giovanni about the cost of living and how much it would be to rent an apartment or small house up in the mountains overlooking Sorrento. She loved Italia. No, there was no sadness about the vacation winding down. I knew we were going to come back some day.

I didn't think about my dad as I pondered the last few days of our trip. I hadn't thought about him at all since the second day in Rome.

I snapped my last image; finally secure that at least one of my twelve shots would come out the way I wanted it. Fact of the matter was that eleven of the twelve would come out perfectly. It was hard to mess up here. And I was a much better photographer than I gave myself credit for.

The Mamiya signaled the end of the roll and I rewound the film canister. I popped it out of the back of the camera and started dismantling the tri-pod. As I did this, I saw Giovanni pull into the hotel driveway below. He was an hour early, like he always was. He would go into the hotel restaurant and have cappuccino each morning until we were ready to go.

I collected my camera equipment and nestled the Mamiya inside the camera bag as if it was an infant being placed in a crib. I gently pulled open the sliding glass door and crept back inside quietly so as not to wake the girls. The sun streamed though the glass and caught Stacy's face. I paused for a second, fixed upon her. Thirty-seven year old Stacy still looked twenty-seven. What a beauty. I can't believe I am married to her! I was still some lonely, shy, awkward teenager inside my mind. I couldn't believe that someone like Stacy would have even considered marrying someone like me. Lord, what did I do to deserve her?

There had been many times in my life where I felt that life's material luxuries and rewards had passed me by. We didn't have the magnificent, showcase home. There were no Cadillacs or Mercedes in our driveway. I had a difficult, often painful, usually thankless job trying to repair years of abuse and neglect in the children and families I saw. There was no glamour in my life, and, by American dream standards, I sometimes thought I had failed to attain the good life.

But on this moment, with the sun streaming across Stacy's face, I knew I had the greatest gift of all. My fortune was always there, on the faces of my wife and children. Nothing else really mattered. Relationships are everything. I said a prayer to myself. Thank you, Lord, for helping me realize again what is important and what is not.

The alarm went off and Stacy smiled as she opened her eyes. She said what she always said every morning in Massa Lubrense, as each day I had been out on that balcony when the sun came up. "Get some good shots, honey?"

"I hope so." I wasn't feigning modesty. I really didn't know how any of my shots would come out until the film was developed.

As Stacy got the girls up, I carefully put the used roll of film away inside the room's refrigerator. I had a certain ritual I went through with exposed film. Put the roll inside two sealed zip-locks, then inside a black, x-ray proof bag, then inside a black hard-sided plastic container, then inside a large zip lock bag, then inside a cooler, then back inside the refrigerator. I had anticipated every possible catastrophe that could befall my precious film:

heat, light, water, x-rays, theft, and being crushed. I had all the disasters covered. I guarded the film like I did my children.

I put the most recent roll of film away, respecting the prescribed ritual. As I did this, I saw the now five plastic containers, each holding six rolls of spent film. The containers were all marked, with nostalgic reminders of the days passed. I smiled greedily as I read the labels. I knew I had plenty for the L'Images Di Italia show at Verna's gallery. "Roma, Firenze, Sorrento, Amalfi, Positano, Ravello, Massa Lubrense, Capri, Vesuvius, Pompeii, Vietri sul Marie." And there was still more to come. Today we would go to Paestum. Giovanni had promised us a life changing experience. And he was always true to his word.

It seemed like it took forever to get the girls ready for the day, but in real time only 45 minutes passed before we were in the hotel restaurant having coffee and rolls for breakfast. Breakfast always seemed to be Miah's favorite meal in Italy, as she loved bread. The waitress smiled as she placed one basket of bread in the middle of our table, and another one in front of Miah, just for her. Then the customary pat on the head, the customary smile, and the expected words. "Bella bambina."

Giovanni came over to the table. It was 8:20. Although always relaxed, he was always very punctual. "So, Senorina Miah, buon giorno. Are you and Lupe ready to go to Paestum?"

Miah nodded and smiled, her mouth stuffed with bread.

"I will let you finish your breakfast and then I will be waiting for you just outside in the Mercedes." Giovanni then bent over and whispered to me. "Signore Garrett. Today I promise you, your best day yet in Italia. You will have one of the greatest moments. Beyond your greatest imagination."

Giovanni was anxious to get started. He seemed as excited on these adventures as we were. I was so excited now I could hardly stand it. Giovanni hadn't failed us on any of his promises yet.

We hurried to finish our breakfast and packed up the remaining rolls for Miah to eat later. If she didn't like the lunch menu, she could be happily sustained all day on bread and juice. As we left our breakfast table to make our way out the hotel entrance, it seemed as if the entire Francischiello family approached us to send us off. "Buon giorno, signore, buon giorno, signora. Buon vaggio!"

Giovanni had pulled the Mercedes right up to the curb. You could hear his tape of "Vaggio Italiano", by Andrea Bocelli, as he opened passenger door to let Stacy and the girls in.

"Bocelli?" I inquired.

"Si, Garrett. You know him?"

"We have all his albums, I think."

"Maybe not this one. It might be hard to find in the States. This one has all the old Italian classics on it. "Santa Lucia, O sole mio, Core n' grato. Today we shall listen to it, si?"

"Si." And with that, we were off on another adventure, Bocelli, Giovanni, and his adopted Turke family. We were heading south today, through the now familiar Amalfi Coast, through Positano and Vietri sul Marie, through Salerno, and down to Paestum.

I was excited. Paestum was the home of twenty five hundred year old Greek ruins, which supposedly were extremely well preserved, away from the pollution of the big cities and even away from most tourist pressures. Giovanni also told us that Paestum was in the center of Italy's buffalo mozzarella cheese industry, and that we would be buying bread and a softball sized block of fresh buffalo mozzarella cheese for lunch. I could hardly wait.

About an hour down the rugged coast, Bocelli had finished his last encore, and Giovanni turned off the stereo. I knew what was coming. Each morning Giovanni turned off the stereo and gave us an Italian lesson. The outcome would always be the same. Stacy would master the phrase and pronunciation perfectly, and I would butcher at least 50% of the words, sometimes so badly that it was impossible to understand even a hint of what I was supposed to be saying. But Giovanni had expressed great confidence in me, and said I was improving. I was his loyal apprentice.

"So today, Garrett, we will practice some words and then you will go into a store and order a loaf of bread for our lunch." I felt a surge of anxiety, but pushed it back down.

"I'm going to order the bread? Me, in a store, ordering some bread...?"

Giovanni finished my sentence for me. "By yourself. We shall be anxiously awaiting your return in the Mercedes."

"By myself."

"Si, Garrett. You can do it. You must have confidence in yourself!"

For the next hour Giovanni drilled me on the phrase, "Vorrei il pane, per favore." Translation: "I would like a piece (loaf) of bread, please." And then I would say, "Quanto costa?" or, "how much is it?" I had already decided I would give the clerk so large a bill that I wouldn't have to worry about being short.

"Giovanni, that's really easy. Even I can do that." And for the next hour or so, I would periodically sing out, "Vorrei il pane, per favore. Quanto costa?" Giovanni was going to be so proud of me. "Vorrei il pane! Vorrei il pane! Quanto costa, quanto costa?!" And then my crowning glory, which caught Giovanni completely off guard. "Parlo l'Italiano!" (I speak Italian!)

Giovanni beamed. His elementary Italian student had passed his class. "Well, Signora Stacy, do you think Signore Garrett is ready to buy our lunch?"

"He's as ready as he's going to be."

Giovanni drove a few more minutes, then came off the road at a little village. He parked the Mercedes next to an unpretentious little bakery. "Here is a little store, how you say it, a bake store, that bakes the bread, fresco, every day. You go in and ask for a piece of bread."

I nodded dutifully. The master was going to be proud of me. One last rehearsal before I go in. Proudly, and in my very best Italian, I said what I thought were the magic words, "Vorrei il pane, per favore. Quanto costa?"

Giovanni burst into uncontrollable laughter. He was like a little kid. He'd try to suppress it for a few seconds but then would erupt again uncontrollably. Finally he composed himself, but only a little.

"Garrett, my friend, I have come to love you, but..." Giovanni erupted in laughter again. He couldn't stop.

"What, what? What I do? What I do? Votrei il pane, quanto costa, quanto costa! What's the matter? Perfecto, perfecto!!!"

"No perfecto! No perfecto!! What you say is... what you say..." Giovanni couldn't even get it out. He was laughing so hard I thought he was going to have a seizure. And now Stacy and Shani were laughing hard in the back seat.

"What did Dad say, Mom?"

"What did he say, Giovanni?"

"He say....he say..." Giovanni couldn't get it out. He was holding his side he was laughing so hard.

"He say..." Giovanni still couldn't do it.

Then Giovanni took a deep breath and blurted it fast enough to get the whole sentence out before erupting again.

"He say, 'I'm going to kill you by stabbing!!!!'"

Now the whole car was laughing uncontrollably, even Miah.

"I can still do it! I'm going inside for the bread."

"No, my friend, I can't let you do that. The carabinieri will come for you!" Giovanni opened the door and started walking toward the bakery entrance. He started laughing out loud again before he even reached the door.

Giovanni returned with the bread, a big, crusty Italian loaf. "Now we must go to the mozzarella store." He was still giggling periodically.

We got back on the highway and soon got off again, stopping at what looked a lot like a green Burger King or McDonalds. "This is the buffalo mozzarella store. They are very popular, and they are all over southern Italia. All they sell is the buffalo cheese. I'll come back with our 2 kilos of mozzarella."

I opened the passenger door. "I'm coming in with you!"

Giovanni burst into laughter. "Oh no you're not!"

"Oh yes I am!" And I got all the way out of the car.

"Well OK my friend, but you must promise me one thing. You must promise not to open your mouth in the store. Not even a single word!" Giovanni started giggling again.

In the store we continued to embarrass ourselves, giggling with each other like a couple of 10 year old boys. We laughed again in line when the person in front of us said, "Quanto costa?" The clerk and the other people in line looked at us like we were a couple of lunatics.

Giovanni and I would laugh about this day for the rest of our lives. I had bonded with him over this one incident. I would consider him my friend forever.

We continued on our journey to Paestum. Giovanni instructed me to tear off a big hunk of bread for everyone, then top it with some of the cheese. I asked him what could I slice the cheese with. He started laughing uncontrollably again. "There's a... there's a ... there is a knife in that compartment!" He didn't need to add another line. It was already a joke. The whole car would laugh all the way to Paestum.

The afternoon at Paestum brought wonder and enchantment. Giovanni had made good on his promise. Paestum was not only incredible, it wasn't even crowded. Just a few groups of well behaved students on field trips. The ruins stretched out for several football fields in all directions. Huge, magnificent salmon colored buildings made from marble, incredibly intact given their age. The Temple of Neptune. The Temple of Ceres. Virtually empty. I could take all the shots I wanted with no tourists in the image.

Giovanni nudged me. "Go on, go on. Be free. I will walk the girls through. We will see you at the end of the day. Just don't speak to anyone!" Giovanni and I started giggling again.

I glanced over at Stacy. "You heard him, Garrett. Go on, you're free."

And with that I spent the whole afternoon in wonderland. I was transported back in time, two thousand, six hundred years ago. And while I could have felt like a fly-spec next to the gigantic marble pillars, I didn't. I felt connected to everything good about life again. My mind was clear. My mind was transcended. My mind was free.

One hundred ninety six shots later, I found Stacy and the girls on a bench, eating some gelato. Giovanni had headed back to the Mercedes, ready to pull it around to pick us up.

"Isn't this place incredible? I can't believe there's almost nobody here. Nice shots?"

"I can't even begin to tell you where I've been."

Stacy didn't quite get it. "Well, we knew you were in there, somewhere."

"That's not what I meant. It sounds stupid, but I really wasn't here all afternoon."

Stacy thought I was just being dramatic. It didn't bother me that she didn't quite understand.

On the long ride back to Masssa Lubrense, the girls fell asleep in the back seat. I fell asleep for awhile, then woke up from a bump on the road.

"Hey, Giovanni."

"Si. Garrett?"

"You were right. This has been my greatest day in Italia. That promise you made, about Paestum, you were right, it was beyond my greatest imagination."

"I'm glad for you, amico. But Paestum was not what I was referring to. We are on our way to the place beyond your imagination right now."

I couldn't speak. What could possibly top what I just experienced?

"I have timed this just right. When we get there, the sun will be low."

Two hours later we were coming back into the Amalfi region. We climbed back up the cliffs I had grown accustomed to all week. I was beginning to feel disappointed. This magical place must have been something we had already passed before on our other excursions.

I was right. We would be stopping at a place we had already passed. Lots of times. But I had never really seen it. You couldn't see it, from the road. Giovanni pulled off the road just before a large bridge that hugged the cliff. The back seat woke up as we rattled to a stop on a dirt driveway that dead-ended into the mountainside.

"Hurry, hurry. Get your tri-pod and cameras. We must beat the sun. Stacy, you hold Miah's hand. Be careful, Shani. Be careful, here. The rocks are slippery."

Giovanni led us down a short path, until we were level with the bridges arch. "Now look to your right."

We all stood there with our mouths open. No words were necessary.

After a few minutes Giovanni explained where we were. "This is a fishing village. You cannot see it from the road. Almost no one knows it's here. It's so small it doesn't have any name. It's just a few families. They have been fishing here for hundreds of years."

The village was about four or five stone dwellings built into the cliff. They had a light salmon and adobe colored finish, and were several stories tall. Below them were a score of small, but incredibly brightly colored fishing boats, blue, red, and yellow. They were all pulled up from a dried out lagoon, which Giovanni said filled up when the tide came in. The image was startling and beautiful. It was like those National Geographic shots of the classic Italian fishing boats. Only this was better than any image I had ever seen in any magazine or gallery. There was nothing like this village anywhere on earth.

My hands were shaking so hard I couldn't get the camera mounted atop the tri-pod.

"You don't have to worry mi amico. It's not going anywhere. Besides, it's too early yet. We have at least ten minutes."

My nerves calmed enough to get the camera mounted. I ran through my mental checklist. Lens open and cleaned. Check. Focal point. F32, I want everything in focus. Check. Shutter speed. Better be set extremely slow, there's not much light in here. Check. Good thing there's no wind to shake the tri-pod. Then the ground shook a little, jarring the tri-pod. Shit, the cars coming across the bridge rattle the tri-pod down here. Don't worry, it's not that often. OK. Shutter speed. Oh my, the meter shows we need a shutter speed of 4 seconds. Whoa. It will be hard to keep the tri-pod still that long.

"Signore, Garrett? Your shutter speed, you won't need it that slow."

What does he know? Hey, I've got to get this exactly right. How does he know what the meter says? "Why do you say that, Giovanni?"

"You'll see in about two or three more minutes. Patience."

What's going to happen? The tides going to come in or something? There was so much drama in the anticipation I could barely stand it.

"Here it comes!" And with those words the miracle unfolded. The sun had come down below the bridge, and was streaming through the arch. It was surreal, the single most beautiful image my eyes had ever seen, or ever will.

"This will be your masterpiece, Garrett. There will be no one on this earth that will have a shot like this, I am pretty sure of it."

"The light will stay like this for 15 minutes. Take your time. Italia says she is yours today."

I took the image every way I knew how. Long depth of field, short depth of field. Fast shutter, slow shutter. Polarized filter, UV filter, no filter. Nikon F-4 and Mamiya 645.

After 15 minutes, it was over. The light was gone. I popped the film out of the camera backs and clutched them all the way back to the hotel.

Although we would have two more days with Giovanni, including a wonderful pizza dinner high up in the mountains over Naples and a day at the Castle at Caserta, nothing could come close to the moment at that tiny fishing village.

We had come to Italy as strangers seeking some respite from life's responsibilities and the pain that came from caring for my dad. We left Italy belonging to her.

Giovanni would remain our friend. He would call us every holiday when we got back to the States. I would laugh with him each time he called. "Vorrei il pane."

Two months after our return, I had a big display at Verna's gallery. I called it what I had always dreamed I would call it, "L'Images di Italia," or "The Images of Italy." Although I had many images I was proud of, the Duomo at night in Florence, the ruins at Paestum, the cliffs overlooking Sorrento, the images of Capri off our balcony, and the street scenes in Rome, my showcase image was a huge 30"x 40" printing of the little fishing village on the Amalfi Coast.

The fishing village image at Verna's gallery was my second printing. The first print was already on the wall of Giovanni's bedroom.

I titled the photograph: "For Giovanni."

We will see you again, my friend.

49 { Return to Earth

It was cold and cloudy the morning of our return from Italy. It had been a long drive home from Detroit's Metro Airport. As we pulled into our driveway, there were still remnants of the spring snowstorm that had blanketed Michigan two weeks before. We had been in a subtropical paradise on the Amalfi Coast just 30 hours before and now this. An abrupt return to the Michigan "spring," which in most places would still be called "winter." Back to the clouds and the cold. Back to work in a couple days. Back to my responsibilities as caregiver. Back to reality. Time to re-enter the orbit and return to earth.

All the makings of a quick plunge into post-partum depression were there, but I didn't succumb to it this time. Italy had cleansed me. I felt relaxed. I felt that our connection to Italy was just beginning, not ending. I felt like a part of my family again. I didn't feel so all alone. It was all right to be back. And I was ready to go again.

As I started to unload the suitcases from the back of the van, I realized that I hadn't really thought of Dad for the past two weeks. Now, no less than five minutes after being home, I was starting to preoccupy myself with thoughts of Dad again. He no doubt had missed me. Everyday he probably got up and wondered where I was, until Tiffanie or Mom reminded him that I was on vacation.

I wondered how Tiffanie had done with Dad's care giving. I was sure that had been difficult, too. As I thought about Dad, I wondered when the resentment and the fear and the thoughts of him being dead would return to haunt me. But they didn't return on this day. All I could think about was how much I had missed my dad. I wanted to get over to see him as soon as I could.

"Thinking about your Dad, honey?" Stacy interrupted my thoughts as she locked her hand in mine.

"Yeah, how did you know?"

"Well, you've been standing behind the back of the van, just staring into space for the past couple minutes."

We lugged the heavy suitcases inside and down the basement steps to the laundry room. After sorting the dirty clothes and starting the laundry, I came upstairs to find a mountain of mail awaiting me on the kitchen table. It was sorted into two piles, our mail that the neighbor kids had brought in, and Dad's mail that Tiffanie had collected from his PO Box. Atop Dad's pile was a sticky note from Tiff.

"Welcome back, Garrett! Call me right away about Dad. He's OK, but I am really worried about him. Love, Tiff"

I was hoping to take today off from any responsibilities and to ratchet things back up tomorrow, on Sunday. Guess again. Looks like I'm going back to work right now.

I quickly filled the kitchen garbage bag with three pounds of junk mail that I had angrily ripped up. At the bottom of Dad's pile were the legitimate letters, including two from Arthur, five bills, and two strange looking letters were addressed in Dad's handwriting. Both of these letters had "Return to Sender, Address Undeliverable" stamped on them.

I looked at the letters more closely. They appeared to have been sent by Dad, because I recognized his handwriting. One was addressed to "Mr. George 'Goober' Lindsey, care of TV-Land, Channel 45, Hollywood." The other was addressed to "Mr. Rod Steiger, in care of TBS, Channel 19, Hollywood."

Well, this is kind of odd. I guess I could understand what Dad was attempting to do with George Lindsey. He was an acquaintance of ours in Los Angeles who Dad met at a Hollywood party. "Goober" had been to our house a few times in L.A., and even once in Traverse City, when Dad arranged for him to star in a comedy at the Cherry County Playhouse for summer theatre. OK, OK. I can understand Dad wanting to get in touch with him, and the address, well, sort of a naïve attempt to locate him, tinged by Dad's disease.

But what about Rod Steiger? Rod Steiger, Rod Steiger....Wasn't he a famous actor from like the 1950's and 60's? But isn't he dead?

I called over to Stacy, who was making the girls a sandwich. "Hey Stacy, Isn't Rod Steiger a famous actor?"

"Yeah, honey. From the 50's and 60's. He starred in "On the Waterfront" and "In the Heat of the Night." Why do you ask?" Stacy approached the letter and picked it up.

"Looks like your Dad's at work again trying to make friends with famous people. He's gonna tell you that he knew him in LA, or had dinner with him in Singapore."

"Yeah, you're probably right. Think I should open it?" Up until now, I had always respected Dad's privacy with his mail, opening up his personal letters with him sitting right next to me. Unless there was some question of him being exploited by mail fraud.

"Garrett, I keep telling you. He's getting more and more impaired. You have power of attorney. I think you have to start opening his mail."

I didn't want to go there, as that meant Dad had fallen down another rung on the ladder. But Stacy was right, and this time I opened the letter.

I got the creeps even after reading just the first few lines. The grammar was intact, but there was nothing intact about the content:

"Dear Rod,

I've known you since we were young boys growing up in New York. I have always admired you and I consider myself a close friend to you. You have made a good life for yourself and you should be proud of your accomplishments. I understand that you are depressed right now and feel like you can't go on. Please, please, let's get some help for you! I can help you, if we just talk about it. I don't want you to kill yourself. You have so much to live for! I am sure you'll feel differently after we've talked awhile.

I saw you trying to take your own life in the ocean. Just walking out deeper and deeper, into the blackness, with the waves crashing against you. You are still a young man, please don't do it! I beg of you to reconsider!

I am here to help you. I can only hope and pray that this letter reaches you in time, before it's too late!

 Faithfully yours,

 Your friend and confidant,

 Walter"

"Oh my God, Stacy. This is so crazy."

"Honey, that image of him committing suicide in the ocean. I'm pretty sure that's a scene from one of his old movies."

"Huh?"

"Yeah, I think that might even be from On the Waterfront. One of his movies ends with Rod Steiger's character walking out into the ocean. It's implied that it's a suicide"

"How could Dad think..."

"Honey, you need to open the other letter. The one to Goober."

I didn't think twice about it this time. I opened the letter to George "Goober" Lindsey.

"Dear Goober,

How great it was to see you today! My oh my, you are looking good! Have you been exercising a lot? You look so young and so fit. How is your job going at the gas station? You've been working there a long time; I think they need to give you a raise!

Remember our parties that we used to have? Those were fun times. I'd like to do that again some time!

I hope you can come out and see me. Please write me back as soon as you get this. I miss you!

Your best friend,

Walter"

"Well this one isn't quite as disturbing." Denial and minimizing. I was doing what I always tried to do when I watched Dad fall down another rung.

"Honey, it's just as bizarre as the other letter. It's as if he saw them, personally, moments before he wrote these. Do you think he's hallucinating?"

"Stacy, can you finish the unpacking and the laundry? I have to..."

As usual, Stacy read my mind and I didn't have to finish the sentence. "Go. Call me when you get there."

Stacy hugged me but I didn't take the time to really hug her back. I was already preoccupied. I was back to work. Back to being the caregiver.

I called Tiffanie again. Still no answer. I left another message. "Hey Tiff and Don. We just got back. Its 12:15, and I'm heading over to Dad's. Call me over there when you get this."

I went downstairs and pulled Dad's present from Italy out from the suitcase. It was a marble replica of Michelangelo's David.

I came back upstairs to overhear Miah talking to Shani. "Shani, where's Dad going? We just got home."

"He has to take care of Grampy."

"Why does he have to go now?"

"Because Grampy needs him."

I said my perfunctory goodbyes and left out the door. I put the seatbelt around David to keep him from rolling off the seat.

Dad was already standing by the front door when I got there. "Come in! Come in! I was just watching, you know, I was just seeing our, our, our friend. Yes our friend on the, the thing that you, you know the whatchamacallit." Dad drew a large rectangle in the air with his index finger. "You know, the thingama.."

I pointed to the TV.

"Yeah, that's it! All of our old friends are there."

I went into the living room and saw the channel icon in the lower left part of the screen. He had discovered TV-Land when I was in Italy.

"There he is, there he is!" Dad sat down, absorbed and mesmerized by the images on the screen. "There he is, our friend, looking better than ever! My God, he hasn't aged a bit after all these years!" Dad was giddy with excitement. I was stunned, starring at the screen.

It was an episode of Mayberry RFD. From about 1964. Our friend, as Dad put it, was Andy Griffith's sidekick, Goober. Aka George Lindsey.

The phone rang, which was fortunate. I had to have some bearings on reality. Dad raced to get it. It apparently was Tiff.

"Hi there, sweety. Yes, yes, I'm doing fine. I'm just watching...our old friends here, on the whatchamacallit, with our friend, you know the one, he was gone and now he's back...yes, Garrett. Garrett is here again! So are you coming over to join us? Oh, OK, yes, love you too. Garrett, here, it's for you. It's your, ah, friend."

Tiff seemed almost out of breath. She was anxious. She raced to the point without any small talk. "Hi Garrett. Hope you had a nice time on vacation.

Thank God you're back. It was really rough with Dad. I had trouble with getting him to shave and to wash, you know I couldn't go in there and bathe him, Don was able to get him to shower a couple times…"

"I'm sorry. I'll get him to shave and wash today."

"No, no, that's OK, that's not it, there's more…"

"What? You sound out of breath."

"Well he's discovered TV-Land, and that old movie channel. All he wants to do is watch…"

I cut her off. "But that's OK, it keeps him bus…"

She cut me off. "Garrett! He thinks the characters on TV are real! He thinks what's on TV is really happening! Garrett, listen to me. This is freaking me out. We have to do something. He thinks those old Mayberry shows are really happening. Right now. He talks to the characters on the screen! He thinks Goober's a young man. And he watched some movie last week where the actor commits suicide, and now he thinks he has to prevent it."

I was stunned, silent.

Tiff started crying. "Garrett, Garrett. What's happening to our father? We're losing him. Can't we do something? Can't we do anything? I'm not ready for this. Can't we call Dr. Jahnke, maybe get him on more meds, something, isn't there anything we can do?"

I reassured Tiff as best I could. It was bullshit, we both knew it, but we had to get us back to functioning mode. "I'll call Dr. Jahnke and see if she can get him in this Friday. She'll adjust his meds."

Tiff settled. I went into repression of feelings mode and turned on the caregiver switch. I told Tiff I would take care of things for the rest of the day with Dad.

It was time to return to earth. A lot more time had sifted through the hourglass while we were in Italy.

I decided to pick up some beer on the way home. I wasn't much of a drinker, but tonight I felt like I needed it. Standing in line, I thought about how wrong it was to self medicate with alcohol when under stress. I could pray instead. I could talk to Stacy some more, go get some exercise, play with the kids. Lots of healthier options. I didn't have to escape through alcohol.

When I reached the clerk, I had a strong impulse to go put the beer back on the shelf.

Screw it. I pulled out a ten, bought the beer, and drove home.

50 { Free Falling

The warm Italian sun glistened off the beautiful Amalfi shoreline. I was on the dock, watching the colorful fishing boats coming back in from the morning run. I imagined them to be full of shrimp and lobster, and was salivating at the thought of an al fresco seafood lunch. I could hear the seagulls calling and smell the wisteria blossoms.

I was lost in a daydream, triggered by an impressionistic painting of an Italian fishing village in the lobby of Dr. Jahnke's office. Dad was asleep next to me. We hadn't been in the office long, but Dad's brain had already gone into hibernation mode while I was inside the painting.

"Walter, come on back, Dr. Jahnke's almost ready for you." Dr. Jahnke's nurse, Carolyn, broke my thoughts. Although she called for Walter, I instinctively responded as if I was the one being called. Dad and I were nearly one person now, at least in public.

I nudged Dad to wake up. He responded like he always did when I woke him up from an Alzheimer's induced hibernation. You would think he would wake up disoriented, maybe scared, maybe anxious. But he didn't. He usually woke up looking totally peaceful, with a tranquil smile on his face. Like he had been someplace wonderful.

Dad stirred a little as I gently moved my open palm against his already stubbled face. "Hey, Dad, Dr. Jahnke's ready for us."

Carolyn was kind, like everyone in Dr. Jahnke's office, but she didn't waste time on small talk. "So, Garrett, you called for today's appointment. You're having some concerns about Walter's functioning? "

"Yes. He seems to have dropped off a lot lately." I was uncomfortable talking about Dad's status in front of him. Carolyn was not.

"How has he dropped off?" Carolyn started testing Dad's reflexes with the familiar rubber mallet.

I looked at Dad. He was smiling, oblivious to it all. There were days now where he didn't even realize we were talking about him.

"Well, he's getting his times all mixed up, his self care skills are deteriorating, he can only fix himself jam sandwiches to eat, otherwise I don't think he would eat, and, then there's this really strange behavior..." I looked again over at Dad, uncomfortable with where I was going. Dad was still smiling. He was somewhere else.

"He watches a lot of TV when I'm not there, and, well, he seems to think the TV shows are real and that he's interacting with the characters as if its real life."

"So he's personalizing what's happening on the TV, and his reality is breaking down. Do you think he's delusional?"

My brain responded with an instant, "Yes," but when I opened my mouth I choked and teared up.

Carolyn looked over at me. "It's part of his disease, Garrett."

"Dr. Jahnke, has told me about your wraparound team. She tells all of her families about the incredible job your family is doing, caring for your father."

I choked up. "I took my family to Italy for two weeks and I think Dad nose-dived while I was gone. He's just free falling now."

Dr. Jahnke knocked once and burst into the room, a bundle of caffeinated positive energy. "Hi Garrett. Why, hello there, Walter." She lit up as she came into the room and approached Dad.

"So Walter, Garrett tells me he went to Italy with his family. I bet he had a wonderful, no magical time. You know, after all of his hard work, I think he not only really needed that trip, but he deserved it. I bet you would agree." Dr. Jahnke had a wonderful, clever way of talking to me through Dad, so he was included.

"Garrett, he's... he's... he's my son! The greatest, he is just the greatest!"

"I know, and you are so lucky to have him by your side." Dr. Jahnke continued to talk to us as she began Dad's physical exam.

Dr. Jahnke completed her finger-agnosia test and had pulled Dad up to his feet. "Push on my hands Walter, that's it, hard as you can. Now walk with me, come on walk with me, that's right, now let's have you walk backwards, yes that's it, now take a few steps to the right, now to the left..."

Dad started dancing as if there was music playing. Having two left feet his entire life, his version of dancing always mimicked his Karate "forms," which was what he was doing now. Dr. Jahnke stood in front of him and danced with him.

"So, Garrett, Carolyn's notes say you're concerned about his functioning dropping off and some possible delusional behavior."

"Yes, Dr. Jahnke, he seems to think TV characters are real, he talks to them on the screen and he's tried to mail a letter to at least two of the actors."

Dad piped in, suddenly at least partially connected. "They're my friends. And one of them, oh what's his name, he's... he's... he's really depressed and I have to get to him before he...."

"He thinks Rod Steiger's going to kill himself. It's apparently a scene from one of his movies."

"That's the one!!! Rod Steiger! See, Garrett knows him, too. He's trying to kill himself! We've got to try and save him!!"

Dr. Jahnke saw Dad was getting worked up. So she reassured him, by joining Dad's delusion from the inside. "You don't need to worry, Walter. Garrett's got it all under control. He's been in touch with Mr. Steiger, and, thanks to your concerns, he's talked to him and he's now getting the help he needs. You and Garrett," Dr. Jahnke looked over at me and winked, "You and Garrett saved his life."

"Garrett, is this true? You saved him?" Dad seemed more relaxed already. Dr Jahnke's strategy was working.

I continued, showing Dr. Jahnke I understood the technique: "Well, that's not quite right, Dad. I didn't save him. Dad, we saved him. If it wasn't for your letter he never would have gotten the help he needed. You are a wonderful friend to him."

Dad teared up, and Dr. Jahnke hugged him. You could tell she still had all the respect in the world for him.

"Now Walter..." Dr. Jahnke pulled back and returned to clinical mode. You know what we have to do next, that little test..."

"Oh no, not the little test..." Dad actually seemed a little anxious about the Mini Mental Status Exam. I was more anxious about it. Last time Dad only scored in the lower 20's out of 30, and he had dropped to the mildly impaired range. I thought this time he would certainly drop a couple more points.

I braced myself, ready to take the test with Dad, and to send him the right answers telepathically. After all, I was his other half.

Dad fumbled his way through the first sets of questions. It was brutal. As much as I tried to will him the answers telepathically, he didn't receive them.

Dad didn't know where he was, what month it was, what season it was, where he lived, or even that he was in a medical office. He thought the year was 1967.

Dad couldn't retrieve the words, "apple, table, penny," after being told these words seconds before.

He couldn't spell "world" backwards. He could follow directions to pick up a piece of paper on the floor and fold it in half. He could still copy simple geometric designs, although for the first time, he sketched them hesitantly instead of confidently drawing out the shape in one motion.

And he could still write. He could write as if he wasn't even impaired. His handwriting, grammar, spelling, all intact. The goddamn disease hadn't reached the writing centers of his brain yet.

When asked to write a sentence, Dad continued to write down his heartfelt thoughts, like he always did on this test: "Dear Dr. Jahnke, You are the best doctor in the world. I am so proud of you. Fondly and with respect, your friend and professor, Walter Turke."

When it was all said and done, Dad had scored a 14. Fourteen! I was devastated. I expected a 19 or a 20. Fourteen was in the moderately impaired range. And I remembered Dr. Jahnke's words from a previous visit, that the goal in medically managing an Alzheimer's patient was to keep their mental status scores from dropping, or at least from dropping quickly. Once the drop had occurred, you couldn't bring the patient's functioning back up.

Dr. Jahnke sat down and pulled her chair up across from mine. She was in angel mode now, and spoke right into my soul. She grabbed my hands gently as she spoke. "Garrett, I'm afraid the disease has accelerated again. We can increase his Aricept, that might slow it down again, that's what I would do because he still has good quality of life and seems happy. You will have to monitor him even more closely. I know this will tax you even more, and I am so sorry for that. I know you have already got Power of Attorney and have his wills and finances in order and out of his control. But right now, I must tell you he is completely, and legally, incompetent to make any responsible decisions on his own. I will draft a formal letter stating such."

Dr. Jahnke clutched both of my hands. "Garrett, he is getting close to the point where he will need around-the-clock care. I think he's still OK for a while because of your wraparound team, but maybe not that much longer, six months, maybe a year, but that's all. A lot of the care facilities, the good ones, have pretty long waiting lists. So you might want to start looking around now. All these facilities say they do the same kinds of care, but what you need to look for is whether the staff seems to sincerely care about the residents. They need to see the patients still as real people, not just empty shells."

All I really heard was "six months to a year." Dad's death sentence.

Dr Jahnke looked me square in the eyes. Right through the surface and into my soul. "Garrett, remember our promise to your Dad. We must never, ever, forget who he is. We must never stop loving him. You must hold on to this. This is what you must keep."

51 { Dear Arthur

May 17

Dear Arthur,

My name is Garrett Turke, and I am Walter's son. It is with great sadness and regret that I have to write you.

My father was diagnosed with Alzheimer's disease two years ago. He is still doing well, and he is happy. As you know, he has moved to the East Lansing area to be with his children and grandchildren. This has given him great joy and comfort. We have been blessed that Dad does not seem all that aware that he is even impaired, although it is obvious to those of us that are caring for him that his functioning is dropping off quite steadily.

Dad still loves to write, and he writes remarkably well for someone who is increasingly impaired. He may not seem impaired at all to you in his letters. This will eventually change as his Alzheimer's progresses. I am so sorry to have to tell you this, but I felt that you should know in the event that his correspondence with you starts to show the effects of his disease.

I know that you and my father have a very special relationship that he values tremendously. He talks of you in such positive terms every time I see him. He lights up each and every time that he receives a letter from you, which of course, has been often. He has a deep bond with you that cannot be broken, no matter what life events may occur. Please know that my father loves you and cherishes your relationship.

I hope and pray that you will continue to write to my father. I will see that he gets your letters and that your relationship with him is respected. I would be happy to keep you updated as to his status, if you would like. I will enclose my address and phone numbers with this letter. I am sorry to intrude like this, but I felt that you should know.

I know this letter will undoubtedly cause you distress. I am so sorry for that.

God bless you, Arthur.

Semper Fi.

Sincerely,

Garrett L. Turke

Walter's son

52 { Dear Garrett

It was the Saturday after mailing Arthur's letter. As I opened the door to the post office, I hoped that I would find a return letter from him. It had been only six days since I had mailed the letter, and I figured if Arthur was going to respond right away today would be the first chance it could arrive. I pulled out a mountain of mail and paper that was crammed tight into the PO Box and went over to the recycling station to dump out the junk mail. As I sifted through the advertisements, community announcements, and the requests for donations, a small 4x6" card sized envelope slipped out and fell to the floor.

I recognized it immediately, as it had U.S. Navy and Marine Corps stickers all over it. The return address label was an American Flag design, with the words Semper Fi beneath the name and address. It was from Arthur. It was addressed to me.

Arthur must have written this the day he received my letter. My hands shook a little as I opened the envelope. I was surprised how nervous I was.

"*Dear Garrett,*

I received your letter this afternoon. I very much thank you for writing me. These must be some very tough times for you. I am glad that Walter has you to help look after him. I know how that is, having to look after someone who is chronically ill.

I would very much appreciate it if you could keep me updated about your father. He is a very good man. I cannot begin to tell you how much he has helped me. I can tell from your letter that you are a very caring person, too. I hope you will find the strength to keep on helping your father, especially now that he needs you. Semper Fi.

Tell your father I said hello and that I will write him soon. And tell him my wife said hello, too.

I will keep writing your father. Will you keep writing me?

Stay strong.

Semper Fi, Arthur"

53 { Wandering

When I got off from work at five it still seemed like mid afternoon. I was not feeling burdened by the mounting stress of Dad's care needs today. It was Friday and I was in a good mood. I had cranked up the wraparound one more notch and my family had once again responded impressively. I had taken care of my business with Arthur, and his letters kept streaming in. Dad was right. He was a strong man. He had been hit and hit hard with the news of Dad's disease and hadn't wavered. Arthur was responding to the wraparound, too. His letters were now addressed to Dad and me. Dad was delighted whenever he received a letter from "our" friend. And he continued to bring up the issue of seeing Arthur. I wasn't ready to do that yet. That was an ethical line I still couldn't cross.

With the warm summer sun now becoming a daily occurrence, I had given some thought to resurrecting the farewell tour again for the summer. Dad was markedly more impaired this year, but he was still happy and full of energy. He still didn't appear to have a clue that he was impaired. The periodic torture of Dad's slide was apparently only for those around him. He didn't seem to have a care in the world.

I reached into my pocket, worked around the giant mass of keys that momentarily reminded me of how many responsibilities I had, and found my cell phone.

Stacy answered the phone almost immediately. "Hi Stace. I'm almost to Dad's. Hey I was thinking. It's such a nice day. Why don't we have a cookout and have Dad over for dinner? "

Stacy thought that was a great idea. I knew she would. In all the years of Dad's illness, she never turned me down when I asked if Dad could come over for dinner, or lunch, or anything else for that matter. Not even once.

With my good mood now solidified, I exited the freeway, made the stretch around Park Lake, and turned down Dad's street. As I pulled into his driveway,

I was excited about telling Dad we were going to a cookout.

"Hmmm. That's funny," I muttered to myself. "The door's ajar a little."

"Hey Dad, its me, Garrett!" I didn't see him in his customary position, in his Herman Miller chair in front of the TV.

Hmmm. Funny. He's not in the bathroom either. Oh well, maybe Mom took him out somewhere. Yeah, that's it. They went for a walk and just forgot to close the door.

Wait a minute; Mom's car isn't outside. Shit! I ran outside, and looked down the long block in both directions. No Dad.

Back inside, down the stairs into the basement. "Dad? Dad? Are you down here?" No answer. Now I was really starting to panic. Am I going to find him slumped over dead somewhere in the condo? Or is he outside somewhere? Oh shit! Dad's never wandered before. Oh shit! How can we be that stupid?

But my panic quickly subsided as I came back up the basement stairs. Of course Mom's car isn't outside and there's no Dad. That's because Dad is with Mom, in her car. They must have gone for a drive or to the park or something because it's such a nice day. Yeah, that's got to be it. I went into Dad's kitchen and picked up the phone.

"Hi Stacy, I'm over to Dad's. We're going to be a little late."

"Is everything OK?"

"Yeah, fine. Dad's not here yet. He's out with Mom somewhere."

"That's OK, I haven't started the coals. How long will you be?"

"I don't know. Mom didn't leave a note like she usually does."

"OK. But could you call her to find out when she's bringing him back? Or on second thought, maybe she could just bring your Dad here and she could stay for dinner, too."

"That's a great idea. OK I'll call her and call you right back."

Denial is a powerful mechanism. Mom always left a note if she took Dad out somewhere, she was compulsive about making sure the door was locked after her, and she always left Dad in front of the TV with a movie on. The movie was on, but there was no Dad in front of it.

I called Mom. As the phone rang, it dawned on me that I wasn't going to find her at home. She was in the car with my Dad, or at a park, remember?

She wouldn't have taken Dad over to her place. She never did that. I readied myself to leave a message, rehearsing the words in my head to invite her over for dinner.

"Hello."

"Oh. Ah... hi Mom. I didn't expect to find you at home. I thought you were out driving around with Dad. I see you took him over to your place."

"What are you talking about? Your father's not here. I left him over an hour ago, watching a Humphrey Bogart movie that he likes. We had a good afternoon together."

"Dad's not with you?"

"No, Garrett, I just said that. Maybe he's with your sister."

No time for niceties. The panic was back. "I'll call you back, Mom."

I pulled out my cell phone as I slammed the front door behind me. I was so scared I couldn't think straight. "OK, OK, call Tiff. What's her number? 349, no that's not it. 655, 47..., no that's her work number. Damn it! What's her number, what's her number? For God's sake, I call it everyday. 339-3402... No, that's not it either. 339-4312. That's it!"

"Hello?"

"Tiff, its me. You have Dad?"

"Was I supposed to? I thought it was your day?"

"Yeah it is my day. He's not here!"

Tiff wasn't panicked, yet. "Well he's with Mom then. It's a nice day, they probably went out..."

"Tiff, he's not with Mom, the door was open, the TV's on, he's gone!! Come down here, please, now!" I barked out the order like a cruel drill sergeant. I didn't wait for a response and hung up.

I started running down the block. No, stupid! Get into the van!

I raced through Dad's block and started combing through the side streets. It was a new housing complex and there were lots of woods undeveloped all around the neighborhoods. My mind flashed to all those stories in the news about elderly citizens wandering off and being found, weeks later, dead. When I couldn't find Dad on any of the side streets, my panic had escalated to the point where I could actually hear my heart racing inside my chest. The panic was starting to mix with despair. Dad was gone. And it was my fault. I had not built any wraparound precautions for this. I readied myself to call the police.

I pulled out of the condo subdivision at its southern edge, and was ready to get on Park Lake Road northbound to circle back to Dad's place. As I stopped at the intersection, I saw a hazy figure of a person walking southbound along Park Lake Road maybe 150 yards to my right. I turned right and gunned the engine, then slammed on the brakes as the figure came into clarity.

It was Dad.

I pulled over just ahead of him and opened the passenger door. Dad was walking as calm as could be. He saw me, smiled, and then became elated.

I couldn't downshift my feelings so fast. I unleashed a fury on Dad he didn't understand, much less deserve.

"Damn you, Dad! Damn you! Where the hell have you been! I've been looking all over the neighborhood for you! You're supposed to be at home! You left the door open and the TV on! I thought you were dead!"

Dad didn't know what to think or do. His bottom lip started quivering as he got into the van. Like some guilt riddled little kid who knew he was about to be punished.

"I was just walking. It's a nice day. I was just on my... on... on my..."

"On your way..."

"Yes! On my way back home when you came. Why are you so mad at me? I'm very glad...I'm very ..." Dad was fighting back tears now. "I am very glad to see you. Aren't you glad to see me?"

"Dad, I am glad to see you." I reached over and hugged him. "I'm sorry I yelled at you. It was just that I was so worried..."

"So, what will we be doing today? It's been kind of a slow day."

A slow day? For God's sake, Dad, you scared the shit out of me! "Well Dad, I know it's been kind of slow, so I thought we'd have a cookout!"

"Really? A cookout? With me?"

"Yeah, with all of us. Stacy and Shani and Miah. And we could invite Rosemarie and Tiffanie and her family."

"Really?"

"Yep. All for you. It's like a party just for you."

"Oh come on. I don't deserve it."

"Oh yes you do. We all do!"

I turned around on Park Lake Road and headed back northbound to Dad's condominium complex entrance. It was only four hundred yards and one minute away. But it felt like we were coming back from being lost for weeks in the Sahara.

Less than two minutes later, we were at Dad's driveway. Tiff's car was there, door open. She was down the block, but came running back when she saw us. She raced into Dad's arms and held him ever so tightly, sobbing.

Dad comforted her. "Why are you crying, Tiffie?"

"I missed you so bad. I'm just so happy to see you!" Tiff clutched him hard and wouldn't let go.

Dad wrapped his great big arms, still strong from his youth, around her. "Garrett and I were on a long trip together. But now we're back. And we're going to have a...a... a cooking party together. Want to come?"

"Sure, Dad." Tiff had started to calm down, but she was still gripping him tight. A minute or two later they separated. I could see how much Tiffanie loved him. And I could see how much she would miss him when the sand in the hourglass finally ran out.

From that day on, until Dad's residential placement, I could never fully relax when I wasn't with him. I was always afraid he would wander off. I would call him constantly during the day and wouldn't sleep very well at night.

Please, dear God, watch over him. I can't always be there to keep him safe.

54 { False Positive

June was here and so was summer. It was now sunny nearly everyday and not only warm during the day, but also at night. This particular morning, it was already rather hot and sticky when I pulled into Dad's driveway at 10 AM. As I parked the van, I could see Dad peering around the front door. God knows how long he had been waiting there, with the door ajar, looking for me. It might have only been a few minutes. But it might have been a few hours.

Dad emerged from behind the front door as soon as he had noticed it was me. As usual, he was excited and captivated at my arrival. A hero's welcome every time I saw him. I thought to myself, this is nice, but I really don't deserve it. I was still reeling from Dad being lost in the neighborhood the previous weekend. And I knew it could happen again. Easily.

Dad climbed into the van. It was already 88 degrees and muggy outside. I had on shorts and a t-shirt. Dad had on a heavy, long-sleeved Navy sweatshirt, and his Navy starter jacket. We were creeping into yet another phase of his disease, the inability to recognize what level of clothing matched the weather outside. In his mind, it seemed to always be a cool, fall day. From this point on, he would be ill prepared for a very cold day in winter or a very hot day in summer.

The sweat started to trickle down Dad's brow as he got into the van. "Geez, Garrett, it sure is hot in your car, can't you turn down the heat?"

"Dad, it's practically 90 degrees outside. Let's get your jacket off, and maybe your sweatshirt, too. " I cranked up the air conditioner, got out of the van, and came over to the passenger side. Dad gave up his Navy jacket willingly, but only reluctantly gave up his sweatshirt. Underneath his sweatshirt he had on not one, but two U.S. Navy t-shirts. He apparently had forgotten he had put the first one on.

"Hey, Dad, I can see why you're so hot; you've got two shirts on. Here, let's get one of these off." I tried to help lift the outer t-shirt off, gently pulling it up to get it over his head. Instead of helping me, Dad looked pissed.

He snapped back, irate. "What the hell are you doing? I'll freeze to death without that." Dad angrily yanked the outer t-shirt back down around his waist. "Now wait a minute, you hold off there!"

Dad looked at me, glaring. I was a stranger who was trying to accost him. I backed off immediately. For a moment, Dad had seemed to lose track of who I was, and what I was trying to do.

"OK, OK, sorry! Sorry, Dad. It's me, Garrett, your son. We can leave that on." I tossed his jacket and sweatshirt onto the seat behind him, and then changed the subject. So what if he's got two shirts on? It wasn't worth the hassle.

"So, Dr. Fang, where are we going today? Are we going to see my…my… no our friend, what's his name, he's a big guy and he lives, you know, way up?"

"Arthur?"

"Yeah, Arthur, that's the one!"

"No, no, not today, Dad. Today we're going to see our other friend, Dr. Jahnke. But I did finally reach Arthur."

"How's his wife doing?"

I made something up. "She's doing fine these days."

Dad looked relieved, and satisfied. "Whew, that was a close one. I mean, with his wife."

What the hell does that mean, I wondered? But I didn't want to go any further down this road. I had to get Dad oriented for his six week follow-up with Dr. Jahnke.

"Yep, Dad, it sure was, a close one. So, today we'll be seeing our other friend, your old student, Dr. Jahnke."

Dad looked distant and confused. He no longer immediately recognized Dr. Jahnke's name as a familiar person. I worked hard to get Dad's memory to snap back in.

"You know, Dr. Jahnke? She works up in Saginaw, she loves seeing us, we see her on Fridays; she was one of your favorite students…"

You could see that Dad was in memory retrieval mode, but nothing was coming up. Finally, he seemed to connect with something. "Oh, the one with those goddamn questions I hate! Well, I think we can do without her today, don't you?" Dad was starting to get irritated again. It was unusual for his mood to be so negative, and I was getting a little worried.

"Oh, don't worry about those questions, Dad, not today. We're just going for a nice drive to see her…"

More lies. And as I watched Dad calm back down, I thought about how I might need to start using my new Alzheimer's strategy on an ever-increasing basis. Say whatever you had to, to keep him calm and happy. And no matter what, keep him connected interpersonally and interacting. The content of my speech was becoming much less important than the form of how I said it. It didn't matter anymore if what I said was true or not. He would forget most if not all of what I said within a minute anyway. It was more important to get his mood in a good place, and keep it there.

I wondered if my lies to Dad would ever catch up with me, that he would notice and call me on it. But that never seemed to happen. How could it, given the state of his memory? He was increasingly only living in the immediate present. No future, and no past.

I thought about our last visit to Dr. Jahnke's office. She had given me a directive to find Dad a suitable residential care facility. I wasn't ready for Dad to go into residential care. I equated residential placement with Dad's death sentence.

Other than calling that one nurse at Burcham, I hadn't followed through with anything that Dr. Jahnke had said. Open your eyes and think, Garrett. He was a 14 on his last Mini Mental Staus Exam. He wandered away just a few weeks ago. We're losing him. He's not safe. We can't keep him at home much longer.

I reached over and held Dad's hand for a second. He had drifted off to sleep. "Hi Dad, we're just about there. Our friend, Dr. Jahnke, will be sure glad to see us."

Dad looked interested and smiled some more. "Oh, she's coming down to see us today?"

"Something like that."

We had found our parking spot in the Med Arts complex and were walking toward Dr. Jahnke's office. Dad seemed to recognize where we were, and it helped re-orient him.

"Oh, it's this place. You know, the two women who just talk, talk, talk! They're pretty nice, but they ask all those stupid questions."

"Well, it's going to be like a reunion today, Dad, so not to worry. They've invited us, and they just want us to sit down, visit for a while, and maybe have some lunch. They want to see their old professor. That would be you! They are our good friends. In fact, they are our guardian angels!" I didn't have a clue why I said that last line. But in a string of lies designed to protect Dad, it was the only statement that was true.

We were only seated a few minutes, but it seemed like an eternity to me. I was already squirming anxiously, thinking about my agenda. OK, talk to Dr. Jahnke about Dad's risk for wandering, ask her if he is able to do some more Farewell Tour trips with me again this summer, pray he rebounds on the Mini Mental Status Exam, and please, please, please don't bring up residential care. I'm going to delay that one until later in the year, maybe even early next year...

Dr. Jahnke, apparently well tanked on caffeine, burst in with Carolyn. Dad had drifted off to sleep during our three minute wait, but again woke up with a smile on his face. Dr. Jahnke launched into her exam of Dad, while simultaneously weaving in a conversation with me.

"Hey Walter! How nice to see you, and your son, Garrett, today." Dr. Jahnke pulled Dad to his feet. "Now walk with me Walter, hey we're dancing, two steps forward, now two steps back. Now push on my hands, that's it, now pull me back, push me forward, pull me back, push-pull, push-pull, very good. Now Garrett, we talked last time, how have you been doing in your search to find a residential facil..."

The first question out of the shoot is this one? Quick, say something, say something so you don't look like you've been doing nothing!

"Well, I've been checking into three places that are in the East Lansing area. They all look pretty good, but there's this one place, its called Clare Bridge, which might be the best. Its right around the corner from my house, I could even walk there if I wanted to."

That wasn't exactly a lie. I had made a list of facilities from the phone book, but the way I said it made it sound like I was on a more active search. I hadn't contacted any of these places, except for the Burcham Hills facility in East Lansing that I had called last year.

"That's great, Garrett! And as soon as you've selected the right one, make sure to get him on the wait list."

Dad was oblivious to what we were talking about. Dr. Jahnke now had Dad's right hand behind his back, performing the finger agnosia exam. "Now what finger is this, and this one? And now, do what I do." Dr. Jahnke placed her thumb and index finger together and opened and closed the gap between the two. "All us women do is talk, talk, talk. Now you do it."

Dad tried to get the coordination down, but he couldn't do it very well. He used to do it easily, but not any more. And this time, he didn't get the verbiage right, either. "All women do is quack, quack, quack!"

Dr. Jahnke and Carolyn started administering the Mini Mental Status Exam in between questions directed at me. "So, Garrett, any changes in your father's functioning?"

"He seems about the same. He still thinks characters on TV are real, that it's happening in real time, Tiff and I have to prepare all his meals, and I have to help him wash. He chooses clothes that don't fit the weather; you'll notice he has two shirts on today. I had to crank up the wraparound some more, and oh yes, I found him wandering down the street once, just this past weekend. He said he was out on a walk going home, but he was going the wrong way..."

"That must have scared you."

"Out of my mind scared."

"He doesn't have any history of wandering, does he?"

"Not until this particular time. Well, not that I know of."

"It's a tough predicament. Wandering is so hard to safeguard unless they're in residential care. Do the neighbors know to look for him?"

"Yeah, in the past I talked with them. Maybe I should revisit this issue with them. It's a delicate balance. I don't want for them to feel pressured, or responsible for him, or that there's someone unsafe living in their midst."

"I understand. You're in that risky and tricky phase right before they need residential care…"

Shit. There's that word again. She said it twice in 20 seconds.

Dr. Jahnke had refocused on Dad's MMSE that Carolyn was administering. Carolyn was still on the first tier of questions.

"And where are we talking right now, Walter, I mean what city are we in right now?"

"Well I can tell you we're not in East Lansing anymore."

"So where are we?"

"I believe we're in Saginaw. In your office. In Med Arts One. Answering these stupid questions you know I hate."

What? He got it right? He got two items right in one sentence? A two-pointer coming in cold? Way to go, Dad!

"So, Walter, what's this?"

"A watch, you know that!"

And this?

"A pen. You're kidding me, right? "

"And so, Walter, can you spell "world" backwards?"

"You know I hate this one. World. OK, lets see…D, L … lets see…D, L…W-O-R-L-D…OK, its ah…D, L, R… O…"

Come on Dad, come on! Even Dr. Jahnke was totally focused on the moment.

"W!!"

Dad jumped up and high-fived everyone in the room. It was like a game to him. "Now can I go?"

"Just a few more, Walter, and we're done. Carolyn completed the test while Dr. Jahnke and I cheered him on. Dad still failed most of the remaining items, but he did manage to draw the geometric shapes correctly, and to write an intelligible sentence, which he always personalized:

"This is a very nice office. You two are fun to be with! But I hate taking the stupid test!"

Dad's MMSE sentences were becoming more child-like, but they were still intelligible and organized.

When all was said and done, Dad had scored a 17. Not exactly a great score, still in the moderately impaired range, but up from his last score of 14. Dr. Jahnke said that maybe the increased Aricept dosage was working a little, but she also clearly warned me that the score could just as easily have been a false positive, and to not read a whole lot into it

I only heard that the increased Aricept was working. "So, Dr. Jahnke, you think Dad could handle a few trips up north with me this summer? His friends all want to see him again..."

Dr. Jahnke answered my question at face value. "I think a few trips up north would be great for him, and for you. You still have some time, I think. Make the most of it. Maybe we'll look at residential care later this year, in the fall or the winter. But get him on the waiting list now."

Dr. Jahnke read my thoughts, despite all my attempts to conceal them, and it was all right with her. Thank you, guardian angel. I wasn't joking. I meant it.

Dr. Jahnke summed up the results of today's exam, like she always did. "Looks like your Dad is holding his own again right now. But remember, this could be a false positive, he's still quite impaired, and he will eventually slip downwards again. But for right now the increased Aricept might be working a little. There's a another drug on the market now for early and middle stage Alzheimer's patients, its called Exelon and we might want to talk about this next time we see Walter. It works a little differently, so there might be some benefit in trying it. But for right now, the increased Aricept seems to be working, so let's stay the course."

Dr. Jahnke continued as I hurriedly wrote all of her advice down. "You guys are doing such a wonderful job caring for Walter. A lot of families, maybe most families, would have started to let go by now. His improved functioning is probably a testament to your exceptional care giving. As for his wandering, it's always a risk, but he doesn't show a pervasive pattern or history of this. I'd alert his neighbors again, and get him one of those medical alert bracelets, you can get it from a program called Safe Return, and I'll get you some information on it. That way, if others find him, they will be alerted who to call. So, let's keep up the wraparound, you get him on a wait list for residential care for later next fall or winter, and we'll see you in three months."

Three months? That means stability in Dr. Jahnke's world! That's the longest Dr. Jahnke ever went in between appointments.

We left the office with the some more Aricept sample packs, and a Safe Return brochure. I vaguely recalled that maybe the Safe Return program was the one that the Alzheimer's Association recommended at that introductory meeting we attended so long ago.

Before heading back on the freeway, we stopped at Taco Bell for burritos. While in line, Dad reminded me he didn't want cheese on his. I thought it strange that his hatred of fish and cheese was withstanding the ravages of his memory loss and the disease.

55 { Safe Return

I didn't want to see the notice in the Lansing State Journal, but it was too late. I had already read the header. "Safe Return to register Alzheimer's patients this weekend."

The Safe Return brochure from Dr. Jahnke's office was upstairs in our roll top desk, buried somewhere in the "unfinished business" pile I kept. I wasn't ready to deal with it yet. Instead of looking at the bracelet as a fail-safe net to protect Dad, I viewed it more as a brand. The kind of brand that was burned into cattle hides. The kind of brand that turned something into a possession.

The Safe Alert bracelet was a fantastic safety net for somebody else's dad. To me, it marked my dad as an object. He was no longer a competent, strong human being. He was no longer a complete person. No longer free. And no longer The Champion.

It probably didn't matter what I felt, anyway. There was no way Dad would ever wear that bracelet. He'd look at the back of it and see the words "Memory Impaired," and rip it off. "What the hell is this for?" he would say. "Garrett, did you have something to do with this? Is this how you see me?" The bracelet would destroy Dad's blissful denial of his Alzheimer's disease and only create pain and anxiety for him.

Bullshit. All the bracelet would actually do is eradicate more of my denial. And that, pure and simple, was the reason I hadn't signed Dad up yet. It was irresponsible not to sign him up.

I finished cutting out the advertisement and left it out on the counter. I wasn't sure I had enough courage to go sign Dad up this weekend. But I knew if I left it out on the counter, Stacy would see it. And she would make sure I signed Dad up.

True to plan, Stacy came home from the Y and within minutes saw the announcement. "Hi, hun. Hey, isn't this the Safe Return program that Dr.

Jahnke told you about? Huh. It's gonna be at the Haslett library this Saturday. You're gonna sign your Dad up, right?"

"Yep." I said with an unenthusiastic, resigned tone. I knew she'd force me into it.

Stacy came in and hugged me. All I could return was a lifeless hug and a few mechanical pats on her back.

That Saturday I took Dad to the Haslett library. I told him he was going to receive a "major award" from the township for all of his contributions to the ALFA Center. The lies were coming easy now. Anything to protect him.

As I stood in line with him, I worried that he would either find out why we were really there, or that the person registering these mothers and fathers would blow my cover. But neither happened. Dad passively waited while I filled out the paperwork, and the person registering us was very discrete and professional. She measured Dad's wrist size with him while I filled out the emergency contact information. I paid a small fee, and all was done. Dad never seemed to have any awareness of what we were doing, other than I was ordering him a nice silver bracelet.

Yeah, a major award. I felt like shit. I had not only pulled off one of my biggest lies to date, but I was about to declare him incompetent to the entire world.

Just a week later, the bracelet came in the mail. I went over to Dad's, told him his "major award" had arrived, and put the bracelet on his left wrist. I told him it was sterling silver and that it never needed to come off. Dad not only accepted it, he loved it. He had won the award, and was proud of it. Although the words "Memory Impaired" were clearly etched into the plate, he never looked at it.

Dad's easy acceptance of the bracelet brought no relief for me, however. I felt I had branded him.

56 { Things Fall Apart

I sat halfway up a fifty foot sand dune, looking out over the turquoise blue waters of Lake Michigan. It was a sunny, warm, late summer afternoon, not very muggy, with a stiff westerly breeze that was churning up some nice 4 to 6 foot waves. If you didn't know you were in Michigan, you might think you were somewhere tropical, far, far away, like off the coast of Baja, or somewhere in the Caribbean.

Dad was inside our rented beachfront condo with the girls. Stacy had sent me outside for a break. I was starting to lose it inside the condo from all the stress. I had been fused to Dad at the hip for the past five days. I didn't know I needed a break until I was outside, alone. It was the first time I had been alone all week.

I watched a 30 foot sailboat clear the lighthouse at the end of the breakwater. The crew pulled up the main sails, the wind immediately filled them, and the boat raced off into the choppy open waters. You could see the waves break over the boat's bow in great plumes of spray as it headed out. I thought about what a sense of freedom those folks on board must be experiencing. I imagined myself on board with them, holding tight to the rail lines as the boat ventured gallantly into the oncoming waves.

I smiled, then shook my head.

We had come up north for one final week away before school started. Dad was with us, at my insistence, but things weren't going very well. He was disoriented much of the time, and he had trouble sitting through the simplest of activities, like a dinner out, or even a walk on the beach, because he would get so confused and anxious.

It was a wonderful idea to bring Dad with us, but it was a mistake. No one verbalized it, but I knew it, Stacy knew it, and my kids knew it. Dad should have remained in East Lansing with my sister, my brother-in-law, and my mother watching over him. But I wouldn't have it.

My holier than thou attitude was stressing everyone out. I was stressed out, but would not acknowledge it. I could see and hear myself talking to my family, edgy and angry, bossy and controlling, unrelenting that we needed to keep Dad in our sights at all times. But my fleeting insight didn't curb my behavior. I had taken our successful wraparound support system, balanced with breaks and respite for everyone involved, and turned it into a dictatorship.

All summer long, I had approached each day as if it had life or death stakes attached to it. And what was once a smooth running, happy, loving family, was now starting to show signs of wear. Dangerous wear. I was becoming a walking razor, short fused, angry, and impatient. Angry and impatient with everyone and every thing. Things were falling apart.

The warning signs had been there all along this summer. Earlier in June, I had great plans and great expectations for the summer with Dad. I had counted on another summer like the year before. I had planned the Farewell Tour II, complete with several trips up north, another sailing adventure, reunion lunches with Dad's old friends, maybe even another concert. Perhaps even a tour of the Upper Peninsula. Up across that mighty Mackinac Bridge to freedom and escape. Just like in that Bob Seger song that I loved so.

In late June, I was up for it, and feeling hopeful and full of promise. One more run with Dad. Yeah, it was gonna be great. But now, in late August, the dream of another Farewell Tour with Dad lay at my feet, having fallen from its perch into a bunch of broken, jagged little pieces.

Too much time had passed though the hourglass. The Farewell Tour was a nice idea. For last year. Dad just couldn't do it this year.

It wasn't as if I hadn't tried. In early July, I had attempted a trip up to Traverse City alone with Dad. The cherries were ripening and it was time for the National Cherry Festival. I hadn't been to the Cherry Festival with my dad in 25 years. It was a crazy time in Traverse City, but it was a fun time. It was a time to forget your worries, kick off your shoes, and play in the Lake Michigan sand and sun. Willard Scott and the Today Show would be there. And so would two hundred fifty thousand other folks, who would descend onto this pretty little resort town of fifteen thousand. What a perfect way to kick off another Farewell Tour.

Dad and I never made it to Traverse City that weekend. About three hours up, in the middle of that forest outside of Kingsley, things started to go wrong. The perfect plan, the perfect organization, the perfect supports all started to break down.

Dad woke up in the van and started talking about needing to see his girlfriend. I had tried to distract him, and to steer him away from his preoccupation. It usually worked. But it didn't this time. He had to see his girlfriend. Now. He looked anxious, and was getting more and more agitated. And for the first time with this disease, he wouldn't allow me to distract him.

Dad was referring to Tiffanie, and he was increasingly adamant that we had to change course to go see her.

"Damn you, son of a bitch! We've got to go see her, right this minute!" I had to block Dad's arm as he tried to grab the steering wheel. He sounded so distressed, so completely confused. For the first time riding with Dad, I was afraid he was going to cause an accident.

"Dad, it's me, Garrett, your son! It's OK, it's OK!" I was scared, and feeling like I was losing control. Not just losing control over the situation. Losing control over my strategy, my way of dealing with Dad, and my way of dealing with life.

"My girlfriend is waiting for me, and you're going the wrong way! Damn you, you've got to get me back to her. You know I've got a date with her!" I discretely glanced over, and out of the corner of my eye could see Dad's eerily detached look on his face. He looked like some sort of deranged stranger.

For a second, I thought of what the experience was like for Dad. A stranger who was kidnapping him. A stranger who was stealing him away from his love. He was intensely angry. I was certain he would try to grab the wheel again.

"OK, OK, OK!!! We're going to head back, Dad. I forgot, I'm sorry, I forgot you had a date with your girlfriend. OK, see, we're getting off the road now so we can turn around. OK, we're heading back now. See, look at the compass, we're heading south again." My hands and my voice trembled.

"My girlfriend loves me, so why are you trying to keep me from her. Ah ha! Maybe you just want her for yourself!"

Dad's paranoia and agitated demands had catapulted me right into the middle of an anxiety attack. I was spinning in a panic driven vertigo.

"Dad, Dad, it's me, Dr. Fang! We're heading back, we'll be there soon. Everything is fine. We'll be there in plenty of time for your date. What did you have planned?" I did the redirect by lying but this time it was different. This time it wasn't just a little charade to keep Dad happy and the conversation moving. This time the redirect seemed to have life or death consequences attached to it. I was trying to prevent Dad from crashing the van.

"Oh no you don't! I see what you're up to. You are trying to trick me!"

"No, really Dad, I just forgot, but I remember now. You put it on the calendar. A date with Tiff. Yep. We're heading to her now. Don't worry, we'll be back in plenty of time."

"Then why are you still going the wrong way?! Damn you, whoever you are, turn this thing around now!"

"OK, see? We're getting off the road and going a different way now. See? Yes, this is the shortcut to Tiffanie's place. Just a little longer and we'll be there." I glanced down at the odometer. "A little while" would be another 140 miles.

For the next hour and a half I was on eggshells with Dad. Three times I had to pull off the freeway and head down a secondary road in order to convince him we were changing course. At first I prayed to God to return my Dad. Then I prayed to God to just have him fall asleep.

I glanced down at the speedometer. We were still going 60. Better push it. I pressed down on the accelerator and we sped up to 75.

Somewhere around Mt. Pleasant, Dad quieted a bit, then fell asleep for the last hour of our trip. My heart wouldn't relax, however, until we were back in East Lansing and heading down Dad's street.

When we pulled into his driveway, Dad awakened, with a faint smile on his face. He had no memory whatsoever of what had transpired up north. I hadn't been so lucky.

I startled when a tender hand tapped me on my shoulder, bringing me back out of my long, posttraumatic flashback. "Hey, Dad." It was Shani, a fifth grade kid when this whole thing started, and now a grownup looking 12 year old. "Mom wants you. It's Grampy. He's starting to get all stressed out again."

"Tell her I'll be right in." Shani turned, and dutifully trotted back up and over the dunes to the condo.

The Farewell Tour II was over before it had even started. The events of this summer should have humbled me. It should have taught me I couldn't handle Dad alone anymore, that I needed help. But instead of reaching out to others, all I could do was retreat more into martyrdom. Dad couldn't be without me anymore. He couldn't ever leave my side. I couldn't go anywhere without him.

I took one final look out over those beautiful waters. The late afternoon August sun shimmered through the Lake Michigan haze, relentlessly eating up time as it made its inevitable path toward the horizon. I shook my head again, as if someone was conversing with me and I disagreed. The summer that held such promise just a couple months ago was now fading really fast. And, I thought, so was my dad. Things had fallen apart.

The sailboat I had been watching came back in. Their little excursion into freedom was over, too. It had become too rough out there.

I picked myself up, dusted the sand off my shorts, and went back to the condo to take care of my dad.

57 { The Choice

Dad's wraparound team continued through the fall, and we continued to have meetings as a family. Dad continued to go to the ALFA Center. And I continued to come out twice each day to look in on him. Dad wasn't doing very well. He was more and more delusional. At the ALFA Center, he was no longer the staff psychiatrist. He began to feel he was being detained there against his will. There were days where the ALFA staff had trouble convincing him to stay. Twice he walked away from the building, and I had to be called at work to come get him. Stacy saw the erosion, too, but the rest of my family didn't. They thought that Dad was still holding his own.

Instead of trying to convince the rest of my team that Dad was floundering, I further entrenched myself in the role of martyr. Although I kept scheduling wraparound meetings, I quit pouring my energies into the wraparound team, and started viewing the team meetings as a perfunctory obligation. Essentially, I had already decided to just take care of Dad myself. If my mother and sister and brother-in-law didn't get it, to hell with it. To hell with them. It was too painful to have to check in all the time with the family to try to convince them. I stopped talking to everyone about Dad's deteriorating status. I quit talking to everyone about how stressed I was. Eventually, I just quit talking about Dad, period.

When I'd get home at 7 or 8 each evening and Stacy asked how it went with Dad, I said, "fine," and changed the subject. When Stacy prodded me to open up, I snapped back angrily and said I had had enough, talking about him all the time. Although I was still physically around my family, I really wasn't there. I wasn't trying to be cruel, or cold, or distant, but I guess it came across that way. Bullshit! I knew it came across that way! But I just couldn't mobilize anymore. Fuck it! Fuck the world! Yeah, that's right, fuck the world! I was inside a shell now. Almost all the time. And I would only come out to take care of Dad.

Upstairs on my roll-top desk was an increasingly large pile of unfinished business. There were cards I had bought for Dr. Jahnke and for Arthur. There were lists of things I wanted to do for me, and for my family. There was a brochure from a pool building company, and some travel magazines highlighting places I wanted to go, and for places we wanted to go as a family. There were five or six catalogues from companies that sold artists' booths, waiting for the day when I would take my images out on the road. There was a letter to Cindy, virtually finished, but never sent. All my hopes and dreams and responsibilities were in that pile. Grounded. Because I was too busy taking care of Dad.

I told myself everything in that pile would have to wait. Some of my responsibilities would have to wait until I had time to do them. Some of the plans might have to wait a few years. Some of my dreams I chalked up as lost forever. I was in danger of passing my prime. Maybe I had already passed it. But it didn't matter. Dad needed me, and me only. It was he and I from here on out. Everything else just wasn't as important. Dad was always at the top of the priority list, and there just wasn't enough time, or energy, or resources to do anything else.

I had resigned myself to being a martyr. The outside world would see me as a saint. But to the inside world, I was paying an ultimate cost. I was sacrificing my children, my wife, the rest of my family, and my well being, for a dying man.

I was too stubborn to let Stacy pull me back into the real world. I didn't want to join the real world, because I knew what that meant. Rejoining the real world meant feeling more pain. Rejoining the real world meant letting go of Dad.

God could have brought me back. But I was too stubborn and full of anger. And so I stopped talking to God as well. My soul was now officially adrift. Lost, isolated, and disconnected.

At the bottom of that pile of unfinished business on the roll top was the answer to getting my life back. The answer to finding my soul. The map for finding my way back home. I knew it, but I couldn't face it. For it meant not only severing my role as martyr with Dad. It meant severing my life with him.

At the bottom of that pile was a short list I had compiled the list many months ago, at Dr. Jahnke's request. It had three phone numbers on it. They were the phone numbers of the three residential facilities in the area. Calling those numbers meant the end of my time with Dad. I already knew what the outcome of those calls would be. It was Dad's death sentence.

It also meant getting my wife, my children, my life, and my soul back.

It was up to me, and me only. It was my choice.

58 { 2:28 AM

The fall was unusually short this year, or so it seemed. It was already Thanksgiving again, but it felt like mid winter to me. It was already unusually cold for November. At bedtime this particular evening, the temperature outside was 15 degrees, with a stiff wind howling outside our bedroom windows. There was an icy draft coming in over our bed, and I curled up with Stacy to stay warm. It was a Sunday night, and we had turned in early in order to be fresh and rested for the start of the workweek. I used to like these very cold nights in the winter. I would burrow under the covers and sleep like a baby.

At 2:28 AM, I awakened. A couple seconds later the phone rang. I don't recall when I noticed I had this talent for awakening just before the phone would ring, but I had had it for many years, going back to at least my adolescence.

"Damn Youth Center," I mumbled as I slowly came to life. By the third ring I had mustered enough consciousness to pick up the receiver.

"Hello, it's Dr. Turke." I normally didn't answer the phone so formally, but in the middle of the night I did, because it was almost always the detention center with a distraught or suicidal kid.

The voice on the other end wasn't one of the accustomed Youth Center night shift staff. It was a familiar voice, however. It was my dad.

"Hello, Doctor, er, ah, Garrett, ah, no, I mean, Dr. Fang." Dad not only sounded confused, he sounded out of breath. "Ah, say, do you know where, ah, where he is?"

"Where who is, Dad? Who are you looking for?" I was starting to wake up a little.

"You know, the man. The big guy who picks me up to go to work?"

"You mean your Spec Tran ride to the ALFA Center?"

"That's it! So, I've been waiting out here a long time and the son of a bitch isn't here yet!"

"Dad, its 2:30 in the morning. He won't be there until morning. Go back to bed."

"Really?"

"Yeah, Dad. It's way too early. Where are you waiting?"

"I've been outside. It's really, really cold out!"

"I know it is, so just go back inside, lock the door, and crawl into your nice warm bed. I'll call you in the morning when its time for your ride."

"OK, if you think so, you mean I won't miss my ride?"

"No, you won't miss your ride. Now go back to bed."

"OK, I love you, Fang."

"Go back to bed, Dad, right now. I'm going to hang up, OK?"

"OK, I'm going to bed."

I hung up the phone and tried to fall back asleep. Stacy groaned as if she was annoyed. She was still mostly asleep.

2:48 AM. The phone rang again. I didn't have to wake up this time, because I never fell back asleep. It was Dad again. I could hear him shivering. "Dr. Fang, is that you?"

"Yes, Dad."

"Where the hell is my ride? It's so cold outside!"

"Dad, I thought you were going back to bed. We just talked about this."

"We did?"

I snapped. I was really getting angry. Dad was ruining my chance to get some sleep. My only escape from all of the stress created by him. How am I going to function at work tomorrow?

"Damn it, Dad! Listen to me. It's the middle of the night. You'll freeze outside, it's probably below zero by now. Stay inside and go to bed. I'll call you in the morning, when its time to go to work."

It was much too much of a sequence for Dad to follow. And still I got angry at him. "Dad! Go inside, now! Its time to go to sleep."

"OK, Fang." Dad hung up the phone.

3:05 AM. Still not asleep. The phone rang again.

This time, Stacy woke up all the way. "Honey, I think you need to go over there."

I picked up the phone. I was too irritated, too sleep deprived, to be sensitive. Dad was still shivering. "Fang. You said you were going to call for my ride to work. Son of a bitch isn't here yet. Some help you are!! What are you trying to do, get me to freeze to death?"

Before I could answer him, Stacy sat up in bed. "Honey, it's near zero outside. He could die if he stays out there. He could try to walk to work. You or Tiff have to go over there."

Stacy was right. He could die out there. And I was worried about getting enough sleep! "Dad, I'm sorry. I couldn't get a hold of your ride. So I'm coming over to take you to work. Will you please go inside and wait for me?"

"Sure, sure. So you'll be here, soon?"

"Dad, I'll be there in 13 minutes."

"OK. I'll wait for you. You're going in to work too, right? You're going in with me?"

"Yep. We've both got the early shift together."

"Great. So we'll be working together. I'll see you soon. But hurry, OK? It's pretty cold out."

I hung up the phone, raced into my jeans, threw on my heavy parka, and climbed into the van. I did the math inside my head. OK, 13 minutes to Dad's, half an hour to lie to him and to get him back to bed, 13 minutes home, lets see, it will be about 4:15 when I get back. Yeah, OK, that will give me two hours of sleep before I have to get up to go to work.

Although there was absolutely no one on the roads, I still managed to get stuck behind some railroad tracks as a long train came through. It was hauling automobile factory supplies in from Flint. At 3:10 in the morning. I came to a stop, looked up at the crystal clear, sub zero sky and just lost it. It was a furious, blinding anger, an accumulation of the last two years of pain and frustration and rage that just poured out, unchecked, uncensored, and un-modulated.

"You mother fucking son of a bitch, you're wrecking my life, my family, my world. All my plans, you've killed them all, you sad, sorry, mother fucking bitch!!! You mother fucking bitch!! You hear me! You hear me, Dad! Why don't you just fucking die already? This is what it's going to be all the time for me, isn't it? Isn't it? What do I have to look forward to anymore? You bastard! Why did you have to get so sick? Who are you? What are you? This is going to be my life from now on? You'll be calling me up all night? And I'll have to drive over whenever you trip out? Where's my life, you bastard! And you too, God? Why are you doing this to me? Why don't you just take him? Just take him, damnitall to hell! He has no quality of life and it's killing my quality of life! What are you waiting for? So you can torture me some more? You hear me? You hear me, God!!! I don't want this life! This is no kind of life for anyone! Just take him! I'm ready!!!"

The last clickity-clack car went by, and then the caboose. The gates lifted. I was now pumped full with an entire football team's worth of adrenalin. I had scared myself. I was so far over the line. I was out of touch with reality for more than just a moment. There was no denying how stressed I was. There was no denying how much pain and anger had accumulated. It frightened me that I had lost such control.

When I came into Dad's neighborhood, I could see Dad standing in his driveway. He had on his lightweight Navy windbreaker, suitable for a 60 degree day. The van's outside thermometer read 6 degrees.

My dad was ice cold when I got to him. I put my arms around him and took him inside. He was shivering and his lips were blue. I made him some hot tea; got him dressed back into his pajamas, and told him work had called and given us the day off. I tucked him in bed, not unlike a parent would do with a little kid, and told him I would see him in the morning. He soon fell asleep and was snoring. I stayed with him, and kissed him on his forehead. I thought of a line from a Bob Marley song, which was a variation of a Bible verse, "Once a man and twice a child, and everything's just for a while..."

I thought about slipping out and going back home. Instead I called Stacy and told her I wasn't coming back home tonight. I found a blanket and curled up on Dad's sofa. I was exhausted. I tried to go to sleep, but I couldn't.

59 { Unfinished Business

I grabbed the pile of unfinished business off the top of my roll top desk. It was early in the morning, and no one was up yet. The unfinished business pile had gotten pretty large, and it took two hands to carry it. I had to balance the pile as I made my way downstairs, careful not to wake anyone up. It was not even 5 AM yet.

I had told myself today was the day I would quit procrastinating and clean up everything in that pile. There were cards to Arthur I had purchased but never got around to sending. Arthur was still writing Dad at least weekly, and almost every trip to the post office would yield at least a card or letter from him. Semper Fi. Dad was still writing him back, as I oversaw that process. But I had reneged on my promise to keep in touch with Arthur, to keep him apprised of Dad's status. It wasn't just a lack of time, laziness, or simple procrastination. It was just too painful to tell Arthur, and everyone else, of Dad's decline, over and over and over again.

In that pile was a letter to my sister Cindy. It had been started, but wasn't quite finished. I wanted to write a letter that said I loved her and wanted her to come back to the family. That was hard enough. But I figured the letter would also need to address Dad's failing functioning, and that was just too hard to bear. It would no doubt bring up all the old questions, and all the old family ills. I had fantasized what Cindy's response might be to my report on Dad. "Good! I'm glad that bastard is dying! It's about time! The one you hold in such high regard abused me! And now, I'm going to tell you everything! See how that fits in with your image of The Champion!!" I didn't know if this would be her response, but I feared it.

The pile also contained reminders of my hopes and dreams, all delayed, deferred, or otherwise brutally postponed by Dad's disease. A brochure from a local pool building company, as I had always wanted to build an in-ground pool in our backyard. There were brochures from places I still wanted to visit, including China, Sicily and Sardinia, Greece, Israel and my ancestral homeland in Germany and Turkey. Also in that pile was a big stack of art booth catalogues I had sent away for. My fantasy had always been to finance our family's world travels with money I made from selling my photography at various art shows across the country. My images were selling pretty consistently at La Bella Galleria. Verna and Barb told me that I should take my work on the road.

On the bottom of the pile was what I had really come to take care of, however. The list of geriatric residential facilities in the area. I was still struggling to convince myself that despite all the warning signs, it was too soon. Dad didn't need intensive residential care yet, and if he was floundering, it was only because I wasn't doing everything I could to help him.

But beneath all the rationalizations, all the denial, all the psychological smoke and mirrors, I really did know what Dad's status was. He was floundering. His time frames were all screwed up, he didn't recognize most people outside of the immediate family, he was delusional much of the time, and he wasn't able to care for himself at all any more. Bringing down that big pile from the roll top was just a cover up for what needed to be done next. All I needed from that pile was the small list at the bottom. It was time. I had a decision to make.

I pulled out that list and stared at it. What is it going to be, Garrett? Your family or your father? Your dreams or your care-giving? Your life returned, in exchange for Dad's residential placement? Your life returned, in exchange for Dad's death sentence.

It looked so simple on a scrap of paper. Just three names and three phone numbers. The first was Clare Bridge of Meridian, part of a national geriatric health care chain, and within walking distance from my house. It was modern, nicely landscaped, and "homey," from the outside at least. It had been built just within the last few years, and I drove past it each day coming home from work. The second was the county's regional geriatric care facility, about five miles away, well established, but more institutionalized looking. The last was Burcham Hills, a continuum of care campus in East Lansing that had living accommodations ranging from independent retirement apartments to an assisted living complex to nursing home level residential care. Burcham Hills was the facility I had contacted back in 2000, and where a nurse had told me that Dad would most likely need to be placed within a couple of years. Well, 2002 was already here.

I used all my psychologist skills. I pictured what life would be like for me if Dad was in residential care. I pictured myself playing with my kids on Saturdays, outside in the sun, instead of being over at Dad's all day and scheduling 30 minutes in the late afternoon to be with my children. I pictured Stacy and me back in Italy, in some romantic little villa, with a bottle of wine and Bocelli in the background. I pictured myself with my camera and tripod, rugged and adventurous, hiking up the Great Wall of China. And I pictured myself with a big, beautiful, relaxing pool in my backyard, even bigger and more magnificent than the one we had in California. It didn't matter to me we would only be able to use the pool four months a year, because Michigan's climate would only make us appreciate it even more.

I also pictured Dad living in a residential care facility. I could see myself stopping by on my way home from work each day to visit him. But I couldn't create an image of my dad inside the care facility that had any semblance of positive connotation. The image I ended up with was a nightmare every time. Dad crying and pleading with me to take him home whenever I stopped by to visit. Dad sitting alone, depressed, in some isolated corner, while staff neglected him. Dad urinating and defecating on himself, sitting there in diapers, festering in a pool of stench. Dad just lying there, helpless, lost, alone, just waiting to die.

I had to make a decision. I knew it couldn't be just my decision. Tiff and Mom, and Stacy and Dr. Jahnke all needed to be a part of this. And yet I knew the deciding vote probably was mine. I had seen to it that I was the lead caregiver. I had wanted that role, that responsibility, that status. Sure, I would call a family wraparound meeting to discuss and make the decision. But I knew my family and the wraparound team would ultimately respect what I felt Dad needed. Dad's ability to function hinged on my care giving. He was in my hands. This was going to be my call.

The ambivalence was torturing me. The way I saw it, I would be getting my life back at the expense of pulling the plug on Dad's life support system. All sorts of images flashed through my head. 1965: Dad and I holding hands, jumping the waves at Zuma Beach. 1966: Going sledding up in the mountains above Palm Springs. 1967: Dad buying me my first tie-dyed hippy pants. 1968: Dad coaching my YMCA softball team. 1974: Sailing around Marion Island with Dad in Grand Traverse Bay. 1990: Dad going to Senegal, West Africa with Stacy and me, and with my first tour group. 1997: Dad winning his minority students appreciation award at Michigan State, with Tiffanie and I proudly by his side.

I got the kitchen trash container out from under the sink and brought it up to the table. I had made my decision. I was angry about it, as I knew I would be.

I threw out the travel brochures. I threw out the artist booth catalogues. I kept the cards for Arthur. I kept the half completed letter to Cindy. I threw out the list with the residential care facilities names and phone numbers on it.

I couldn't pull the plug on my father.

I went into the living room and lay down on the couch in the dark. I started crying. It had been a while since I had done that, as I hadn't allowed myself to let go. I cried because I had let Stacy down. I cried because I had let my kids down. But most of all, I cried because I had let myself down. I had just thrown out all my dreams in the kitchen trash for a dying man. A dying man who had changed so much that I couldn't even tell if he was my father or a stranger.

Stacy came down and found me sobbing on the couch. She hugged me, like she always did. This time I hugged back. "Whatcha doing, here, honey, in the dark?"

"Thinking about Walter." It was the first time in my life I had called him by his first name.

60 { Angela

The days and weeks after I made the decision not to place Dad in residential care haunted me. It was a wrong decision. It was a wrong turn back into the forest. Back off the trail. Back into the darkness. No one, except me, knew that I had stepped to the plate to make a decision and backed away. Tiffanie, Don, and Mom all thought the wraparound was still working adequately. They had not been privy to all of Dad's recent failings, as I had really not stressed to them the magnitude of his decline. I didn't want to. Tiffanie was reveling in her new, recently built house. I didn't want to mess with that, although on a lot of levels I resented that she seemed happy. How could she be enjoying life with our dad flailing so? And my mom, always looking for the positives, kept insisting that Dad was still lucid and responsive in their weekly trips down memory lane.

Stacy knew Dad was struggling so, but she did not know that I had got up that fateful morning to make a decision and had failed. I kept the failure to myself, and it festered inside me. I had chosen to neglect the living and damn myself. Just in order to stave off Dad's inevitable placement in residential care a little while more.

Christmas soon was gone, and so was New Years. This year the holidays went by quietly. Stacy and the girls knew I was depleted and didn't try to cheerlead me on. I was getting depressed again. The dark, cloudy, snowy winter days, normally a time of rest and introspection for me, became unbearably symbolic of Dad's last days before what I figured would be his death sentence and execution. And no matter how hard I tried to be kind to myself, I continued to see myself as the executioner.

How had I allowed myself to get this depressed again? I had managed to get through the previous years of Dad's disease by finding renewed meaning in my relationship with my father, and to value every speck of remaining time with him. I had gotten through with my spirituality and my faith and belief in God. I had gotten through by trusting other people. And now I was lost again, unable to find my link with other people, and with God. I was still trying to push and control things. But the solution to my woes could only be found by letting myself be pulled again.

And now, I was close to just plain giving up.

It had been a long time since I had been visited by one of my guardian angels. I thought about how long it had been since I had been uplifted by one of those kind souls, those charismatic spirits that I had come across so frequently in the past two years. They seemed to have left me during the last six months, alone, and I wondered if they would ever return.

On a particularly gray Monday in early winter, when it wouldn't clear and it wouldn't snow, I set out for my afternoon consultation at the detention center. I had thoughts on the ride over that I wasn't up for working in that place today, and I contemplated bailing and calling in sick. I never did that, and so I thought if I avoided my responsibilities just this one afternoon, no one would question it. But by the time I had given this escape plan any real thought, it was too late. I was already pulling into the detention center parking lot. It was a good thing, too, for inside the walls of the building that day was an angel who was waiting for me. Angela.

Angela had been an employee at the detention center a couple years. She worked the afternoon shifts. I saw her at least twice each week, on the days when I consulted in the afternoons. I was always in "competent doctor mode" when she saw me, and I rarely let my guard down. She was always in "competent child care worker mode" when I saw her, and she rarely let her guard down. But I liked her and she liked me. I had to call her "Miss C," as was the detention center protocol, and she had to call me "Dr. Turke." These formalities were set up primarily for the kids, as it was very important to set clear relationship boundaries with them. We typically talked shop, which in the detention center usually involved how to care for the troubled kids who resided there. Once in awhile, Angela shared bits and pieces of her life with me.

Angela was about 30 years old. I knew she was from the south side of Chicago. I knew she was deeply spiritual, and deeply religious. Southern Baptist, I believe. Angela had been trained in the National Guard before finding work at the detention center. She was an interesting blend of Jesus inspired, Bible quoting, African American maternal warmth and a regimented boot camp sergeant. She was no nonsense and about business whenever she was at work.

Angela had a way about the kids. She could keep them in line, yes, but she could also melt them. There were not many people who could earn these kids' respect while still finding their way into their hearts.

I pushed the intercom button. "Good afternoon. How can I help you, sir?"

I recognized the voice as Angela's. She must be working control today. "Hi, it's Dr. Turke."

The voice brought life to the drab gray intercom box. "Oh, hi, Dr. Turke, how are you doing? God bless you and come on in."

Angela was at the helm in the Control Room. She was monitoring a hundred switch control panel that opened and closed security doors throughout the building. It would be her job to keep the building and all its people, staff and kids, safe today.

"Dr. Turke, how are you? It is always so nice to see you! How are your wife and kids? May God bless you on this fine day."

"Hi, Miss C. How's it going inside the fort today?"

Angela motioned for another staff to take over the control board for a moment. She stood up, and came over to me, discretely. I knew immediately something was wrong.

"Dr. Turke, somebody, an older gentleman who seems to know you, has been calling here for hours. He says his name is Walter. We have been trying to locate you, but you apparently have your cell phone turned off."

I pulled my cell phone out of my pocket. It was turned off. How the hell did that happen? That phone was my emergency hotline, both to the detention center and to my family. I never turned my cell phone off.

"Dr. Turke, this gentleman sounds really distressed. He doesn't always call you Dr. Turke, either, it's really rather strange, he calls you Garrett, Gary, and then sometimes he calls you fang, or something like that. Do you know who he is? He says he's been outside a lot, looking for you, you are supposed to be driving him somewhere?"

I turned completely white. I was immobilized. Angela noticed, immediately, that I was suffocating in stress. It was flooding me.

"Honey, please, sit down. You're not OK, are you? Sweet Jesus, we need you here. Right now, Lord! What is the matter, Doctor Turke? Who is this person that keeps calling?"

I couldn't even begin to get back into competent doctor mode. "It's my Dad, Angela. He has Alzheimer's disease. I'm so stressed out. I'm trying to take care of him and it was working and now I just can't seem to do it anymore. I can't do it anymore! I'm so tired. He's not safe, he's calling for me all the time, he's out in the snow and in the night looking for me. I just can't keep up with it anymore. I promised myself I would always take care of him. I promised! And now it seems like I can't hold on anymore. He's slipping from me and I can't hold on to him. I try and I try and I work harder and harder and harder and he still is slipping away!"

"Honey, we have to get you some help taking care of your father. Child, this is God's business, it's not yours. You are not letting go of him. You need to let God take care of him. You cannot do this alone! I know you want to, but you can't anymore. It's just too big for one person. How can I help you do this?"

I looked down and away for a second, trying to avoid. It was a strange juxtaposition of roles for me. I was the therapist, and I was the caregiver. I was supposed to be the one holding everyone else up.

Angela grabbed my hand and held on. "Dr. Turke, you are a wonderful son to your father. But he needs more help than you can give. It sounds like he needs people with him, around him, all the time now.

"I don't know what to do, Angela. My family is doing all they can. My sister has a new house and she has a family and can't always..."

"What about your family, Dr. Turke? Your wife and kids? You all need more help than this."

"I don't know what to do. Hire a stranger to live with him? I don't know if I can trust anyone like that."

"Dr. Turke, I can help take care of your father, if you need someone. My family is all in Chicago. I'm not that busy here. I will help you. My church will help you. Please, Dr. Turke. You can't do this by yourself anymore."

"I don't know you well enough to impose like that. And I can't impose on your church."

"What do you mean, Dr. Turke? I do too know you! You and I have been working together for years. And the church is a family. It's my family. And it's your family. We are all God's children, I know you know that, Dr. Turke." Angela gripped my hand tighter again. "Honey, it seems someone needs to be with your father all the time now. It's getting to be his time. It's not just you and him anymore. It's between God and him. God will take care of you and your father. You will see."

Angela let go of my hand and went over to the Control Room's computer station. "Go back home and be with your Dad. Things are OK in here today, it's calm and the kids are all acclimated. Go be with your dad and talk to your family. I will help you. You just call me and tell me what you've decided. My church will be ready when you are."

Angela pulled up a blank Word "page" on the computer screen and started typing. "Now Dr. Turke, you get your coat on and get your things together. I'm going to type up a note to post to the staff, so when your dad calls again, they'll know what to do."

I didn't argue with Angela. I collected my things and put my coat and gloves on. The other staff in Control either patted me on the back or hugged me. They didn't have to say much. They all knew.

Within a minute or two Angela had finished her note and it was coming out of the printer. She showed it to me before posting it up for the staff.

It read,

"To all Staff.

This is very important. Please read and be ready to assist. Dr. Turke's father has Alzheimer's disease. His name is Walter. He is a very nice gentleman but he gets confused easily. If he calls the center looking for Dr. Turke, tell him that Dr. Turke is on his way, and tell him to stay inside to wait for him. Then call Dr. Turke at home or on his cell. If you can't reach Dr. Turke, then call his sister, Tiffanie. Their numbers are in our Rolodex. It is very important that we keep Dr. Turke's father calm and safe until we can contact Dr. Turke. This could happen at any time, day or night. We need to always be ready.

Remember, this isn't just Dr. Turke's father. He could be any of our fathers, any of our loved ones. We must treat him like we would any of God's children.

Please pray for Dr. Turke and his father, and God bless you.

Miss C."

I drove back to Dad's condo and found Dad pacing by the door waiting for me. We went out for dinner, I got him relaxed and calm again, and performed the 45 minute day. I tucked Dad in for the evening, prayed he would stay inside all night, and prayed for God to keep him safe.

In the van I prayed again, this time to give thanks for putting Miss C in my path today.

On the ride home, I thought about what Angela had said to me. She was sincere in her offer to assist with my Dad's care giving and to involve her church. She was right. Dad did need 24 hour care, if not now, very soon.

When I got home I asked Stacy to join me in the living room. I took her hand, and tearfully told her I had made a decision. It was time to place Dad in a residential facility. I swallowed my belief that it was Dad's death sentence. I had to do this for me, and for my family.

I told Stacy we would call a wraparound meeting and discuss this as a family. I knew that my sister would take it hard. I knew my mother would only see the positives.

I never needed to call on Angela and her church after making my decision that day. I didn't need to. I had gotten her message loud and clear, punctuated by that spiritual presence rippling down my spine.

"We are all God's children." "This is between your father and God, not you." "It's his time with God." "You're not letting go of him, you need to let God take care of him." "God will take care of you and your father. You will see."

Miss C has since left the detention center to move back to Chicago. She wanted to be closer to her family. I hope that someday she will read these words, as I have never properly thanked her.

God bless you, Angela. Thank you for helping me, and for restoring my faith.

61 } The Epiphany

The epiphany came to me early the next morning while I was praying, before I had even opened my eyes in bed. I began thinking about all the things that had happened to hold me up and to prevent Dad from falling down. All of the people in his life who reappeared after all these years to help him. All of the strangers who arrived in Dad's and my life at precisely the right time to help with critical decisions. The seemingly magical events that provided me with rather profound insights and lessons. The return of the Webbed Tentacle after nearly 50 years. The eagle that stopped time for Dad and me on Old Mission Peninsula. Selling enough photographs at precisely the right time to fund the phenomenal Italy trip. Arthur refusing to disappear and relentlessly and mysteriously pounding Semper Fi into my head. Dr. Jahnke emerging as a kind hero from the seemingly insensitive managed care system. And the prophetic words that first came from that out of place woman at the Secretary of State Office, now emphatically drilled into me by Angela: We are all God's children, we are all in God's hands. There were too many of these events to be left to chance.

Was God sending these people, these angels, to help ease us along the road that Dad was on? Maybe God wasn't sending them at all. Maybe God was simply uncovering them along the way. Were the angels always around Dad and me? Were the angels always around all of us?

In the months after my epiphany, I came to believe in angels. I also came to realize that the angels were not guiding me. They were pulling me. Was I on a journey that was leading somewhere? A journey that was purposeful and deliberate, intended if not planned? I wasn't quite sure yet where Dad and I were going, but would it lead to someplace good, someplace kind, some place safe?

I was afraid to tell anyone about the epiphany. I didn't want to sound preachy and I didn't want to look foolish or naïve. But by the end of a long winter, I felt myself getting stronger and stronger. There was a force at work that was greater than me, greater than my Dad, greater than his disease process, greater than anything else that life could throw at me.

All I had to do was let it pull me.

62 { Betrayal and Redemption

Monday morning. I had already called in sick the night before. I was exhausted and knew a night's sleep wouldn't have helped. I hadn't slept at all. Lying in bed, I continued to replay what had kept me awake all night.

I had delayed Dad's death sentence for over a year after Dr. Jahnke had first instructed me to find him a "memory care facility." But now, Dad's wait in line was up. I couldn't stay the execution anymore. And it was going to be me, the one who had loved and supported and propped up The Champion, the one who had worked so hard to delay the inevitable, who would deliver the final verdict. I was going to be the executioner. I was going to be the one to betray him.

My often cruel conscience tried to take the lead, like it had so many times before. It now seemed bigger than just my conscience. It was like an invader, a demon intruding into my soul, always appearing without warning: You're sending your Dad to his death sentence. Don't give me all that you are trying to help him shit. You know full well what you are doing. You know residential care, if that's what you want to call it, will kill him. That's right, kill him. And it will be you who sets the whole thing up and betrays him. Simple as that.

The cruel demon invader was countered by another voice within my head. This voice was soothing, kind, and enveloping. Why are you beating yourself up so? Have you not heard, did you not listen, did you not heed your lessons? Your father's time is drawing near. This is not up to you anymore. You carried him this far, and now your journey is coming to an end. It's time to go back home, to be with your family again. You have done enough. It's time for me to carry him now. You have heard this before. Now it's time for you to listen, and to follow.

The cruel demon voice tried to regain control. But the soothing, all enveloping voice pushed it back again. You have been a great son to your father. You are a great son! Your father will cherish you forever. Your family understands that you needed to care for him. Things will be all right. You will see. There are still lessons to be learned, for you, and for your father. But now you must trust. You are too tired to carry him anymore. Everyone is too tired to carry him. I will carry him the rest of the way. All you have to do is let go.

Stacy's voice momentarily broke up the war inside my head. "Hurry up, Shani, it's time to go! Miah and I will meet you in the car!" I could hear Stacy's voice resonating throughout the house. I could hear Shani scrambling down the steps, the garage door opening and closing, then the car door closing and the sound of the car pulling out and away from our driveway.

I was back alone with my thoughts. I had made the decision for Dad to go to Clare Bridge for residential placement a few days before. I had been warring inside my head ever since. I knew that the only cure for my painful rumination was to enact the decision.

Although I had never been inside the walls of the Clare Bridge Memory Care Facility, I already knew that it was going to be Dad's next stop. His final stop. For the past several years, I had driven by the facility four, five, six times each day, dropping Shani off at the middle school, on my way to work, on my way home, and whenever I went into town. The facility was attractive from the outside, there were flowers out front in the spring and summer, and a nicely landscaped fenced-in courtyard. The building was single story, and nicely kept up and painted. It looked much more like a large home than an institution. And it was less than a five minute drive from my house. I could even walk it on a nice day if I wanted.

For someone who used to be all about science and logic, I made the decision for Dad to go to Clare Bridge without really conducting any research about cost, level of care, reputation, or suitability to Dad's needs. And for someone who prided himself in fairness, team play, and democratic decision-making, I had also made the decision completely autocratically. I suppose I could have unconsciously made the decision based on how the building looked, or its close proximity to my house. But those explanations really didn't feel like the reasons for my decision. It was more of a spiritual, intuitive pull toward the building. I would not be able to explain it logically, because logic never entered into my decision. I just had a strong feeling that Dad, if he had to be placed somewhere, had to be placed there.

An hour later I had showered, shaved, brushed my teeth, took my anti-hypertension medication, and weighed myself. 215 pounds. Not exactly fat, but not the trim 185 pounds I had been prior to Dad getting sick. I knew that all of that weight was due to the stress of Dad's care-giving. I thought someday, after all this was over, that I would take that weight back off again.

I thought I would make a little trip to the Meijer grocery store, where I would pick out something good for dinner tonight. Yeah, that's a good idea; I'll make a gourmet dinner for Stacy and the girls. I haven't done that for a long time.

As I headed down Marsh Road, I had a very strong impulse to put my blinker on and pull into the Clare Bridge driveway. Why not? I was going right past the facility anyway. I could stop in and get some information, maybe even be brave enough to schedule an appointment to discuss Dad's potential admission there. I felt a surge of panic race up from my stomach to my throat, but it didn't stop me. I put my blinker on, and pulled into the left turn lane.

Then "it" returned. The demon-intruder side of my conscience. The entity that called me, "the executioner." It was cruel, as was its nature, and it tried to stick me, razor sharp and lethal, right through the heart.

I thought we already went through this! So now, you're ready to go in there and make plans to end it all for him. Put him away for good. So you won't have to be bothered by him anymore. I knew you'd cave in! Can't deal with the pressure. He's counting on you to protect him and instead you're going to send him to his death sentence.

I turned off my left blinker, checked the rear view, put my right blinker on and got back onto Marsh Road. Clare Bridge was soon behind me.

The intruder didn't want to relinquish control. *That's better. Well, finally you made the right decision. Now go on, get out of here. You've got to go make a nice dinner for your family. And don't forget to invite your father. What do you think he was going to do after he got home from the ALFA Center? Fix his own dinner? Come on now, you know better than that.*

The demon-intruder was relentless. I pictured myself screaming inside my own mind. But instead of reeling, this time I fought back. Fuck you! Fuck you, whoever, whatever you are! Fuck you! You hear me, fuck you!!! I'm not doing this anymore! I'm done! I'm not listening to you! Fuck you! You think you are so powerful, you can try to torture me, go ahead, go ahead! This time I'm going to fight you back! I'll tear you up, you son of a bitch! Fuck you! You can't hurt me, God is protecting me! Go on, try it! You're not going to hurt me anymore!

It was the first time I had really stood up to the demon-intruder.

I pulled into the Meridian mall parking lot and turned around, now heading back north on Marsh Road.

I'm warning you, if you step into that facility, I swear I will never, ever, leave you alone. This will be your fatal mistake! How'd you like me, the intruder-demon as you call me, to stay with you, forever! Well, just do it and find out!

I turned on my right blinker and slowed down. My heart was racing. I couldn't think. Please, please dear God, protect me. Please, please, dear God, get this voice out of my head.

I entered the foyer, where there was a welcome sign, a calendar of activities upcoming at the facility, and a big bowl of fruit. Peering through the entrance door, I could see a group of residents sitting around in a circle, doing some sort of activity with one of the staff members. I pushed the intercom button, and a simulated doorbell chime sounded. A beautiful young woman, with tight braids and an East African accent, opened the door. Although the accent wasn't the same, she immediately reminded me of Angela.

"Why good morning, sir! Come right in. We are so happy to see you on this fine day! Are you here to see one of our residents?" The beautiful woman had the same aura as Angela. Come to think of it, she had the same aura as all of the other angels that had pulled me during the past two and a half years.

"Well, no, actually, no, I'm not...I'm, I'm not actually... here for somebody that's placed..." I was stammering, and so full of panic suddenly that I couldn't speak fluidly. Two and a half years of pent up trauma was coming out. No, not here, stay composed, stay composed! Please God, help me hold it together. I can't let down here! This isn't appropriate...

"Sir, are you alright? My name is Eunice. And you are?"

"Garrett. It's, it's about...I'm here because...Well, I thought I'd stop by to see about...I'm sorry...It's, it's... it's my father."

"You poor child, come-come, you must sit down. Come, I'll get you some coffee or some tea or some juice. You just sit down and rest." Eunice grabbed my hand and had me sit down in the lobby, right in the midst of the residents' group. "You need to talk to our director. His name is Charles, and I will tell him you are here. But first, let me get you some juice. You just sit and relax."

As I waited, I watched the morning's activity. I was among about ten residents, sitting around what looked like a large living room. Big band music from the 40's was playing softly in the background. The group was playing some sort of trivia game about entertainment stars from the 1930's and 40's. I knew most of the answers, because I had watched all the movies and listened to all the recordings from that era with my dad.

"Harry James!" shouted out one of the residents.

"Duke Ellington!"

"Judy Garland!"

The residents actually seemed to be enjoying themselves. They were all clean. Most looked actually kind of cheerful. Some looked really impaired, in wheelchairs, drifting in and out, but a lot looked relatively intact, like my dad. It was nothing like the nightmare I had been designing for months inside my head.

The staff group leader, a perky young woman named Heather, had stumped the audience with the next question. "Who was a famous clarinetist from the 30's and 40's? Come on now, I'll give you a hint. First name starts with a B."

The audience was stuck. They looked around at each other for help.

"Garrett, here's your juice. I have let Charles know that you're here." Eunice touched my shoulder and smiled. I melted.

"Thank you, you are so kind."

"We are all God's children. Every one of us. Our parents here, they are also in God's hands, as are you." The kind soul with the tight braids and pretty face swept her hands across the air in front of her, as if to make sure I understood she was including every one in the room.

It was pretty much the same message; no it was exactly the same message, which had been delivered by Angela at the detention center.

"Come on now, everyone!" exclaimed the group leader. "We can't end our game here! Who was the famous big band leader who played the clarinet? First name starts with a B?"

I could immediately picture my father dancing to one of his old records. It was a comforting image, and it lingered and hung in my mind. "Benny Goodman!" I shouted it, full of enthusiasm, and with a great big smile. The demon intruder voice was nowhere to be found.

"That's right! Let's give the gentleman a great big hand and welcome him to Clare Bridge!"

The audience, well those that were higher functioning, all looked over at me and smiled. The man next to me extended his hand. Several clapped their hands. The man next to me asked me if I had seen his car, telling me it was due for an oil change.

"Who's father, or son, or brother are you here to see?" said another one of the residents. He looked like he was about a hundred years old, with huge ears and huge glasses. I later found out that Bob was 97.

I answered proudly, "I am Garrett, and I am Walter's son. He is not here yet, but he will be, soon."

I had found Dad's new home. No, I hadn't "found" Dad's new home at all. It had found me.

I had been pulled to it.

63 { Charles

The office door behind me opened and a slender, boyish looking young man emerged, scanning the day room. He had a stylish goatee, and a baby face that made him look very young. I pegged him to be about 18 or 20. Although the sign on the office door from which he came said Director, I was sure this man was a young employee, or maybe one of the residents' grandkids, who had been talking to the director. The young man's face finished scanning the room as soon as he found me.

"Hello, I'm Charles. I'm the director here."

I was stunned. "Hello, I'm Garrett Turke." The words out of my mouth were appropriate, but my mind was already racing off in another direction, filled with silent questions. What on earth, they have a kid as the director?

"Nice to meet you, Garrett. Why don't you come back to my office and we can talk?"

"That would be great." But before I could even stand up, Charles had whisked one of the residents to her feet, and was dancing around the resident-audience like a hyperactive butterfly. Heather turned up the boom box, and Glenn Miller's horns filled the room with swing.

Charles was laughing with delight as he swung around one of the residents in a sophisticated dance step. "Why hello there, Doris, shall we show them what we've got?"

Doris was enthralled by him, her face aglow, like a young woman at her first prom. I could hear whispers from the audience.

"Is that her husband?"

"No, no, no! He's married to that woman over there, I think!" The man pointed to the group leader, Heather.

"I wish he was my husband."

"He is so handsome."

Charles was humming out loud to the music as he danced with Doris, who was dressed in attire that might have been appropriate for a ballroom dance in the 1940's. Soon Charles had taken Doris' long boa from around her neck and put it around his neck, draping himself like someone at an amateur burlesque show. It was hysterically funny.

Charles' face was full of joyful expression. He pranced and dipped and swayed as he danced Doris around the perimeter of the audience. It was clear he loved these residents. Charles was single-handedly breathing life back into Doris. She had been transformed back to her prom night in 1947.

"Can I have the next dance?" asked a very frail 90 year old woman a few feet away. For the moment, she was no longer 90. She was a shy 16 year old.

"Why you most certainly may. But first, I have to meet with this kind gentleman here." Charles pointed over to me.

Charles finished his dance with Doris by twirling her, and then the finale, an exaggerated dip, with Charles swinging his head back and holding a pose. The audience clapped and roared. And Charles, again in exaggerated fashion, bowed several times to the audience. I was in awe of how the room had been transformed. I thought to myself. Man, this guy is not your ordinary guardian angel. He was like some guardian angel prototype.

"Come right this way, Garrett. Whew! That was hard work! I'm all sweaty." Charles fanned himself with his hand, then led me to his office and closed the door. "Sorry for the interruption out there. We try to make the most of every moment here, and, well, I felt the spirit move me." Charles laughed a little as if to make it clear he was joking. Looking back in retrospect, I don't think he was.

"That was amazing. No, really. How you brought that woman to life."

"Oh, you mean Doris. It's not that hard, really. They are just like anyone else. They need love, that's all. It's so easy to forget that when they get dementia, they still need what all of us do."

"Do you do that for all the patients, er, I mean, residents, or whatever..."

"We don't look at them that way. They are not patients, and we don't really like calling them residents, either. This is their home. And we are their family. We just can't stop loving them just because they got sick! That's what's wrong with our culture. These older people, they have so much to give us, even if they have dementia. They have wisdom and experience, and they will be the ones to pass over before it is our turn."

Huh? What does that mean, pass over? What is he talking about?

Charles then leaned forward toward me, to emphasize his next point. "This is not Doris or Bob or Jim the patient. They are somebody's parent, and somebody's son. Bob is someone's father and someone's son, just like you. They must be treated like human beings, with the respect that is owed them, not just discarded somewhere."

I had a shiver run my spine like I had never had before. It was like there was a holy presence in the room, hanging there, permeating, and enveloping the both of us.

Charles continued. "I create a biography for every one of our family members here, and I put it in their file. The staff must read them. And then we kind of test each other at staff meetings. We must know our family members as real people."

"Now, Garrett, it's your turn. Tell me about what brings you to Clare Bridge."

"Well, my father is Walter. He is 72. He got sick ..." I paused, as I was getting choked up. I fought it at first. I wanted to stay in control. But I couldn't. There was too much pressure backed up behind the dam.

"Garrett, please don't worry. You are not alone here. You are coming to us just like all the other sons and daughters do."

I wept. Not just a few fought back tears that managed to sneak through. I wept, hard. I opened the valve that had been holding the dam waters back.

"I see that you love your father very much."

An hour later Charles knew my whole story. He gave me a brochure and told me to look it over. It asked him how long the wait list was. He said that they had two immediate openings, that two previous residents, ah family members, had been in hospice and "passed over." I didn't want to clarify what that meant, even though Charles had said it twice already.

Before I left, Charles gave me a tour of the facility and introduced me to almost the entire staff, from Therese, the head nurse, and Heather, the activities director, to all the direct care staff, and Peter, the cook. I noticed that most of the direct care staff were African immigrants. They had a range of different accents, some with Christian names and some with Muslim names. I didn't know it just then, but Charles and his staff were going to be my teachers. There were a lot of lessons to be learned inside Clare Bridge.

Charles finished his tour and escorted me back to the front door. He punched a numeric code into a box near the door and a green light came on.

"So, Charles, that code unlocks the door?"

"None of the doors are locked here. That just releases the alarm that will go off if the door has been breached."

"None of the doors are locked?" I sounded concerned, because I was.

"No, they can't be, for the type of license we have. It would violate our fire codes. We just have alarms that go off, to alert us in the event that someone tries to wander off. Then the staff will orient them back into the building."

I was still uncomfortable, and increasingly perplexed. "Wait a second. The doors aren't even locked? For dementia patients?"

"They really don't need to be."

"Then why aren't they all trying to escape?"

"Escape?" Charles smiled knowingly, as if he had had this conversation a million times before. "Why would they want to escape? This is their home."

64 { Nowhere to be Found

My guilt for deciding to place Dad in a residential care home had been evaporating all week. And my self-debasing, all punishing conscience, the one that said I never did enough to help Dad, had vanished. I wasn't confident that the voice was gone for good, but it no longer had the upper hand, and it wasn't calling the shots. I had slept well every night since that visit to Clare Bridge and my meeting with Charles.

I had tomorrow's wraparound meeting all scripted out. I was going to tell the family that I had an introductory tour set up at Clare Bridge, just to give everyone an idea of what one memory care facility out there was like. I wasn't going to push Clare Bridge, just get them in the building and let the facility sell itself, precisely like it had happened with me. Yes, this was going to be a good week. I had resolved Dad's residential placement, I finally felt good about it, and nothing was going to go wrong for a change. Amen!

Despite my gentle nudging, Dad was still asleep next to me. "Dad, hey Dad! Wake up. Dad, come on, the movie's over. Time for dinner." I had to shake him rather hard to get him to stir. Finally he did.

"Huh? What are you doing? Cut it out!" Dad raised his forearm as if to block a punch. As he became more oriented, he recognized it was me, and the familiar smile returned to his groggy-looking face. "Oh, it's you. Doctor, ah... Doctor, Doctor..."

"Dad, I'm your son, Garrett."

"My son? I have a son? My son, if I had one, he is a young boy."

"You sometimes call me Dr. Fang, too."

"That's the one! Yes, it is you, Doctor Fang! I know who you are! You're the one who works with, you know, the whatchmacallits, those, the... the... gang people! You work with them, trying to get them to change, and you are the greatest!"

"And I'm also your son!"

"I don't think I have a son, Doctor. And if I do, he's nowhere to be found."

I felt an incredibly sharp pain tear through my heart.

65 { The Last Wraparound

"You guys have been amazing. We have been amazing. We have sacrificed so much to not only help and support Dad, but to keep him propped up and functioning as best he can. We helped him retire with dignity, we helped him move down here to be close to us, we got all his affairs in order without making him feel diminished as a person. He has been happy, he is still happy, he loves us, and there is no question he knows we love him. I have had some of my best times with him, I mean across my whole life, over these past two years."

As I glanced around the room, I noticed Tiff was starting to well up with tears. She knew what was coming next.

"As you know, Dad's functioning has been dropping off lately." My voice choked. Stacy held my hand. Tiff's eyes were filling. A few tears ran down her cheeks. I was choking up, my voice cracked, but I kept going, because I felt like I had to. It was always so important to stay in control.

"I saw Dr. Jahnke with Dad this week. You guys, he has dropped all the way to an eleven on the MMSE. He can't even follow instructions to fold a piece of paper in half anymore."

Tiff's face was now flushed, tears streaming down her face. Mom and Stacy both put their arms across her back.

Tiff tried to defend against the reality. "Garrett, sounds like he was having a bad day when you took him to Dr. Jahnke's. He can do better than that. I don't think he's that bad."

"Tiff, he no longer knows me as his son. I am now his trusted companion, who he calls Doctor. And you, you are his girlfriend. That's why he keeps trying to hold your hand the way he does."

Tiff started crying out loud. Mom and Stacy rubbed her back. It was brutal. I knew it would be. "Garrett, what are we going to do? He is our father.

He's still our father! Garrett, what's happening to him? What will happen to him?"

"Dr. Jahnke wants us to get him in a memory care facility." Now I welled up with tears. Stacy moved over to me, and started rubbing my back. I wanted to flinch and bristle, in order to maintain my distance and stay in control. But Stacy was more powerful. This was no place and no time to be in control. This was the place and time to let go.

I had one more thing to say before I let down. I stammered as the tears flowed. But I had to push it out, somehow. I caught my breath and forced out the words that were once delivered by the first guardian angel. "You guys, we must remember, this is just the beginning of the next stage. It is not the end. Far from it. We must remember, never stop loving him as our dad, as our loved one. That is how we keep his identity alive."

I broke down and cried. Tiff kept on crying. Don put his arm around Tiff. Stacy put her arm around me. Mom took the lead. I knew she would. She was not overcome with emotion like the rest of us. She was ready to deliver her lesson. She had been waiting to do so all morning.

"This is part of life. Maybe I will be the next in the family to need care. Someday it will be Garrett's turn, Stacy's turn, Tiffanie's turn, Don's turn. Someday it will be my grandkids' turns. Think of it as a natural course. It is painful, yes, but your father is feeling all this love for perhaps the first time in his life. You know his childhood. And when I was married to him, he didn't know how to receive love from someone else. Love to him was superficial, it was sexual, it wasn't deep, it couldn't carry him. Now he is feeling it for the first time. It is his lesson, before he dies. Whether he knows exactly who you are or not doesn't matter. You see, it's so much bigger than that. All that matters now is learning what he didn't learn before. He may not know that you are his son or his daughter anymore, but he does know that he is loved. That is his lesson, and that is your gift to him."

Mom wasn't finished. "Garrett and Tiff, my children, and Stacy and Donald, you are my children, too. You are loved more than you may know. Life's lesson is all about kindness, love, and forgiveness. You need to have learned these things before God will allow you to complete your course. Your father is getting ready to go on a journey to the next phase of his life. No, I'm not talking about his going to a memory care facility. He is getting ready to leave this earth, to go be with the Almighty, whatever you choose to call it or define it as. We can't stop the process, we can't control it, all we can do is help him get ready."

Mom had silenced the room. The tears had stopped. For a moment, there was no time and no place. For a moment, there was no pain and no sorrow. Everything had been transcended by Mom's powerful message.

Don brought us all back to the pragmatics. "So, what do we do next, Gart?"

"Well, we need to start looking at the different care facilities in our area. There are many, but I suggest that we stick to only those that are close to where we all live, because we'll need to be visiting Dad a lot."

Tiff was welling up with tears again. Mom resumed rubbing her back. Don put his arm around her.

I pressed on. Almost home. "There are three in our area. I think we'll find they all cost about the same. So, we have to figure out which one has the right fit for Dad, and for us. We need to find a place that he will call home, a place that treats him with respect, a place where he is still a person and not a patient."

Tiff was streaming again with tears. "I don't think there is such a place. You know what nursing homes are like. And how is he going to afford it, these places are like fifty thousand a year."

"I know, I know. I have the same concerns. As for the money, though, look at it this way. It's costing him sixty three thousand a year now, just to live in his condo. This would be less than that."

I kept going. I had rounded third, and was heading home. "What I suggest we do first is go check out the place that's closest to home. That would be Clare Bridge, right there on Marsh Road. It's almost next door to Haslett High School. And it's only five or ten minutes from any one of us."

Stacy knew what I was doing. She knew I had been to Clare Bridge, and that I had already made up my mind. She had warned me, however, that this needed to be a democratic process, with the decision made and accepted by the whole team. The stakes were huge. One bad move, especially if controlled and orchestrated by me, could have permanent, disastrous results.

Stacy spoke, careful not to betray me, or the team. "I think we should look at all the facilities in our area. I think we all have to agree. That might be tough, but it might come together just fine also. Why don't we check out Clare Bridge first, after all, it's right around the corner for all of us. It's a newer facility, and it looks really warm and inviting, at least from the outside. We could go Monday, right after work, if that's OK with everyone."

Tiff barely let her finish. "This Monday? I don't know about that. We're so busy. I was thinking maybe in a few weeks." Tiff was trying her best to delay the inevitable. But I didn't get angry. How could I? I had delayed the decision over a year already.

Don interrupted in so I wouldn't have to be in an awkward spot. "Honey, we're not that busy. I can get my parents to watch the kids. We're just going to see it, not check your Dad in that day. Let's just go look at it and see what it's like. Then we can compare it to the other places. Monday is fine, Gart."

Don had stepped up and all but cemented the decision.

Then my mother made sure of it. "I think Monday is a great idea. What time?"

"Let's shoot for 4:30." I figured Charles might leave at 5:00, and I certainly wanted him to be around. "Agreed?"

We went around the room, one by one, to ensure consensus. It was how we did things in the wraparound.

"Agreed."

"Agreed."

"Me too."

"I'm in."

Tiff answered last. "Agreed."

Unanimous.

God works in mysterious ways. Amen.

66 { 4:30 Monday

Stacy and I had been waiting in the Clare Bridge parking lot for over 15 minutes, and I was getting antsy. "Where the hell is everyone, Stacy?"

"Garrett, honey, would you relax? It's just 4:30 now, they're not even a minute late yet. Geez, both of them had to come all the way from work and then go drop off the girls. They'll be here."

Stacy was right of course, but I had trouble acknowledging it. "Maybe they're not going to come. Maybe they got cold feet or something."

"Garrett, just stop it!" Stacy's voice had a twinge of anger in it. That always told me I was crossing the line into the unreasonable.

"OK, OK already. I'm just a little anxious. It's a big thing, this visit."

And at that moment, my Mom's royal blue Ford Taurus turned into the lot, pulling up next to us. I opened up my door as Mom approached.

"How are you doing my son? I have a feeling this is going to go very well."

Instead of building on her confidence, I built upon my already escalating worry. "I'm OK, but I'm worried Tiff isn't going to come. I think she might have gotten cold feet about this."

"There you go again, always worrying! Stop throwing such negativity out into the universe! Of course she'll be here. She had to drop off the kids and meet up with Don. You never give her enough credit for all she does." Mom's voice had just enough judgmental tone in it to shift me from anxious mode to slightly pissed-off mode. I suppressed the temptation to snap back at her. This was not the time or place. Besides, she was right.

Don's silver Grand Am turned into the lot and pulled in alongside Mom's car. Tiff and Don stepped out. Don smiled, but Tiff looked really anxious and conflicted. I checked my watch. 4:37. Late, as usual.

Stacy and my mother both noticed I was checking my watch. Either one of them could have reprimanded me. This time, it was Stacy. "Good God, Garrett. You're actually checking your watch after they've arrived! What does it matter? They're here now. Why are you always keeping score?"

Stacy got out of the van, now also a little miffed at me, and began addressing our family. "Hi everyone, how's everyone doing? It's such a nice, spring-like day for March." Stacy was taking the lead. She knew what she was doing. Tiffanie and I were too anxious and too conflicted to be in the lead. Stacy knew the magnitude of what we were about to do.

Stacy held serve. "So, OK, this is an important moment for us, I guess we're all a little anxious, and rightly so, but this is going to go well. Everybody ready to go in?"

I could tell that Tiff and Mom were slightly peeved that Stacy was in the lead. I think everyone expected one of <u>our</u> family to guide us. But I was glad Stacy took charge. And, damn it all, she was one of our family.

As we walked down the entrance sidewalk, I could feel the demon intruder voice trying to find its way back to a position of control inside my head. Then, as if summoned, the kind, all enveloping voice emerged. It gained strength as it spoke within my head. You can leave now! Go on now, leave him alone! Get out of here! As soon as he goes through that door, its over for you. You are nothing but harmful to him, and he doesn't want or need you anymore. Besides, you have no real power. Your only power is to prey upon people who don't have any faith. Go on now, go! I am banishing you!

Stacy had pushed the intercom button at the entrance door, and soon a young, kind, pleasant-looking face was at the door. We could see her punching in a code that de-activated the building's alarm.

The demon-intruder voice was still there, but fading into the background. You can still turn back, right now, betrayer! It's not too late. But this time, my voice talked over the demon-intruder, out loud.

"God is with us, you guys. This will go just fine."

And with that, the door opened. We were inside and the demon-intruder was not.

The kind face belonged to a young, sandy-blond haired woman named Devin. She looked barely 21, but she was very confident. "Hi. Welcome to

Clare Bridge. Are you here to visit one of our residents?"

"No, actually we have an appointment with Charles and Therese."

"Sure. I'll go get them. You'll have to excuse us, we're getting everyone for dinner right now and it takes awhile to get them all situated. Please, have a seat in our living room here."

We took a seat in the living room area. It was warm and inviting, with fresh flowers on the fireplace mantle and nice, soft pastel paintings of landscapes everywhere. There were a few residents seated around us. They smiled at us. I recognized Bob, the nearly 100 year old man I had seen the last time I was here.

"Hi there! How are you doing today?" I said, trying to pass some time while we waited. Bob was seated next to a potted plant, a philodendron. Bob responded to me, I think, but he spoke directly to the plant.

"Why hello there, my dear little friend! How are you doing today? Philodendron adamantinum, from the genus Araceae. Native to South American rainforests and now used commonly as houseplants. I'm fine, thank you. And how are you?"

Bob was talking to the plant. Tiffanie looked over at me, looking uncomfortable and ambivalent. I translated her look to mean, "We're going to put Dad in a place where people talk to plants?"

I smiled over at Tiff, also feeling awkward and anxious. But I was soon rescued from the moment by Charles.

"Hello, everyone. I see you've met Bob here. He used to be a botanist at Michigan State. He's almost 100 years old. We're going to throw him a big party on his birthday. So, you all must be Walter's family. I'm Charles, the director, I'm glad to meet all of you."

Charles looked even younger today. I could see Tiff glance over at me out of the corner of my eye. I interpreted this look as, "Oh you've got to be kidding, Garrett. This guy's the director? He looks like he just came out of high school."

"Come on over to the office. Our nurse, Therese, will be joining us. Oh, here she is now. Therese, this is the Turke family. Their father, Walter, might be joining us here."

We exchanged handshakes and were escorted into a cozy, but friendly looking office. Charles and Therese sat down next to us. They leaned in toward us, with their arms outstretched, as they spoke. "So, let us tell you a little about how we work around here, so you can see if you think Walter will be a good fit for Clare Bridge. And then maybe you can tell us a little about your father, and we can begin to get to know him just a bit. Then we can give you a tour if you'd like."

"That would be great, Mr. Rich..." I was cut off.

"Please, call me Charles. We are not very formal around here."

I smiled in return. I was starting to relax and gain confidence.

"Well, I've been the director here for the past five years..."

What? Five years? This guy must be some sort of child prodigy.

"And in case you're wondering, because a lot of people think I'm too young to be doing this job, I'm actually 34."

Charles continued, "Yes, I'm nearly 35, and I have one daughter, she's 8. I was really close to my grandparents when I was growing up, and people have always told me that I get along so well with elderly people, well, I guess that's why I'm here; it's my calling."

I could see Tiff starting to relax. She sat back in her chair, and her muscles began to loosen up. Clare Bridge was about to work its magic. I could feel it. The melting process had begun.

"I believe we need to run this place like one big family. You see, in this country, we are always so busy conducting our own lives that we forget how important our elderly are. They have given so much, they have contributed so much, and they bring wisdom and perspective to our lives. We as a society should be judged on how we take care of our children and our elderly, not in terms of how much money we have or how much we have achieved individually. I'm not trying to sound preachy, and I hope you are not offended."

"No, not at all! Please go on." Tiff leaned forward in her chair. The Clare Bridge magic was already working.

"Everyone here is part of our family. This is our home. We want Clare Bridge to be an extension of your family. Our family here, they are not patients here, no! They are at home here. And the staff here, I've picked almost every one. They have to feel the same way in order to work here. Bob isn't a man with dementia. Bob is someone's father, someone's grandfather, and someone's husband. He is somebody important here, and he still has an identity here. If Walter came here, he wouldn't be Walter the Alzheimer's patient. He would be Walter, Tiffanie's father. Walter, Garrett's Dad. Walter, Stacy's father in law. These folks need our respect. We must keep their dignity and integrity. They are valued here. That is our commitment."

"And, it may bug some people, but I'm a little compulsive. The staff have to know each person here as individuals, too. We prepare a biography on each resident, which the staff have to read and learn. Each month, at staff meeting, I quiz the staff about each resident's life before they came here, so we always know who they are, where they came from, what their purpose was here in this life."

The "what their purpose was in this life" line drew raves from my mother. "I feel exactly the same way. This is so refreshing to hear."

Next it was my turn. "I really like the biographies idea. You know, Dad wrote a book about his life as a psychiatrist. It's called, 'Messages from the Interior.' He has boxes of these books in his basement."

Charles seized on this, as if it was some kind of grand opportunity for Dad to be properly introduced to Clare Bridge. "Well, if you wouldn't mind, if Walter came here, maybe we could have a few of his books distributed to the staff so they could learn about him. Heck, he might enjoy it if we did a little book-signing event with the staff! Wow, I can even picture it in my mind…"

I sheepishly looked over at Mom. That book contained some negative recollections about her life with Dad. However, the comment about the book seemed irrelevant to her. She was still enamored with Charles and his message about respect for the elders and their life purpose. Thank God.

Therese, the resident nurse, then took the lead. "We try to make each day here meaningful for our residents. As you will see, some are in the last stages of dementia, but many are still pretty high functioning. It sounds like your dad, if he came to Clare Bridge, would be one of the higher functioning individuals here."

I interjected anxiously. "I'm actually worried about that. I think he'll start realizing what kind of place this is and refuse to stay here. We had the same problem with his day respite program, the ALFA Center, over in East Lansing. We had to sort of lie to him to get him to go, we told him he was going to be their staff psychiatrist and that he would get paid. I've been telling him each week his checks have been direct-deposited."

Charles looked really intrigued. "I wouldn't call that lying to him. I would call that brilliant! Whatever it takes to maintain their safety, their identity, their sense of being needed is what we have to do. We too lie to our people here, but we don't call it that. We call it redirecting them. As for your fear or worries about how he'll accept this place, as long as you can get him in through the front door, we'll take over from there. We're really good at getting people acclimated here, we're used to that problem, and it's easier than you think to resolve. You see, they quickly realize this is a very friendly, kind environment, and that they don't need to make any difficult or stressful decisions here. It's really a completely stress free environment. None of the activities are too difficult for them to succeed at, and everything we do is tailored to be at their own level. There is no sense of frustration or failure."

Therese and Charles were in a near perfect rhythm. I wondered for a second if we were being taken by a couple of really slick salespeople. But I quickly discounted this. They just seemed too sincere, their investment in the residents too genuine and heartfelt to be feigned.

Therese took her turn. "You know, Garrett. We could tell your Dad that he's coming in for a job interview, that we need a geriatric psychiatrist, if that's what you guys want, if that's what it takes to get him here. He really could meet with all the residents as if it was his job. They'd like that, and we could tell your dad he can occasionally spend the night here if he had to work late."

I looked around the room for indications that we were exploiting Dad by manipulating him in this way. Instead, everyone nodded approvingly.

Then Charles erased any trace of ambivalence that remained. "Now, if your Dad comes here, and I'm not trying to pressure you, we want you all to know that Clare Bridge becomes your home, too. We want you to come over here, as often and as long as you want. We suggest you not take them out of the building until they're well established here, but once they are acclimated, we encourage families to take them out for an hour or two whenever they want. We'll be taking them out too, the higher functioning ones. On Thursdays, for example, I often take a group of residents out for lunch, like to Bill Knapp's, or the Olive Garden. Sometimes we go down to the lake for a picnic."

"The services here are for you, too. We have parties and special events. We'll get a band in here and have a dance. We have Christmas parties, Thanksgiving dinner, beach trips, all sorts of fun things, to which you will all be invited. And you can also consider this place a drop-in counseling center. We know how stressful it has been caring for your dad. We know you might feel guilty some days for placing him here. We know you still have a lot of grief and you may just want to come in and talk and even cry a bit. We know all this. This is what we do. We want Clare Bridge to be your refuge, too."

This sounded too good to be true. My family not only looked at peace, but they looked mesmerized by the guardian angel-director. He had taken every one of our fears and eradicated them. He seemed to anticipate every one of our questions. Within half an hour, there was no fear and no ambivalence remaining.

Tiffanie asked the one remaining, potentially threatening question. "So Charles, not to sound too gloomy or anything, but what happens when the residents are too low functioning or too frail to be here any more. Then we'd have to move Dad again?"

"Tiffanie, if your dad likes it here, and you like it here, your dad can spend all the rest of his days at Clare Bridge. Residents usually pass over, you might say pass away I suppose, while they are here. It might take many years, and I'm sure that will be the case with your dad, but they can die in peace and dignity here. We call in hospice services, the whole family can stay here during that time if they need to, and their loved ones can pass over peacefully when it's their time."

Don, as expected, asked the most pragmatic questions. "So how much does this place cost, and how soon can you take him?"

Charles handed us a few brochures. "You can all go through this after you leave. The costs are right here. It depends what kind of room you want, and what kinds of care services he needs. We assess their care needs every three months. You'll find our costs are about the same as everyplace else. You can save a little more if you want him assigned a roommate, which often goes well. To put the cost in perspective, compare it to what his cost of living is now, living independently. You'll see it's actually very fair and reasonable. And, we have our own doctor, podiatrist, clergy, and even hairstylists that come to the building. You can still keep your old service providers, but it's so much easier having all these professionals come here."

Therese finished off the second part of Don's question. "We have two openings right now. We could get him in soon, in just a couple weeks, maybe the second week in April. But you shouldn't feel pressured. Go on home and think about it, call us if you have questions before you make a final decision. If you decide to go with us, then we would probably want to have him move in within a couple weeks."

We had no more questions. Charles and Therese had melted each and every one of us. We were now in their protective hands. And soon, Dad would be in their hands as well.

"Now, if you don't have anymore questions, tell me about your father's life…"

An hour later we had shared an overview of everything we could think of about our father. His childhood. His travels. His marriage. His falling out with my sister. His strengths and his shortcomings. His successes and his failures. Our feelings about his disease. How we developed and ran the wraparound. And the crowning jewel of our experiences with Dad, how we helped him discover what real, unconditional love was.

I was amazed how open we had become with what used to be taboo, well-defended family secrets. Just two years ago, we would never have discussed any of our history outside of the family. It was too threatening, too embarrassing, too scary. Now the skeletons could come out of the closet. And they weren't nearly as frightening as any of us had thought.

I was proud of us. I felt a twinge of sadness that my sister Cindy hadn't been a part of today's meeting. But I also felt a twinge of optimism that perhaps someday, she would be. I still had that image in my head of our dad and her walking arm in arm.

Therese had taken notes throughout the family interview. I glanced, as discretely as I could, at the summary section she was now completing. All I could read was her last line, which she underlined twice. I will never forget it, because for years I had not believed what she had just written down about my family:

"Exceptionally supportive, loving family."

We had our tour but the decision had already been made, silently and collectively. As we made our way along the sidewalk, Tiff came up to me, put her arm around me, and pulled my head down to her level with a gentle tug. She said, softly but reassuringly, "I don't think we need to look at any other facilities."

67 { Ghosts

I could feel the condo was haunted as soon as I entered. It gave me the creeps. At first I didn't know why. I had been in Dad's condo hundreds, maybe even a thousand times in the last two and a half years. I had had many powerful moments inside that condo. Times when I felt scared, pressured, stressed, frustrated, angry, happy, safe, relieved, worried, apprehensive, joyful, panicked, sad, exhausted. I thought I had experienced all imaginable feelings within the walls of Dad's home.

But I never felt haunted by the ghosts in there until this day.

I should have known they would be waiting for me. I should have brought Stacy with me to protect me from them. But they weren't waiting for Stacy. She would not be able to see or feel them. No, these ghosts had lain in wait only for me.

Tiff, Don, and Dad had gone out to lunch. Dad's delusional brain had made sense out of the threesome. Don went as Dad's brother, so Tiff could still be his girlfriend. They would have a leisurely lunch, and then would go to the movies. I had over four hours to myself.

I had come in expecting to take a few things off the wall to dress up Dad's new room at Clare Bridge. C-4. I had been out to the room earlier in the morning to size up how much space I had to work with. All morning I was preoccupied with how I was going to collapse the nine rooms of Dad's condo "museum" into one 12 by 15 foot room at Clare Bridge. It seemed impossible.

All morning long I thought about what items, what pictures, what mementos would be representative of Dad's entire lifetime. He probably had several hundred memories affixed to his walls, maybe even more than that. What to bring, what to bring? They had to be the right items. Because Dad's room at Clare Bridge would be the last home Dad would ever have.

I didn't plan on meeting the ghosts this morning. But they had planned on meeting me. They had been waiting for this moment for almost three years. The painful, conflict-laden apparitions were in every room. In Dad's study were letters and cards to Cindy, some finished but never sent, some started but never finished. I knew they were in there, but I never read them. Not that I didn't want to. I told myself that it wasn't my business, I shouldn't intrude, and it wasn't right to snoop. But the simple truth wasn't about ethics or morality or interpersonal boundaries. I was simply afraid to look at them. Did they contain the answers to Dad and Cindy's ten year falling out? I wanted to know, but I was too scared to look at them. I told myself it wasn't right for me to look at them. They had already settled their business in an exchange of letters about a year and a half ago, as Cindy had told me over the phone that one Christmas. Leave it alone, Garrett, I told myself. Leave it alone.

But I still had unfinished business with Cindy. This was not just about my dad and her; it was also about her and me. After Cindy severed her ties to Dad, the rest of the family's ties to her were cut, too. She was angry with all of us for not supporting her in her banishment of my father.

Now, things were maybe changing. After that phone call over a year ago, I had the opportunity to follow up with Cindy and start working to improve our relationship again. Since that Christmas phone call, some positive momentum had been created. The door was open, and the next move was mine.

But I hadn't taken the next move. I was afraid. Afraid of what I might hear if I did open things up with her.

I had talked to Cindy by phone a few times over the past year. A couple times my mom kind of forced me to call her on holidays or family get-togethers. Once or twice Cindy called me. Once or twice I had mustered enough courage to call her. Both times I had to have two beers in me before I felt relaxed enough to even talk to her. The outcome of all these calls had been the same. I was only able to talk about benign things, like the weather, our kid's accomplishments, and the day to day routine. Never about Cindy's relationship with Dad. Never about my relationship with Cindy. Never about her estrangement from our family.

Cindy had done her part. She even talked about getting together for a family visit. She was telling us that the door was opening back up.

Also in Dad's study was a big stack of letters from Arthur, Dad's cherished but enigmatic patient turned best friend turned Navy blood brother. I still didn't know what to do with this, either. There was no one in Dad's life outside the family as important to my dad as Arthur. Dad had nothing but love and compassion for Arthur, and Arthur seemed to have nothing but love and admiration for my dad. He was so loyal, so kind, and so consistently supportive. The relationship changed somewhat after I informed him that Dad was sick, with Arthur assuming more of the lead in the relationship, offering words of encouragement, hope, to keep going, to stay the course, to never give up. But Arthur and Dad were Semper Fi. Always faithful. They had meant so much to each other.

And there was something else that was bothering me about Arthur. I knew from conversations with Dad that something was wrong in Arthur's home. Dad kept alluding that Arthur was such a strong man, that he was a caregiver for someone he loved and that he was worried about the strain and toll this was taking on him. I could never tell if Arthur was taking care of someone who was impaired, disabled, or ill, and if whoever was afflicted was a friend or a family member. I could have found out by asking Dad or by reading Arthur's letters. But I couldn't do it. It wasn't appropriate, I told myself. I didn't want to pry. But that wasn't the real reason, either. I was afraid of opening up Pandora's box again.

In Dad's bedroom were a whole bunch of photographs of Dad's second wife, Teri, an ill fated marriage built on a sexual but otherwise weak foundation that lasted only a year or two. Dad's relationship and marriage to Teri had haunted me for two decades. Dad married this woman in the late 1980's, after a long, tumultuous courtship that included multiple break-ups and reconciliations. They had met in Traverse City at a party about 1979 or 1980. Teri was still married to her husband Mark when they met. Following Dad's and Teri's divorces, which suspiciously happened in close proximity, the two of them moved to Arizona within three months of each other. I had my blinders on, and let myself believe their relationship had started after my dad's divorce. They moved in together and married shortly thereafter, in 1988.

I didn't want to face whether Dad was having an affair with her before he separated and divorced my mother. I also didn't ask Dad or Mom about this. I could only lose by asking. Why would I want to tarnish the image of The Champion? But the price for not asking about this relationship was just as scary. I would be forever preoccupied about whether Dad was unfaithful to my mom when we were in Traverse City. When I was Dad's caregiver, I could distract myself from this painful issue. But not anymore. My role as caregiver was ending, and all the suppressed, backed up feelings, problems and unresolved shit was starting to come back up, like regurgitated vomit. The haunting had begun.

Also in Dad's bedroom were photographs of several of Dad's girlfriends, spanning a whole decade of Dad's life after he was divorced from Terri. None of these relationships lasted more than a year. Why? Because Dad couldn't handle relationships with women? Because he couldn't handle intimacy? Aside from his sometimes gregarious exterior, Dad must have been very lonely inside. Thinking about this made me sad. How come he could never attach to any woman in a mature way?

Down in Dad's basement were boxes and boxes of memories from Dad's marriage to Mom. Although these items never made it to his walls, they were kept and arranged by my dad as if they were still important to him. They were stacked neatly and meticulously along a wall off by themselves, separated from all the other stuff in his basement. I would check on these boxes whenever I had to go into Dad's basement to reset the fuses or change the furnace filter. I would notice that sometimes the boxes had been rearranged or left open. Dad was apparently going into them periodically, but not removing anything. I thought that maybe his relationship with my mother still mattered, that it still meant something to him.

Those boxes also contained memories that mattered to me. I could have easily looked through them when I was alone in the basement. I had lots of opportunities. But I never did that, either. All those feelings about my turbulent years as a teenager when my parents were fighting. All those memories from my childhood. Our lives in hippy culture Los Angeles. Our escape to Michigan. Those memories and feelings were in there. And maybe some more answers. But I was afraid to open them, too.

Back upstairs in the Dad's living room were family pictures of my sisters and Dad's grandchildren. Tiffanie's and my family's pictures were all current and nicely framed. Cindy's family pictures were all ten years old. But Cindy's pictures were not tucked away in some quiet corner of the room. They were included up front and center, right alongside the other family photographs. Cindy had remained very much alive in my dad's life. How he must have missed her after they stopped speaking.

I began to survey the walls, thinking of specifically what to take for Dad's room at Clare Bridge. I was hoping it would distract me from the haunting. I selected what I thought were the most important reminders of his identity, items that I hoped would someday make me smile and not cause me to feel sad.

I wasn't sure if I was selecting the most important things to him, or to me. University of Iowa paintings and mementos. Dad's U.S. Navy photographs, showing him smiling in full officer's uniform. Dad's Karate black belt and the cherished photo of him and his sensei after receiving that honor. The photos of Marilyn Monroe, David Niven, and Humphrey Bogart, complete with Dad's delusional, Alzheimer's induced comments to himself scrawled across the bottom of the images. The photograph of Dad with his friend George "Goober" Lindsey, complete with a real autograph and a legitimate personalized note. One of my huge, framed photographs of the Mackinaw Bridge, symbolic of our escape to northern Michigan. And, lastly, the family photographs, Cindy's included, from the living room. I loaded each and every keepsake with painstaking care into the van, treating each one as a treasure, and cradling everything with towels so they wouldn't get scratched or damaged.

I thought about rearranging the remaining items on Dad's walls so Dad wouldn't be distressed by the missing items when he returned home. But why do that? Dad's walls were already so skewed, so cluttered, so disorganized by his constant reorganizing it was barely noticeable that anything had been removed. Besides, how was Dad going to remember what was there to begin with?

After loading all of the mementos into the van, I took out the two laundry baskets I had brought with me. I filled them with Dad's spring and summer clothes, which not unexpectedly, pretty much reflected the same themes I had just taken off the walls. U.S. Navy attire, Iowa Hawkeye shirts, shoes and jackets, a Humphrey Bogart sweatshirt, and an "I love you Grampy" shirt that Tiff's kids had made for him and signed. I also took an "I love Grandpa" mug designed by my kids with their pictures on it. Finally, I took a red, heart shaped pillow that had been signed by all of his students and work colleagues after Dad's triple by-pass surgery.

After gathering up the last basket of clothes, I stopped by the wipeboard on my way out. Everything was already done for the day except for the evening's agenda "6:30 PM: Garrett over. Time to plan our next adventure!" I checked my watch. 1:43. Plenty of time to get to Clare Bridge, unload, and dress up Dad's new room up with Stacy before I had to be back.

I picked up the laundry basket and headed to the van. I was surprised how full the van was and worried if all the things would fit into Dad's new room. They had to fit. Everything I took mattered.

I started the van, put the transmission in reverse, and carefully backed into the street. Driving away, I had an eerie feeling, like I wasn't alone, like something was there, pressing on me.

I wasn't alone. The ghosts had come with me.

68 { C-4

The room seemed so small. Although I had been in C-4 several times, it seemed even smaller than I had remembered. And now the walls felt like they were closing in, ready to suffocate me.

Outside the door were all of Dad's things that I had taken from his condo. The Clare Bridge staff had helped me unload the van and had placed everything along the hallway wall. Dad's things lined an entire hall. How would they possibly fit into this tiny little room?

I looked at my watch. 2:30. Stacy would be here any minute. I wanted to wait for her before I got started. I sat on the bed and tried to relax a little. But I couldn't. I could feel the weight of all the family problems and unfinished business I hadn't tended to over the years. Not only did I have to deal with the pain of placing Dad at Clare Bridge, I had to deal with the ghosts. My ghosts.

I thought to myself, what direction will my life now take? I knew that once I checked Dad in, he would never check back out. My days as caregiver, and a whole identity I had built for myself over the last few years, would be over in about 15 hours. I was expecting to feel relieved by this, maybe even happy, but all I felt now was sadness, emptiness, and confusion.

I thought I was doing the right thing by placing Dad here. Now I wasn't sure. And I wasn't sure for selfish reasons. Placing Dad at Clare Bridge might have been the right thing for him. But I wasn't sure it was the right thing for me. I was a lot less ready than I thought I would be.

There was a quick tap on the door and it slowly opened. For a split second, I thought it might be Stacy. It wasn't. The person who came in scared me. It was a 75 or 80 year old woman. She didn't look or act like she was welcoming me. She looked disoriented and crazed. She shuffled in, spotted me, and came right up to the foot of the bed where I was seated.

"Well, hi there, deary. I've been looking all over for you. We're late, and they're waiting for us at the banquet. All of our friends are there, waiting for us. So, are you ready?

I felt a rush of panic surge up from my gut. My heart started to race. I had a surreal feeling of estrangement, like I was detached from reality, trapped in another plane of existence.

The old woman continued to speak. "Oh, come on now, what kind of husband are you! We're supposed to be together now that we're married. So how about it, deary?" Now she was pulling on my hand to get me up off the bed. "Let's go to the banquet, and then later, maybe we could have a little koochy coo."

The old woman was getting angry. "Come on, Bill, I already told you, they're waiting for us! It's time for the banquet. Why are you always so stubborn? Come on, its time to go."

A beautiful, 20 something year old woman with mahogany skin entered the room. Trailing behind her was Stacy. The two of them were smiling and laughing as they entered. The 20 something woman spoke first, in a melodic accent.

"Oh Francis! There you are. Come on now, its time for Lawrence Welk in the parlor. Come-come, you go with me now. Let's leave Walter's son and daughter in law alone. They're getting ready for our newest family member who will be arriving tomorrow. Come on!" The beautiful woman took Francis by the hand and gently escorted her out.

Stacy then entered, coming up to me and giving me a big hug. I didn't stiffen like I sometimes did when Stacy hugged me. I hugged her back, and nestled into her arms. I needed her. I felt my anxiety attack subsiding.

"Stacy, I'm scared. I thought I was ready for this. Instead, I'm sitting in here having panic attacks. I thought this was the right thing. This place is fucking bizarre. There are people in here that are walking around like zombies. That woman that was in here, she called me Bill, she thought I was her husband! It was like some scene out of The Shining!"

"Honey, they all have Alzheimer's disease. They're not all that different from your Dad. The people who work here, I talked to several just since I came in, they are all so kind. They really seem to care about the patients here. They treat them like they are all part of their family."

"My Dad is not a patient!"

"Honey, he is an Alzheimer's patient. It's OK. You've been fighting so long for your Dad. It's time to rest now. Your Dad will be just fine here. I bet he'll start liking it here sooner than you think. Honey, it's now time for you to rest. You're going to get your life back again."

"That's what I've been thinking about." I wanted to cry, but bit on my lip and pushed it all down. "I'm scared I'm not going to know who I am anymore. All I've been doing is taking care of Dad for the past three years."

"Garrett, honey, you are much more than just Walter's caregiver. You are Shani and Miah's Dad. You are my husband. You are your Mom's son. It's time to come back home. We've all missed you."

Stacy hugged me some more. Biting my lip no longer worked. I cried in her arms, burying my head into her shoulder. After a minute or two, I started to feel better, that eerie detachment was gone and I felt connected again. I looked up at Stacy's face. She had been crying, too.

Stacy pulled up the window shade and the afternoon sun streamed in. You could see some tulips starting to bloom just outside the window.

"Well, we've got only a couple hours. Let's get your dad's room set up. Come on, honey, this will be all right. You'll see."

Stacy and I spent the next hour and a half setting up Dad's room. We dedicated the wall space over Dad's bed to the University of Iowa and all of his Hawkeye memorabilia. We threw an Iowa Hawkeye bedspread over the bed, added a couple pennants, and Dad's beautiful framed painting of the Iowa Union. The room transformed into what could have passed for a 1950's college dorm.

Next, we took on the wall space to the right and left of his window. On one side went his U.S. Navy mementos, including his officer's bars and two pictures of him in officer's attire, circa 1962. On the other side we put up his Karate black belt and the picture of Dad and his sensei, circa 1968 Los Angeles.

On the large wall adjacent to his bed went all the family photographs. I put Cindy's family pictures right in the middle. Next to the family photos was space for his heroes. Humphrey Bogart, David Niven, Marilyn Monroe, Jackie Robinson, Woody Allen, and of course, George "Goober" Lindsey.

Over his dresser went my photographic masterpiece, a 24 x 32 image of the Mackinaw Bridge, taken from Fort Michilimackinac, framed in cobalt blue, which highlighted the sky and water around the bridge. This image always reminded Dad of our escape from L.A. to northern Michigan.

We collected our hammer and picture hanging kit and closed the door behind us. I took a deep breath and let out an audible sigh. I didn't feel good, but I was no longer anxious. Stacy grabbed my hand and we walked through the hallway into the main living room area by the front entrance. The facility was pretty quiet, as most of the staff and residents were watching the Lawrence Welk Show in the TV Parlor. Another beautiful 20 something staff, this one with sandy colored hair and creamy skin, saw that we were moving toward the front door.

"All set? Are you two ready to leave?"

We smiled and nodded. The staff member punched in the code for us and opened the door. She smiled as she spoke.

"You're Walter's family, aren't you?"

"Yes we are."

"Well, we are sure looking forward to your Dad joining us here tomorrow. I've read his book."

"You've read his book?" I was truly amazed. I didn't think that Dad had actually sold any copies.

"Yes, our director, Charles, had each of us read Walter's book. We've been passing it around the past couple weeks. We all feel like we know your Dad already. What an interesting life you all have had. Your father has helped a lot of people. I'm a med student and his book was an inspiration. Well, we'll be looking forward to seeing him tomorrow."

Stacy and I walked through the foyer and outside into the bright spring sunshine. She pulled me closer and gave me a kiss. "Well, I guess we'll see you after dinner."

I didn't have to think before answering. I had already decided to change the plans for the evening. "No, you're going to see me in about 5 minutes."

Stacy looked perplexed. "Aren't you going over to your Dad's?"

"Nope. Tiff can get Dad set up for the evening. I've had enough today. I'm coming home now."

Stacy smiled, but still looked perplexed. Almost never had I broken the routine with my Dad. "Are you sure? You always get your dad set up in the evening. And this is his last night in the condo."

"Yes I'm sure, I'm coming home instead. Tiff has got him set up for the night before. I want to be home with you guys tonight."

Stacy still looked confused. "Really? You're all right with that? Well OK, I was going to make gnocchi with a cream sauce. It will be nice to have you home with us tonight."

"Well, get used to it, because I'll be home now every night."

Stacy came up to me and kissed me again. She whispered, "Welcome home, honey."

69 { My One Ringer

Stacy was already downstairs. She had made the morning coffee and was getting breakfast ready for the girls. I heard the anchor for the Channel 10 Morning News in the background. "Good Morning. It's Monday, April 15th." Time for Stacy to go back to work. Time for the girls to go back to school. Time for me to place Dad at Clare Bridge.

I came up behind Stacy and gave her a big, enveloping hug. She turned and smiled, widening her brown, almond shaped eyes as she spoke. "Good morning, honey. Today's your dad's big day." She nested for a moment in my arms. I felt connected and secure.

The pain and conflict of moving my Dad to Clare Bridge had diminished again. I was mobilized today. I was ready. I thought for a moment how I was able to banish all those ghosts and lay my haunting conscience to rest, for I wasn't plagued by any of those feelings and internal voices this morning. It had a lot to do with the person I was hugging. It had a lot to do with the prayers I had said yesterday.

"Are you ready for today, honey?" Stacy gently broke our embrace and looked up at me.

"Actually I think I am. I feel so much better today. You know me, I worry and worry and worry, but when its time to actually do the thing I'm scared of, I somehow always seem to mobilize. I feel like I can do this."

"I know you can. It will go fine. I have a very good feeling about this. Is Tiff going to go over to Clare Bridge with you?"

"No, she has to work, and we thought it would be better if we didn't make too big a deal about this so Dad doesn't get anxious. She's going to stop by and get Dad set up with breakfast and his meds, as usual, and then go on to work. She'll come over to Clare Bridge around twelve and have lunch with Dad and me."

"Do you want me to be with you?"

"No, no. You go to work. I'm fine. Really, I'm not just saying that, I'm really OK. I'm ready. This will be a good day. Yesterday I was kind of screwed up, all those memories going through his condo, then setting his room up with that elderly woman wandering in thinking I was her husband. But today I'm really clear headed, I feel like this is definitely the right thing to do."

"Well, honey, I've gotta go get the girls up and get ready. What time are you going over to your Dad's? Do you want me to drop Shani off? I have time to do both girls today. That way you can put all your energies into your Dad."

"That would be great. We're due at Clare Bridge about 9. So I thought I'd go over around 8 and make sure he's ready."

"Well, I want you to call me as soon as you get your Dad situated over there, OK? I mean it; I want you to call me."

"Fine, fine, fine. I'll call you." Even though I truly appreciated Stacy's concern, I still acted like she was pestering me. "You don't have to worry, really. I'm doing OK this morning."

We both completed our morning routines. Stacy got the girls up and then put on her make-up for work while they ate. I showered and got dressed. I called the switchboard at work and reminded the receptionist that I had one more day off. I said my perfunctory good mornings to the kids when I came back downstairs. None of us were big talkers in the morning. Shani came up to me and said "Good luck with Grampy today." Miah kind of grunted over her bowl of cereal. That was it.

At 7:55 I left for Dad's place. I was still feeling strong, focused, and confident as I pulled out of the driveway. While I was driving, I said a prayer, thanking God for all of those guardian angels he had placed in my path to helped guide, then pull me, over the last three years. I thanked God for protecting my dad, and for protecting me from my harsh and often cruel conscience. I thanked God for my wife, my children, my mother, my friends, my work colleagues, and for all of Dad's friends who helped me get through this. I prayed for my sister Cindy to resolve with our family. I prayed for Arthur, now that his doctor-therapist-blood brother-friend was slipping from him.

And I prayed for my dad's soul. I didn't know if Dad had turned his soul over to God before he got sick. I didn't know how God communicated with someone who had Alzheimer's. And if he hadn't made peace with God, how is that accomplished after being ravaged by dementia?

Thirteen minutes after I had left I arrived at Dad's condo. It would be the last time I was ever at his condo with him.

I got out my key and opened the door. I could see Dad off in the living room, sitting in his Herman Miller chair, dozing in front of the TV.

But before I could get to Dad to wake him up, I saw it. I stopped in my tracks.

It was Dad's wipeboard in the entrance hallway. The daily agenda that I had written the day before was still there. But at the bottom of the wipeboard was something added, a sentence written in the handwriting of what could have passed for a seven year old child's. It was just one simple sentence, a sentence that would haunt me for months to come. It had been written by Dad the night before.

"No help for Walter today."

Although Dad was delusional, disoriented, and out of touch with reality most of the time, the message didn't need interpretation.

My confidence evaporated almost instantaneously. I had built Dad's wraparound. I had overseen Dad's routine for three years. I was as dependable as clockwork. I was the one everyone counted on, especially in the clutch. Except last night. I had wanted to return home to my family a day early. I just couldn't do it that one last time. It was just too painful.

I was stunned by the words on the wipeboard. I was devastated. I had trouble breathing in any kind of rhythm after I saw it. And as noxious as that board was for me, I couldn't turn away from it. My eyes were locked upon it. I tried, but I couldn't pull them away.

I should have just written it off. After all, how could one night, even if it was a mistake, color my whole care-giving journey with Dad? I knew what I had done for Dad these past few years. If he had been well he would have appreciated everything I did. He did appreciate everything I did, actually. He just didn't remember it. No, Lord no, I shouldn't be beating myself up over this.

But I was. The words stung. "No help for Walter today" was being burned into my memory bank. How the hell would I ever erase these words from my conscience? It tormented me. I just laid in wait for the demon intruder voice to return.

I finally mobilized enough to go into the kitchen, retrieving some Kleenex to wipe the board clear. But for some ridiculous, unnecessary, self-deprecating reason, I couldn't do it. I kept those haunting words up there, as a sort of self inflicted punishment. A brand that would remind me and everyone else who saw it that I had failed Dad on that last critical night. Oh why, God, why?

I thought of Stacy and her insistence that I call her. She had acted as if this morning was going to be extremely tough for me. I had begun the day feeling focused and ready. I was going to be well defended against the pain this morning. I was going to feel relieved when the day was done, maybe, secretly, even a little happy. I was going to get my family back today. Then I was going to get my life back.

But now, standing in Dad's hallway, I felt all the pain, all the guilt, all the ghosts, all the internal conflict pushing their torturous way up to the surface. I should have called Stacy. She would have told her co-workers she had a family emergency and come right over. It was an emergency, but I didn't call her. For some reason I was content to punish myself.

I knew I couldn't stand in that hallway forever. I did the only thing left to do. I prayed.

Please, please, please dear God, don't let it end this way. Please, show my dad I love him. I did make the commitment, I did take care of him, I do love him. Please let that be the last thing in his memory before he leaves me, not this! Please, please help me, I don't know if I can do this without you. Please show me the way. I know I have to let go and be pulled but....

My prayer was interrupted by the phone. It rang, once, and I startled. I went to go answer it, but it didn't ring again.

I knew who had called. A "one ringer" was code in Stacy's family. The code had been employed by Stacy's mother when Stacy was in college. It was a way to say "I love you" without words. It was originally designed to convey the message without the cost of a phone call on a tight college budget. But the one ringer soon evolved into a family tradition, a powerful symbolic message that could be implemented anywhere, any time.

This one ringer gave me strength. I knew Stacy was behind me, there if I needed her.

I mobilized again. "Come on, Dad, time to get up, rise up and shine. Rise up! We've got a new job to start today!"

Dad opened his eyes and turned around as I entered the living room. Although still groggy, his eyes soon found my face. He smiled. "Oh there you are, doctor! I've been looking for you all year! And now, finally you're here. There's something big going on today, I don't know who or what it is, or where it is, but something big is about to happen. You know, the whose-is-whatses, the pretty one, well she is my girlfriend. She told me something about a big one. I think its happening today!"

"That's right, Dad, today is the big day. We start our new jobs today! You and I, side by side at work, just like the old days! We're due there in about forty-five minutes, so let's get ourselves showered and shaved. I'm feeling great! This is going to be a great day for us!"

I didn't really feel great, the wipeboard was still bothering me, but I was no longer emotionally incapacitated. My "one ringer" had given me all the strength I needed.

Dad was excited! He couldn't wait to get into the shower and get ready. He let me shave him with no hassles, and then he got dressed in his favorite attire: "Navy blues" (his everyday dark blue slacks), a blue and gold Navy t-shirt, New Balance athletic shoes (Dad thought the "N" on the shoes stood for Navy), and of course, his ever-present U.S. Navy windbreaker.

At 8:45 Dad was looking spiffy and ready to go. We climbed into the van and pulled out of the driveway. It was the last time I was ever at the condo with Dad. I thought about that as I was pulling away. I could have cried, easily, but it wasn't the place or time. I pushed down my feelings and continued on. I was still in caregiver mode.

"Boy, Dad, I just can't believe it! You and I, together again, on the job! This is going to be great! And, I don't know if I told you this already, Clare Bridge is going to give us our own office-apartment! It has a bed in case we have to work into the night, like in case of emergencies with our patients. And we have our own bathroom, I was out to see it yesterday and our office is perfect for us! Oh is this ever going to be fun!"

"You know it, Doctor! Why you seem almost as excited as I am! Who... who do we meet first today? You know, he's the one high up, or will it be that pretty one?"

"Why I think it will be both of them, Dad. Charles, the administrative director, will be there. And I think Brenda or Therese, the nurses, will be there. Maybe both of them." I patted Dad on the shoulder, and readied my next set of lies. Anything to help him feel secure, needed, and connected. "You know, Dad, I think both of them kinda like you."

"Really, Doctor?"

"Yep. Sure do! So, how does it feel having all these women doting on you?"

"It is the greatest, Doctor. Today, you and I, we are on top! That's the way it should be! You're the greatest, my, my....my whatchamacallit..."

I prayed Dad would say "son" one more time. But he couldn't find the right word. I wanted to fill in the blank, but it wouldn't mean anything to me if I said "son."

"....my...my....my greatest friend!"

I knew what word Dad was searching for. I smiled internally, but it was a bittersweet smile, because the sadness and pain were also pushing up. But I knew, at least for one brief moment, that Dad had meant to say "Son."

As we were driving, those painful words on the wipeboard lost some of their sting. Heading off to Clare Bridge with Dad was going a lot better than I had ever imagined. Maybe this was going to be OK after all. Maybe I wouldn't have to fake my way through the day.

Dad couldn't wait to get out of the van. I gently put my arm out in front of him, symbolically restraining him in his seat.

"Hold on a minute, Dad, we're a bit early. Let's call Stacy and tell her everything is going fine."

I punched in Stacy's cell number. She must have been expecting my call, because she answered it before the first ring had finished.

"Hi, honey, how's it going with your Dad?"

"Unbelievably well. We're here in the Clare Bridge parking lot, ready to go in right now. Dad can't wait to get started, I can hardly hold him back!"

"He thinks he's starting work today?"

"No, we're starting work today!"

Stacy laughed. "I see. I'm so glad for you, honey. I knew it would go just fine today. It will probably still be a struggle for you for awhile, but I think your dad is going to do just fine."

I thought of telling Stacy about the wipeboard, but it wasn't the time. I was feeling mobilized and focused again. And, besides, Dad was itching to get inside.

"I love you, Stacy."

"I love you, Garrett. Call me later this morning, once you guys have acclimated a little."

"Will do. Hey, Stacy?"

"Yes?"

"Thanks for that phone call earlier."

"Phone call?"

"You know, the one-ringer. That really meant a lot to me. It came at exactly the right time."

"Garrett?"

"Yes?"

"Garrett, honey. That wasn't me. I didn't call you."

70 } The Welcome

"Welcome to your new job, Doctor Turke!" Charles' voice resonated with enthusiasm and confidence. He shook Dad's hand and then mine, and with a sweeping forearm, led us to a group of Clare Bridge staff assembled in a single file line. Always the showman, Dad smiled broadly as if he was about to go onstage before an adoring audience. It was just like his days as a mentor-professor for incoming medical students. I smiled, too. The old Dad, my dad, was back again, if only for a moment.

The welcoming line was an interesting mix of different worlds. There were young American college students who liked the flexible hours that this care-giving job allowed. They thought the experience and the 11-dollar an hour pay was great for a part time job. Then there were a few older workers who needed this job to make ends meet. Perhaps they had had the American dream pass them by, or perhaps they were committed to caring for the elderly. Their 11-dollar an hour pay probably barely allowed them to pay rent and scrape by.

But these two groups were not the majority of caregivers employed at the Clare Bridge facility. I was struck that most of the Clare Bridge staff greeting us this morning were African immigrants.

I didn't know it yet, but the African staff at Clare Bridge were also going to be my teachers. They were the next wave of guardian angels there in place to help me. They were going to help me better understand my circumstances with my dad, and to embrace my family again. They were going to help put my life in a clearer perspective. They were going to help me find, and then reclaim, my soul. And they were going to help me let go and be pulled.

The African teachers were all assembled in a row, like welcoming gatekeepers. I recognized some of their names as West African, perhaps Senegalese. Some had Swahili names, pointing to an East African origin. Some of the names were Christian. Some of the names were Muslim. Their kindness in welcoming us was powerful for me. It was a mixture of humility, heartfelt empathy, and social confidence. It was unexpected, and yet it was familiar and comforting. I had seen this kind of welcome before in my life. In West Africa.

"Good morning, Doctor Turke, I am Hadiyya." "Good morning, Doctor Turke, I am Eunice." "Hello Doctor, I am Abdulai, nice to meet you." "Hi, Doctor Turke, my name is Devin. Welcome to Clare Bridge." Dad was busy shaking hands as he made his way down the welcoming line. He was in all of his glory, smiling, often bowing slightly, humbly, as he worked his way down. I trailed right behind him, his loyal sidekick, his work companion, his trusted protector. Dad was in his own world. He didn't have a clue that he was being admitted to an Alzheimer's care facility. I had twinges of guilt thinking about how we were deceiving him. But my guilt was insignificant and easily banished this time. Because the alternative to the deception, the truth, would only create unnecessary pain, fear, and confusion for Dad. It was best to just let him be Don Quixote. And I was more than comfortable playing the part of Sancho.

Charles bubbled over with enthusiasm. "Well, Doctor Turke, it looks like you've already made quite an impact on our staff. What a welcome!" Although it had all been scripted out, the welcoming was still heartfelt and sincere.

"Your staff, I mean...I mean...my staff, well no, that's not right... our staff, yes that's it! They are so wonderful." Dad was starting to tear up.

"Yes they are. And it's so wonderful that you have chosen to work with us here. And to have your son working here as well, why, how did we get so lucky?"

"My son? My son works here? I don't think I have a son..."

"Your son, Garrett, is right here, right along side of us." Charles motioned over to me, Sancho, standing dutifully just off to the side.

"Oh, now you're talking! You mean the doctor. I don't think he's my son, but he is a good one. No, better than that. He is... the...the... he is the greatest!"

It was no use trying to fight off my feelings. I felt sad. There was no doubt that Dad had lost my identity, and there was no retrieving it. Maybe I was the greatest, but he couldn't even occasionally claim I was his son anymore.

Charles tried to resurrect the memory. Maybe he was just doing it for my sake. "Yes, he is the greatest! He is the greatest son!" Dad again looked confused, and then, mercifully, Charles changed the subject.

"How about a tour of the clinic, Walter, may I call you Walter?" Charles locked his arm again with Dad, and started leading him through the facility. "First, Dr. Turke, I mean Walter, I want to show you the parlor, that's where we do most of our work with the residents. We have two of these parlors, one on each side of the building. This might be a good place for you to see your patients..."

Although I was standing right alongside Charles and Dad, I felt like I was trailing behind them, watching them from afar. For Dad, the change in roles had already happened, swiftly, effortlessly and painlessly. I was no longer leading Dad. Charles and the Clare Bridge staff were. Dad no longer needed to exclusively depend on me; he was now arm in arm with the Clare Bridge director and his staff. I was no longer the center of Dad's world. I was no longer his co-star, just one of the supporting casts. It suddenly hurt.

Most painfully and perhaps most significantly, I was beginning to worry that Dad would no longer look for me. Would he no longer search for me to provide him with guidance, direction, or security? He had found his safe haven. This environment was tailor-made for him. He would no longer have to make a decision about anything. He appeared to be enveloped by a sea of unconditional love.

I should have been happy. I should have been grateful. I should have been relieved. Hell, I should have been rejoicing that Dad was adjusting so well. But instead, I ruminated on my worries that soon, Dad wouldn't need me anymore.

Charles and Dad remained arm in arm, smiling and chatting away. "And over here, Walter, let me show you the dining room. This is where we serve the residents their meals. We have a great chef at Clare Bridge; he runs this place like a restaurant. And, of course, we want you to dine with us whenever you're here at work..."

"Really? All this comes with the job?"

"It sure does. Let me find out what they're serving at lunch today."

"Remember, I don't eat fish!"

"Oh, we know, Walter. Don't worry. No fish and no cheese! Hey, you're in luck, Walter. Lunch today is spaghetti and meatballs."

I pulled up a little and let Charles and Dad walk out in front. I didn't realize how symbolic this was until I watched them up ahead of me. Dad was now putting his arm around Charles. They were already buddies. He not only already seemed accepting of being here, but he already looked happy and secure. This was a good thing, but I didn't feel it.

Why was I having so much trouble letting go? The answer was not going to be found dwelling on my own jealousies, sadness, and worries. I was getting mired again in my own selfishness. Hadn't I learned anything through my journey with Dad? Geez, I had only heard the same message from the guardian angels about a million times.

Charles and Dad had made their way all the way around the facility and were now nearly back to the front entrance. As they rounded the corner, Charles made a sharp, unexpected turn to the right, down one of the four residential hallways.

"Walter, let me show you your office suite." Charles was still arm in arm with Dad.

Charles took his master key and opened the door. "Walter, Garrett took the liberty to dress up your office a little. I think he did great job, don't you?"

Dad was sincerely choked up. "It's so...so...so beautiful! What a surprise! You did this for me, doctor? "

"Yeah, Dad. Just for you." My voice was flat and lacked enthusiasm. I made a weak attempt to fake it, but it didn't go over very well.

Charles and Dad began the tour of Dad's mini-museum. I knew in advance how that would go, because I constructed Dad's "office" just the way Dad always designed his home museums. Draw the curious visitor in and wow them. Then humbly begin talking about your travels, your adventures, your exploits. Then watch the visitor's amazed reactions. I had witnessed Dad's routine hundreds of times.

Dad may have forgotten I was his son, but he had not forgotten his museum shtick. Within a few seconds, he had Charles wrapped around his finger. The stories were all more than a bit distorted. Dad's guided tour to see the Mudmen of New Guinea became Dad's daring solo adventure to infiltrate the "madmen of the Sahara." Nice try, Dad. And Dad's story of being chased by a crocodile in Australia, always a tad suspect in the first place, became a fantastic story about a great white shark that had chased Dad into a bay, then snatched another person who was walking atop a sea wall. Good old Dad. He was back again for a little while at least. Too bad he couldn't be back with me as his son.

Charles was enthralled, or at least acted like he was enthralled, by all the adventures advertised along the walls of Dad's room. He and Dad walked through what seemed to be Dad's entire life. Although I was standing right there, pretending to be interested, I had already tuned out, feeling sad, resentful, jealous, and sorry for myself. Charles eventually noticed something was wrong.

"Hey, Garrett, why don't you take a break for awhile? Walter and I are doing just fine here. Why don't you hook up with us again at lunch? Tiffanie's coming over then, right?" Charles was doing his best to reassure me that Dad was acclimating just fine. But that wasn't the problem. I was the one who needed the help acclimating.

"Right, she'll be by at 12. I guess I could come back then." I put on a fake smile and politely excused myself. I tried to act like it didn't bother me.

I did the redirect by lying but there was no emotion behind my words. "OK, Dad, it looks like the staff really need me on the other side of the building. I'm going to go help them out a while, and then I'll rejoin you at lunch? Tiff is coming over, too. Sound OK, Dad?"

Dad looked at me, smiled, but didn't answer. He wanted to show Charles his picture of the Brooklyn Bridge.

I turned and headed for the door. I thought I was keeping my composure. I bit down on my lower lip, hard, to keep it from quivering. I wanted to just hold it together long enough to get outside.

I didn't make it. That damn security system made me wait at the front door.

Hadiyya came up to me, took my hand and turned me around gently. "You are Walter's son, yes? I know this must be very hard for you; I can see it on your face. You have some time? Here, you sit down for a minute. I cannot let you leave upset like this. You know we will take very good care of your father. You know he is not just a patient here. We are like a very big family and your father, Walter, is joining us. You and your family will be joining our family, too. Your father is a very nice man, I am told he helped a lot of people in his day. You must be very proud to be his son."

"That is the problem. I am not his son anymore. And I no longer care for him, you do."

"Nonsense! You are always his son, and you will always care for him. You must respect that it is his time. He is getting prepared to leave from this place, and we must help him be ready. You have your whole lifetime with your father, it's all locked in your mind and it will always be there. But you also have many days left with your father here. Use them wisely."

She continued before I even had a chance to think of a response. I was struck how forward and self-assured she was, like everyone seemed to be at this place. "You must trust that we can be like a family to you. You see, the staff here are very kind toward the people that are old. They have given so much. They are just tired. They are just awaiting their turn."

"How do I know he will be all right here?"

"Because the staff will come to know you, if you let us, that is."

"How will that help with my father's care?"

"Because the staff will come to know Walter as your father. He will never be just a patient that way. He will have his identity and he will have yours. You understand?"

"Where in Africa are you from?"

"I am from Ivory Coast."

"I have been to Senegal several times."

"Then why are you resisting? You already understand."

Hadiyya punched in the code, smiled, the green light came on, and she opened the door for me. "So we will see you later, then?"

"I'll be back for lunch with my sister."

"Very good! Clare Bridge will be waiting for you."

71 { Lunch at Clare Bridge

My ears were still ringing when I pulled back into the Clare Bridge parking lot. I had passed the time before lunch cranking up my stereo to near airport runway level decibels. I had taken a little hiatus to Zion with my friend Mr. Marley. It had been a long time since I had had a simulated concert in my living room. It felt good to find that my old self was still in there.

When I arrived back at Clare Bridge, Tiffanie was already there, waiting for me in her car. I could see her smile at me through the passenger side window when I parked alongside of her. A very beautiful woman, she had a pained expression on her face that overtook her forced smile. I immediately felt bad for her. I had worked, struggled, so hard to get my own head right after Dad got sick that I had put very little effort into taking care of my sister. Yes, she had her husband, Don, her circle of friends, and our mother to help her get through Dad's disease. But I was probably the only one who really felt what she was going through. We were in the same boat. And although we were in the same boat, I had only been concerned with keeping myself afloat to help Dad. Maybe that was all I had energy for.

Tiffanie was always very close to our dad. She looked up to him and idolized him as a child. She was, in some ways, very similar to Dad. She liked expensive things and growing up often liked being the center of attention. And it was always my dad who provided her with that attention. My mom used to say Dad was spoiling her by showering her with superficial compliments and material things. But she was secure with Dad, and they became inseparable when she grew older. Before Dad got sick, Tiff would visit him just about every other weekend at his condo in Bay City. That was a lot more than I did.

My other sister Cindy and I sometimes thought Tiffanie was indulged by Dad. We thought that Tiffanie had it much easier than we did. She wasn't expected to work as hard as us, wasn't expected to achieve in school like we were, and she wasn't pushed toward academic or career success like we had been. We thought she had been pampered. Maybe it was a sign that by his third child, Dad was relaxing a bit more with his parenting and expectations. Or maybe he was distracted, preoccupied with his own needs, his increasingly troubled marriage, and ultimately his affair with Teri. I knew my mother subscribed to the latter hypothesis. In retrospect, however, it seems that perhaps Cindy and I were just a bit jealous of Tiffanie's close relationship with our dad and his sheltering, protective orientation toward her.

Tiff got out of her car, locked arms with me, and pulled tight. "I don't know if I can do this, Garrett. How is he? Weren't you going to be here all morning? Is he scared in there? Oh God, Garrett, Oh my God, this is our father, Garrett. He's in there, all alone now, without us."

I responded to Tiffanie superficially, although I knew what Tiffanie was saying was much deeper. "Tiff, I was with him all morning, until they sort of kicked me out to give me a little break, because Dad was doing so well. Tiff, Dad thinks he's at work in there, he seems to love it, he's getting all kinds of attention, and the staff..."

I hadn't responded to her SOS. I was answering her up on the surface. She was really hurting, and was trying to tell me to get deeper with her. She made sure she hit her mark on the second try.

"Garrett, our dad, what's happening to him? We're losing him. Oh my God, Garrett, I'm watching him slip away right in front of me! He's already in care. I can't believe it! I can't believe it!! I don't know what to say to him when I see him. I don't know if I can face him. I can't talk to him the way you do. I can't tell him how I feel; I don't want to hurt him! What do I do?"

Tiffanie was pleading, but I truly didn't know what to do. The reality was crashing down on her.

I pulled Tiffanie in closer, and steered us toward the Clare Bridge entranceway. I felt like that big brother again. I was reminded how much I loved her. Good God, all the years of Dad being sick and I had taken so little time to tell her that I loved her.

I tried to muster up some big brother reassurance and confidence. "Tiff, everything is going to be all right. You are going through exactly what I went through. Trust me, I know how much it hurts. But you will get through this. You have to go through it, we all do, I know it's scary, but you'll be all right. I will help you and God will help you. There is a presence about us, God's presence, it's with Dad too, and things will be all right. I know that things will be all right."

I wouldn't allow Tiffanie to catch her breath. There was a lesson in this, and it was my responsibility to impart it. "Listen to me. When we go inside in a minute, you're going to see some things that I know you don't expect. Not bad things. Wonderful things. These people who work here, they are so kind toward Dad. It's almost like a miracle. They seem to know all about him. I think Charles must have told his entire staff a lot about Dad's life. They know his history, what he did for work, who he was as a person, what he likes and dislikes. They even know a little about us. Tiff, the staff here are taking him under their wings. It is so touching. You'll see. This is the best possible thing that could have happened. Those people, I mean the staff in there, they are like angels..."

Tiffanie interrupted me, tears streaming down her face. "What are you talking about? You almost sound crazy, Garrett! They won't take care of Dad the way we do! They don't love him the way we do! I can't believe you said that! Garrett, I know we had that meeting with Charles and everyone seemed really nice, but they won't take care of Dad like us, they are not our family, they are not his family..."

Now it was my turn to interrupt. I didn't know anyway else to do this, other than to lance the wound. "Tiffanie, Dad has advancing Alzheimer's disease. He is very sick. We have to face it, damnitall! We can't do it alone anymore. It's too much for us. We did all we could, way more than the average family I am told, and now we have to let go and let others help us. I am not crazy. Come on, let's go in. You will see. The staff here, they are like a family to Dad already. Ready or not, like it or not, they have already adopted him. And, they have already adopted us."

"I don't know how you can trust people so quickly! You're talking crazy! You don't even know them! Geez, what's wrong with you, Garrett! These people are strangers to Dad. Half of them aren't even from this country! I can't believe you just trust people so easily! They've adopted him? What are you saying? That's crazy! You know what people say about these nursing homes."

"Tiff, I know what people say about nursing homes. But this place is special. I know it is. I can feel it. And Tiff, we already made our decision." I took her hand and pressed tightly to emphasize my point.

"Tiffanie, it's already happened! He's already in there! I know it all seems so unreal, but it's all done. Tiff, he has Alzheimer's disease. He has it! And there is nothing we can do about it other than to support him. Tiff, he is slipping, fast if you ask me. But he's all right with what's happening. In fact, he seems as happy in there as I have seen him in a very long time. We are the ones who have to accept it now. Not just face it, accept it! We have to let go! I do know what you are going through. But I also know Dad is safe in there."

Although the 50 foot walk from the parking lot seemed to take an eternity, we finally made it inside the vestibule. Devin came to the door and punched in the code. She opened the door. Like all the staff at Clare Bridge, she smiled, ever so warmly, as we came in.

"Hi, Garrett." Devin already acted like she knew me well. "Hey, is this your sister? Hello, my name is Devin. Your father sure is making his mark here today. He's already made a lot of friends. Everyone likes him. He seems so kind and so friendly. Are you here to have lunch with him?"

"Yes we are!" I said emphatically and enthusiastically. Tiff had a look of barely controlled panic on her face.

"Well, follow me this way to our dining hall. I think Peter made spaghetti and meatballs today."

Devin escorted us to the dining room. Everyone had assigned seating, according to their needs for assistance and according to their chemistry with the other residents. On the left side were people who were in the latter stages of the disease. They had to have their food pureed and had to be helped with eating. A few of them were slumped in their chairs, asleep. I would learn that my analogy of a laptop computer going into hibernation when not in use was completely accurate. For the advanced Alzheimer's patients, if they were not being directly and actively stimulated, they would fall asleep in just a minute or two. Sometimes it was just a matter of seconds.

To the right were the higher functioning patients. There were some who were like Dad. They still retained a lot of their self-care skills and were still able to carry on a meaningful conversation, well at least bits and pieces of a meaningful conversation. This side of the room seemed like a chatty, energetic, social club.

Dad was seated next to a man named Anthony when we approached his table. He was talking away, something about a car that needed some repair work done. I could tell that Dad was in a supportive role, telling Anthony not to worry, that things would be all right.

Devin escorted us over to the table. There were two more place settings, presumably for Tiff and me. Dad looked up and beamed when he saw us. It was that same look I had seen hundreds of times at his condo when I came over, like I had been overseas for ten years and had just returned home. Funny thing, though. This time Anthony had the same look upon his face.

Both Dad and Anthony stood up, excited. Anthony spoke first, with an unexpected air of familiarity. "Why hi there, gee it's been a long time! We are so glad to see you two! How is our family back home?"

Tiff looked distraught. I instinctively kicked in my "redirect by lying" skills. "Why hello there, ah, ah....."

Devin helped me out. Like all of the Clare Bridge staff, she was also an expert in the redirect by lying technique. "It's Anthony, Garrett. Anthony."

"Why hello there, Anthony! Our family's great! We just thought we'd come by and have lunch with you two. Dad, how on earth did you find our long lost family member here? Boy oh boy! What a coincidence! Unbelievable. All these years and now, at last, re-united!"

Dad patted Anthony on the shoulder. "Old Navy buddy, this man here. Wow, after all this time."

Anthony whispered over to Dad, as if Dad was his trusted confident. "So, do you think they could help us? You know, I mean, I mean, with, you know, the thing that's broken? Oh shit! What the hell do you call it, you drive it for God's sake. Shit, I can't think worth a damn anymore."

I continued to play along. Tiff was quiet.

"You mean your car?"

"Yes that's it, that's it! By God, you got it right on the first try!"

Dad was all excited, too. "I told you, I told you! He is, he is… oh what do I call him? He is… the greatest!"

"He sure is the greatest," echoed Anthony. "Who is he, your brother?"

Dad leaned over and whispered back. "I don't really know exactly who he is, but he is a good one, well, he comes over and he works with me and he is the greatest." Dad looked at me and smiled, tearing up, like he always did when something touched him.

"So. About my car." Anthony reached into his back pocket and pulled out his wallet. "My car is somewhere on the west side of Chicago. It needed an oil change or a new transmission or a tune-up or some blasted thing. I've got to get going. Your brother and I have got to get out of here, I mean it's been very nice and all, but we need our car."

Anthony then opened his wallet and took out two green bills. "How about a couple of twenties? Do you think that would do it, I mean, to take us over to my car?"

Anthony handed me the two bills. They were twenties, all right. Twenties in Monopoly money.

I could tell that things were starting to get a bit too weird for Tiffanie, so I tried to change the subject. "Anthony, that's more than enough, but we can talk about that later. Right now, let's have some lunch; it's been a long time since we've seen you and we came all this way."

"Oh right..." said Anthony, seemingly acting as if he had offended us. "Sorry. Well, aren't you going to introduce us to your pretty wife here?"

"This is Tiffanie, you're right, she is pretty, but she's not my wife. She's my sister."

Dad interrupted. He was so proud to tell Anthony all about her. "She's my pretty young friend. She comes over to see me all the time. We go... we go out, to those big screens together, she comes over for dinner, we have a great time together." Dad reached out for her hand.

Tiff forced a smile, but it only fooled Dad and Anthony. She had tears streaming, welling up in her eyes. While I was playfully bantering away with Dad, Tiff was recognizing that her identity had slipped away.

"Garrett, I don't think I can do this, this is too weird."

The meal came, with nice portions of spaghetti, meatballs, garlic bread and green beans. I was very hungry and ate everything. Tiff just picked at her food.

Dad and Anthony continued to chat away. Dad was talking to him about the Navy, while Anthony continued talking to him about his car. It didn't seem to matter to either one of them that they were simultaneously talking about two different things.

After we finished our meal and had a small dessert, Tiffanie abruptly stood up and said she had to get back to work. She looked very sad and very uncomfortable. I felt bad that I didn't feel the same. I had actually enjoyed my lunch with Dad and his new buddy. Anthony was going to become Dad's loyal companion and sidekick at Clare Bridge. They would continue to talk about the Navy and Anthony's stranded Buick in Chicago for months.

We politely excused ourselves and headed for the front entranceway door. Dad and Anthony got up and followed us like two puppies. I already knew how to find our way around the building and showed Tiffanie. It was easy. Everything was in a circle and took you past all of the facility's main rooms. It was designed for the memory impaired. It was impossible to get lost.

When we reached the front door, Devin was waiting for us.

"Tiffanie, your father will be well treated here. He is already very well liked by all of us. If there is anything we can do to help you, to make this easier for you, you let us know. This is Walter's new home, but it is also your new home. You may stop by any time to see your father. You do not need to call. And if you feel sad, we can sit down with you and we will listen."

I said "thank you" for both of us. Devin got ready to punch in the code, but before she did, she explained how to separate.

"When I open the door, it's best to have said your good-byes and then go straight out. Don't look back, or your father may try to go with you, and then that sometimes causes problems. So, maybe say your goodbyes right now and then I will punch in the code.

"Dad, I will see you later. My shift is over now but I'll be back after dinner with Stacy and the girls. See you later, alligator?"

I hugged my dad and separated. It was easier than I thought it would be. Dad smiled and chirped, "After awhile, crocodile."

Tiffanie was clamping down on her lower lip, barely holding it together. She hugged Dad tightly, lovingly, and clung to him for a minute, like it was her very last goodbye. She turned, Devin punched in the code, and we left.

Per our instructions, we didn't look back. I could hear Devin in the background redirecting Dad and Anthony back into the interior of the facility.

Tiff tried to compose herself, asked what time we were coming over to visit tonight, and said she had to hurry back to work. We hugged. Mine was heartfelt but rather perfunctory. Hers was a tight, help-me-I'm scared kind of embrace. I got into my van and Tiff got into her car.

As I backed out into the driveway, I could see Tiffanie's face through the passenger side window. She was crying.

72 { "Won't You Come Home, Bill Bailey?"

I held the door to the vestibule while Shani, Stacy, and Miah filed in. It had been a pleasant spring day, but now, as the sun was going down, it was getting really cold outside. Miah was shivering as we entered. Shani, independent and mature beyond her years, tucked the handful of piano sheet music she was carrying up under her arm and took Miah's hand. She then pushed the black entrance button that summoned the staff. The simulated doorbell began to chime, which immediately caused a stir of activity on the other side of the door.

Stacy and I had talked about whether it was appropriate to bring our children to Clare Bridge tonight. Could they handle a whole facility of Alzheimer's patients? Up to now, they had just been exposed to only their grandfather's disease. It had been such a gradual process, or rather erosion, that it hadn't seemed to cause either one of them a great deal of distress yet. But could they handle Clare Bridge? They would see many patients in the latter stages of the disease, not being able to communicate, some confined to wheelchairs, some not even able to hold their heads up anymore. And the ones that could still communicate often said really strange, bizarre things. Would they be frightened by this? Would there be some lasting trauma because of what we were about to expose them too?

And the smells. While the overriding, dominant smell at Clare Bridge was a clean, disinfectant or air freshener kind of smell, there were frequent waves of other smells that might be troubling to the kids. Feces, urine, vomit. They were unavoidable life smells that accompanied the disease. This would undoubtedly affect the kids as well, and form a painful lasting impression.

We thought that Shani could probably handle Clare Bridge. She was a very precocious 12 year old who had never seen a "B" on an assignment or report card in her life. Shani was already talking about wanting to become a pediatrician or an obstetrician. Before Dad got sick, she had had a number of conversations with her "Grampy" about what medical school was like. Shani had a thirst for knowledge and an incredible drive to understand things. If she didn't understand something or something made her uncomfortable, she would relentlessly ask questions until she felt resolved. Yes, Shani, we thought, probably would be able to handle Clare Bridge. And she would certainly tell us if seeing her Grampy or anyone else in residential care caused her distress.

But what about six year old Miah? She was a regular little kid, happy, spontaneous, full of life and energy. She didn't stop and analyze things the way Shani did. She was a "doer," who experienced things first and thought about it later. But Miah didn't ask questions the way Shani always did. If something bothered, troubled, or perplexed her, it was hard to tell right away what was going on inside her head. Stacy and I weren't sure if visits to Clare Bridge were appropriate for a six year old. If something distressed her from a visit inside the facility, we might not know it for days.

Despite the risks, we decided to bring Miah on the premise that it would be wrong to separate her from the rest of the family, to shelter her from an obvious reality that would be discussed daily in her home, and to keep her from having contact with her grandfather. We talked to Miah about going, and she didn't express any ambivalence at all. Although Miah had awareness that her grandfather was sick, and couldn't take care of himself anymore, she didn't seem particularly troubled by his decline. Instead, she just innocently talked about wanting to play with him. Miah's innocence was a beautiful thing, but that was exactly the issue that troubled Stacy and me. Taking Miah to Clare Bridge was a gamble, for we were certain that with each visit there, a little more of her innocence would be taken away.

A few of the residents noticed us standing at the front door. I could see them sort of huddling and pointing at the door. Two elderly women came right up to the entrance and peered at us through the entrance door window. They started to speak to each other.

"Look, there's someone's whole family at the door. Do you think they're here to see us?"

"I don't know, but they look familiar. Are they your children or mine?"

"I don't really know just yet, but it looks like they want to come in. Let's just open the door. Why it's so rude to just let them stand there. Look at the little one, she's shivering it's so cold out there. Please, can't we just let them in?"

"No! Don't you ever listen? We can't just let them in, it's, it's, you know, it's against what we are supposed to do, it's, why you know, it's, it's against the law!"

"Oh, that's right. Geez, thanks for reminding me, I could have been in big trouble."

"Big trouble? Bigger than that! You could have been arrested!"

Suddenly, Charles, the ever-effervescent director, emerged from the left side of the living room. He parted his way through the group of residents and came up to the door. By now, the whole living room seemed alive with excitement that there were visitors waiting to come in. We didn't know this just then, but Charles would later tell us that family visits in the evenings were rather rare. Many families admitted their loved ones to the facility and soon disinvested. They would rarely visit and left the final months and years of their loved one's lives solely to the care of residential staff. It was a sad commentary on our society's lack of investment in the elderly.

Charles spoke with an enthusiasm that matched the buzz in the living room behind him. "Excuse me, excuse me! Look everyone; we have some very special guests tonight!"

"Who are they?" came an elderly male voice from the back.

"Why its Walter's son, Garrett, his daughter in law Stacy, and their two children, Shani and Miah."

I smiled through the window as Charles punched in the code. My God, how the heck does he remember my children's names? He's never even met them before.

"Come on in, come on in!" Charles extended his hand to Shani, and made a dramatic sweeping motion with his arm as if to say the living room belonged to her. He then crouched, as he got down to Miah's level.

"Why hello there! You must be Miah. I have a daughter who is just about your age. She was just over here yesterday. She has a lot of fun here playing with everyone."

Miah smiled cautiously but sincerely. I relaxed. If Charles brings his little girl in here then it must be OK for Miah.

Charles engaged Miah effortlessly. "Hey Miah. You see that giant beach ball over there in the corner? It's almost bigger than you! Why don't you go over there and bounce it around a little? You can play beach ball with your grandpa and the other residents if you want. Go ahead, check it out, it's really fun."

Miah looked back at both of her parents for approval, both Stacy and I nodded, and Miah went over and picked up the ball. It was about three, maybe even four feet in diameter and could probably contain her easily if she was inside of it. Miah began dribbling it as if it was a giant basketball, with the bounces coming up to her eye level each time. Within seconds Miah had mastered her task, dribbling it easily and fluidly with both her right and left hands. She then started going underneath the giant ball in-between dribbles, picking up her dribble each time after she passed underneath it. It was rather amazing little stunt, and the whole facility, residents and staff alike, were momentarily captivated by what she was doing.

I beamed. "We call her 'the natural,' Charles." Miah was the natural, at least athletically. Shani had played organized basketball for years and had become a good player by virtue of her sheer drive, practice and determination. Miah had picked up a basketball at age 4 and with no instruction whatsoever could dribble immediately and effortless with either hand. At one point Stacy and I even wondered if she was actually left-handed.

Soon Miah was playing volleyball with the staff and residents, gently hitting it to the residents that were seated around the living room. Although the ball was so light it couldn't hurt anything or anyone, I asked Charles if there was any risk in hitting the ball around.

"Oh certainly not. That's exactly what we do with that ball. The residents love it. Actually, on Wednesdays I think it is, we play a sort of indoor volleyball game with the residents. It's really kind of fun, we have teams, the staff and I play too sometimes. Wow, look at that! Miah's really got command of her audience!"

Stacy and I glanced over. Miah had positioned herself across from about four residents, and was taking turns hitting the ball to each one in turn. The residents were all smiling and actively engaged. Miah was smiling, and occasionally, giggling.

Charles was smiling, too. "Look at her over there. Miah is fitting in very nicely. A lot of adults think children shouldn't come in here, that it's too scary for them to see people in this condition. But you know what? Every child that comes in here plays with the residents, just like Miah is doing right now. This is very good for the residents, and it's very good for children to see that their grandparents or loved ones are still valued and happy here. It's very natural, and it's very innocent."

Charles continued on with his lesson. "You know, the parents that think their children can't handle this place are really telling us something."

"What's that, Charles?" I inquired, curious, but careful not to let on that he had obliquely hit upon my issue.

"They are telling us that it is they, themselves, that can't handle this place. They are the ones with the fears and the worries. That's why you don't see too many families visiting in here."

Charles then abruptly left us to be impacted by his statement. He had spontaneously hooked arms with Shani and was escorting her toward the piano that was against the far wall. "Shani, I see you brought some of your music with you. What do you like to play?"

"Mostly classical. You know, Mozart, Beethoven, Chopin. But I like other kinds of music, too. Today I brought some ragtime, and some turn of the century songs that some of the residents might even remember." Shani answered politely and articulately. If I wasn't looking right at her middle school frame, I would have thought she was an intelligent young college student.

Charles pulled out the piano bench for Shani to sit on. Then, completely unexpectedly, he sat down next to her, and began playing a complex ragtime piece with such precision and rhythm that it was obvious that he had taken many years of lessons.

"I used to play, too, Shani. It's amazing how it all just comes back to you." Charles continued to talk while he played. It seemed effortless for him. "I think it's really cool that you came out here ready to play. The residents are going to love you."

Charles finished his piece, which had drawn in most of the residents who were not in the living room at first. Dad and Anthony came in too, having completed another lap around the facility. Anthony was still concerned about his car being fixed in Chicago, and Dad was still telling him not to worry, that things would be all right.

Charles left the piano seat and began rearranging the remaining open sofas and chairs in the living room to face the piano. It was turning into a special event for the facility. There was going to be a concert at Clare Bridge tonight! Charles instructed us to sit down, and positioned Dad and Anthony to sit next to us. The evening staff then gathered up the remaining residents and had them take a seat as well. One of the staff got Clare Bridge's turn-of-the-century looking popcorn maker going. The whole place was alive and festive. Charles made an announcement welcoming Shani and the concert was ready to begin. Shani looked more than a little nervous, but had her play list all organized. Poor girl had entered Clare Bridge expecting to just play quietly in the background.

Anthony was squirming anxiously next to us. "Oh boy, what's going on now? Can't anyone take me to my car? It's been ready for days."

Dad intervened. "Just relax. We'll get your car fixed later. Right now there's going to be a show. You need to be quiet. That's my, my... my sister up there, and she is marvelous. Now shhhhhhh, just listen."

Shani started playing. The room was quiet. Miah had put her beach ball to the side. Other Clare Bridge staff who had been busy in other parts of the building came in and sat down.

Shani played as well as she had ever played in her entire life. She opened with a Scott Joplin song, and then smoothly moved into "Bill Bailey." I looked around. The entire room was mesmerized. It was almost as if they had been transported back in time, to an era when things made more sense to them.

Listening to Shani's performance, I began to realize how exhausted I was. Exhausted from the day. Exhausted from the week. Exhausted from the past several years. It had been a long time since I could let down. It had been a long time since I had been able to rest without wondering whether Dad was safe or not. A minute or two into "Bill Bailey," I found my head starting to nod downward. I fought it for a little while, but soon lost the struggle.

Surrendering, I put my head down on Stacy's shoulder, with my eyes closed. I then heard a faint, but increasingly perceptible, elderly voice, singing clearly and right on key:

"Won't you come home Bill Bailey, won't you come home? She moans the whole day long. I'll do the cooking, darlin', I'll pay the rent. I know I done you wrong."

73 { Where Are My Parents?

It had been a hard day at work. One of the kids I had worked with in the past had killed himself in jail. I thought to myself that never would have happened in our Youth Center. I had learned a cruel reality through my years at the Court. As soon as a kid turned 17 he was no longer considered a victim of abuse and neglect anymore. He was now a threat, a perpetrator, someone that society no longer wanted to help but instead wanted to remove. And when a kid turned 17, he became a number in the adult system. A number that represented someone that had lost value, someone that didn't matter anymore, someone for society to be afraid of. And today, that number had committed suicide.

Almost like some sick ritual, I automatically added this kid's name to the running list in my mind. Number 21. Twenty one senseless deaths in my 18 years with the Court. Suicides, homicides, accidental shootings, gang drive-bys, reckless car accidents, alcohol and drug overdoses. A drive-by that inadvertently killed a six year old from a stray bullet. A drowning in a river while being chased by the police. A fatal car crash while high on speed and acid.

I startled with the blare of the car horn behind me. I had zoned out in a left turn lane and had failed to recognize that the green turn arrow had come on. I made the left turn from East Grand River onto Marsh Road, and headed north, toward my house. In a few minutes I would be home, to emotional safety, and in time for a nice dinner and then some basketball with the kids in the driveway. But instead, I glanced at my watch. Only 4:10. I had left work early due to the stress of today's news. I had time to stop and see Dad before going home. That was the blessing and the bane of Dad's placement at Clare Bridge. He was always on the way home.

The Clare Bridge entrance door opened as soon as I came in the foyer. "Why hello, Walter's son! Your father has been looking for you all day today.

He is having a most difficult day. Not to worry, lots of our residents go through this, it will pass and things will settle down again."

I stepped inside hesitantly, not knowing what to expect. Shit! I was on my way home. I had had enough for one day. Why did I have to stop?

Masudi grabbed me by the hand, put her other arm behind my back and gently began walking me along the circular corridor that ringed the facility. I had no choice but to submit and follow his lead.

"What's wrong, Masudi?"

"Your father, he is scared today. He is looking all about for you, and his parents. He has taken his room down, he says he needs to go home. He says he can't find his mother and his father. It is a bad day for him. No one seems to be able to console him and distract him. But now you are here. Perhaps God has seen to it that you are here exactly when you are needed? Ah yes, we all know how that works in this life. God is great!"

Needed? For Dad? I thought that role was pretty much gone forever when Dad checked in here.

Masudi opened the door to Dad's room. His room was bare. Dad had taken down everything that had been upon his walls. His photographs and mementos and memories were all neatly lined up against the hallway wall. Next to them was the Japan Airlines flight bag, a vestige from our 1968 trip to the Orient, overflowing with clothes and underwear he had stuffed in.

Dad was sitting vacantly on the bed. He stood up immediately when he saw me, but he didn't have that welcoming, "it's so good to see you, you're back from overseas" look on his face that I had grown accustomed to. Instead, Dad looked desperate, lost, and disconnected.

"I have got to find them. They are missing from me."

"Who, Dad?" I approached him and put my arm around his back.

"I've got to get out of here. We have to go home. I've got to find them."

"OK, we can go look for them, sure. Who are we looking for again?"

"My, my, my…" Dad was starting to cry. "Where are my parents! I need to find them. I don't know where they are. I don't know if they are alive or dead. I've got to find them, to talk to them, I…I… I left them with bad things going on and now I can't seem to find them. They are waiting for me, I think, they are at... that place, you know, with the big white walls, you know it, the place we were always at, where we watch our movies, you know, our home? I want to go home to be with my parents. "

Dad was trembling. I flashed back to when I was 4, and had gotten lost in a grocery store. Although I was only one aisle away, I remember the dread panic of being unexpectedly separated from my parents and not feeling like I could ever find them again. Dad was having that same experience right now.

Masudi interrupted my memory. "Walter has taken his room down many times in the past couple days. We keep putting it back up, but it keeps coming down again. Each time, he is saying he wants to go back home and be with his parents."

"I understand. Can I take him out for a while? Maybe if I get him out I can settle him and then we'll come back."

"Sure you can. I will have his room back in order when you come back. Here, let's get his jacket, it is so cold out for so late in the spring. I am wondering when it will finally be warm every day. This is a lot different than my country. Brrrrr! Africa has never seen a day this cold. And here it is May."

Masudi went into Dad's closet and pulled out his U.S. Navy windbreaker. "Here you are, Doctor Turke, we need to zip you up, it's chilly out today."

I helped Dad put on his windbreaker. Dad jumped at the opportunity, apparently still equating putting his jacket on with going somewhere.

"We're, we're, we're going somewhere, someplace out?"

"Yep. Sure are, Dad. We've got some business to take care of. With your parents."

Dad's face immediately brightened. "You've found them? Then they are alive? Oh, thank God! This is so good, so very good. I've got to go see them right away. My mother and my father, I was angry at them, for something, I don't even know what it was anymore, it was something, something big, but now, now it seems so small. I don't want it anymore, I just want to see them and to tell them that all is ... it's all better, I just need to tell them I love them and it's OK for me to come home."

I was starting to tear up, but held it back. What was Dad trying to tell me? That he had unfinished business with his parents? Even as impaired as he was, he seemed to be struggling to resolve something. Maybe he wasn't always in an oblivious bliss after all.

I instinctively made the switch back to caregiver mode. As much as I had fought to lose this identity, I welcomed it back. It gave me purpose with my Dad. I was needed again.

"Come on, Dad! Time to shove off! Anchors away?"

Dad looked up and tears welled in his eyes. It wasn't that desperate, sad, teared-up look that he had had moments before. It was the teared-up look that Dad always had when he was touched by something. He was coming back.

I took Dad by the arm and escorted him back to the circular interior corridor. We wound our way around the interior until we came to the front entrance. By then, we had picked up an entourage of people who wanted to come with us: Mildred, the vocalist from Shani's concert night, a woman named Joyce, who wanted to know if we could drop her off in Oklahoma, and Anthony, who of course wanted us to take him to his car in Chicago.

Masudi punched in the code, distracted the entourage, and Dad and I left the cocoon for the world outside.

The outside world seemed like a scary place with Dad. I immediately realized how unsafe it actually was given Dad's impairment. My God, this is the world I maintained Dad in for three years with his disease. I couldn't believe we had managed it. I couldn't believe he had come through safely.

Dad looked happy and excited to be outside again. "There it is, the big silver one!" He couldn't wait to get into the van. I opened the door and he climbed in, like an excited little kid going on a field trip.

I buckled Dad in and we headed north on Marsh Road. I didn't know where to go. I thought going back to his old condo would only open up a Pandora's box of problems that would confuse Dad. Besides, if we went back to the condo I would have to see that "No help for Walter" message up on his wipe board again. That was sure to bring up ghosts I didn't want to face.

I decided to just start driving aimlessly to the north and east, out into the countryside. Pretty soon we entered our old stomping grounds, the Rose Lake natural area.

"So, Dad, about your parents…"

"I need to find them, to talk to them. Are they alive?"

My first impasse. What do I do? Tell him the truth that both of his parents are dead and traumatize him? Then deal with all the anxiety and desperation this would bring? Or do I go straight to the redirect by lying as a strategy, and then try to put him at peace.

The answer was obvious and now instinctive for me. "Dad, I've been in touch with them. You will be seeing them, soon. But I can give them a message in the meantime."

"You can? Oh that is so wonderful. Doctor, you are the greatest."

"What do you want me to tell them?"

Dad's response was as fluent and articulate as I had heard from him in many months. "Well, it's a very long time ago and I was mad at them for something that happened. I don't remember it, but it was bad and it was big once. I think I was gone for a long time and I didn't want to see them, but now, now... now I need to see them."

"You will, Dad, you will. What do you need to tell them?"

"That the things I was mad at, the things that made me so mad, well now I don't want any of it, it seems so small now, I don't need it, I don't even remember it. I want to tell them I love them and I can be at home again, with them."

"Your parents did the best they could. They had a hard life, too."

"Yes, that's it, that's it!"

"You are saying you forgive them, I think."

"Yes, you got it again! That's why, that's why... you... you are the greatest!"

"You know what Dad? I think your parents, your mother and your father, will be so happy when I tell them that. You know what? You don't have to worry about any of this anymore. You have worked it out! Yes, you have! Your parents will be happy and you will be happy."

Dad teared up and his bottom lip trembled. He was smiling and crying at the same time. I reached across the console and grabbed onto his hand. He clutched my hand in return.

We drove around the natural area for about an hour and then headed back toward Clare Bridge. Dad was chatty and happy the entire time. It seemed like he had resolved things. Despite the ravages of his disease, he too had ghosts that apparently still clung and pressed on him. Maybe I was wrong. Maybe Dad wasn't completely lost in an oblivious bliss. Maybe some things still bothered him. Maybe some things still mattered. Maybe some things could still be resolved.

On the way back to Clare Bridge, I prayed to tell God thanks. Thanks for helping my dad get back to a safe place in his mind. But also thanks for helping me. I was still needed in my Dad's life. Dad still needed me to protect him and to guide him. Only the playing field had changed. I wasn't protecting and guiding him from potential physical harm anymore. The playing field was now a psychological, maybe even a spiritual one. Maybe I could help pull Dad's soul to a place of safety. Like all those guardian angels did with me so many times before.

74 { Three Seasons Later

Three seasons had now passed since Dad's placement at Clare Bridge. I was settled into a new routine with him, a quiet, reflective phase that was free from day-to-day care-giving duties and the physical and emotional stress that came with it. I had gotten used to Clare Bridge as Dad's new home. His physical needs were now met by others and not me.

I was more like a psychological support for Dad now. I relished this new role, because it gave me back a little of my old identity as a caregiver, but without the stress of the mundane, day-to-day physical grind of performing the "45 minute day" countless times. What I didn't yet fully appreciate, however, was that my new self-assigned role as Dad's psychological support was going to be just a starting point. I was about to begin my evolution to a new caregiver's role that carried stakes and responsibilities far greater than my duties had ever seen as Dad's physical and emotional caregiver. I didn't quite realize it yet, but my transformation was now going to entail being a spiritual guide for Dad.

Dad still recognized me and lit up every time he saw me, but no longer seemed to have any idea who I was. Dad's mind would try to assign me an identity each time he saw me. Sometimes I would be his brother, sometimes his entrusted friend or buddy, sometimes "The Doctor," sometimes his father. But it changed every time I came over to Clare Bridge. I had long ago given up trying to remind him that I was his son. It was going on two years since he last called me "Son". It was just no use. I accepted that, but it still hurt. It wasn't an overpowering hurt anymore, just a nagging one.

I had built a nice weekly routine with Dad over the past nine months, one that I could live with, and one that didn't involve the neglect of my own family or my own time anymore. I was beginning to enjoy my dad again. On Wednesdays the kids and I would bring Dad ice cream and hang out with him at Clare Bridge. Shani would bring her music and play on the piano for the residents while I socialized with Dad. Miah played a sort of volleyball game she invented with the higher functioning residents, utilizing the oversized beach balls in the central living area. She was only six years old but acted like the residents' coach at a volleyball practice. I would socialize with Dad while all this was going on, asking him about work, how his patients were doing, and what we were going to do on our next vacation. The subjects were all fantasies, of course. But Dad lived inside of these fantasies, and sometimes, I lived inside of Dad's fantasies with him.

On Wednesdays I also began to learn of the facility's social gossip and politics. Although most of the residents were so very impaired, Clare Bridge was still a community complete with its own soap opera. Residents would believe they were married to each other, that they were buddies from some war, or that they were brothers or sisters to one another. It was amazing to see that despite their impaired thinking, they still created a social order and community that made sense to them.

On Fridays I would pick Dad up around noon and take him out to lunch and then to the movies. We always went to Sultan's, his favorite restaurant, and ordered the same meal, a falafel combo plate, with tabouli and hummus. We always had the same waiter. I never got his name. Dad just called him "our favorite friend." Our waiter would smile and say, "the usual again?" and Dad would say, "of course."

Dad still loved going to the movies. It seemed, however, that he liked the anticipation of going to the movies more than the actual films. A year ago he could sit through the whole show and vaguely follow the plot. Now, he couldn't really follow the themes or plots anymore. I imagine that a movie now seemed more like a disjointed collage of images to him. Dad often mistimed when the movie ended. He frequently stood up about an hour into the show and abruptly exclaimed, "Well that was a great movie! Shall we go home?" He would then try to get through the aisle to leave. At first I could settle him back down and get him to sit through the rest of the film. But lately, getting him to stay through a whole movie was an exercise in futility. It was easier to just file out of the aisle and go home.

Home was now Clare Bridge. That was a good thing, I guess. Clare Bridge was his safe cocoon, almost a perfect, self enclosed world for him. I already knew Clare Bridge was going to be Dad's last home until he died. I accepted that too, but it also brought a nagging hurt. Not a fatal, debilitating hurt, just a twinge of psychological angst that reminded me there was hardly any sand left at the top of the hourglass.

On Saturday or Sunday afternoons I brought Dad to our house for dinner. A lot of times Mom would come over too. We would put on one of Dad's old favorite movies, very often a musical. Dad still loved Evita, South Pacific, West Side Story, and Man of La Mancha. Like in the theatres, he would have trouble with the plot, but ironically, could recall and even sing many of the songs without any loss in fluency. Sometimes, for a brief moment during the songs, Dad wasn't impaired anymore. "I am I, Don Quioxte, the Lord of La Mancha!" Dad would sing boldly, often tearing up during the song. "Isn't this wonderful?" he would then say, as his eyes filled up with tears and his voice cracked.

Stacy loved to cook for Dad. She usually made one of her Italian dishes she had learned in Italy. Dad loved Stacy's cooking, especially those meatballs she made with homemade, Italian-seasoned breadcrumbs rolled in. Dad still retained his aversion for fish and uncooked cheese. We could still joke with him about that. "Hey Dad, we're having fish and cheese sandwiches tonight!" Dad would just shake his finger at me and start laughing. Once he pulled out a whole pocketful of sliced American cheese at dinner and said, with an air of disgust, "Could you please take care of this for me?" He apparently had taken it off a sandwich he was given at Clare Bridge earlier in the day, and hid the cheese in his pocket. Bet he did that when he was a kid.

Dad's visits to Dr. Jahnke continued every three months on Fridays. Dad no longer recognized who Dr. Jahnke was and had dropped to an "8" on the MMSE. You could see that Dad's decline really troubled Dr. Jahnke. Dad had once been her revered professor, her mentor, perhaps even a father figure of sorts. She had suffered watching Dad's decline, too. I admired how she could be a physician and retain her compassion, her humanness, her kindness. She had been one of Dad's original guardian angels, steering him toward help and guiding our wraparound team in the early years of Dad's disease. I will never forget her for that.

Dad's mental status score didn't much matter anymore. Twelve months ago, a score of 8 would have been catastrophic for me. But now, I could easily recognize that the MMSE screen was designed to be a measure of a person's ability to function in the <u>outside</u> world. Dad was no longer in the outside world. Inside Clare Bridge, the environment was so ordered, so controlled, so predictable that one's mental status score didn't really matter. There were no real decisions to make, no situations to test one's judgment, no real risks or consequences or dangers. Kind of like a utopia, I suppose, if one was able to see it that way.

There were administrative changes going on at Clare Bridge. Charles was being groomed to take over another facility and then maybe move up to regional director. He would be leaving Clare Bridge soon, and I wondered what this would do to the Clare Bridge family. I wondered how much of that wonderful chemistry, which had made Clare Bridge what it was, had been directly cultivated by Charles. I was already mourning Charles' departure well before it even happened.

The past three seasons had brought about change in me, too. I had learned I had the guts to face all the neglected areas of my life. I was gaining confidence in myself. I had contacted Arthur, who was writing me regularly now. All of his letters were very short, always hope infused and inspired, and usually included some spiritually tinged message that things would someday be better again for Dad. I was beginning to really like Arthur. Although I had originally continued the relationship as an obligation to Dad and to Arthur, it seemed that I was beginning to form my own relationship with him.

I finally figured out what Dad had meant by referring to Arthur as a "strong man who was going through so much." Running parallel to my life as caregiver for Dad was Arthur caring for his wife. I learned she had had cancer and had passed away just before Dad went into Clare Bridge. Arthur must have sensed I needed to know; he sent me her memorial booklet one day many months after she had passed. This cemented my pen-pal relationship with Arthur. I told him I would be honored to stay in touch with him for Dad.

I had opened the doors back up to my sister Tiffanie. She was still in the throws of grieving the loss of the father she knew. There wasn't much I could do, other than provide support and reassurance, and be more emotionally available. But I was doing that, and not just watching things play out from the sidelines. I was no longer resentful that Tiffanie didn't grieve according to my schedule. It was her time to grieve now. I was learning. Everything in its own time.

Mom was regularly coming over for dinner and we were talking about other things beside Dad. She kept nagging me to go on a trip with her to someplace exotic. She chastised me for always worrying about the money.

"You can't use your money when you're dead," she would say. I was beginning to realize that this trip wasn't about her finding a companion to go with. Mom wanted me to go on an adventure for me, and would be happy to go along. She kept saying I deserved it for all I had gone through. She said I needed it. I was beginning to think that maybe I did. New Zealand, Australia, or China. Hmmm... I had always wanted to go climb the Great Wall.

And Cindy. I was calling her periodically now, without the beer. Things weren't completely resolved, but we were talking, mostly about our kids. We still had that awkward pause at the end of our conversations. Neither one of us had yet said "I love you." Cindy kept bringing up that maybe we could all get together someday. She continued to bring up renting a cottage on an island off the coast of Maine. But I wasn't there yet. I continued to struggle with my need to have Dad and her walk arm in arm one more time, a symbolic healing of sorts. Then I would hear Stacy's words inside my head, bringing me back to reality. Dad arm in arm with Cindy? Forget it. That's your fantasy, Garrett, not Cindy's. Besides, even if this could happen, how could it be meaningful? Dad wouldn't even know who she was. Forget it.

Dad's condo was all cleaned out and packaged up. It was just sitting there. I had thought about selling it many times, and just rolling the money into Dad's estate. There was still a lot of work to do on the condo. All the mementos were neatly packed up or distributed, but it was still full of Dad's furniture.

I thought of the irony about how my parents ended up in life. Dad had all the money but now wouldn't be able to enjoy it because of his disease. Mom had very little material wealth but was spiritually and physically healthy. There was an obvious lesson there. Mom was already primed and ready for "the next life." Was Dad?

I was torn about what to do with the condo and all of its contents. My mother had been screwed in the divorce, a victim of my dad being able to afford a high priced, high powered lawyer. Most of the furniture in Dad's place had belonged to Mom too. Since their divorce, Mom had lived in a small one bedroom apartment, while my dad had lived in luxury.

Our family's financial planner thought there shouldn't be much conflict as to what to do. Just sell it and invest the money back into Dad's estate for our family's future.

I looked out the window at the late February twilight. The snow was falling, ever so gently, and there was no wind to disturb it. I smiled. Not a forced or a transient smile. It was a deep, drawn from within my soul kind of smile. I had come to a decision.

We were going to give the condo to Mom.

75 { A Promise of Hope

It was going to be yet another warm, sunny, Indian summer day, with temperatures predicted to be in the upper 70's. I couldn't believe I was going outside in October wearing just shorts and an old Bob Marley and the Wailers t-shirt. It still felt like summer, and only the orange and red hints of color on the trees reminded me of the inevitable change in seasons. Summer was hanging on this year, and so was the promise of hope for my family's future.

Several years had now passed since Dad had moved to Clare Bridge. Nearly six years had now passed since Dad was diagnosed with Alzheimer's disease. Things had changed a lot over this time. Things had changed a lot just this past weekend. And things were about to change a lot more today.

Tiffanie's marriage ended once Dad was placed inside the protective cocoon of Clare Bridge. The warning signs had been there for several years, festering, and it came as no surprise. She and Don had grown apart, despite working together so well as part of Don's wraparound team. Don's decisions to drink his way through the marriage didn't help matters, and was the final straw.

Tiff had landed on her feet, as she always did, and in so many ways, just like Dad always did. After a year or so of being single again she met a wonderful man named Mike. They had married on a pristine beach this past weekend. It was a beautiful ceremony on a beautiful sunny day, with the azure and turquoise streaked waters of Lake Michigan as a backdrop.

The house was completely still as I locked the garage door and got into the minivan. Stacy had gone to work, and the kids were already in school. The neighborhood was quiet. The only sounds that gently disturbed the silence were the birds singing softly in the background. They thought it was still summer, too. It hadn't been cold enough yet to trigger their migration south.

I was glad I had taken a few extra days off from work. I didn't need any more distractions than necessary as I got ready to make that familiar, 13 minute drive.

Marley's "Three Little Birds" came on as soon as I started the ignition. I had left the classic Exodus album in the van's disc player over the weekend. The song was fitting for today. "Rise up this morning, smiled with the rising sun. Three little birds, pitch by my doorstep, singin' sweet songs, of melodies pure and true, singin' this is my message to you: Singin' don't worry, about a thing. 'Cause every little thing, is gonna be all right…"

There was still lingering evidence in my mind that things would work out for my family, despite my proclivity for worrying. This weekend had already given me plenty of cause for hope for our future. I turned up the Chrysler's 6-speaker stereo, by far my favorite accessory in the van, and merged with Marley's song. "Singin' don't worry, about a thing. 'Cause every little thing, is gonna be all right…"

If this past weekend was a gauge, there shouldn't be any grounds for continued, obsessive worrying. The weekend, the one I had dreaded for months, went far better than I had anticipated. Saturday turned out to be a joyful event, just the way it was planned.

My family had been reunited on Saturday, largely due to my sister's wedding. Cindy had come out for the wedding.

I drifted in and out of that simple, uplifting song. I pulled into the condo driveway. It was now my mom's condo. Cindy must have been looking out of the window. She emerged from the front door as soon as I pulled in.

I put on my best fake face, trying to mask the lump in my throat that was threatening to choke me.

"Hi Cindy." I kind of stammered as it came out. Although we were at the wedding and reception together, other people had buffered us. This was the first time we had been alone since she had arrived. We were going to have lunch together.

Cindy looked pensive and preoccupied, like she needed to talk. And as soon as the van door shut, she started talking.

"So Garry, I've changed my mind. Mom and I were talking. I'm thinking now that I should go see Dad. I mean I came all this way, not to see him of course, but I'm right here, and I probably won't ever have the chance to see him again."

I glanced over at Cindy, my poker face not revealing any of the underlying turbulence. I knew Mom was behind this.

Cindy continued before I could speak. "But I'm not really sure, Garry. I've worked so hard to get where I'm at with him. Those letters Dad sent me were really healing for me. I thought I had convinced myself that it was all done, that I wouldn't have to see him anymore. I'm at peace with him and I want to leave it that way. It's so weird, I still hate him on some levels and yet I feel so sorry for him. He didn't have such good parenting. I can kind of understand it."

I couldn't believe what I was hearing. I said nothing, and just let her go. She was working it out right before my very eyes! And she was working it out by herself. I was so relieved that I didn't have to get involved and take a stand.

That relief lasted less than three seconds.

"So Garry, what do I do?"

I was frozen, virtually immobilized. She was coming to me for help about her relationship with Dad. What do I do? I could give her advice that would feed right into my fantasy. But that was what I wanted. And what if that advice was wrong? I could make things worse, way worse, catastrophically worse, and it would be entirely my fault.

Cindy kept going while I remained immobilized. She hadn't noticed yet that this was troubling me.

"So, I could go see him, that's maybe the right thing to do, the risk is that by seeing him I might open things back up inside my mind, and then I'd start ruminating about stuff all over again, like I have been for the past 15 years. That wouldn't be so good. But then again, this will probably be the last chance I get to ever see him. If it's the right thing to do, this is my only opportunity."

Maybe she will work this out on her own. She's getting there, I think. Oh please God, please help her through this. I don't want to take a stand; I'm done being caught in the middle…

"So. Garry. I'm really torn. You are really good at solving these sorts of problems."

What? I am?

"Garry, I'm asking you! What should I do, I just can't make up my mind on this. You are the one who's good at making tough decisions."

I quickly replayed my tape of Stacy's speech, covering a whole page of advice in a nanosecond. She would say, this is between Cindy and her father, not you, it's none of your business, leave it alone.

And with that internal replay, I made my decision. Well, sort of. "Cindy, you'll be here for two more days. Dad is just down the road, he's always there, and we can just go over there on a moment's notice. It's entirely up to you, it won't bother me if you choose not to see him."

I recognized that last line as a lie as soon as it came out of my mouth, but I thought it was for the greater good. I had gotten so good at that.

"But Garry, what do <u>you</u> think? This might be my last chance to ever see him."

"I think it's entirely up to you, really, you've already done what you needed to do in talking with him a couple years ago, so I can respect it if you don't want to see him. Don't put so much pressure on yourself."

"Yeah, he was really lucid in his letters. At first I didn't believe you that he had Alzheimer's disease. Those letters helped me get closure on everything; I really hadn't thought I'd ever see him again. I was all set to just let things be. But now, I'm here, and I really don't know what to do. I keep going back and forth on it."

"If you obsess on it, all you're going to do is tie yourself up in one big, anxious knot. Trust me, you don't want to go there. I know all about obsessing on things. So you're gonna have to make a decision. You have two more days here, you have a little time, and like I said, he's not going anywhere; he's just down the road."

There was an awkward pause, as I had again tried to dodge what she had asked me to do. I couldn't stand the silence, and had to say something.

"Cindy, you're just like me, we both think too much."

Cindy laughed, hard. "I know we do! I think it runs in our family."

"Tiff and Mom don't do this. Just you and me... Well, Dad used to obsess like this, too."

Cindy laughed some more. My attempt to just fill dead space had successfully broken down more barriers. "Why do we always do this to ourselves, Garry?"

"I don't know; it's just the way we are. We got it from Dad. But I don't think that we should always be worrying about changing every little thing about ourselves, we should just accept who we are. I don't really want to spend another thirty years trying to figure it all out. I am what I am. Besides, I kinda like myself."

"You are so at peace with yourself."

Ha! What little do you know. "Well, actually, Cindy, there are a lot of things you don't…"

Cindy interrupted me. This time she looked different, like she was about to cry. I was starting to really feel for her. Just like me, she was trapped inside her own head.

"So this is really bugging me, Garry. What do I do?" Cindy's response, now increasingly desperate, was starting to scare me. I thought I had it all nicely deflected, or rather avoided, but she now looked like she was on the verge of unraveling.

"It's really your decision. I can't make it for you." I copped out again.

We had reached the intersection of Haslett and Marsh roads. It was pretty clear to me now that the lunch with Dad idea was purely the result of Mom's interfering. Raising the issue had done nothing but create severe conflict and anxiety for my sister. Good going, Mom.

I thought about how to seal this issue back up. Maybe just go on to my house with Cindy and fix her something to eat there. Maybe lunch would distract her a little.

But I tried anyway. "So, do you want to come over to my house for lunch? I could make a Greek salad or something, and we could talk some more. Or we could go somewhere. I know a lot of nice little restaurants in East Lansing. We could get some Mediterranean food, or I know this little Ethiopian place…"

"I think we should talk some more. I don't care where we go." Cindy was now sounding more and more dejected. I anticipated the next stop would be defeat.

I envisioned us having lunch at my house. That was safest. She was going to break down in tears any minute. I sure didn't want that to happen in a restaurant.

The light turned green for the left turn lane. I had only a few moments to make the decision. OK, straight through the intersection and home within five minutes. I'll make a nice Greek salad and we'll regroup there.

"So, Garry, what have you decided for lunch?"

"I think we'll just go over to my house and I'll make something there, Cindy."

"That's fine, whatever. I can't even think right now." Cindy seemed dangerously close to shutting down.

The light turned green for our lane. But instead of going through the intersection, toward my house, I put on my blinker and turned right. We were now going south on Marsh Road, away from the house.

A shiver had run down my spine at the intersection, and I paid attention to it.

"Isn't your house the other direction?"

I didn't have an answer for her. We were going away from my house, and for reasons that were not yet fully apparent to me.

We had traveled a few blocks down Marsh Road when I put on my left turn signal and got into the turning lane. I slowed down, waited for the traffic to clear, then pulled into the parking lot.

"No, wait! I think I'm ready. Can we still go eat with Dad at the nursing home?"

"We're already here, Cindy."

Cindy just looked at me. Her wide eyes spoke for her. She thought we were just turning around to go back to my house.

"We're here? This is Clare Bridge? But this doesn't look like a nursing home. How did we end up..."

"This isn't a nursing home. This is Dad's home. Welcome to Clare Bridge."

Amidst all of the obsessive rumination, all of the ambivalence, all the avoidance, all the dodging of questions and the pathetically shallow, noncommittal answers, we had just driven straight from the condo to Clare

Bridge. I hadn't driven that route since I moved Dad years ago.

Maybe mom's directive had unconsciously pushed us to Clare Bridge. Or maybe we had just been pulled there.

76 { The Elegant Caregiver

The vestibule door closed behind us as I pushed the black electronic doorbell, triggering that familiar, simulated doorbell chime I had grown so accustomed to. As soon as we entered the vestibule, my confidence grew and expanded. I was secure and safe now. I was at home here. There wouldn't be any worries when in the accompaniment of angels.

Cindy stood anxiously by my side. She had made a decision today that would prove powerful enough to change at least one life forever. Mine.

I pressed up to the entry door glass and peered inside. It was 11:50, and most of the residents had already been escorted to the dining room for lunch. A few residents were still back in the main living area, sitting comfortably on the pastel, rose and teal colored sofas. They were past the ability to anticipate what activity was coming next, but yet they looked tranquil and peaceful. We could see two elderly men sitting with their backs to us. One of them was our dad.

Joyce got up from her seat when the staff weren't immediately available to answer the door. At mealtime, there often was quite a long wait for visitors at the entrance door. Escorting the residents to the dining room, and then keeping them there until the meal was served, was an arduous task. It was difficult for any of the staff to break away from their responsibilities to let visitors in.

Joyce tried fervently to get the attention of everyone around her. It was a big deal when somebody visited Clare Bridge. It really bothered her not to be able to let us in.

"Oh my Lord, someone's here, someone's here! It's not my mother, but it's somebody's mother and father that want to come in. Well, let's not stand here, let them in!" Joyce looked at Dad. "Come on, you're the big man around here, you let them in."

Joyce walked over and pulled at Dad's arm. He stood up and turned toward the entry door. He looked like he usually did these days, largely confused, distant, and vacant. I could see Anthony, his entrusted sidekick, also get up. He was whispering to Dad and pointing at the door.

I pushed the doorbell button again. I wasn't perturbed by the wait, but knew that I had to be persistent at lunchtime. "It might be a few minutes, Cindy. They're getting the residents situated for lunch."

Cindy was getting impatient as the doorbell chimed again. "Yeah, I suppose...But still, how can they supervise anyone if they're not even around?"

Cindy wasn't the only one who was getting antsy. Dad seemed to be getting impatient, too. He was still whispering back and forth with Anthony. They appeared to be hatching some sort of primitive plan.

Dad and Anthony came up to the door and stared right at us through the glass. It was kind of funny and kind of eerie at the same time. Their faces were only three or four inches away from us and yet they seemed so distant. It reminded me of looking into a huge aquarium.

Both Dad and Anthony appeared bewildered and perplexed as they gazed at us through the glass. Then Dad's face suddenly brightened. The vacant look was gone. He had recognized me.

Motivated by the recognition of my face, I could hear Anthony and Dad trying to problem-solve. There was now some urgency underlying their voices.

"Do you think we should let them in?" queried Anthony. "I don't know who they are, or if they are even legal. I don't want to make a mistake and then get arrested by the big chief."

"For God's sake, you know who that one is!" answered Dad, pointing right at me. "He's a good one, you already know that! He's either my father or my brother. And there's somebody with him, she looks familiar too. I think this is something big!"

"Well then, let them in! We just can't keep them waiting! Oh, blast it all, where's the key when you need it! Don't you have one; you're one of the top dogs around here."

Dad searched his pockets. All he found was a stick of deodorant. "I don't suppose this would help, would it?"

Masudi came racing across the dayroom, heading to the entrance door. Just as I thought, the staff were overextended at lunch. Masudi was a little embarrassed we had been waiting there, but he already knew I would understand.

"I am sorry, Mr. Garrett, Walter's proud son. Please forgive us for keeping you. As you know it is very busy around here at lunchtime. It is our big meal of the day."

"No, no. That's OK, that's OK, Masudi. We knew you would be busy. Is it too late to join Dad for lunch? My sister and I would like..."

"This is Walter's other daughter? Welcome to Clare Bridge! I am Masudi!"

"I'm Cindy."

"It is so nice to see you here. What a big day it is now! Yes, yes, of course! Come in, come in! Yes, certainly, you and Cindy will be having lunch with Walter today!" Masudi seemed very excited. This was a big deal.

Dad was standing off to the side, like an eager puppy that had been told to stay but was barely able to hold off his impulses.

Masudi continued. "Just give us a few minutes to set up the table, and then we will come get you. Why don't you visit with Walter now, walk around, see our home here, and we will come get you?"

Dad saw this as his opportunity to join in. He may not have known exactly who we were, but he sensed that this was a special visit.

"Thank you, good man!" Dad saluted Masudi with a crisp hand to his forehead.

Masudi saluted back and chuckled. "Yes, sir, Walter." Masudi looked at me and smiled. "Walter is always in the Navy."

Dad put his arm around Masudi. "This one, he is a good man. He is...my... my....my best friend! I really like you." Dad choked up and fought off tears, just like he always did when something touched him.

"I like you too, Dr. Walter." Masudi smiled back warmly. He meant it. "Now. You visit with your oldest daughter and your only son. Your daughter has made a great journey to be here today. Where are you from, I think I remember it is Maine, or is it New York?"

"It's Maine." Cindy looked baffled that he knew something about her. She glanced over at me, with a "how did he know that?" look on her face.

"So you have made a long trip here. Will you be staying in Michigan long?"

"No, not too much longer, just another two days."

"It is so very nice for you to come here and see us, and to visit your father. So, Mr. Garrett, Walter's proud son. Three for lunch? We are having roast beef, carrots, and potatoes."

I put my arm around Dad and started walking around Clare Bridge's inner perimeter circle, thinking that would give Cindy a quick tour of the home. Cindy was at Dad's other side, and Anthony trailed a few steps back. Soon, Betty and Mildred were tagging along just behind Anthony. We had formed an entourage. I was worried that Cindy might get creeped out a little. It was a pretty strange experience for anyone not used to it.

"Hey, Betty, hey Millie! Are you guys joining us too? Come on! So nice to see you two this morning, and what a great day this is! I see the two of you are all dressed up, looking fine! This is Walter's daughter, Cindy, she's visiting today all the way from Maine, so come on and join us!"

I could hear Betty talking behind us. It was sort of like gossip, but at a Clare Bridge level.

"Who'd he say that was? I didn't know he was married?"

"Well apparently so. Why don't they tell us anything around here?"

"I don't know, but where are we going right now?"

"I'm not completely sure. I think he said something about going to a show."

"But I'm not dressed for it! I thought we were going to church."

The entourage rounded the bend and we headed down the corridor that led to Dad's room. Cindy got closer to Dad and spoke to him for the first time. The first time in 15 years.

"Hey, Dad, remember me? I'm Cindy."

Dad smiled. "You are... you are his sister?"

"And I'm your daughter."

"You are? I have a daughter?"

I anticipated a rush of disillusionment and anxiety for her, so I interjected. "Cindy. Its OK, he does this with me all the time. He doesn't recognize..."

"Yes, I've come to visit with you. We have some things to talk about. We've had a lot of memories together."

Oh-oh. No, Cindy, no! This is not the time or place! He doesn't know who you are, there are all these distractions here, he's not tracking, he's not going to remember anything you want him too. He has <u>advanced</u> Alzheimer's disease, remember?

Cindy didn't get it. But how could she? She didn't have experience with Alzheimer's disease, and she hadn't seen Dad's deterioration over the years like I had. She didn't have any baseline, any reference point, as to where his functioning was at. I chalked this up as being my fault, of course. I hadn't done a good job prepping her.

Dad tried to respond to Cindy, but he didn't seem to comprehend. The input from Cindy was just too complicated. Dad was now functioning on maybe a four or five year old level, on a good day. I had done an MMSE on him recently and he had scored a 4, at the bottom of the grossly impaired range. There were only a few grains of sand left at the top of the hourglass. But to impart that to Cindy now would be unnecessarily cruel. So I just let things be. Like Tiffanie and me, Cindy had to go through it for herself.

"So Dad, I'm here from Maine. I'm your oldest daughter. My name is Cindy. Do you remember now? And I'm here to see you. Garrett has told me all about how you have been and how you are doing here."

"Garrett?"

"Yes, you know, your son and my brother."

Cindy looked at me for help. "Maybe he knows you as Garry." She tried again.

"Dad, your son, Garry, has told me all about you here."

"You have a son named Garry?"

"No, not me, <u>your</u> son Garry. He's right here."

"Oh, him. You mean...ah...um....the good one!" Dad patted me on the back like a buddy.

Cindy was struggling but remained upbeat and persistent. She was searching for the old Dad, and still believed he was in there, somewhere. I didn't have the heart to try to tell her that what she was asking of Dad stopped being possible about two or three years ago.

Fortunately we were interrupted. Eunice called to us from behind.

"Miss Betty and Miss Millie, time for lunch, come on, time for lunch. I see we have special visitors today. You must be Walter's oldest daughter. Hello, and welcome! I am Eunice. You are most welcome at our home here. Yes, you have a fine father here. He is U.S. Navy man all the way! And your brother here, he takes such good care of him, really, you have a fine family. But tell me, where is the youngest sister, the youngest daughter?"

"She got married this past weekend, Eunice." I answered.

Dad blurted out happily, "to the big guy! He's a good one, too!" I immediately thought, my God, maybe Dad is still in there, maybe he can still follow things a little.

"Oh, that is right. I knew she was getting married! Of course she is on her honeymoon right now. How happy for her!" Eunice smiled, and then continued.

"We will be eating soon. Why don't you finish your tour and just end up at the dining room? Come on Millie, come on Betty, let's leave them be for a few minutes. You too, Anthony. Come on."

Millie and Betty departed with Eunice. Cindy, Dad, Anthony and I continued down the hall until we got to Dad's room.

Dad had been moved to a double room in the past year to save money. He had no trouble adjusting to the double room, primarily because he was never in there. Dad roamed Clare Bridge all night, typically trying to assist the staff and trying to be helpful. He no longer slept at regular times, getting by with just catnaps in chairs and couches all over the facility. We had tried lots of different tranquilizers and sleep medications, but nothing could get him into a regular rhythm. Now, staff and I just accepted that he would roam, and sleep whenever and wherever.

I tried to open the door to Dad's room. It was locked.

"It's OK, Garry, I don't need to see his room."

"No, no. It's not a problem, Cindy. I have a key."

"They pass out keys here to the residents' rooms?"

I smiled back a smug, proud little smile. "They do with me."

"You act like you are one of the staff in here. You seem to know everyone."

"I do."

"This is nothing like I expected."

"I know, Cindy, I am at home here. Everyone in here is like my family. You are starting to notice that."

"Are all the staff African?"

"About half, it might be more than that today, but it's just by chance."

"That's why you are so at home here! I always thought you were an African in a past life!"

I laughed quietly as I unlocked the door. I thought she was joking.

She wasn't. "This place has an African cultural feel to it, doesn't it?"

"You see that too."

"How can you miss it? It's all for one and one for all. The boundaries are different in here. Everyone is one family. There is a great sense of belonging."

I got Dad's door opened, and peeked in to make sure the room was unoccupied.

"That's why you said I have to have lunch! It would be disrespectful to turn a meal down as a guest."

"You understand! Finally, someone else gets it!"

"We have some East African refugees who were relocated in Portland. I know a little about their culture. Wow! This must be perfect for you and Dad!"

My sister and I were truly connecting. Aside from Stacy and my mom, I had not met many Americans who understood the connection between African culture and Dad's care.

I escorted everyone inside Dad's room. The room was clean and tidy, but the faint smell of urine occasionally wafted through the air. It reminded us of where we were.

"Wow, this is really very nice, Garry."

"Yes, we did the best we could to make it look like Dad's place. Forgive the urine smell, they scrub the floors down but the men in the building sometimes just urinate up against the walls or into the drawers when they have to go. When I first got here a woman had ruined the copy machine because she thought it was some kind of toilet. She squatted over the paper trays and peed right into the machine. Sounds pretty weird, I know."

"Oh, I don't mind the smell, it's not too bad. You'd expect things like that, I guess, in a place like this."

Cindy went around the room, studying everything upon the walls. There were photographs of all the family members. Cindy's family was represented, although most of her photos were quite old. There were a few newer ones that Mom had given us, including some shots of Cindy's two children, now 17 and 15. I had only met Cindy's oldest child once, when he was 10 months old. Cindy didn't say anything about her pictures on the wall, but I was glad she noticed them.

Cindy looked at Dad's karate section, his New York section, and his Iowa Hawkeye section. She then stopped at my huge photograph of Fort Mackinac, with the gigantic Mackinaw Bridge spanning across the Lake Michigan - Lake Huron straits in the background. It was one of my best photographs, and one that Dad loved. I had waited two hours to take that shot without any tourists in the picture. My reward was a shot that captured two eras in Michigan's history, 300 years apart, without any distraction.

Cindy stared at the image intently. Of all the things on Dad's walls, I had no idea that this one would be the one to evoke a response from her. "This for some reason reminds me of good times with our family, when we first moved to Traverse."

Dad couldn't stand not being the center of attention for more than a few moments. He wanted Cindy to see the "U.S. Navy section." He interrupted us like an excited little kid and motioned Cindy to the other side of the room.

"U.S. Navy, U.S. Navy!" Dad pointed to the pictures of him in full uniform and then pointed to his chest. That brief period of life from 1960 to 1963 sure must have been important, because it was the last identity to stay with him.

Cindy smiled and patted Dad gently on the back. She had backed off from the intense set of first questions directed at him. I wondered now, however, if she had backed off too far. Yeah, those first questions were too much for him and probably way over his head. But now, all she's willing to offer is a safe, unobtrusive pat on the back. I worried a little that maybe they wouldn't connect at all.

"Cindy, this will sound strange. You see where Dad's functioning is at and all, but he is really happy here. In fact, I often have conversations with Stacy and Tiffanie that this is the happiest we have ever seen him, I mean in my whole life history with Dad. It's the first time he doesn't seem lonely. It's the weirdest thing. Everyone notices it; some of the other families that visit even say they are jealous of Dad's condition. One woman said, 'I wish everyone could be where your Dad is at. It's like he is always living in Pleasantville.' It seems so bizarre to say that, I mean when he's plummeting cognitively..."

"It's because all he has is love in here. There is nothing but love here for him. You can feel it."

The conversation was getting too intimate for me to handle. I smiled an awkward smile and changed the subject.

"Well, we better get back over to the dining room for lunch. They're probably waiting for us now."

"Anchors away?" Dad looked at Anthony.

"Anchors away, sir." The two of them saluted.

The entourage left and I closed the door behind us. We met Constance as soon as we merged into the inner perimeter corridor.

"Ah ha, there you are, Walter's son! So. Garrett, this must be your sister, our very special guest who has come all the way from Maine to see your dad."

"Yes, this is my sister, Cindy."

"Ah, Cindy. That is a lovely name. I am Constance. We are so pleased to have this day for you. Yes, we are ready for you when you are ready for us, in the dining room."

"OK, Constance, we're on our way. We'll be right there."

Constance went over to Dad. She was one of the staff that was most connected to him. She was originally from Zambia, leaving her ailing father at his request to come to America. Dad called her "the pretty one," and sometimes, "my other girlfriend." When it was her shift, he tagged along side her for hours at a time. Constance, like most of the staff, exuded nothing but love, kindness and respect. In her presence, I couldn't help but think that this is the way God had intended all of us to be.

Constance locked arms with Dad and started walking with him. "Yes sir, Dr. Walter Turke, U.S. Navy man! Lunch with your oldest daughter and son. How wonderful."

Dad looked at her intently and saluted. She saluted back. It wasn't a joke kind of thing. It was a taking what you had and transform it into respect kind of thing. Beautiful.

Constance moved ahead of the pack with Dad, and the entourage followed behind.

Cindy inquired, curiously. "Constance is her real name?"

"Yes, it's Constance all right. She and her sister Cleo work here."

"Those aren't Muslim names."

"That's right. They are probably Christian."

"I thought all the African staff here were Muslim."

"No, its about half and half. Often they are from the same country, like Kenya, Tanzania, or Senegal."

"They all treat Dad the same? I mean, in the same way."

"Yep. But they treat everyone that way, not just Dad. They all bring the same message." I didn't appreciate the magnitude of what I had just said, until after I said it.

We continued our little tour, accelerated some because of our need to get back to the dining room. On the way, I showed Cindy the two smaller parlors where they did specialized activities, the hair styling salon, the central courtyard with its pretty gazebo, and the back patio, with the remnants of the summer's garden.

We had our lunch together, the four of us. Cindy didn't eat everything, being a vegetarian, but she made an effort to make it clear that she appreciated the meal and the welcome. Just about every resident who was ambulatory made an effort to welcome Cindy during lunch, as did just about every staff member.

After lunch we started walking around the inner perimeter again. I put my arm gently around Dad, to steer him, while Cindy stayed close by off to his right. The walk was bitter-sweet, as I knew we would be leaving soon. Goodbye was always the hardest part.

While we were doing our laps, with Anthony trailing of course, Cindy stopped me.

"Is there a place where Dad and I can walk alone, or sit down together? Maybe without all the distractions?"

"Sure. Let's take our walk outside. I'll let the staff know."

"You mean the courtyard or the patio?"

"Well, that would be OK if you want to, but I thought you meant outside, like go for a walk up Marsh Road or something."

"Out there? Won't he try to run away? Is it safe? How will we get him to come back?"

I laughed. "Sorry to laugh, Cindy. You sound just like I did when Dad first came here. He won't run away or resist coming back. Why would he? This is his home. This is where his friends are. This is where his family is. You said it yourself; there is nothing but love for him in here. Why would he want to leave?"

"Excuse me. Abdulai?"

"Yes, how can I help you, Walter's son?"

"Hey. Walter and my sister and I are going to go out for a walk for half an hour. Could you code us out?"

"Of course. But first, let me get a light jacket for Walter. I know it is warm out today, but he gets a little chilly sometimes."

Soon Abdulai returned with Dad's U.S. Navy jacket. "Here you go, Walter. U.S. Navy, Lieutenant Commander, Walter Turke, sir." Abdulai saluted, and Dad returned the salute.

Abdulai punched in the code on the security system, the green light came on, and soon we were outside. It was in the middle 70's, but Dad put his hands inside his jacket pockets as if he was cold. Soon we were on the sidewalk, heading up Marsh Road.

Cindy came up to Dad and locked arms with him. I dropped back about six feet and trailed from behind.

The image I saw in front of me was exactly the image I had harbored in my mind all these years.

"Dad, we have some things we need to talk about…"

A powerful shiver ran down my spine. I dropped back even further, so I couldn't hear what they were saying. It was none of my business.

God is great. This day had been planned for them, or maybe for us, all along.

Cindy walked with Dad for about 15 minutes. They were smiling and still arm in arm when we returned inside Clare Bridge.

On the ride back to the condo, we were both quiet, and emotionally spent. Finally, Cindy said something.

"You know, Garry, you've been dealing with Dad's disease for years now. I never could have done what you've done for Dad."

After a few minutes, Cindy touched my arm gently, to get my attention. I didn't expect that she was about to hit me with the most powerful compliment of my entire life.

"I know who you are now, Garry."

I looked over at her, still silent.

"You are the elegant caregiver."

Cindy didn't realize how profoundly important that was to me. In one short sentence, she had taken all of the pain and hurt and suffering that had been the past seven years and made me feel valued and needed. Like I mattered. Like I belonged. Like the struggle had been worth it. Cindy had given me my identity, and my purpose.

The elegant caregiver. I loved the title so much that when I got home, I wrote it down immediately on a sticky note, as if I might forget what she said. But that was ridiculous. I would never forget those words as long as I lived.

I found a place to put that little sticky note. It went to my most cherished spot, that special box that Mom had made for me all those years before. The box was now crammed full of little sticky notes and index cards, each one of them containing a cherished memory that had occurred in my life with Dad.

The next day Cindy and I said goodbye. We went through all the usual, ritualistic niceties that people do when they say goodbye after a pleasant visit. We vowed to get together again. The next visit was planned for Cindy's home in Portland. We again talked about renting a little rustic cottage on an island off the coast of Maine.

Then we said goodbye. Cindy spoke first.

"Love you, Garry."

"I love you too, Cindy."

As I watched her go up the escalator to the boarding area, I choked up and fought back tears. Like I always did when something touched me.

77 { The Christmas Prayer

"Oh come all ye faithful, joyful and triumphant..." Perry Como's voice sounded rich and alive, even though the sound was coming from a tiny, three-inch clock radio speaker. I thought to myself, my God another year has almost passed. It was now over seven years since Dad was diagnosed, and almost four since he had been placed at Clare Bridge.

I could see the red LED illumination on the clock radio. 5:10 AM. I rolled over, found Stacy's hand, and laid there quietly. It sometimes took Stacy awhile to wake up even after the clock radio went off. I usually woke up seconds before it went off.

Laying there in bed, holding Stacy's hand and anticipating the promise of another Christmas morning, I was visited by the familiar shiver that ran up and down my spine periodically.

I thought for a minute what that sensation had meant to me across my lifetime. I had had that certain kind of shiver come over me for over 40 years now. For years I never knew what to call it or how to really define it. But I did know that it always came with an enveloping peace, a comfort, a sense of security and safety.

I used to think the familiar shiver was just my body signaling me that I had been touched by a vestige of a fond childhood memory or perhaps a primal remembrance of childhood security. But in adulthood, I came to view the experience differently. I began to believe that I was being visited by some all-encompassing presence, something that wasn't just associated with comfort, but rather something that brought comfort. And as I grew older, I began to believe that when this presence came, it didn't exist as a separate entity. That shiver running up my spine was an indication that the presence was merging with me. I even had a trite little name for the experience, coined during my young adulthood. I called it, "the theory of merging consciousness." Perhaps also known to some as the Holy Spirit.

I couldn't remember if I had ever had this experience on a Christmas morning. It always showed up unexpectedly and almost never when I tried to summon it.

Dear God, please hear my prayer. I don't usually try to ask for anything from you other than to keep me and my family safe. But today I do need to ask you something, please. I need you to do something for me, please God, for my Dad's sake. Thank you for steering my dad, guiding him to all these angels that are now caring for him. I know he is in good hands. But now he is nearing the end of his journey and I am worried for his soul. I don't know where it is, whether it is lost, or where it has gone. I don't know if Dad turned himself over to you before he got sick. Maybe he did, but he was so private, I just don't know. I never asked him about his belief in God, or in an afterlife. I should have, but I didn't. And now I am scared for his soul.

I know you are kind and accept everyone, but I don't want my dad to be lost. So, please, dear God, would you take him in, would you count him among your flock? Would you allow me to turn him over to you if he hasn't done it himself, or if he can't do it? Please, please, can you help me? Will you let me know?

I waited for a heavenly response manifested by another shiver running down my back. Instead, Stacy stirred, rolled over, and smiled.

"Merry Christmas, honey. Let's get up now and get going before the kids wake up."

And with that, my prayer and transcendent connection with the ethereal ended. I launched myself out of bed, brushed my teeth, and met Stacy downstairs. Soon I was spitting out the reindeers' carrots and celery into the freshly fallen snow. Stacy handed me a mimosa and we toasted the promise of the day. I got the camera ready, and waited for the kids to make that excited little trek down the stairs.

Christmas turned out to be beautiful this year. Miah, now almost 8, fell for the chewed up carrot and celery routine again, hook, line and sinker. We opened our presents and ate cinnamon buns. Amidst all of the great gifts, that in most places of the world would be considered rather opulent, one stood out that year. It was a $1.49 little statue that Miah had bought for me in her school store. I opened the little box it came in, teared-up, and had to fight back the impulse to start sobbing.

It was a little ceramic statue of a bald eagle.

The kids were flying high by 9 o'clock, and so were we. I brought Dad over later in the morning and we opened some more presents. Mostly all of his gifts were "U.S. Navy" apparel I ordered from the Naval Academy store in Annapolis. We got him Navy shirts, athletic shoes, a new windbreaker, and an "official U.S. Navy Officer's watch," all slightly embellished and exaggerated in stature, of course. Dad loved it, but after an hour or so, had had enough. He wanted to go back home to Clare Bridge, to see his "girlfriend" on the "big day."

All day long I waited for the shiver to come back, to signal that my request had not only been heard, but was accepted.

It never came.

78 { Carnival Day

Winter had come and gone, and spring had come early this year. It was already early June, and it was going to be a hot summer. It had already been in the 90's several times, and dry as a bone. Dad was doing well at Clare Bridge. He didn't seem to have any worries, anxiety, or insecurity whatsoever. Unfortunately, I could not say the same. I still had not received a reply to my Christmas prayer. I was beginning to worry that it would never come.

Today was Carnival Day at Clare Bridge. Carnival Day was another one of Clare Bridge's many family events, designed to help normalize life for the residents and their families. I was getting accustomed to these affairs. The staff had put on a huge Christmas party with live music the previous December, an Easter egg hunt in April, a spring picnic at Lake Lansing in May, and now a summer carnival. Each event had a different theme. The Clare Bridge staff would plan the event for weeks, and the facility would be lavishly decorated in accordance with the season's particular celebration to help get the residents excited with anticipation. These recurrent events usually drew big crowds, and were very well attended by staff, their families, and the residents' families alike. It was one of the few times during the year when the residents' families came out in droves to visit their loved ones. Maybe the "normalcy" of the event allowed them to be temporarily distracted from the Alzheimer's induced haze that their loved ones lived in.

There was a big spread of food, music, and games for the residents and the many children in attendance on his special day. Shani and Miah were already off at the game booths with my dad, and Miah had a handful of fun little prizes she had won. Everything was going great, well, except for the dunk tank.

It was Brenda's turn to take her perch up on the ledge. Stacy and I watched as Clare Bridge's nurse climbed apprehensively up the wobbly, ten foot ladder to the precarious metal seat that awaited her above the dunk tank. Although this early summer day was relatively warm, already in the upper 70's, the tank had been filled with extremely cold water.

Some of the other Clare Bridge staff had already taken their turn up on the perch, but none had yet been dropped into the frigid water below. The residents just didn't have the strength or accuracy to hit the target with enough force to drop the seat. I was beginning to think that the dunk tank was a wonderful idea, but a complete flop.

I held Stacy's hand and smiled as we watched the residents wait their turn in the pitching line. To trigger the seat release, the "pitchers" would have to hit a 4-inch diameter target with a baseball with substantial force. Most residents could only generate a feeble toss that typically fell many feet short of the tank and nowhere near the target. Some residents appeared to have completely forgotten how to throw a small ball. Probably some no longer had any recollection what a baseball was for.

Many of the African staff had gotten in line to try their luck at plunging their bosses into the drink. But they were not much better than the residents. It looked like most of them had never thrown a baseball in their lives. Hassan, the youngest and most athletic looking of the Clare Bridge staff, had thrown the ball the hardest. His effort was so wild, however, that the ball not only went over the entire dunk tank, but over the courtyard fence and out into Marsh Road. That drew a big laugh from the crowd.

"You couldn't hit the broad side of a barn!" shouted Brenda, feigning a smug, mocked arrogance from atop her perch.

"Oh yeah? Take this one! Here's a high hard one, right at you!" said Bill, pushing 85 years. He wasn't feigning anything, but his ball landed harmlessly about ten feet short of its target.

"Missed again! Your mother could throw harder than that! Like I said, you couldn't hit the front of a barn! Next!"

Dad was about seven residents back. He had been off with Shani and Miah at the game booths, and had just now gotten into line for the first time. Dad had a very serious look on his face. He was staring at the dunk tank, like he was deep in thought and intently focusing on something.

The trash talking in the background was broken up by Stacy's voice in the foreground. "Oh look, Garrett honey, Jim's up."

Stacy and I now knew the names of practically every resident. In fact, after a year and a half of coming to Clare Bridge, Stacy and I had at least a capsulated biography on damn near everyone in the building.

Jim and Dad were always in close proximity. Some days they got along, but most days they acted like they hated each other. No one seemed to know exactly why. There was some kind of competition going on between them, like two Alpha dogs competing for dominance over the pack. Both Dad and Jim always wanted to be at the center of attention. Dad hated it when Jim got any attention before him.

Dad now had various descriptive adjective-noun combinations that he assigned to just about every person in the facility. He no longer could recall anyone's names, but ironically, could recall the descriptive identities he created with great accuracy and consistency. He always called Jim, "the Big Error."

I could hear Dad's voice toward the back of the line. "Oh Geez, here we go again. He's up there now. I don't know why we have to watch him, All he does is talk, talk, talk. What's the point? It's always about him, the Big Error."

Stacy laughed, hard. "Your Dad calls him, "the Big Error?"

Jim stepped up to the pitching line and was handed two baseballs. His 80 year old arm launched a feeble, 20 mile per hour slider into the patio concrete four feet in front of him and twenty feet short of the dunk tank. The second pitch went about the same distance and was way right.

"Jesus Christ! Blasted thing! Son of a gun!" Jim angrily shook his finger at Brenda perched atop the tank. "You're going to pay for this!"

Brenda continued her trash talking. "Hey Jim, you call that a pitch? Next time bring your A-game!"

Stacy shook her head. "This is way too hard for them. All this is doing is frustrating the residents. And Bob's up now. He's way too old for this activity. He can't do this, Garrett."

Bob was the nearly 100 year old man who had been some kind of botanist at Michigan State University in his younger years. He was the guy who always seemed to be talking to the plants whenever I visited Dad. Bob knew all of the houseplants' Latin names, and how to care for them, but couldn't remember much of anything else. I remember the staff telling me that he probably didn't have Alzheimer's disease, just age related dementia. Dad really liked Bob. He often walked with him, attending to what he thought were Bob's needs. Dad called him "Good Man," and sort of looked out for him.

Bob "hurled" both of his pitches into the ground exactly one foot in front of him. The experience wore him out. He was done pitching for the day. Maybe Stacy was right; this activity was much too hard for the residents.

"Garrett, I'm telling you, I think this is way too much for them. I'm worried some of them are going to get hurt."

Stacy was probably right, but I discounted what she said. "Come on, Stacy, it's all right. No one's going to get hurt." My reply lacked eye contact and any semblance of emotion, because I wasn't really paying much attention to her. I was still studying my dad, slowly working his way up the line. He still had a very serious, intent look upon his face.

"All right, Joyce is up! Hey-hey Joyce, come on now, we can do this, come on Joyce, let's go!" I clapped like I was a coach trying to get a rally started. Joyce was another "character" at Clare Bridge, who was always at the center of the facility's social web.

Joyce was originally from Oklahoma. She talked about getting picked up by her mother and going home to Oklahoma City almost every day. Most mornings she even packed a small suitcase that she would leave up by the front door. She would say that her mother was going to be arriving soon to take her home. Dad called her "the Oklahoma Schooner," after the University of Oklahoma football team's nickname. Only it was really the Oklahoma "Sooners." Dad got the name mixed up, but "Schooner" somehow stuck inside his mind and he couldn't be convinced otherwise. Pretty soon, even the Clare Bridge staff were playfully calling Joyce the Oklahoma Schooner, like she was some sort of majestic ship.

Joyce thought she was married to Jim, and after awhile, Jim came to believe he was married to her. Joyce was always trying to sit next to him and put her arm around him. Although he thought he was married to her, Jim couldn't stand Joyce. He called her "the Old Battleaxe," and was forever trying to push her away.

The dynamics became more complex when Dad arrived at Clare Bridge. Joyce would try to make Jim jealous by flirting with Dad, which only served to make the conflict between Jim and my dad worse. Dad got along with

Joyce, but wasn't interested in her romantically. And there was this new resident at Clare Bridge, Myra, who was becoming part of this mix. Myra was a 70 year old woman who I'm sure was quite attractive in her day. She wore only expensive clothes and often traipsed around with a frilly blue boa around her neck. Although Myra thought she was married to Dad, she came on seductively to every man that crossed her path.

Joyce took her turn throwing the baseball. She at least got her pitches up in the air, but like everyone else, way short. Stacy was right. This was way too hard for any of them.

But I could have cared less about the residents' pitching at this particular moment. Some drama was about to go down, and I knew it was coming. I continued to giggle. Stacy elbowed me in the stomach thinking I was making fun of the residents. I was.

The drama began when Joyce went over to Jim and latched on.

"OK Stacy, watch this. Here it comes."

Joyce wrapped herself around Jim's arm and tried to pull him close. Jim responded immediately by trying to push her off, but Joyce just tightened her grip. Then she started scolding him. "For the love of God, why are you always so ornery? Can't I ever get any affection from you?"

"Get off of me, you Old Battleaxe! Jesus Christ, why can't a man get a little peace in this world? Why don't you go make yourself some dinner and then go off and eat it all by yourself?"

"There's no time for any of that. Have you forgotten, sweetie, we're going to be leaving for Oklahoma any minute now. My mother is coming up from Oklahoma City to take us back home."

"Take us? Oh no you don't. I might be married to you, but I'm not going anywhere with you, or your scary-looking sister."

Myra was eyeing Dad and hurried her pitches. One went straight into the ground in front of her; the other was released way too early and actually went behind her. Just about every resident had lost their ability to know when to time the release of the ball so it could go in some semblance of a forward trajectory. Myra then went over to Dad in line and started stroking his arm.

"Excuse me, what are you doing? Do I know you?" Dad looked really uncomfortable.

"You're always teasing with me, dear. You don't have to tease, everyone already knows you're my man."

"I can't be your man! I'm not old enough for you, for God's sake! My God, You're old enough, you're old enough to be, my, my... oh whatchamacallit, my, my.... my grandmother! Are you insane? I'd never marry someone as old as you!"

Dad then pointed over to Jim. "There, that's your man over there! He's the one for you! He's with his mother now, and then he'll have time for you. Just go on over there and stay there!"

Fortunately, Constance, the new Clare Bridge staff directing the pitching line, came over and peeled Myra off Dad. Like all the staff at Clare Bridge, she was a master at distracting and then redirecting the residents. "Come on Miss Myra, let's go over here, I think there's someone over here who's waiting to see you."

Myra was shuttled off, and Dad seemed greatly relieved. I smiled and looked over at Stacy with my eyebrows raised. Stacy looked back at me like I was being really disrespectful, but then smiled wryly too. We both had secretly enjoyed watching the little melodrama unfold. Sometimes you just had to laugh at what the Clare Bridge residents' collective impairments brought. It was kind of cute and usually more than a little funny.

Next up to pitch was Anthony, Dad's old Navy buddy. Dad called him, "Old Navy."

A few months ago, Anthony and Dad had actually launched an "escape" from Clare Bridge where they were going to retrieve Anthony's car from the west side of Chicago. They were a little short on the details, like how they were going to make the 200 mile trek to Illinois, but they weren't short on motivation. And on one bright, sunny Saturday morning, they had a little meeting and just walked out Clare Bridge's front door, bound and determined to make it to Chicago. The alarm system went off immediately of course, and within seconds, a small entourage of Clare Bridge staff was trailing them.

Rather than risk any physical conflict, two of the Clare Bridge staff, Abdulai and Abdul decided to just walk with them. Dad and Anthony made it about 600 yards up the road, and then began to complain about how hungry and tired they were. Using the tried and true "distract and redirect" technique, Abdulai and Abdul told them they couldn't make it all the way to Chicago without lunch. They said they would treat them to lunch at a nice restaurant. And within a minute or two, they had Dad and Anthony turned around, and lumbering very willingly back to the facility and into the Clare Bridge dining room. Dad and Anthony were convinced they were in a restaurant, and quickly forgot about their once urgent escape plan.

Fortunately, Anthony and Dad's incessant talk of finding Anthony's car had dissipated in recent months. Their daily conversation was now replaced, however, by a mutual delusion that they had fought together in World War II. Anthony actually had been in the Navy as an ensign, and he now thought that Dad, being a lieutenant commander, was his superior officer.

Dad and Anthony eventually came to believe that they were in the Pacific together during the war, aboard a ship that Dad commanded. Dad's three year stint as a Navy psychiatrist had now mushroomed into a persistent delusion that he had a lifelong career as an aircraft carrier commander, and that he had been some sort of hero during a war that had actually ended when he was 14.

Anthony's tosses made it all the way to the base of the dunk tank, but with absolutely no velocity. The two balls rolled harmlessly at the floor of the tank. Brenda reacted with absolutely no sympathy.

"Ha! That's your pitch, Anthony? Looks like I'm going to stay high and dry all afternoon. Hey Walter, is this the best your team can do? My grandparents could do better than you guys!" Brenda was merciless. Normally one of the kindest staff in the building, the dunk tank had transformed her into Cruella Deville.

Dad's turn in line finally came up, and Constance handed him his first baseball. Like everyone else, I expected him to just casually toss the ball, but maybe with just a little more mustard than the other residents. I was secretly hoping that I could brag a little about his pitching exploits in high school before we went home.

Dad studied the target intently, almost like he was looking in to get a sign from his catcher. Then, to the absolute amazement of everyone watching, he went into a full pitcher's wind-up. He kicked his left leg high up into the air, and came down with a release that sent the baseball hurling through the air with what seemed to be the intensity of a major league fastball.

The spectators gasped in awe. The ball missed the target by only inches, and made a thunderous clang as it hit the back of the dunk tank.

"Oh shit!" Brenda was so startled up on the perch that she had no time to censor her reaction. The spectators laughed. Brenda repositioned herself on the metal seat, suddenly anxious about the next pitch.

Dad had the intensity of a 17 year old pitching ace playing for the New York City League Championship. He took his second ball from Constance, studied his target, kicked his leg up high in a wind up, and hurled. Dad unleashed another beauty of a fastball, straight as an arrow...

Clink! Dad's fastball nailed the target; the trigger was released and down went Brenda before she could even brace herself. She came up drenched from the frigid water, shivering and gasping for breath.

The spectators, all suddenly re-energized by Brenda's plunge, were elated! Dad was doing a little dance, the residents were patting him on the back, and staff were high-fiving him. Even staff from inside the facility came out to see what all the commotion was about. Brenda hurriedly climbed down from her perch and immediately instructed one of the other managers to take her place.

Constance raised Dad's arm into the air, as if he was some sort of champion, and the spectators cheered some more. Even Jim, Dad's arch nemesis, participated in the celebration. Dad acted like he had just won the national title. Maybe in his own mind he had.

But there was one person there who was beaming even more than Dad. His proud son.

"That's my dad! That's my dad! Wow! He's amazing!" I ran over and high-fived him, then hugged him. It might have looked ridiculous, but I didn't care.

Despite the ravages of time and his disease, my dad was still in there. He was still The Champion.

79 { The Gift

I reached over and held Stacy's hand as we headed east on Haslett Road toward Tiff's new place. Another year had passed, and I wondered how much time was left with Dad.

This morning the roads were empty, presumably because a lot of people were still in church, but it gave me a kind of lonely feeling. My kids were in the back, both already listening to music on their headsets. Next to Shani, cradled and protected by white tissue paper inside a simple red decorative bag, was Dad's gift.

Today, Sunday, June 25, was going to be Dad's birthday party. Dad's actual birthday had fallen on the Friday before, but Tiffanie and I had agreed to celebrate it later in the weekend at her new home. It was a good thing we had delayed the celebration until Sunday, because we had gone into the start of the weekend without a gift for him. It wasn't as if we had procrastinated buying a present for Dad this year. We just couldn't think of what to give him that would still hold some importance for him. In years past, even well after he had been stricken with Alzheimer's disease, shopping for Dad at Christmas, Father's Day, and birthdays was effortless. University of Iowa. Michigan State Spartans. U.S. Navy. Upbringing in New York. World traveler. Physician and psychiatrist. Healer. He had so many identities and interests that shopping for him was easy.

Even with Dad deep in the throws of his disease, I had gotten him what I then considered was his best gift ever from me two years before. He was at the peak of his delusional, Alzheimer's induced U.S. Navy identity then, and I had been browsing around on-line for something that represented the Navy. I found a company that produced hundreds of different types of military commemorative medals, including scores that represented the Navy. I bought a set of four medals and some oak leaf officers' pins for Dad, and they arrived in a special, felt-padded 4x6 inch case that was very impressive looking. Stacy created an official looking little sign that we attached to the top of the inside of the box: "Walter Turke, MD, U.S. Navy Lifetime Achievement Award."

I made up a little white lie that the Navy was honoring him for 50 years of service and had a mock little ceremony at Clare Bridge. This of course fed right into Dad's delusion that he was still an active, high-ranking officer and special figure within the Navy. But I didn't care. It made Dad extremely happy, and reinforced his sense of purpose and belonging. Dad was so enthralled with that gift that he had taken that 4x6" medals case and crammed it into his front pants pockets, proudly removing it and showing it off to everyone he passed at Clare Bridge. That case would be carried around with him each and every day, for well over two years, until the case's outer covering was nearly worn off and virtually all of his pants' pockets had been ripped.

I thought the "U.S. Navy Lifetime Achievement Award" was going to be the most meaningful, cherished, and impressive gift I would ever give my dad. At least I thought that for the next two years. Until this birthday.

This year I had really struggled with what to give him. Dad had almost no real identity left. His disease had robbed him of all of his ties to the University of Iowa and to Michigan State. He no longer knew he had been a physician. His childhood upbringing in New York had also been erased. And so was his knowledge and memory of his family and our relationships with him. Perhaps most painfully, however, over the past six months Dad had lost his last real vestige of an identity, his link to the U.S. Navy. That was a terrible blow to me, because along with the loss of Dad's Navy identity came the loss of Dad's interest in those Navy medals.

Dad had a vacant, detached look on his face much of the time now, and if he wasn't actively being stimulated, he would drift off to sleep within a minute or so. He had gone through a weeklong stretch in March where he was nearly catatonic and refused to come out of his room. He had pulled out of that, but it was an ominous foretelling of what may lie ahead. Although our family was still trying to hang on, it had become clear that there were only a few precious grains of sand left at the top of the hourglass. I had been preoccupied this birthday with making those last few grains of sand count, before Dad's time on this earth was over.

I had racked my brain for most of May and the first two weeks of June as to what to give Dad for this birthday. He didn't need clothes or mementos or wall hangings. This birthday had to be more special than that. In fact, I was growing obsessed that this birthday had to produce the greatest gift of all, one that would venerate and define my dad's life before he passed on. But how could I possibly top the Navy commemorative medals? That seemed to be an impossible undertaking. I told myself I should just resign myself to letting go. It was too late to get him the greatest gift ever. I had already done that, two years ago.

But, true to form, my mind wouldn't quit nor capitulate. There must be a way, there must be. I was unable to give in. In the end, Dad's life would have to be marked by something more than just a box of commemorative Navy medals that were spawned by an Alzheimer's induced delusion.

What could I give him? What could I give him? Something that had meaning. Something that would still matter to him. Something that I would cherish, that we as a family would cherish. Something that he could take with him to the next life.

That last line had been haunting me for some time now. It was the real reason I needed such a special gift. I still had that one final, troubling piece of unfinished business eating me. It had been quietly haunting me for over a year now.

Everything else had resolved so nicely. I had fought hard to get my life back. Cindy was back connected with our family. Tiffanie had found her soul mate. Dad was in the accompaniment of angels at Clare Bridge. But I couldn't fully rejoice. I kept going back to that talk I had with God two Christmases ago. What was the state and condition of Dad's soul? Was it still present? Or was it in limbo somewhere? Had he handed himself over to God before he got sick? Or did he wait too long, only to be overcome, and now lost, within his disease? I had prayed and prayed for an answer. I had felt God's presence with Dad and Cindy. I had felt God's presence with the caregivers at Clare Bridge. I had felt God's presence when our family pulled together on that beach up in Traverse City.

But I had not received an answer to my question about Dad's soul. Maybe those stakes were just too high, and just too personal. Maybe that was just between God and Dad. Maybe I was forcing it. Maybe it was none of my business. Maybe it was no longer within my control. Maybe it was never within my control.

I woke up at 3AM the morning of Friday, June 23, which was Dad's actual birthday, and couldn't get back to sleep. I had had an epiphany.

I emailed Tiffanie as soon as it looked like a reasonable hour to send an email out, seemingly waiting, minute by minute, until it was 5:45 AM. I didn't want Tiff to see an email sent at 3 AM, for fear that she would think I was mentally ill. 5:45 was probably the earliest time I could get away with.

"Tiff, Hi. Have you gotten Dad a present yet for his birthday? I really have been thinking hard about what we could get him this year, but it's so hard to think of something that would still be special to him. I don't want to get him just clothes or practical things, but rather something that is meaningful. Well, I thought of something! How do you feel about...."

I finished the email, clicked "send," and prayed that Tiffanie would agree with me.

Getting through my four hours at work that Friday seemed like an eternity. When I came home from work early that afternoon, I opened the garage door and raced straight to the computer. Sure enough, there was an email reply from Tiffanie, waiting for me.

It read, all in caps, "THAT IS A GREAT IDEA, GARRETT!!! COUNT ME IN! I'LL MEET YOU AT THE MERIDIAN MALL IN THE FOOD COURT RIGHT AFTER WORK, ABOUT 5:30, AND WE'LL BUY IT TOGETHER. LOVE YA! -T"

We turned left on Eppley and made a right onto Barry Road. Within a couple minutes we were pulling up into Mike and Tiffanie's new driveway. Their new home had just been landscaped. Although all the plants were still small and tender, they were healthy and looked well nurtured. It was a beautiful and serene sight, and matched the promise of the early summer day. Everything about their home was new and fresh and filled with the hope for a better future. It was a new start and a new life. It made me smile to think of it that way, because I had had those very same thoughts about Dad when we purchased his gift.

Dad was already inside when we got there. Tiffanie's husband Mike had picked him up a half hour before and brought him over to the house. It was increasingly rare now that we took Dad anywhere outside Clare Bridge, but we had all decided we wanted to do this for his birthday today. Dad was seated in the living room, his eyes fixed upon the entrance door, when we walked in. He looked like he was waiting for us, but then again, he was always waiting now. His eyes tracked us as we came in, but he looked distant and vacant. I went up to him, held both his hands, and kissed him on the cheek. He looked at me blankly, but then smiled. There was a faint recognition. Well, that's what I interpreted in order to convince myself. The fact of it was that, deep down inside, I just wasn't sure if he recognized me at all any more.

I gave the red gift bag to Tiffanie. As soon as I handed the bag over to her, I became so anxious I could barely speak. I had never given anyone such a gift before, and my emotions were overwhelming me.

"Here, Tiff, I want you to give it to him."

"Right now?"

"Yep. I'm so nervous I can't stand it anymore."

Tiff gathered everyone around Dad, who stayed seated on the couch. Dad looked up at us, with what I interpreted was an inquisitive look.

I looked around the room. Our family was still strong, and still standing. When this difficult journey had begun, our oldest kids were still in elementary school. Now Shani and Lindsey were going to be high school seniors next fall. They looked and acted like adults. The experience with Dad had taken some of their innocence earlier than I had hoped, but it had also earned them their adulthood. They were mature now, and ready to take on what life would throw at them.

Next I panned to the youngest kids, Miah, now age ten, and Brityn, age nine. When Dad first got sick they were only three and two. Their entire remembered childhoods were of their parents being caretakers for their grandfather. I wondered how that would affect them. I sure hope it taught them to value relationships, their family, and most of all, how they were linked to and extended from their ancestors.

Tiffanie and Mike were holding hands. Tiff had found happiness and a soul mate despite the trauma of Dad's disease. I thought for a moment that she probably would never have met Mike if it weren't for what we went through with Dad.

Mom was there, too. I went over and gave her a hug. It was a real hug this time, not some perfunctory, obligatory, devoid of emotion hug that I used to give. It meant a lot to me that Mom had come. She had remained there for Dad all these years, despite having every justification not to stay connected. My mom was going on 80 now. She was still standing strong as the matriarch of the family. She had held on to her beliefs despite all the shit that life had given her. Nameste. Mom didn't just talk it. She walked it. I thought to myself, soon it would be time to write her story, for her life experiences had been just as incredible as my father's.

And Stacy. She still looked youthful and beautiful in her 40's, as if life had been kind to her. But her life's journey had been filled with great pain also. Her mother had meant as much to her as my father had meant to me. I knew that each time she gave to me, to our children, and to my father, she touched the pain of losing her mother. And yet, she still gave to all of us. Selflessly. Lovingly. Forgivingly. Stacy, your mother would be so proud of you.

Tiffanie handed the red gift bag to Dad. He smiled. Tiff helped him take out the small gift box, but Dad didn't know what to do next. He no longer understood cause and effect, social convention, or sequences very well. Dad put the box next to his side and gently patted it, as if he was acknowledging that it was valuable.

Tiff interjected, softly. "No, Dad. We want you to open it. Let me help you." Of the two of us, she was the only one who could speak. I was too anxious to say anything. I wouldn't be able to get a word out if my life depended on it. I could hear my heart pounding. I wondered if those around me could hear it as well.

Tiffanie gently undid the ribbon and opened the box. She pulled out a simple, but glistening sterling chain. At the bottom of the chain dangled a simple, two inch silver cross. "Walter" was inscribed on the back.

A powerful shiver ran up my spine, then down, then up again. No one saw it, because everyone was watching Tiffanie affix the chain around Dad's neck. Dad beamed and cradled the cross in his hand. I had been so worried he would resist even putting it on.

"This...this... this is so... so... beautiful. It's for... it's.... just...for... me?" Dad spoke the longest coherent sentence in months. His eyes teared up, like they always did when something touched him.

Tiffanie's and my eyes filled up with tears too. She could still speak. I could not.

"Yes, Dad. This is for just for you, from all of us."

Dad looked around, nodded humbly, and teared up some more.

I had another shiver traverse my spine. My final, remaining worry dissipated with this shiver. My Christmas prayer had been answered in its own time. There was no need to question the state of Dad's soul any more.

In the year following this birthday, Dad had lost virtually everything we had given him at Clare Bridge, including some of his Navy medals, three pairs of glasses, his wallet, numerous clothing items, one of his Navy rings, and countless cards and photographs.

He never lost, nor removed that cross.

Dad's soul could rest now.

I could rest now, too. I found my way out of the forest.

80 { My Son

Six years, two weeks and three days had elapsed since I began this book. I have written chapters while at home, on vacation, in the Michigan State Undergraduate Library, in the Michigan State Union Building, in a rented condominium on Lake Michigan, in a small hotel room in Traverse City, in the basement of my brother-in-law's home in Chicago, and even inside my Chrysler mini-van. I have written chapters while angry, intensely sad, depressed, tearful, anxious, and ecstatically happy. I have written chapters at four in the morning and at 11 at night. I wrote one chapter when I was drunk, after one of my friends insisted that I try my first Long Island Ice Tea. I have written chapters on most Saturdays and nearly every Sunday morning. I have written when my soul felt lost, and when I felt powerful shivers running up and down my spine.

When I first started this book, I was an angry, sad, disconnected 40-something year old man who thought his best days had already passed him by. Back then, the future looked bleak. Dad's course was going to get worse, his fate was inevitable, and I was going to go down with him. I had gained almost thirty pounds since first being told of Dad's diagnosis. Although I still managed to exercise, I was worried I would succumb to the stress and just let myself go.

Aside from Christmas and Easter, I had not been to church since Dad got sick. At first I stopped going because I was angry. Actually, angry didn't begin to describe it. I was furious, furious at what God had given me. When I started writing this book on Sunday mornings, I was quite conscious and aware that I was doing it during "church time." It started as a sort of fuck you to God. It ended with me embracing God. In the end, this wasn't just about me and Dad. It was about me and God.

Today, on a cool but sunny Easter Sunday, I find myself laying down the final words of this book. As I write down these final words, I am feeling joyful and in touch. In touch with the world, my family, my loved ones, and with God. I am now over 50, many long years since my dad was first diagnosed, but I am beginning to feel that my life is just beginning. I feel youthful and alive again. I am losing my weight and all that emotional baggage that I had carried, not just over the past seven years, but which had accumulated over my entire life.

I am feeling unsaddled and unchained. "I once was lost but now I'm found." I know that I am flawed and imperfect. I am stubborn and moody and have compulsions and sometimes still get angry at things I should just let slide. But I am happy again, and I am at peace with myself. Love, acceptance, and forgiveness is all that can and will prevail. Amen.

Today my dad sits at Clare Bridge, drifting in and out of sleep, waiting. He is waiting for his time, for his trip out of this life and into the next. He has a vacant look on his face most of the time. It is not a sad look, nor a lonely look. It is more of a distant, preoccupied look, like he is off somewhere else, maybe making plans, maybe making plans with the angels for his transition. He still smiles when someone comes up to him and offers even the smallest token of kindness. He still tears up when something touches him. He still feels. And, thanks to God, all he seems capable of feeling is love. For that is all that surrounds him.

A number of Clare Bridge residents have "passed over" since my Dad arrived at Clare Bridge. Anthony and Bob and Myrna are now gone. Joyce's family actually did come get her and moved her to Oklahoma. When Dad first got to Clare Bridge, he was among the highest functioning residents there. Now, years later, he is in the last stages of the disease. The next, and final stage is what the staff call "hospice," where the body starts to shut down as the neural pathways that control body regulation begin to fail. I have seen so many residents now go through this hospice stage before they died. Their deaths usually occur quietly, peacefully, naturally, in their rooms at Clare Bridge, in the accompaniment of all those angels that work there. Sometimes their families come to participate in this experience, but most times not.

I used to mourn the passing of a resident at Clare Bridge, as I knew so many of them quite well. I used to dread that every death there meant my dad was one step closer to his end. But I don't feel that way anymore. The residents' passing is just another step on their life journeys. Their energy is just taking a different shape and form. I believe Albert Einstein taught us that energy can never be created nor destroyed. Well, it's not just confined to the material. It applies to the spirit as well.

I have taken over Dad's role with Arthur, sending him cards and an occasional picture. His wife, for whom he was care giver, has passed over too. Arthur, like my dad, never gave up. He remained loyal to my father and his wife all the way through. Sempi Fi, Arthur, Semper Fi! You will be the first to receive this book.

My dad is waiting for his hospice. I will surely be there, along with all of those guardian angels, when his time on this earth is done. I am not afraid anymore. I know my father is in good hands. I know the guardian angels will lead my dad to the next life.

Some months ago, I went to Clare Bridge on a Saturday morning to bring Dad over to our house to watch the Army - Navy football game. I knew that Dad wouldn't understand what was going on in the game, but I wanted to honor our tradition. When I got to Clare Bridge, Dad wasn't in his usual chair, asleep in the living room, so I had to search for him. I rounded one of the inner perimeter corners and almost bumped into him. He was having a rare, active day, and was walking around the perimeter, like he always used to do with Anthony.

I gave my dad a quick hug, as I was physically upon him after turning the corner. My dad's bristly cheeks brushed up against mine, and some of the Old Spice aftershave that Abdul had put on his face rubbed off onto my face. As I pulled back from the hug, Dad looked at me, smiled, and said, "My son." I will never forget that moment as long as I live. Why, after years of not knowing who I was, did he experience that brief moment of lucidity? How could that possibly be? Maybe the moment wasn't meant for my Dad. Maybe it was meant just for me.

Earlier in the year, I had given Dad the greatest gift for his birthday. And on this grey day, in early December, Dad had given me his greatest gift. I was still his son. Somewhere in there, inside the fog, Dad still knew me.

Dad might never again be that lucid, at least while on this earth. Maybe it was Dad's farewell to me, before he makes his journey.

Throughout the writing of this book I always knew what the last paragraph would entail. It would take me back to where the book started, back to that little black and gold box my mother had made for me years before. The box was now crammed full of little sticky notes, index cards, and folded pieces of paper that documented my life with my dad. The box was so full I had to hold the cover in place with a rubber band, as if I was afraid that I would lose some of the precious memories held inside. It's time now to dump out the contents of the box and replace all the scraps of paper that previously held together my life with Dad. Inside will go a copy of this book, Dad's remaining Navy medals, and a condolence letter from Arthur. Semper Fi.

Dad, I will always love you. Farewell, and I will see you on the other side.

Epilogue: { A Message in a Bottle

My father and Dad, Walter Turke, M.D., born June 23, 1930, passed away on June 22, 2013, minutes before his 83rd birthday. In the end, perhaps just like the beginning, he transitioned over peacefully and serenely. His hospice physician, a wonderful man named Enrique Lopez, told him, "its OK Walter, all of your family is here, they are ready, you can go on to heaven now," and he passed over. He was wearing his cross when he died. There was no struggle. If I had to describe his passing in one word, I would say, "beautiful."

In October the following season, our family had a Memorial for Dad at the Michigan State University Chapel, a serene place that Dad loved. The title we gave the Memorial was, "A Life That Mattered," for his life truly did. Dad would never accept such a title being applied to him. He would have interrupted me and said, "We all matter, my son, I am no different than anyone else."

I would like to share my memorial eulogy with all my readers. At the memorial I was so anxious I thought I wouldn't be able to speak at all, but that all-enveloping shiver visited me again. The words flowed out, easily, actually effortlessly.

"On July 5, two weeks after my father passed, my family launched a bottle off the Frankfort Pier into Lake Michigan. Inside the bottle was a handful of rice to weigh it down and to keep the precious contents dry inside. For inside that bottle was a copy of my father's obituary, written as his life story, a man who had travelled to all of the continents and who spread his brand of compassion wherever he went. Also inside was an impassioned hand written letter by me and signed by our family, hopefully inspiring whoever found the bottle to learn a little more about Dad and his legacy.

Carefully wrapped around these documents was a twenty-dollar bill placed there to attract the finder, with a note to please use this money to brighten someone's day, and with instructions to repack the bottle and send it back on its way. I pictured the bottle somehow magically making its way to the ocean and traveling all around the globe. The whole implausible, slightly fantastic plan was so very much my dad, part symbolism, part fantasy, part Don Quixote-esque idealism, and 100 percent compassion and heart. We watched the bottle, nicely weighted down by the rice, bob up and down in the wavy, turbulent water as the Betsie River current took it out into the rough seas of Lake Michigan. I never realistically expected to hear again of the bottle, but it was a nice symbolic gesture. It would certainly be a nice memory in memorial for Dad.

I will smile when I remember the times I had with my father:

- Calling me Baby Fang as a little kid because I had one snaggle tooth. Later, as I grew older, my nick-name became Fang. When I was 28 he called me Fang and I said, 'that's Dr. Fang now, Dad'. He laughed and called me Dr. Fang from that day on.

- I remember so vividly jumping the waves in the Pacific Ocean when I was a kid. Dad taught me to not be afraid of the mighty ocean, not to fight it but to move with it. Years later, because of my total comfort in water and high waves, I began being called versions of "Sea Turtle," by various friends. First the "Flappy Happy Sea Turtle," then the "Wise California Sea Turtle," and then the "Turtle Prince."

- I remember my Dad hugging me with such awkward force that his whiskers reddened my face, and left a scent of Old Spice that would remain with me the entire day.

- My dad loved baseball and as you can read was drafted by the Pittsburg Pirates only to turn it down. He loved the Brooklyn Dodgers and Jackie Robinson, later following the team to Los Angeles where I too fell in love with baseball. My favorite Dodger game we went to at Dodger Stadium was a 3-0 win by Sandy Koufax where he struck out 17 batters and gave up just a few hits. I hope I am remembering it right.

- My dad saved my life twice. I had an appendicitis misdiagnosed as the flu when I was 12. Dad didn't believe the diagnoses and demanded a white blood cell count, which saw an explosion of the infection eating cells. I was rushed into surgery as my appendix was about to rupture. They got it cleaned out and removed just in time.

- When I was 10, I swam into a mass of seaweed at Zuma beach outside of Los Angeles. Tangled up inside the kelp was a massive colony of 3-foot wide Portuguese man-o-war jellyfish. I ran out of the water screaming with a burn covering my entire torso. My Dad took me to the water's edge and rubbed wet sand into my chest to draw the poison out. He never hesitated and my thoughts and fears of dying soon evaporated with my father's confidence. The lifeguards came and poured ammonia all over me. They told me my dad just saved my life.

- There are so many other memories I wished to share in detail but time will not allow me. I remember the luau we had in our backyard; complete with a pig roast in a pit we dug. I remember our trip to the Orient, 11 countries in 30 days! I remember you blasting all the show tunes and the big band music that now even my children have come to love. I remember how you held Shani so tenderly, and how you helped teach Miah to swim. I remember the movie stars you knew and when we met Elgin Baylor and Jerry West and Wilt Chamberlin. I remember all those bets we made playing H-O-R-S-E and how you excused my multiple thousand dollar debts wracked up from all my losses. I could never beat that hook shot of yours from the corner!

- But my greatest memories are when you faced death and your own mortality. Facing emergency triple bypass surgery, my dad was raced to the emergency surgery room in 1996. When he was wheeled down the halls of the very hospital he taught at, both sides of the aisle were lined up with medical students and hospital staff. They were from all walks of life, young and old, male and female, black, brown and white. And each one touched, held, and kissed my Dad all the way down the aisle to the operating room.

- Even when you were stricken with Alzheimer's disease, and eventually placed at Clare Bridge Memory Care, you continued to be YOU. Dad carried around a clipboard each day and went to every single resident to talk. He wrote a treatment plan for each resident. They were all the same; written in what now looked liked child's handwriting and grammar. Each carried the same message. "This patient is a good man or woman. She is sad because of what is going on. I am prescribing what she needs daily... love."

But most importantly, I will remember what you taught me. I promise Dad, I will continue your legacy by applying everything you taught and that I have learned:

- "Share everything."
- "It's only money."
- "Treat everyone with respect and dignity, even people who are angry and hurting and down and out. Remember, we are all one breath away from where they are."
- "The difficult ones, the angry ones, the ones that will give you a hard time, remember that they need love the most."
- "Don't do anything half assed…if you are going to do anything, do it as good as its ever been done."
- "If someone in a position of power treats you unfairly or meanly, turn them into a patient inside your head and give them therapy."
- "Never bully or start a fight, but if some mean person traps you and starts fighting, kick the shit out of them!"
- "Teach everyone and anyone all you can about respect and dignity. Humanize the disenfranchised, the lost, the mentally ill, and the angry. And always teach with kindness, they won't learn a goddamn thing if you are yelling at them."
- "Spectacles, testicles, wallet, and watch!"
- And finally, "All there is and all that ever matters is love," spoken after the ravages of Alzheimer's had claimed virtually all of his memory.

My Dad always called me "the Greatest." I was always embarrassed when he said that. Now I wish I could hear him say it just one more time. Thank you Dad, you were a wonderful father to me, for you made me feel like I was uniquely special. And maybe, just maybe, I might now be able to feel as if I really am the Greatest.

You might be wondering what happened to that bottle we tossed into the waves of Lake Michigan. On August 19, six weeks after the bottle was launched, I received an email from a man named David. He and his family found the bottle 40 miles north from where we tossed it, along the Leelanau Peninsula. David took the 20 dollars and he taught his young children about charity. They donated it to a mental health center. Then the family repacked the bottle with another 20-dollar bill, and sent it off the Leland Pier.

On September 4 a woman named Phyllis emailed me with the subject line, "a bottle of love." They found the bottle at the tip of the Leelanau peninsula while vacationing there from Colorado. They took the bottle home to Colorado, and gave it to their adult children, who were leaving for Spain.

I want to believe that my dad's story is now floating south along the cold current from the coast of Spain down toward the coast of West Africa. Even after death, the man who loved to travel and touched so many lives along the way continues to do just that.

I will remember you Dad, whenever we think of love, respect, dignity, kindness and compassion. You mattered to many in this world. May your journeys and teachings continue in your new home."

Author's Final Notes:

I was recently reminded of the 5 stages of bereavement, first researched and described by Elisabeth Kubler-Ross in 1969. These stages in sequence include denial, bargaining, anger, depression, and acceptance. I cannot help but notice that now, at the conclusion of this book, I passed through all 5 stages, in order, during my journey with Dad.

Whatever explanations or framework one chooses to describe my dad's life and our journey, his story remains the same. I am grateful that he brought me along on the trip. And I am, unquestionably, a better person for it.

A special remembrance goes out to Barbara Jahnke, MD, my father's physician who guided my father and my family through the course of his disease. She passed away unexpectedly while I was in the process of publishing this book. Dr. Jahnke was a kind, invested, humanitarian physician and the first of my father's guardian angels to arrive. I am deeply saddened by her passing, and hope and pray that my father was there to greet her when she entered the eternal.

Please Contact Me

I would love to hear from anyone touched by this book. I am not a very high tech person, and part of me worries our high tech culture will further de-humanize us. But this high tech world also allows me to get my message out to all of you without greed, and without self-serving interests. I am grateful for the opportunity to share my experience.

I would welcome your response! My email address is gsturke@comcast.net. Please simply address the subject line as "497 Nails" so I will prioritize it.

The publication of this book has inspired me to write a sequel of sorts, A Window to Heaven, about my dad's "out of body" experiences, which I now view as more of a visit to the afterlife. I hope to have this book ready by 2017. I challenge all who "doubt" to read it.

I feel like with this new book my journey with my dad is beginning again, and with that, Dad is still alive within me. And the dad that's in there is not the sick dad, but rather, a restored Dad.

I am also in the process of writing a third book, entitled American Shoes, about my mother's World War 2 experiences and her courageous relocation as a refugee fleeing war-torn Europe, alone, at age 15. I hope to have this book also available in early 2017.

Please visit my website: www.GarrettLTurkePhD.com or connect with me on Facebook.

Garrett

Made in the USA
Charleston, SC
17 July 2016